TENTH ANNIVERSARY EDITION

THE NEW BHAGAVAD GITA

KOTI SREEKRISHNA
HARI RAVIKUMAR

PRAISE FOR THE NEW BHAGAVAD-GITA

"Simple, articulate and accessible,
The New Bhagavad-Gita takes a unique approach
to present a modern translation of this ancient text."
N R NARAYANA MURTHY
Founder-Chairman, *Infosys Technologies Ltd.*

"I'm sure that The New Bhagavad-Gita will stand out among thousands of other translations. The New Bhagavad-Gita is indeed new, because it presents the eternal truth in modern language, so everyone can understand and learn from it. I highly recommend this book and congratulate the authors on their great achievement."
DR. L SUBRAMANIAM PHD
Violin Maestro and Composer

"The New Bhagavad-Gita not only gives the modern reader access to this ancient sacred Hindu text but also provides gems of wisdom for contemporary seekers and guidance for all of us on how to live in a world of turmoil. With the aid of the translators' illuminating commentaries throughout, I felt I was listening in on a private conversation between a supreme god and a mortal struggling with the same questions that confront us today, including what are best actions when confronted with danger, aggression, and violence. The New Bhagavad-Gita can be read through or opened to any page to receive your enlightening message for the day."
PATRICIA SMITH
Poet, Photographer, and Founder, *Peace X Peace*

"I enjoyed very much reading the translation. The efforts to bring the translation closer to the original are evident. In particular, the notes are clear and help the reader understand important details. This book is a welcome addition to the literature on Bhagavad-Gita."

PROF. M G PRASAD PHD

Formerly Board Member, *Hindu University of America*

"The New Bhagavad-Gita will appeal to the younger generation that has generally been exposed to a liberal education."

M R SRINIVASAN PHD

Former Member, *Planning Commission*, Government of India

"Human problems change with time, but what we call great works are precisely those that will always have something important to say in every age. I therefore welcome this translation by two authors of the new generation, and I applaud their decision to make the translation in simple, current English so that its message is directly absorbed."

PROF. RODDAM NARASIMHA PHD

Aerospace Scientist and Fluid Dynamicist

"The Bhagavad Gita is not only a basic text of Hinduism – it also constitutes a most valuable piece of mankind's heritage. Each generation should therefore come up with its own version of Krishna's answers to Arjuna's questions. The new English version by Koti and Hari will gain international recognition in Century 21."

GABRIEL MINDER PHD

Formerly Member, *Swiss Academy of Engineering Sciences*

"A sincere and devoted effort in bringing the English version of the Indian sacred work, without sacrificing the essence of message, at the same time retaining the colloquial nature of the friendly conversation between the charioteer and the archer sitting in despondency. The precise and exact nature of the work is commendable and deserves full credence."

V Prasanna Bhat PhD
Former Advisor, *Saudi Arabian Monetary Agency*

"I was enjoying what I was reading and found almost no places I could add or erase a touch. This book seems to tell us that when we miss the good old days we actually miss great human wisdom as described in the Bhagavad-Gita."

PROF. Huilan Ying
Formerly Professor, *Zhejiang University*

"If you thought Eastern philosophy was abstruse and tedious, prepare yourself for a delightful surprise. In this translation of the holiest of Hindu works, the authors present the most profound spiritual insights in a lucid, lively, and accessible language, while their helpful and witty asides help the reader navigate the text without ever feeling swamped. Scholars and laymen alike are in for a treat."

Chandra Shekhar PhD
Author

"Excellent work. A modern interpretation of a timeless classic, with many original insights. The authors deserve kudos for their initiative and hard work in bringing it together."

Roy Prasad
Entrepreneur and IT Industry Executive, San Francisco Bay Area

"As a complete neophyte I read this translation of the Gita with great interest. It allowed me to access Indian philosophy and to get inspiration to more reading."

Balazs Szeless

Formerly Mechanical Engineer, CERN

"This rendition of the Gita is very articulate. It puts forth the very essence of human existence in a language that is simple and unambiguous. It is a very good book, a pleasure to read, and worth having a copy."

Shanti Karri

Faculty, *Galen College of Nursing*

"The New Bhagavad-Gita successfully attempts to translate the ancient writing into modern-day language, complete with interpretations making the book understandable to the international readership and illustrated with endearing drawings."

Tanja Schulze

Formerly Program Director, *The Melton Foundation*

"The translation is admirably readable and I hope it will bring many people closer to the profundity of India's ancient traditions."

Arun Prasad

Machine Learning Engineer and Sanskrit Aficionado

"...a valuable book which is of great help to the present generation. It is very simple and self-explanatory. Thanks for great work you have done to the society!"

Natesh Magge

Retired Engineer, *General Electric*

The New Bhagavad-Gita

The New Bhagavad-Gita

Timeless wisdom in the language of our times

TRANSLATORS
Koti Sreekrishna
Hari Ravikumar

ARPress
45 Dan Road Suite 36
Canton MA 02021

Hotline: 1(888) 821-0229
Fax: 1(508) 545-7580

Ordering Information:
Quantity Sales. Special discounts are available on quantity purchases by corporations, associations, and others. For details, contact the publisher at the address above.

Printed in the United States of America.

ISBN-13	Softcover	979-8-89356-383-2
	eBook	979-8-89356-382-5

Library of Congress Control Number: 2021924425

Sthitaprajña

The greatest people I have met in my time and station
are those who seem common and ordinary;
quietly doing their work with focus and devotion,
looking for neither rewards nor glory;
enjoying and cherishing every moment of their lives
with a smile on their lips and with a sparkle in their eyes;
neither displaying talents nor voicing opinions,
responding rather than reacting to situations;
observant, conscious, satisfied, tranquil,
unmoved by the forces of good or evil;
bearing no baggages of hate or envy,
holding no memories of pain or sorrow;
thankful for every single day,
unconcerned about each tomorrow;
calm amidst chaos and crises,
untouched by hurdles and trifles;
harming none yet choosing not to beg or to pray,
treating everyone in the same humble way;
unchanged in their spirit yet willing to cope,
unpertubed by despair, unattached to hope;
uninterested in belonging or identity,
eternally in resonance with the eternity;
respecting life yet unafraid of death or destruction,
not lusting behind truths or craving for salvation,
yet find it impossible to tell a lie.

HARI RAVIKUMAR

PREFACE

(TO THE FIRST EDITION)

FROM MY CHILDHOOD, I've been connected to the *Bhagavad-gītā*, one way or another. My father (K S Krishna Tatachar, Sanskrit scholar and author) taught me the recitation of the *Gītā* in the traditional, rigorous way. He would recite a line; I would hear it, see it (Sanskrit verses written in Kannada script), and repeat it twice. He would correct any mistakes in articulation and make me chant it until I got it perfectly right. I had to be attentive, otherwise the session would be prolonged. Nevertheless, I was filled with thoughts of playing cricket, hoping it wouldn't rain and that my friend Lakshmisha would walk around so that my dad would let me go. But that wasn't too common; my friend got dismissed more often than the session!

After I mastered the correct way of recitation, using the text as a guide, I would repeat the verses over and over again until I memorized them completely. Within a matter of one year, I could consistently repeat any verse *ad lib*. By the time I was nine, I had memorized the entire 700 verses of the *Gītā*.

The most thrilling moment with this rote memorization, ever fresh in my memory, was when I won the first prize in '*Six Chapter Gita Recitation Contest*' at my school (*National Middle School*, Bangalore) in 1963. One of the judges of the contest was apparently so impressed that he added ₹10 of his own to the actual award amount of ₹29. I consider that as the most valuable ₹10 ever earned in my life since it was a blessing from HSV (Prof. H S Varadadeshikachar, who was to become my Sanskrit professor in college; he was later known as H. H. Sri Sri Rangapriya Maha Desikan).

Before I left to the US in 1978, I requested my father to say a few words about the *Gītā*, which I promptly recorded. In his brief talk, he said that *Gītā* is a ***sarva-anukūla-śāstra*** (a scriptural guide convenient to everyone). That one phrase said it all. But I always wondered why even those who knew the *Gītā* made life inconvenient for themselves and others. Was that because of 'something else' (divisive ideas and traditional dogma) coming in the way? I kept reading every book on *Gītā* I could lay my hands on; I might have read fifty versions by now. I found some new insight as well as 'something else,' which was not always the same, but was always there, and in disguise at times. All through, I was trying to intuitively make sense, especially of some tricky verses which could be understood in multiple ways; in a way, I was trying to read Kṛṣṇa's mind.

In 1990, my brother K Srinivas gifted me D V Gundappa's discourse on *Gītā* in Kannada, *Jīvana-dharma-yoga* ('A manual for living'). This was a book first published in the '60s, bringing national recognition to the author. I was happy to see that some of my own intuitive understanding was also echoed in DVG's book.

My friend K Vasudevan wanted to bring out an English translation of the *Gītā* and asked me for a recommendation. I couldn't think of one that I wholeheartedly liked. So in 2005, I began working on a translation, trying to keep out the 'something else.' I had just completed a word-for-word translation to be published as a 'one verse a day, self-study manual' and shared the draft with a few, when the best happened. There came along my nephew, Hari Ravikumar, decades younger (only in age) as co-author with brilliant ideas, great depth, unique talents, insights, and style. He wanted to have a modern English version to make the book accessible to any person, from any culture, who wants to know about the *Gītā*.

He put his mind, body, and soul to the cause with such great diligence and dedication that we have this book. I trust you will derive as much joy reading it as we have derived in putting it together.

I have always felt unexplainable joy even while simply reciting verses of *Gītā*. As we celebrate my father's 108th birthday, certainly he couldn't have given me a better gift than this. I must thank my dear wife Shailini for putting up with this 'Gita-nut,' a title accorded to me by my kids!

May 2011 — Koti Sreekrishna
Mason, Ohio, USA

~

In 2006 I wrote the poem *Sthitaprajña* ('the stable one') inspired by my grandmother. At that time, my uncle Dr. Koti Sreekrishna was visiting India and I had shown it to him. He read it and immediately said that he'd like to include it in his *Bhagavad-gītā* translation. Little did I realize at that point that I'd become such an integral part of the project. Working on this book has been so much fun that it has nearly *yogi*fied me.

When I wrote that poem I hadn't read the *Bhagavad-gītā* in detail and today when I look at it I realize that if I had to capture the essence of a text that I had never learned formally, it is because of a higher intuition, of which I am clueless. But certainly it is also because of the great people around me – my family, my *gurus*, my friends – who are always adding something, always inspiring, and always caring. They are, for me, the living *Gītā*.

May 2011 HARI RAVIKUMAR
Bangalore, India

~

ABOUT THIS TRANSLATION

THE translator's task is to translate, not to interpret. But in places where the meaning is unclear, some interpretation creeps in. So, every translation is stained by the translator's understanding and worldview. As translators our submission is that we present the *Gītā* in the light of our own experiences, at the same time taking care to preserve the flavor of the original. We must mention, however, that there is no equivalent to reading the *Bhagavad-gītā* in the original Sanskrit.

While we present just the translation in simple language, in some places we had to include additional notes at the bottom of the verses. We have put the verse number in superscript at the beginning of a verse for those who are familiar with the text and would like to compare with the original.

We have retained the original Sanskrit terms for words that we could not translate easily into English. Since those terms might be unfamiliar, we have explained them the first instance they appear in a given chapter. The *Gītā* uses many names and epithets for Kṛṣṇa and Arjuna. We have avoided translating those where we felt they did not add any value.

In the *Gītā*, all pronouns are masculine. Our translation has retained that in places where it was not possible to have a neutral term. This should not be treated as gender bias but as a convention, just like how the moon is feminine in Spanish or the sun is masculine in French. So, for example, verse 3.21 could have well been – 'A great woman sets an example by her actions. The whole world follows the standard that she sets.'

After initial conflicts between the British and American English spellings, we chose to go with the latter.

In this **tenth anniversary edition**, we have made a number of small enhancements and emendations to the translation. We took this opportunity to thoroughly revise the translation after reading through the Sanskrit text again, particularly in case of verses where we felt that the essence of the original was compromised or could have been expressed better.

We have employed the IAST scheme (see *pp*. 386–87) throughout the book to help the readers get a clear sense of the pronunciation of Sanskrit words.

At the start of each chapter of the present work, we have given the original verses of the *Gītā* (in Deva-nāgarī and IAST) from the corresponding chapter with a view to get the readers to engage more with the Sanskrit text. We have followed the *critically constituted text* of the *Gītā* published by BORI.*

Perhaps for the first time, additional verses of the *Gītā* that are given in the footnotes and appendices of the BORI Critical Edition have been translated into English. This has been given in Appendix 2 along with the Sanskrit original.

* *The Bhagavadgītā* (relevant parts of the *Bhīṣmaparvan* of the BORI Edition of the *Mahābhārata*). Cr. Ed. Belvalkar, Shripad Krishna. Poona: Bhandarkar Oriental Research Institute, 1968

ACKNOWLEDGEMENTS

THIS book would not be in your hands but for the help, encouragement, advice, critique, blessings, and wholehearted support of many people – from our own family members and friends to complete strangers (who have now become good friends). Our sincere thanks to every one of them. It would be impossible to list out everyone who helped shape this work but we owe special gratitude to a few.

Twenty-seven remarkable and diverse individuals from different cultures, age-groups, professions, and dispositions reviewed the manuscript and shared their wisdom and experience, which has made this book what it is: Arjun Bharadwaj, B Ranganayakamma, Balazs Szeless, Dr. Chandra Shekhar, Dr. G Sudesh Kumar, Dr. Gabriel Minder, Prof. Huilan Ying, Dr. Javier Lorca Espiro, Dr. Jwala Prasad, K Srinivas, Dr. M G Prasad, Dr. M K Sridhar, Dr. M R Srinivasan, Narayanan Srinivasan, Preeti Srinivasan, Dr. Ravikumar M V, Dr. Roddam Narasimha, Dr. S Jayaraman, Shana Kaloyanova, Shanti Karri, Dr. Shekhar Borgaonkar, Srikanth Vasudevan, Tanja Schulze, Dr. V Prasanna Bhat, Dr. Varun Prakash, Vaslav Markevitch, and Dr. Vinay Kumar.

Aditya J, our editor, spent endless hours (very often late into the night) reading, analyzing, simplifying, and reshaping the text.

Ashok U, our illustrator, toiled for months before we finalized the superb sketches that you see in the book. We were inspired by his patience and tenacity to ensure that he gave us only the best. Ashok illustrated most of the book, but Shanti Karri and Naethra Sreekrishna also contributed a few lovely sketches.

Śatāvadhānī Dr. R Ganesh, a great Sanskrit scholar and polymath of our times, was so kind as to thoroughly review the final manuscript and check for any failings in our translation; we were delighted and reassured when he mentioned that we had captured both the letter and the spirit of the *Gītā* in our book. He also gave us several clarifications regarding some of the obscure verses in Appendix 2.

Narayan Srinivasan, one of the reviewers, went beyond what we had requested him; he worked closely with us re-working some critical verses, helped manage our Facebook page, and brainstormed on issues that we raised in our blog, *https://newbhagavadgita.blogspot.com*.

Raghavendra G S thoroughly reviewed the translations of the verses in Appendix 2 and gave invaluable inputs.

K Vasudevan, Naresh Keerthi, M S Krishna, Arun Prasad, Malur Vasan, and Prateek Ranganathan gave us wonderful insights and suggestions for improvement. Though the *Gītā* evokes different responses from each of them – ranging from rapturous love to mild contempt – each one of them helped significantly enhance this book.

Sripriya Srinivasan translated our book into Tamil with great interest and dedication. It was published in 2017 with the title '*Bhagavadgītai Tarkāla Tamiḻil*' ('*Bhagavad-gītā* in Contemporary Tamil') and was well received by the readers.

Harini Raghavan explained to us intricacies of *visargha-sandhi* of Sanskrit grammar, which was helpful in presentation of the original verses.

Kanchan B A, Roy Prasad, Anshuman Borah, Divya Tyam, Anirudh Chandrakant, and Avishek Chakravarti offered lots of creative ideas for the book. Jyotsna Pattabiraman, Linda

Spencer, Deepta Rangarajan, S Swaminathan, and Jaikar Mohan enlightened us on the aspects of publishing, business, and marketing. Meeta Gangrade, Sartaj Singh Anand, Vinay Kumar, Siddarth Ramamohan, Arun Ramanuj, and K N Bharat gave several tips on how best we can use the latest technology in connection with the book.

Dr. M P Ravindra and Dr. S Revathikumari not only shared ideas but also gifted *Bhagavad-gītā* books by contemporary authors. Narayan Swamy's manuscript on the *Bhagavad-gītā* helped us revise the translation for some of the verses in this edition. Narayana Kulkarni, Prof. Hema Ravikumar, and Prathigna Poonacha helped with their contacts, shared their views, and often spoke about the book.

Corky and Holly Siegel, Patricia Smith, and Ashish and Elisabeth Khokar gave sage advice and motivation all through.

Special thanks to Dr. L Subramaniam, Kavita Krishnamurti Subramaniam and their wonderful family for always inspiring, encouraging, and supporting.

Needless to say, amidst all the great things that others have contributed, any shortcomings in the book are solely our own and in no way reflect on our reviewers or advisors.

KOTI SREEKRISHNA
HARI RAVIKUMAR

Introduction

Even with our limited ability to peek into our ancient past, we like to believe that we have evolved, refined our senses, heightened our aesthetics, and acquired exquisite tastes. However, we have also hunted, waged wars, spilled blood, destroyed the natural environment around us, and caused a whole lot of trouble to one another. The more we think we have changed, the more we realize that a great deal has remained the same.

As we dive deep into this ocean of human activity—filled with astonishing achievements and abysmal atrocities—in spite of the seeming changes, the basic human qualities have remain unchanged – be it human emotions, desires, or frailties. The 'way we feel' has mostly been the same though it has taken different forms and characteristics.

It is both interesting and beneficial to who we are now to know what the ancient people 'felt' about life, growth, thought, awareness, death, and the universe. The quiet wisdom of our ancestors, often disguised as records of experiences or imaginative poetry, might give us some inspiration and insights into our own lives.

What we call 'scripture' is different from all other genres of literature, for it deals with a different kind of reality and operates at a different level of consciousness, often quite removed from our day-to-day life. It gives us a completely different perspective on things and quite often awakens us to a broader realm of reality.

Bhagavad-gītā is one such scripture from ancient India.

HINDUISM

HINDUISM is the major religion of India with a worldwide following of over a billion people. In its original and purest form, it is a *sanātana-dharma* (loosely translated as 'eternal truth' or 'timeless path') that represents over five thousand years of contemplation, tradition, and continuous development in the Indian subcontinent. One who follows Hinduism is called a 'Hindu' (the term originally referred to a person living in the land of Bhārata).

Hinduism has no single founder. Several ancient seer-sages—*both men and women*—contributed to its scriptures. The Hindu scriptures are numerous and diverse. Many of them are written in the Sanskrit language. Sanskrit, like Latin, is the root language for several languages; both Sanskrit and Latin are said to belong to the same language family.

The word 'scripture' comes from the Latin *scriptura*, meaning 'that which is written,' but the equivalent terms in Sanskrit for Hindu scriptures are *śruti*, 'that which is heard' and *smṛti*, 'that which is remembered.'

Ṛṣis (seers, seekers of truth) of ancient India contemplated on creation, human nature, refining basic instincts, purpose of life, workings of the physical world, and the metaphysical dimensions of the universe. The collective consciousness of the *ṛṣis* is called '*Veda*.' The literal meaning of the word '*Veda*' is 'to know' or 'knowledge.'

Vedas are the foremost revealed scriptures in Hinduism. Every Hindu ceremony from birth to death and beyond is drawn from the *Vedas*. There are four *Vedas* – *Ṛk, Yajus, Sāma,* and *Atharva*. These comprise the ***śruti*** texts. Although any body of knowledge can be called a *veda*, like '*āyur-veda*' (health manual), the term '*śruti*' applies only to the four *Vedas*.

The *ṛṣis* taught this collected wisdom to their disciples, who in turn taught it to their disciples. Thus, this knowledge was passed on, intact, for many generations, without a single word being written down. Even today, traditional students learn *Vedic mantras* (sacred utterances) orally from a *guru* (teacher). A verse from the *Ṛg-veda* poignantly captures the intellectual atmosphere of those times –

Come together, speak together,
let your minds be united, harmonious;
as ancient gods unanimous
sit down to their appointed share.

(*Ṛg-veda-saṃhitā* 10.191.2)

The final portion of the *Vedas*, which are called '*Upaniṣads*' or '*Vedānta*,' contain anecdotes, dialogs, and talks that deal with body, mind, soul, nature, consciousness, and the universe. Of the several *Upaniṣads*, ten are very important: *Īśa, Kena, Kaṭha, Praśna, Muṇḍaka, Māṇḍūkya, Taittirīya, Aitareya, Chāndogya*, and *Bṛhadāraṇyaka*.

Post-*Vedic* texts form another set of scriptures, the ***smṛti***, which were composed by a single author and later memorized by generations. These include *Rāmāyaṇa* and *Mahā-bhārata* (the epics), *Aṣṭādhyāyī* (grammar), *Manu-smṛti* (law), *Purāṇas* (old episodes), *Nirukta* (etymology), *Śulba-sūtra* (geometry),

Gṛhya-sūtra (running a family), and a whole body of texts governing architecture, art, astrology, astronomy, dance, drama, economics, mathematics, medicine, music, nutrition, rituals, sex, and warfare, among others.

The *Bhagavad-gītā* (or simply '*Gītā*'), which is a small part of the epic *Mahā-bhārata*, is an important and widely read scripture of Hinduism. It is one of the most comprehensive summaries of Hinduism.

The Sanskrit word for Creation is ***sṛṣṭi***, which means 'pouring forth.' It is not 'creation' but rather an outpouring, an expansion, a change. The idea of creation is discussed in different ways in the *Veda*s. One poem (*Nāsadīya-sūkta*) proposes a brilliant conceptual model for creation while another (*Hiraṇya-garbha-sūkta*) raises and answers questions about god and creation. Yet another poem (*Puruṣa-sūkta*) describes in detail the process of creation. Amidst all these varied views, there is a single underlying idea: 'one became everything.'

Another contention is that the concept of god is subsequent to creation. Hinduism has many gods but only one Supreme Spirit. The *Veda*s make a clear distinction between god and *Brahman*, the Supreme Spirit, which is beyond all creation and destruction.

Hindu timeline spans trillions of years and *Time is considered to be cyclical* rather than linear; so we have eternal time cycles one after the other with no beginning or end. The *Sūrya-siddhānta*, a treatise of Hindu astronomy explains the staggering timeline –

...twelve months make a (human) year
this equals a day and a night
of the *deva*s (1.13)

360 days and nights of the *deva*s
make a divine year (1.14)
12,000 divine years make one *mahā-yuga* (1.15)
A day of Brahmā spans 1,000 *mahā-yuga*s
a night of Brahmā also spans 1,000 *mahā-yuga* (1.20)
Brahmā's life span is 100 Brahmā years (1.21)

A *mahā-yuga* (Great Age) is made up of four *yuga*s (Ages) – *Satya-yuga* (or *Kṛta-yuga*), *Tretā-yuga*, *Dvāpara-yuga*, and *Kali-yuga*. In human terms, a *mahā-yuga* is 4.32 million years.

A day of Brahmā (the god of creation), spanning 1,000 *mahā-yugas*, equals 4.32 billion human years, which is the time he is active and thus enables activity in the universe. During the night of Brahmā, all creatures are dissolved only to be brought forth again at the beginning of the next day (this is also explained in the *Bhagavad-gītā*; see 8.17–19 and 9.7).

Hindu sects are many and they often follow their own set of traditions and customs. While they seem divergent, they have an underlying unity. Hinduism has a lot of freedom and openness with regard to beliefs, practices, and philosophies of its followers. Take the example of belief in the Supreme: some Hindus believe in god with a form, some others believe in a formless god, while others are agnostics; some believe in one god and some others believe in many.

Hindu values include harmony, tolerance, righteousness, respect for nature, and respect for the Supreme. Hinduism accepts other religions and modes of thought. Here are two verses from the *Ṛg-veda* that bring out these values –

May noble thoughts come to us from every side,
unchanged, unhindered, undefeated in every way;

May the gods always be with us for our gain and
our protectors caring for us, ceaseless, every day.

(*Ṛg-veda-saṃhitā* 1.89.1)

The Truth (Supreme Reality) is one;
the wise call it by different names –
Indra, Mitra, Varuṇa, Agni,
Yama, Mātariśvān, the Divine,
Suparṇa, Garutmān, and so on!

(*Ṛg-veda-saṃhitā* 1.164.46)

Hindu worldview emphasizes conduct more than creed. It celebrates the diversity of existence and embraces the world as part of a big family, as recorded for instance in an ancient book of stories –

"These are my own, those are strangers" –
thus the narrow-minded ones judge people.
But for those magnanimous hearts,
the world is but one family!

(*Hitopadeśa* 1.3.71)

The *Vedas* call humans by a cheerful and hopeful name: **'The children of immortal bliss'** (*Ṛg-veda-saṃhitā* 10.13.1). We are born pure and perfect but over time we accumulate the dust of unhappiness and pettiness. The constant quest is to return to our true nature as children of bliss.

A prayer from the *Upaniṣads* talks about the great spiritual journey from ignorance to illumination –

Lead me from falsehood to truth,
lead me from darkness to light,
lead me from death to immortality.

(*Bṛhadāraṇyaka-upaniṣad* 1.3.28)

Hinduism is perhaps the oldest, most diverse, and most sophisticated system of religious thought and practice, covering nearly everything that comes under the umbrella of religion and philosophy. A human lifetime is insufficient to exhaust the wisdom it has to offer, and accessing even a small portion of this vast treasure enthralls, enriches, and elevates!

MAHĀ-BHĀRATA: STORY AND CHARACTERS

Kṛṣṇa-dvaipāyana Vyāsa is a famous sage of ancient India. He is often called '**Veda-vyāsa**' (or simply '**Vyāsa**') since he organized the *Vedas*. Vyāsa composed several important works, including the 18 *Mahā-purāṇas* and the *Mahā-bhārata*, the great saga of King Bharata's dynasty. Bharata was an important king of ancient India; the official name of India, 'Bhārata,' comes from his name.

THE AUTHOR

Apart from composing *Mahā-bhārata*, Vyāsa appeared as a character in the epic. He was born to Satyavatī, a fisher-girl, before her marriage. She later married King Śantanu, who was a descendent of King Kuru (of the Bharata dynasty). They had two sons but both of them died young, thus leaving no heirs to the throne. And so, Vyāsa fathered Dhṛtarāṣṭra and Pāṇḍu for the sake of the dynasty.

Kuru was a famous king of the Bharata dynasty and his descendents were the Kauravas (or the Kurus). However, the term 'Kauravas' often refers to the one hundred children of Dhṛtarāṣṭra, while Pāṇḍu's five children are called the 'Pāṇḍavas.' It is the dispute between the Kauravas and the Pāṇḍavas that resulted in the *Mahā-bhārata* war, which took place nearly five thousand years ago in Kurukṣetra (the land of Kuru) in Northern India. Almost all major kings from the Indian subcontinent took part in this great war, which was fought for eighteen days.

THE GRANDFATHER

Bhīṣma was the son of King Śantanu from his first marriage. Bhīṣma took a great oath of celibacy for life and helped his step-brothers and their descendants rule the kingdom. He was, in a way, the 'grandfather' of the Pāṇḍavas and Kauravas. In the war, though he fought on the side of the Kauravas, his heart was always with the Pāṇḍavas because he felt they were the more righteous of the two.

Droṇa was a great archer and warrior, though he was born in a priestly family. Droṇa, who was extremely poor, came to the Kauravas seeking a job. Bhīṣma appointed him to teach the art of warfare to both Pāṇḍavas and Kauravas. Droṇa loved the Pāṇḍavas dearly and Arjuna was his favorite disciple. But Droṇa was indebted to the Kauravas for their patronage and fought the war on their side.

THE TUTOR

King Dhṛtarāṣṭra was born blind and before the great war began, Vyāsa offered him divine vision so that he could witness the war. But the blind king refused to see this terrible war between his sons and nephews.

The Narrator

Sañjaya was born in a family of raconteurs and he was Dhṛtarāṣṭra's advisor and charioteer. When Dhṛtarāṣṭra refused to witness the war, Vyāsa gave Sañjaya divine vision in order that he might witness the events on the battlefield as they happened—without leaving the palace—and narrate them to the blind Dhṛtarāṣṭra. The dialog of the *Bhagavad-gītā* is structured in the form of Sañjaya's narration to Dhṛtarāṣṭra.

The Aggressor

Duryodhana, the eldest among the hundred sons of Dhṛtarāṣṭra, was known for his exploits with the mace. His childhood jealousies towards the Pāṇḍavas and his greed for power made him plot against them. Teaming up with his maternal uncle Śakuni and his friend Karṇa, Duryodhana orchestrated many devious schemes to destroy the Pāṇḍavas. One such instance was when he got the Pāṇḍavas invited to a game of dice and defeated them by deceit; it had been decided earlier that the losers of the game would forsake their kingdom, retire to the forest for twelve years and live incognito for a year after that. Having lost the game of dice, the Pāṇḍavas went into exile for thirteen years. When they returned, Duryodhana refused to return their kingdom as promised; he wanted to wage a war to decide that.

THE RIGHTFUL HEIR

Yudhiṣṭhira, eldest of the five Pāṇḍavas, was the personification of nobility. His wisdom and good conduct attracted the admiration of even his enemies. Yudhiṣṭhira couldn't bear the thought of a war, so he pleaded for peace in the land of their ancestors. When the Kauravas showed no signs of compromise, he finally requested for five villages to be given to the five Pāṇḍavas and all would be forgotten.

Duryodhana said in response, "I challenge the Pāṇḍavas to battle! Either I, killing the Pāṇḍavas, will rule over this kingdom or the sons of Pāṇḍu, killing me, shall enjoy this land. I will sacrifice everything but I can't live side by side with the Pāṇḍavas. I won't surrender to them even that much of land which is covered by the sharp point of a needle."

THE HERO

Arjuna was the third of the five Pāṇḍavas, known for his prowess in archery. He was a key player in the great war and spent years honing his martial skills and acquiring new weapons, knowing well that he will have to defend his family from the Kauravas. But just before the war began, he felt sympathetic towards his foes because they were his relatives and friends, and so refused to fight. At that point, Kṛṣṇa, his old friend and mentor, spoke the *Bhagavad-gītā* to awaken him.

Kṛṣṇa, a popular Hindu god, is an *avatāra* (incarnation) of the Supreme. He was related to both the Pāṇḍavas and the Kauravas. When war became inevitable, he declared that he

The Mentor

won't raise a weapon. He allowed his entire army to fight on the side of the Kauravas, as Duryodhana wished. He became the charioteer to Arjuna and gave him the supreme guidance at the time of war. But before the war broke out, Kṛṣṇa tried to broker peace between the cousins because he didn't want the dynasty to be destroyed.

Kṛṣṇa went to Dhṛtarāṣṭra's court and said, "Joy in the happiness of others, sorrow at the sight of another's misery – this has been the credo of the Kurus! Your race, O king, is so noble, that it will be a pity if its scion should do something so improper; and worse still if it were done by you. The evil Duryodhana's misconduct will lead to universal slaughter. Please do something!"

All the elders in the assembly, the many sages visiting the kingdom, and Dhṛtarāṣṭra's counselors told Duryodhana that Kṛṣṇa's words were appropriate for the situation and that peace was the best way forward.

Duryodhana shouted in rage, "Why me? I have done nothing wrong! But as long as I live, the Pāṇḍavas will not get a share of the kingdom. Out of ignorance or fear or some other reason, we had earlier given them the kingdom. But now, I will not surrender to them even that much of land which is covered by the sharp point of a needle."

With anger in his eyes, Kṛṣṇa said, "If you want a war, then you shall have it. In a short time, there will be terrible bloodshed. After so many devious acts, you claim that you have done nothing wrong! You are not willing to give them their share of the land even when they are begging for it! Ignoring the words of the wise and deriding the advice of friends, you can never achieve anything that is good. What you are set to do is dishonorable and sinful."

In an extreme fit of anger, Duryodhana tried to use violence against Kṛṣṇa. A shocked Dhṛtarāṣṭra tried to intervene. Kṛṣṇa calmly said, "O king, if they wish to use violence, let them. On my part, I will not do anything that will bring disgrace."

In response to the violence, Kṛṣṇa just showed a glimpse of his divine form to everyone present. Duryodhana left the place in a huff.

"If war is what they want, let them have it. Now, with your permission, I will return." So saying, Kṛṣṇa calmly went out of the king's assembly.

The war had to be fought.

Peace had lost.

(Appendix 3 of this book has a family tree that explains the relationships between some of the characters of the *Mahā-bhārata*. It also has a map of ancient India.)

BHAGAVAD-GĪTĀ: HISTORY AND CONTEXT

KṚṢṆA and Arjuna had the conversation on the battlefield, standing in the midst of the two armies. Sañjaya narrated it with visual detail to the blind Dhṛtarāṣṭra. Vyāsa wrote it down for posterity and taught it to his student Vaiśampāyana, who later narrated it to King Janamejaya, the great grandson of Arjuna.

As per the traditional accounts, the Kurukṣetra war was fought between 22nd November and 9th December, 3139 BCE and over four and a half million warriors died; only a handful of them survived. The Pāṇḍavas won the war and ruled for about thirty-five years. Then with the death of Kṛṣṇa the previous Age (*Dvāpara-yuga*) came to an end. The present Age (*Kali-yuga*), began on 18th February, 3102 BCE.

Many scholar-saints of India wrote commentaries on the *Gītā* as they considered it an important text (it is traditionally deemed as part of the *prasthāna-trayī* along with the *Upaniṣads* and *Brahma-sūtra*). From what we know, the first of these commentaries was written by the philosopher-saint Śaṅkara (*c.* 7th century CE). His work popularized the *Gītā* and also standardized the number of verses in the text. Some of the other notable scholars who wrote commentaries on the *Gītā* are Rāmānuja, Abhinavagupta, Madhva, Nimbārka, and Vallabha.

Many leaders of the Indian Independence movement (from the mid-19th to the mid-20th centuries CE) translated and interpreted the *Gītā*, including Tilak, Vivekananda, Gandhi, Aurobindo, Rajaji, Bharathiar, and Bhave.

The whole episode of the Kurukṣetra war is so deeply engraved in the Indian mind that for most Indians '*Gītā*' refers to *Bhagavad-gītā* and 'the Great War' refers to the battle of Kurukṣetra. This speaks a lot, given that there are many *gītās* in the Hindu canon like *Anu-gītā*, *Aśṭāvakra-gītā*, *Avadhūta-gītā*, *Devī-gītā*, *Gaṇeśa-gītā*, *Ribhu-gītā*, *Śiva-gītā*, and *Uddhava-gītā* (or *Haṃsa-gītā*) as well as numerous wars.

The influence of the *Gītā* outside India has also been enormous. It is the first Hindu treatise to cross the oceans and reach the continent of America. This is perhaps because the text has such a nice blend of everyday pragmatism and spiritual mysticism. It has something valuable for everybody.

(Appendix 4 has a compilation of quotes about the *Gītā* by different eminent people from all over the world, spanning many centuries.)

BHAGAVAD-GĪTĀ: THE TEXT

THE term '*bhagavadgītā*' is made up of two words – *bhagavat* (of the lord) and *gītā* (song), so '*Bhagavad-gītā*' in English is 'song of the lord.' Chapters 23 to 40 of the sixth book of the *Mahā-bhārata* contain the *Gītā* (of the BORI edition).

The *Gītā* has 700 verses divided into 18 chapters. Though it is structured thus, it is not a systematic manual but a conversation between two friends that is captured in poetry.

The *Gītā* does not present arguments in a linear way; it is circular and often descriptive, with repetitions and clarifications all through. Kṛṣṇa presents many ideas and opinions to inspire Arjuna to fight the war and in the course of the discussion, talks about many aspects of life. Finally, he gives the choice to Arjuna to decide for himself whether to fight or not.

Most of the verses in the *Gītā* are set to the Anuṣṭup meter, with 4 lines of 8 syllables each, like in 2.47 –

ka·rma·ṇye·vā·dhi·kā·ra·ste
mā pha·le·ṣu ka·dā·ca·na ।
mā ka·rma·pha·la·he·tu·rbhūḥ
mā te sa·ṅgo·'stva·ka·rma·ṇi ॥

A few verses are in the Triṣṭup poetic meter, with 4 lines of 11 syllables each, like in 2.20 –

na jā·ya·te mri·ya·te vā ka·dā·cit
nā·yaṃ bhū·tvā bha·vi·tā vā na bhū·yaḥ ।
a·jo ni·tyaḥ śā·śva·to·'yaṃ pu·rā·ṇo
na ha·nya·te ha·nya·mā·ne śa·rī·re ॥

(Appendix 1 of this book has a transliteration guide, which will help in reading Sanskrit written in the roman script. At the start of every chapter in this book, we have given the original Sanskrit text from the corresponding chapter in the *Bhagavad-gītā*.)

Every chapter of the *Gītā* ends with a colophon that includes the chapter number and name, along with a generic description of the *Gītā*. The colophon of the first chapter is –

Thus ends the first chapter '*Arjuna's Despair*'
from the Upaniṣad *Bhagavad-gītā*,
which is a dialog between Kṛṣṇa and Arjuna
on the knowledge of the Supreme and
the art of union with the Supreme.
That's the truth, *Om*!*

Though the colophon refers to the *Gītā* as an *Upaniṣad*, the *Gītā* is not one of the *Upaniṣads*. It is a suggestion that the *Gītā* too is worthy of the exalted status given to the *Upaniṣads*. The colophon is not found in the *Mahā-bhārata* but by convention is used while reciting the *Gītā*.

BHAGAVAD-GĪTĀ IN TRANSLATION

THE *Bhagavad-gītā* is is the most translated Indian book. *Sant* Jñāneśvar composed one of the earliest translations of the *Gītā* during the later part of 13th century CE; his Marathi language translation, along with elaborate commentary makes up the classic *Jñāneśvarī*.

Even earlier, Abu-Saleh is said to have translated the *Mahā-bhārata* into Arabic (11th century CE) and Abul-Hasan-Ali, into Persian (as *Modjmel-altevarykh* in 12th century CE). But the most popular Persian translation, *Razm nama*, was commissioned by Akbar in 16th century CE. All these works contain the *Gītā* either in part or in full.

* *oṃ-tat-sad-iti* । *śrīmad-bhagavad-gītāsu upaniṣatsu brahma-vidyāyāṃ yoga-śāstre śrīkṛṣṇārjuna-saṃvāde arjuna-viṣāda-yogo nāma prathamo'dhyāyaḥ* ।

Under the patronage of king Rāja Rāja Narendra, the poet Nannayya-bhaṭṭa (1000–60) started translating the *Mahā-bhārata* into Telugu but died after working on two books. Many years later, Tikkana-somayāji (1200–80) translated 15 books and Errā-pragaḍa (1280–1350) completed the work.

The poet-philosopher Vedānta-deśika (Veṅkaṭanāthan) (1269–1370) did a Tamil poetic translation of the *Gitārtha-saṅgraha*, a summary of the *Gītā* in Sanskrit, composed by philosopher-saint Yāmunācārya (Āḷavandār) (916–1041).

Mādhava Paṇikkar prepared a condensed Malayalam translation of the *Gītā* in 14th century CE. The great classical poet, Kumāra-vyāsa (Gadag Nāraṇappa), rendered the *Mahā-bhārata* into Kannada in his *Karṇāṭa-bhārata-kathā-mañjarī*, which was finished in 1430. Orissa's 'first poet,' Sarala Dāsa, adapted *Mahā-bhārata* into Oriya in his '*Sarala Mahā-bhārata*' (*c*. 15th century CE). It has portions of the *Gītā*.

Kabi Sañjaya translated the complete *Mahā-bhārata* into Bengali during the first half of 15th century CE.

During the reign of the Koch kings, Rāma Sarasvati translated the *Mahā-bhārata* into Assamese during 15th century CE. Later, King Lakṣminārāyaṇ commissioned Govinda Miśra to translate the *Gītā* into Assamese verse.

The *Gītā* has also been translated into many other major Indian languages like Gujarati, Hindi, Kashmiri, Punjabi, Sindhi, Urdu, *etc*.

The *Bhagavad-gītā* was first translated into English in 1785 by Charles Wilkins, an orientalist and typographer. Soon, his translation was translated into French and German. Later, the German poet August Wilhelm Schlegel translated the *Gītā* into Latin in 1823. Prussian minister and linguist Wilhelm von Humboldt translated the *Gītā* into German in 1826. In 1846, orientalist Christian Lassen translated the work into French and in 1848, Dimitrios Galanos, an Indologist, translated it into Greek.

By a conservative estimate, the *Gītā* has been translated about 2,500 times into over 75 languages.

SHORTCOMINGS IN GĪTĀ TRANSLATIONS

THE reason we embarked on this translation in the first place is that among the existing versions we studied, we found many with translation errors, inappropriate word choices, misinterpretations, and misrepresentations.

The task of a translator is one fraught with challenges and dangers: in trying to be very accurate, one may lose sight of simplicity and by trying to be easily understood, s/he might compromise the contents of the original; in trying to be concise, one might sacrifice clarity and by trying to make things very clear, s/he might end up being verbose and lose out on beauty. The translator's troubles are magnified when dealing with two different languages such as Sanskrit and English.

It would be best to illustrate with a few examples.

Translation Errors In verse 3.24, the word *saṅkara*, which means 'chaos' or 'confusion' often gets translated as 'caste confusion' (*varṇa-saṅkara*), which is incorrect.

In verse 4.13, some people translate the word *guṇa* as though it is *triguṇa* (*i.e.*, *sattva*, *rajas*, and *tamas*). While *triguṇa* represent the three kinds of attitudes, *guṇa* is a general term that pertains to all inherent qualities of a person—aptitude and attitude—which along with *karma* determines his/her *varṇa* in the society. We clearly observe this in chapters 14 and 17 where *triguṇa* is expounded in great detail but there is no reference to *varṇa*.

In 12.5, a sectarian scholar translates the word *avyaktam* as 'Goddess Lakshmi.' Even a basic knowledge of Sanskrit is sufficient to know that *avyaktam* means 'formless,' 'beyond form,' or 'not perceivable.'

Inappropriate Word Choices In the famous verse 2.47, many translate *adhikāraḥ* as 'right' or 'duty,' which makes the first part of verse –

For action alone is thy right but never to the fruits thereof.

This doesn't make much sense in general (Who will work when the fruits of his labour are prohibited!) and is especially meaningless in the context of 2.37 where Kṛṣṇa says,

If you are killed, you will attain *svarga*.
If you are victorious, you will rule over the kingdom.

And so, translating *adhikāraḥ* as 'control' makes much more sense:

You can control only your actions;
you can't control the results.

In 12.19, many translate the word *aniketaḥ* as 'homeless,' 'without a home,' 'unsheltered,' 'whose home is not in this world,' 'who owns no home,' *etc*. Indeed, the literal meaning of the word *aniketaḥ* is 'one without a fixed place of residence' but it seems to suggest that the Supreme is particularly fond of vagabonds. In this context, it must be understood as a person who is not particularly attached to any place as his home while at the same time, he feels at home everywhere.

Simplistic Translations This is often seen in non-Indian translators who are not initiated into the culture of Bhārata or in English-educated Indians who approach the text without grasping cultural nuances. Further, perhaps in a bid to make the text accessible to an international audience, they sacrifice accuracy for the sake of simplicity. An example of such over-simplification can be seen in this translation of verse 7.14:

Composed of nature's qualities,
my divine magic is hard to escape;
but those who seek refuge in me
cross over this magic.

Translating the term *guṇa* as 'quality' may be allowed with some lenience but translating *māyā* as 'magic' is over-simplification.

This verse merely states that it is hard to escape *māyā*, the divine power of illusion. It is only when we recognize a greater force governing the cosmic order that we are able to overcome this divine *māyā* –

It is indeed difficult to overcome
the influence of my divine *māyā*,
which is caused by the *guṇa*s.
But those who submit to me
overcome the influence of *māyā*.

Translating the words *ātman* as 'soul' or 'self,' *brahmacarya* as 'celibacy,' *brāhmaṇa* as 'priest,' *guṇa* as 'quality,' *karma* as 'action,' *pāpa* as 'sin,' *prāṇa* as 'vital breath,' *rajas* as 'passion,' *sāṅkhya* as 'philosophy,' *sattva* as 'lucidity' or 'goodness,' *tamas* as 'dark inertia,' *varṇa* as 'caste,' *Veda* as 'sacred lore,' or *yoga* as 'discipline' or 'physical exercise' are either inadequate or worse, incorrect.

Untranslatables Ancient languages often have words and phrases that are 'untranslatable.' This means that there is no direct, single-word/phrase equivalent in the language into which one wants to translate. To subsitute the original word with a rough, one-word translation not only dilutes the meaning but also implies what is not intended.

For example, if we translate *dharma* as 'religion' or 'duty,' *yajña* as 'sacrifice,' or *puṇya* as 'religious merit,' we will not be doing justice to the original terms. An effective way to deal with untranslatables is to simply give the original term as is and provide a short explanation for it. This is what we have done in the present work.

Literal Translations At the other end of the spectrum we find translators who stick to the letter more than the spirit of the original. They are willing to be authentic at the cost of not being intelligible. They try to adhere to even the form of the original, thus coming up with clunky and unaesthetic renditions in the translated language. A *literal* translation of verse 2.46* would be:

* The original verse is: *yāvānartha udapāne sarvataḥ samplutodake / tāvānsarveṣu vedeṣu brāhmaṇasya vijānataḥ*.

Word-by-word meanings are presented below to give a better idea: *yāvān* (as much), *artha* (use, meaning, value, aim), *udapāne* (in a well or reservoir of water), *sarvatah* (everywhere, surrounded, on all sides), *sampluta* (overflowing, flooding), *udake* (with water) *tāvān* (so much) *sarveṣu vedeṣu* (in all the *Vedas*); *brāhmaṇasya* (of the *brahman*, of the ultimate truth), *vijānataḥ* (who knows, knowing, realized).

As much use there is for a well when water is
overflowing everywhere that much use there is in
all the *Veda*s for a person who knows the *brahman*.

This is not an incorrect translation; however, this is not a typical method of constructing a sentence in English (while it is admirably suited to Sanskrit). To be effective, we have to recreate this idea without losing the spirit and without straying too much away from the letter:

What is the use of a well when there is a flood
and water is flowing freely everywhere?
What is the use of all the *Veda*s
when one has realized the Ultimate Truth?

Using Commentary as a Crutch In some scholarly translations, a verse doesn't make much sense without the help of the long commentary that follows it. Different versions of 18.70 closely matches the following:

And I consider that he who commits this sacred dialogue of
ours to memory, by him I shall have been worshiped by the
sacrifice-of-knowledge – such is my conviction.

When we translate the verse by understanding the spirit behind it, no elaborate commentary is required:

Whoever earnestly studies this sacred dialog –
I consider him to have honored me
through *jñāna-yajña*
(*i.e.*, he has made an effort
to understand my words of wisdom).

Unclear Without Commentary There are some verses that are not easy to translate and even after translation, they require a little bit of explanation without which the meaning remains unclear. Let us take the example of a translation of verse 3.28:

When he can discriminate
the actions of nature's qualities
and think, "The qualities depend
on other qualities," he is detached.

Strictly speaking, this is not incorrect. But this verse contains certain subtleties that requires not just an understanding of Sanskrit but also an insight into the tradition.

The world is always in motion and thus, always changing. Most of us are a part of society and are influenced by it. Our customs, mannerisms, and practices adjust themselves to our surroundings if we let them follow a natural course. If we are perturbed by changing times and cling to practices that are irrelevant, we are bound to be confused and frustrated – this is what the verse is trying to say:

One who has true insight into
the interplay of *guṇa** and *karma*†—
and how they are influenced
by the collective nature of society—
does not get entangled.

Unclear Despite Commentary In some instances, even with the lengthy commentary, a verse does not make much sense. Verses 8.24 and 8.25 explain how the time of death of a *yogin* (a realized person) determines whether s/he is liberated or is reborn. Many versions translate those two verses like this:

* Inherent traits of an individual † Different spheres of action

Fire, light, day-time, the bright-fortnight,
the six months of the northern path (of the Sun) –
there departing the knowers of Brahman go to Brahman.

Smoke, night-time, dark-fortnight,
the six months of the southern path (of the Sun) –
there obtaining the lunar light the yogi returns.

Day and night, as well as bright and dark fortnights are present all through the year; therefore we must understand the metaphor if we wish to truly understand the verse.

The many attributes like fire, light, day, bright, *etc*. can be seen as adjectives to the six months of the apparent northward path of the sun. In a sense, this represents 'light.'

Smoke, night, dark, *etc*. are adjectives to the six months of the apparent southward path of the sun. In a sense, this represents 'darkness.'

The verses suggest that a *yogin* who dies during *uttarāyaṇa* goes forth to reach *Brahman* but one who dies in *dakṣiṇāyana* is born again. From this we may infer that only some of the realized people get liberated while the rest of them are among us, guiding us towards liberation.

Let us take another example. Verse 18.14 speaks about the five factors that govern the outcomes of all actions. There are versions that translate it like this:

...the 'seat' (body), the 'doer,' the various sense organs of perception, the different functions of various organs of actions, and the presiding deity also, the fifth.

What does this really mean? How can one separate the doer (*kartā*) from body, senses, sense organs, and organs of work? Also, translating the word *daivam* in a literal sense as 'presiding deity' only adds to the confusion, especially after Kṛṣṇa says in 5.14–15 that god cannot be held responsible for human actions.

In essence, the verse means:

...the situation, the individual,
the tools he has, how he uses the tools,
and unknown forces.

Force-fitting Some translations awkwardly try to force-fit a given verse to the dictates of a latter-day sectarian scholar of their inkling, at the cost of being dishonest to the original. The result is that the eternal truth is sacrificed at the altar of dogma. One such translation of 3.9 is:

Work done as a sacrifice for Visnu has to be performed,
otherwise work binds one to this material world.
Therefore, O son of Kunti, perform your prescribed duties
for His satisfaction, and in that way you will
always remain unattached and free from bondage.

The verse has been distorted with the use of non-existent ideas. What the original really says is:

Humans are bound by their actions
except when they are performed
for the sake of *yajña**.
Thus, Arjuna, do your work,
free from attachments,
in the spirit of *yajña*.

* In this context, refers to 'an act of self-dedication' or 'service above self.' *Yajña* is also an act of worship; so the message is 'do your work as worship.'

Misinterpretation In 3.35, the word *svadharma* (one's own *dharma*) is often misinterpreted; almost everyone translates *dharma* as 'duty' and some translate it as 'duty that is pertaining to your *varṇa*,' thus reinforcing the misconstrued views about the social structure:

It is better to practice your own duty (pertaining to your caste)
deficiently than another's duty well. It is better to die
conforming to your own caste duty (or religion); the duty
(pertaining to caste or religion) of another invites danger.

Like other Sanskrit words, *dharma* has different meanings in different contexts. Here, it refers to 'the state of mind' or 'innate nature.' And 'one's own *dharma*' refers to 'work in tune with one's inherent nature' and the translation simply yields:

Excelling in one's own *dharma*, even if it is less glamorous
is better than trying to excel in another's *dharma*.
It is better to die upholding one's *dharma*;
following the *dharma* of others is worse than death.

In verse 9.32 translators and commentators often make the mistake of rendering the word *pāpayonayaḥ* (of sinful birth) as an adjective to women, traders, and laborers, instead of treating it as a separate category. Chapter 16 of the *Gītā* has a clear exposition of the traits of sinful people but doesn't have any reference to *varṇa* or gender.

What the verse really tries to say is that although society may perceive a certain individual or social group as being backward or cursed, nothing will come in the way of their liberation once they take refuge in the Supreme. In fact, Kṛṣṇa says that even the worst sort of sinner or criminal can cross the ocean of evil with the raft of wisdom (verse 4.36) – what then to say of people who are not evil but are merely looked down upon by society!

Misrepresentation A major drawback in existing translations is that none of them really address the numerous fallacies of Arjuna. Worse yet, time and again, the orthodoxy has sided with Arjuna's psyche and has offered the justification that 'it has been said in the *Bhagavad-gītā*,' failing to realize that the words of Arjuna are those of a confused person. Arjuna's preoccupations with the outdated post-death rites, *svarga* and *naraka*, disruption of the social structure, and misplaced pacifism have had many supporters. Ironically, all these notions are opposed to the way of life envisioned in the noble thoughts of the ancient Indians.

When we tell someone that we are studying the *Gītā*, a typical question that follows is: "Whose version are you studying?" They might even steer us to a version that reflects their preferred dogma or upbringing.

Such people appear to be more interested in a certain scholar's interpretation of the text or some new-age *guru*'s best-selling book rather than the words of Kṛṣṇa or the text of the *Bhagavad-gītā*!

In spite of the failings of prevalent translations and the divisive mindsets, the *Gītā* has widely inspired and enriched people from all over the world ever since it was first translated into English more than two hundred years ago. We wondered what would be result of attempting to free the translation of the drawbacks and presenting the verses in a pristine state with minimal commentary.

The aim of this book is to liberate the translation from all short-sighted, sectarian, and dogmatic ideas, and to present it in a language that is as simple as the *Bhagavad-gītā* itself, and free from lengthy explanations.

Upon reading the text in an unpolluted form, readers may choose to understand, interpret, and implement it as best suited to them.

This, in itself, will have fulfilled the purpose of our labours.

CONCLUSION

In an ideal world, we don't need any religion by its brand name. We have enough collective wisdom that many of us employ in various aspects of our daily life, irrespective of race, gender, or education. *Our true nature knows right from wrong.* So we could easily light the fire and burn all religious books. But that would be inefficient. Why would we want to miss the opportunity to stand on the shoulders of giants?

We read and enjoy novels written by great authors without worrying about their religious backgrounds, but things change drastically when religion comes into the picture. We get crazy. We simply refuse to learn from each other when it is a matter of faith. In addition, we try to convince others that our brand of religion is the best.

Perhaps the world is not yet ready to absorb the collective wisdom from all religions and philosophies. The best we can do then is to present the most important book in each of our religions and cultures, and leave it at that; readers can draw their own conclusions.

People of a particular religion often take their books for granted and read them with minimal introspection beyond the dictates of their sectarian views. On the other hand, people from foreign cultures might not be very familiar with these books. And so, revisiting such works might give fresh insights to adherents and a totally new inspiration to everyone at large.

There are innumerable spiritual/philosophical treatises in the Hindu tradition starting from the *Veda*s to portions of the *Upaveda*s and *Vedāṅga*s all the way to the *Itihāsa-Purāṇa*s and the huge body of works that come under the *Darśanas*. The *Gītā* is a beautiful synthesis of many of the ideas that appear in these treatises. Diverse religious-philosophical-spiritual concepts are harmonized in the *Gītā* (see p. 428). It gives us the freedom to choose our *iṣṭa-daiva*—'deity of choice'—as well as our *iṣṭa-tattva*—'philosophy of choice.' This is the unique feature of *Sanātana-dharma*. To our knowledge, no other scripture has addressed various fundamental concepts under one cover. This perhaps is the reason for the *Gītā* becoming the most popular work of *Sanātana-dharma*.

The *Bhagavad-gītā* is a great place to start if one wants to know about India's grand heritage, literature, philosophy, culture, religious traditions, and spirituality.

May it protect both of us.
May it nourish both of us.
Let us work together.
Let our work be lit up by vigor.
Let us not hate each other.
May peace prevail, *Oṃ*!

(from the *Kaṭha-upaniṣad*)

Invocation

Salutations to the Supreme Lord,
the teacher of the world, and
the source of Eternal Bliss!

1

धृतराष्ट्र उवाच ।
धर्मक्षेत्रे कुरुक्षेत्रे
समवेता युयुत्सवः ।
मामकाः पाण्डवाश्चैव
किमकुर्वत सञ्जय ॥ १.१

dhṛtarāṣṭra uvāca ।
dharmakṣetre kurukṣetre ।
samavetā yuyutsavaḥ ।
māmakāḥ pāṇḍavāścaiva
kimakurvata sañjaya ॥ 1.1

सञ्जय उवाच ।
दृष्ट्वा तु पाण्डवानीकं
व्यूढं दुर्योधनस्तदा ।
आचार्यमुपसङ्गम्य
राजा वचनमब्रवीत् ॥ १.२

sañjaya uvāca ।
dṛṣṭvā tu pāṇḍavānīkaṃ
vyūḍhaṃ duryodhanastadā ।
ācāryamupasaṅgamya
rājā vacanamabravīt ॥ 1.2

पश्यैतां पाण्डुपुत्राणाम्
आचार्य महतीं चमूम् ।
व्यूढां द्रुपदपुत्रेण
तव शिष्येण धीमता ॥ १.३

paśyaitāṃ pāṇḍuputrāṇām
ācārya mahatīṃ camūm ।
vyūḍhāṃ drupadaputreṇa
tava śiṣyeṇa dhīmatā ॥ 1.3

अत्र शूरा महेष्वासा
भीमार्जुनसमा युधि ।
युयुधानो विराटश्च
द्रुपदश्च महारथः ॥ १.४

atra śūrā maheṣvāsā
bhīmārjunasamā yudhi ।
yuyudhāno virāṭaśca
drupadaśca mahārathaḥ ॥ 1.4

धृष्टकेतुश्चेकितानः
काशिराजश्च वीर्यवान् ।
पुरुजित्कुन्तिभोजश्च
शैब्यश्च नरपुङ्गवः ॥ १.५

dhṛṣṭaketuścekitānaḥ
kāśirājaśca vīryavān ।
purujitkuntibhojaśca
śaibyaśca narapuṅgavaḥ ॥ 1.5

युधामन्युश्च विक्रान्त
उत्तमौजाश्च वीर्यवान् ।
सौभद्रो द्रौपदेयाश्च
सर्व एव महारथाः ॥ १.६

yudhāmanyuśca vikrānta
uttamaujāśca vīryavān ।
saubhadro draupadeyāśca
sarva eva mahārathāḥ ॥ 1.6

अस्माकं तु विशिष्टा ये
तान्निबोध द्विजोत्तम ।
नायका मम सैन्यस्य
सञ्ज्ञार्थं तान् ब्रवीमि ते ॥ १.७

asmākaṃ tu viśiṣṭā ye
tānnibodha dvijottama ।
nāyakā mama sainyasya
sañjñārthaṃ tān bravīmi te ॥ 1.7

भवान्भीष्मश्च कर्णश्च
कृपश्च समितिञ्जयः ।
अश्वत्थामा विकर्णश्च
सौमदत्तिस्तथैव च ॥ १.८

bhavānbhīṣmaśca karṇaśca
kṛpaśca samitiñjayaḥ ।
aśvatthāmā vikarṇaśca
saumadattistathaiva ca ॥ 1.8

अन्ये च बहवः शूरा
मदर्थे त्यक्तजीविताः ।
नानाशस्त्रप्रहरणाः
सर्वे युद्धविशारदाः ॥ १.९

anye ca bahavaḥ śūrā
madarthe tyaktajīvitāḥ ।
nānāśastrapraharaṇāḥ
sarve yuddhaviśāradāḥ ॥ 1.9

अपर्याप्तं तदस्माकं
बलं भीष्माभिरक्षितम् ।
पर्याप्तं त्विदम् एतेषां
बलं भीमाभिरक्षितम् ॥ १.१०

aparyāptaṃ tadasmākaṃ
balaṃ bhīṣmābhirakṣitam ।
paryāptaṃ tvidam eteṣāṃ
balaṃ bhīmābhirakṣitam ॥ 1.10

अयनेषु च सर्वेषु
यथाभागमवस्थिताः ।
भीष्मम् एवाभिरक्षन्तु
भवन्तः सर्व एव हि ॥ १.११

ayaneṣu ca sarveṣu
yathābhāgamavasthitāḥ ।
bhīṣmam evābhirakṣantu
bhavantaḥ sarva eva hi ॥ 1.11

तस्य सञ्जनयन्हर्षं
कुरुवृद्धः पितामहः ।
सिंहनादं विनद्योच्चैः
शङ्खं दध्मौ प्रतापवान् ॥ १.१२

tasya sañjanayanharṣaṃ
kuruvṛddhaḥ pitāmahaḥ ।
siṃhanādaṃ vinadyoccaiḥ
śaṅkhaṃ dadhmau pratāpavān ॥ 1.12

ततः शङ्खाश्च भेर्यश्च
पणवानकगोमुखाः ।
सहसैवाभ्यहन्यन्त
स शब्दस्तुमुलोऽभवत् ॥ १.१३

tataḥ śaṅkhāśca bheryaśca
paṇavānakagomukhāḥ ।
sahasaivābhyahanyanta
sa śabdastumulo'bhavat ॥ 1.13

ततः श्वेतैर्हयैर्युक्ते
महति स्यन्दने स्थितौ ।
माधवः पाण्डवश्चैव
दिव्यौ शङ्खौ प्रदध्मतुः ॥ १.१४

tataḥ śvetairhayairyukte
mahati syandane sthitau ।
mādhavaḥ pāṇḍavaścaiva
divyau śaṅkhau pradadhmatuḥ ॥ 1.14

पाञ्चजन्यं हृषीकेशो
देवदत्तं धनञ्जयः ।
पौण्ड्रं दध्मौ महाशङ्खं
भीमकर्मा वृकोदरः ॥ १.१५

pāñcajanyaṃ hṛṣīkeśo
devadattaṃ dhanañjayaḥ ।
pauṇḍraṃ dadhmau mahāśaṅkhaṃ
bhīmakarmā vṛkodaraḥ ॥ 1.15

अनन्तविजयं राजा कुन्तीपुत्रो युधिष्ठिरः । नकुलः सहदेवश्च सुघोषमणिपुष्पकौ ॥ १.१६	*anantavijayaṃ rājā* *kuntīputro yudhiṣṭhiraḥ* । *nakulaḥ sahadevaśca* *sughoṣamaṇipuṣpakau* ॥ 1.16
काश्यश्च परमेष्वासः शिखण्डी च महारथः । धृष्टद्युम्नो विराटश्च सात्यकिश्चापराजितः ॥ १.१७	*kāśyaśca parameṣvāsaḥ* *śikhaṇḍī ca mahārathaḥ* । *dhṛṣṭadyumno virāṭaśca* *sātyakiścāparājitaḥ* ॥ 1.17
द्रुपदो द्रौपदेयाश्च सर्वशः पृथिवीपते । सौभद्रश्च महाबाहुः शङ्खान्दध्मुः पृथक्पृथक् ॥ १.१८	*drupado draupadeyāśca* *sarvaśaḥ pṛthivīpate* । *saubhadraśca mahābāhuḥ* *śaṅkhāndadhmuḥ pṛthakpṛthak* ॥ 1.18
स घोषो धार्तराष्ट्राणां हृदयानि व्यदारयत् । नभश्च पृथिवीं चैव तुमुलो व्यनुनादयन् ॥ १.१९	*sa ghoṣo dhārtarāṣṭrāṇāṃ* *hṛdayāni vyadārayat* । *nabhaśca pṛthivīṃ caiva* *tumulo vyanunādayan* ॥ 1.19
अथ व्यवस्थितान्दृष्ट्वा धार्तराष्ट्रान्कपिध्वजः । प्रवृत्ते शस्त्रसम्पाते धनुरुद्यम्य पाण्डवः ॥ १.२०	*atha vyavasthitāndṛṣṭvā* *dhārtarāṣṭrānkapidhvajaḥ* । *pravṛtte śastrasampāte* *dhanurudyamya pāṇḍavaḥ* ॥ 1.20
हृषीकेशं तदा वाक्यम् इदमाह महीपते । सेनयोरुभयोर्मध्ये रथं स्थापय मेऽच्युत ॥ १.२१	*hṛṣīkeśaṃ tadā vākyam* *idamāha mahīpate* । *senayorubhayormadhye* *rathaṃ sthāpaya me'cyuta* ॥ 1.21
यावदेतान्निरीक्षेऽहं योद्धुकामानवस्थितान् । कैर्मया सह योद्धव्यम् अस्मिन्रणसमुद्यमे ॥ १.२२	*yāvadetānnirīkṣe'haṃ* *yoddhukāmānavasthitān* । *kairmayā saha yoddhavyam* *asminraṇasamudyame* ॥ 1.22
योत्स्यमानानवेक्षेऽहं य एतेऽत्र समागताः । धार्तराष्ट्रस्य दुर्बुद्धेः युद्धे प्रियचिकीर्षवः ॥ १.२३	*yotsyamānānavekṣe'haṃ* *ya ete'tra samāgatāḥ* । *dhārtarāṣṭrasya durbuddheḥ* *yuddhe priyacikīrṣavaḥ* ॥ 1.23

एवमुक्तो हृषीकेशो
गुडाकेशेन भारत ।
सेनयोरुभयोर्मध्ये
स्थापयित्वा रथोत्तमम् ॥ १.२४

evamukto hṛṣīkeśo
guḍākeśena bhārata ।
senayorubhayormadhye
sthāpayitvā rathottamam ॥ 1.24

भीष्मद्रोणप्रमुखतः
सर्वेषां च महीक्षिताम् ।
उवाच पार्थ पश्यैतान्
समवेतान्कुरूनिति ॥ १.२५

bhīṣmadroṇapramukhataḥ
sarveṣāṃ ca mahīkṣitām ।
uvāca pārtha paśyaitān
samavetānkurūniti ॥ 1.25

तत्रापश्यत्स्थितान्पार्थः
पितृनथ पितामहान् ।
आचार्यान्मातुलान्भ्रातृन्
पुत्रान्पौत्रान्सखींस्तथा ॥ १.२६

tatrāpaśyatsthitānpārthaḥ
pitṝnatha pitāmahān ।
ācāryānmātulānbhrātṝn
putrānpautrānsakhīṃstathā ॥ 1.26

श्वशुरान्सुहृदश्चैव
सेनयोरुभयोरपि ।
तान्समीक्ष्य स कौन्तेयः
सर्वान्बन्धूनवस्थितान् ॥ १.२७

śvaśurānsuhṛdaścaiva
senayorubhayorapi ।
tānsamīkṣya sa kaunteyaḥ
sarvānbandhūnavasthitān ॥ 1.27

कृपया परयाविष्टो
विषीदन्निदमब्रवीत् ।
दृष्ट्वेमान्स्वजनान्कृष्ण
युयुत्सून्समवस्थितान् ॥ १.२८*

kṛpayā parayāviṣṭo
viṣīdannidamabravīt ।
dṛṣṭvemānsvajanānkṛṣṇa
yuyutsūnsamavasthitān ॥ 1.28*

सीदन्ति मम गात्राणि
मुखं च परिशुष्यति ।
वेपथुश्च शरीरे मे
रोमहर्षश्च जायते ॥ १.२९

sīdanti mama gātrāṇi
mukhaṃ ca pariśuṣyati ।
vepathuśca śarīre me
romaharṣaśca jāyate ॥ 1.29

गाण्डीवं स्रंसते हस्तात्
त्वक्चैव परिदह्यते ।
न च शक्नोम्यवस्थातुं
भ्रमतीव च मे मनः ॥ १.३०

gāṇḍīvaṃ sraṃsate hastāt
tvakcaiva paridahyate ।
na ca śaknomyavasthātuṃ
bhramatīva ca me manaḥ ॥ 1.30

निमित्तानि च पश्यामि
विपरीतानि केशव ।
न च श्रेयोऽनुपश्यामि
हत्वा स्वजनमाहवे ॥ १.३१

nimittāni ca paśyāmi
viparītāni keśava ।
na ca śreyo'nupaśyāmi
hatvā svajanamāhave ॥ 1.31

* In the second half of 1.28, many versions have दृष्ट्वेमं स्वजनं कृष्ण युयुत्सुं समुपस्थितम् / *dṛṣṭvemaṃ svajanaṃ kṛṣṇa yuyutsuṃ samupasthitam.*

न काङ्क्षे विजयं कृष्ण
न च राज्यं सुखानि च ।
किं नो राज्येन गोविन्द
किं भोगैर्जीवितेन वा ॥ १.३२

na kāṅkṣe vijayaṃ kṛṣṇa
na ca rājyaṃ sukhāni ca ।
kiṃ no rājyena govinda
kiṃ bhogairjīvitena vā ॥ 1.32

येषामर्थे काङ्क्षितं नो
राज्यं भोगाः सुखानि च ।
त इमेऽवस्थिता युद्धे
प्राणांस्त्यक्त्वा धनानि च ॥ १.३३

yeṣāmarthe kāṅkṣitaṃ no
rājyaṃ bhogāḥ sukhāni ca ।
ta ime'vasthitā yuddhe
prāṇāṃstyaktvā dhanāni ca ॥ 1.33

आचार्याः पितरः पुत्राः
तथैव च पितामहाः ।
मातुलाः श्वशुराः पौत्राः
स्यालाः सम्बन्धिनस्तथा ॥ १.३४

ācāryāḥ pitaraḥ putrāḥ
tathaiva ca pitāmahāḥ ।
mātulāḥ śvaśurāḥ pautrāḥ
syālāḥ sambandhinastathā ॥ 1.34

एतान्न हन्तुमिच्छामि
घ्नतोऽपि मधुसूदन ।
अपि त्रैलोक्यराज्यस्य
हेतोः किं नु महीकृते ॥ १.३५

etānna hantumicchāmi
ghnato'pi madhusūdana ।
api trailokyarājyasya
hetoḥ kiṃ nu mahīkṛte ॥ 1.35

निहत्य धार्तराष्ट्रान्नः
का प्रीतिः स्याज्जनार्दन ।
पापमेवाश्रयेदस्मान्
हत्वैतानाततायिनः ॥ १.३६

nihatya dhārtarāṣṭrānnaḥ
kā prītiḥ syājjanārdana ।
pāpamevāśrayedasmān
hatvaitānātatāyinaḥ ॥ 1.36

तस्मान्नार्हा वयं हन्तुं
धार्तराष्ट्रान्सबान्धवान् ।
स्वजनं हि कथं हत्वा
सुखिनः स्याम माधव ॥ १.३७

tasmānnārhā vayaṃ hantuṃ
dhārtarāṣṭrānsabāndhavān ।
svajanaṃ hi kathaṃ hatvā
sukhinaḥ syāma mādhava ॥ 1.37

यद्यप्येते न पश्यन्ति
लोभोपहतचेतसः ।
कुलक्षयकृतं दोषं
मित्रद्रोहे च पातकम् ॥ १.३८

yadyapyete na paśyanti
lobhopahatacetasaḥ ।
kulakṣayakṛtaṃ doṣaṃ
mitradrohe ca pātakam ॥ 1.38

कथं न ज्ञेयमस्माभिः
पापादस्मान्निवर्तितुम् ।
कुलक्षयकृतं दोषं
प्रपश्यद्भिर्जनार्दन ॥ १.३९

kathaṃ na jñeyamasmābhiḥ
pāpādasmānnivartitum ।
kulakṣayakṛtaṃ doṣaṃ
prapaśyadbhirjanārdana ॥ 1.39

कुलक्षये प्रणश्यन्ति
कुलधर्माः सनातनाः ।
धर्मे नष्टे कुलं कृत्स्नम्
अधर्मोऽभिभवत्युत ।। १.४०

kulakṣaye praṇaśyanti
kuladharmāḥ sanātanāḥ ।
dharme naṣṭe kulaṃ kṛtsnam
adharmo'bhibhavatyuta ।। 1.40

अधर्माभिभवात्कृष्ण
प्रदुष्यन्ति कुलस्त्रियः ।
स्त्रीषु दुष्टासु वार्ष्णेय
जायते वर्णसङ्करः ।। १.४१

adharmābhibhavātkṛṣṇa
praduṣyanti kulastriyaḥ ।
strīṣu duṣṭāsu vārṣṇeya
jāyate varṇasaṅkaraḥ ।। 1.41

सङ्करो नरकायैव
कुलघ्नानां कुलस्य च ।
पतन्ति पितरो ह्येषां
लुप्तपिण्डोदकक्रियाः ।। १.४२

saṅkaro narakāyaiva
kulaghnānāṃ kulasya ca ।
patanti pitaro hyeṣāṃ
luptapiṇḍodakakriyāḥ ।। 1.42

दोषैरेतैः कुलघ्नानां
वर्णसङ्करकारकैः ।
उत्साद्यन्ते जातिधर्माः
कुलधर्माश्च शाश्वताः ।। १.४३

doṣairetaiḥ kulaghnānāṃ
varṇasaṅkarakārakaiḥ ।
utsādyante jātidharmāḥ
kuladharmāśca śāśvatāḥ ।। 1.43

उत्सन्नकुलधर्माणां
मनुष्याणां जनार्दन ।
नरके नियतं वासो
भवतीत्यनुशुश्रुम ।। १.४४

utsannakuladharmāṇāṃ
manuṣyāṇāṃ janārdana ।
narake niyataṃ vāso
bhavatītyanuśuśruma ।। 1.44

अहो बत महत्पापं
कर्तुं व्यवसिता वयम् ।
यद्राज्यसुखलोभेन
हन्तुं स्वजनमुद्यताः ।। १.४५

aho bata mahatpāpaṃ
kartuṃ vyavasitā vayam ।
yadrājyasukhalobhena
hantuṃ svajanamudyatāḥ ।। 1.45

यदि मामप्रतीकारम्
अशस्त्रं शस्त्रपाणयः ।
धार्तराष्ट्रा रणे हन्युः
तन्मे क्षेमतरं भवेत् ।। १.४६

yadi māmapratīkāram
aśastraṃ śastrapāṇayaḥ ।
dhārtarāṣṭrā raṇe hanyuḥ
tanme kṣemataraṃ bhavet ।। 1.46

एवमुक्त्वार्जुनः सङ्ख्ये
रथोपस्थ उपाविशत् ।
विसृज्य सशरं चापं
शोकसंविग्नमानसः ।। १.४७

evamuktvārjunaḥ saṅkhye
rathopastha upāviśat ।
visṛjya saśaraṃ cāpaṃ
śokasaṃvignamānasaḥ ।। 1.47

CHAPTER I

Arjuna's Despair

Dhṛtarāṣṭra

1 Sañjaya, tell me what is happening
in the sacred land of Kurukṣetra,
where my people and the Pāṇḍavas
have assembled, eager to fight.

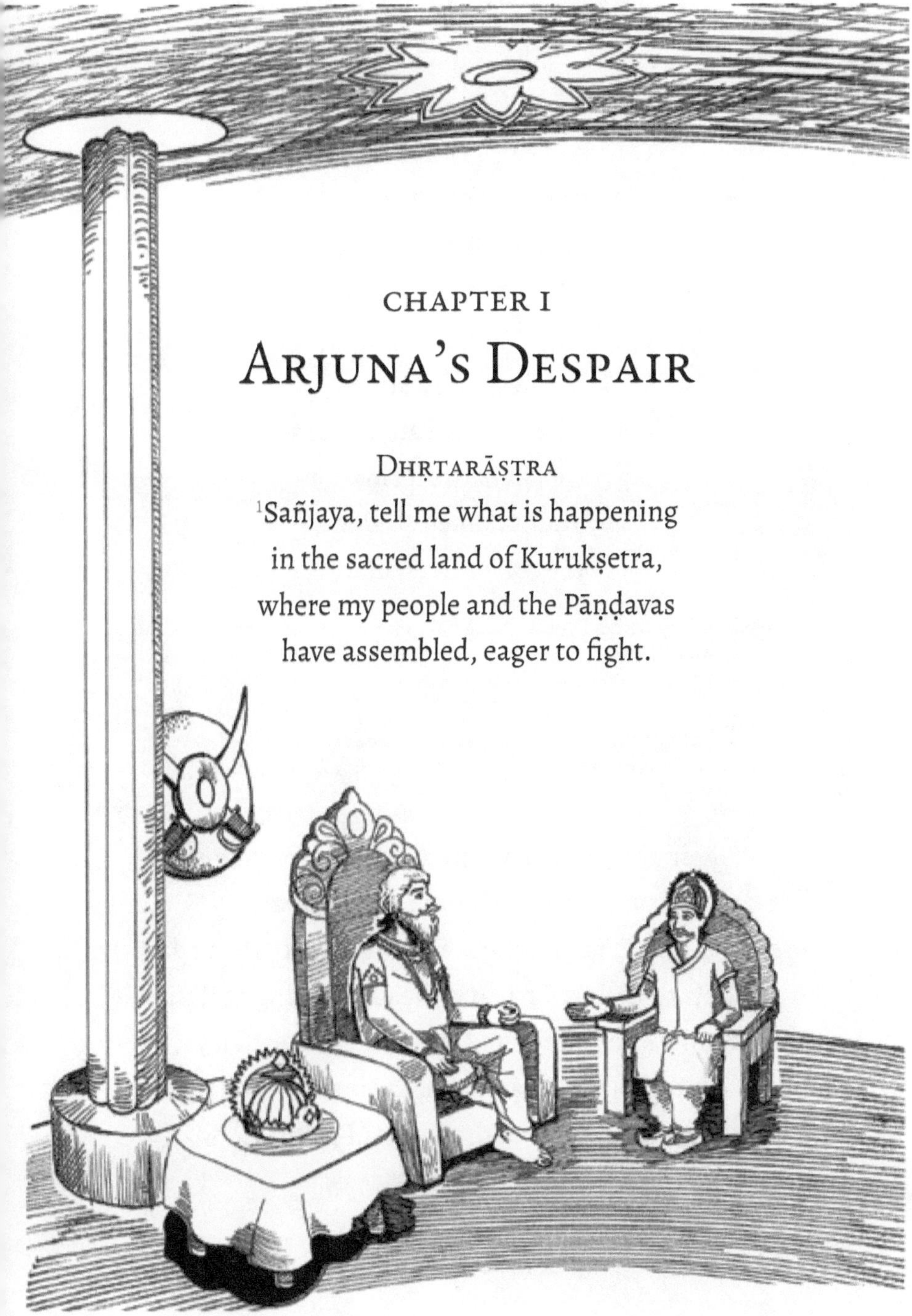

Sañjaya

[2]O King! Prince Duryodhana saw
the Pāṇḍava army drawn up for battle.
Then he went to his tutor Droṇa
and spoke these words:

[3]"Respected sir,
look at the mighty Pāṇḍava army
arrayed in battle formation
by your talented student,
the son of Drupada.

Duryodhana approaches Droṇa although Bhīṣma was the Commander-in-Chief of the Kaurava forces, for he knew that Bhīṣma loved the Pāṇḍavas more and may not fight whole-heartedly. He seemed to have greater confidence in Droṇa to wage the war with all his might. Knowing fully well that Drupada was a sworn enemy of Droṇa, he praises Drupada's son (in this verse) as well as Drupada as a mighty warrior (in the following verse).

[4]"Their army has many great archers and heroes
comparable to Bhīma and Arjuna,
such as Yuyudhāna, Virāṭa, and the mighty Drupada,
[5]Dhṛṣṭaketu, Cekitāna, and the valiant king of Kāśī,
Purujit, Kuntibhoja, and the best of men, Śaibya,
[6]the courageous Yudhāmanyu, the brave Uttamaujas,
Abhimanyu, and the sons of Draupadī.
They are all *mahārathas*.

A *mahāratha* is one who is skilled in warfare and can fight ten thousand warriors at once.

7"Likewise, O best of men, also take a look at
the distinguished warriors on our side.
I shall briefly name the leaders in our army.

8"Besides yourself,
Bhīṣma, Karṇa, the victorious Kṛpa,
Aśvatthāman, Vikarṇa, and Saumadatti.
9There are many other heroes armed
with a variety of weapons,
and each skilled in the art of war.
All of them are prepared
to give up their lives for my sake!

Selflessness has always been an important part of the Indian ethos.
Therefore, Duryodhana's 'my sake' is an aberration;
it is a reflection of his bloated ego.

10"Our army led by Bhīṣma seems inadequate,
whereas their force led by Bhīma looks sufficient!"

Duryodhana is envious of Bhīma's strength and courage.
Thus, he sees Bhīma as leading the Pāṇḍava army
although it is led by Dhṛṣṭadyumna.

Duryodhana's grand description of the Pāṇḍava army implies that he thinks
they are stronger, although they are lesser in number than the Kauravas.

This verse could also mean:
"Our army led by Bhīṣma seems unlimited,
whereas their force led by Bhīma looks limited!"
but given the context, we have preferred our version.

At this point, Duryodhana addresses his side –

11 "Positioned in your designated places, in every move,
give maximum protection to Bhīṣma!"

Having heard Duryodhana's words,

12 to cheer him up,
Bhīṣma, the grandfather of the Kurus,
roared aloud like a lion and
blew his conch with full power.

The blowing of a conch shell signals the beginning of an event.

13 At once, conches, kettledrums, cymbals,
soft-drums, and trumpets resounded
causing a lot of noise and tumult.

14 Then, Kṛṣṇa and Arjuna
seated in their mighty chariot
drawn by white horses,
blew their divine conches.

In those days, warriors blew conch shells to announce the start of battle.
Each warrior had his own uniquely qualified conch shell,
which was either earned as a trophy or was obtained as a gift.

15 Kṛṣṇa blew his conch Pāñcajanya.
Arjuna blew his conch Devadatta.
Bhīma, known for his terrifying feats,
blew his huge conch Pauṇḍra.

16 King Yudhiṣṭhira blew his conch Anantavijaya,
Nakula blew the Sughoṣa, and
Sahadeva blew the Maṇipuṣpaka.

17 King of Kāśī, the supreme archer,
Śikaṇḍin, the mighty warrior,
Sātyaki, the invincible,
Dhṛṣṭadyumna,
Virāṭa,

[18]Drupada,
the sons of Draupadī, and
the strong-armed Abhimanyu –
each blew his conch one by one.

[19]That dreadful sound
echoed through earth and sky,
shaking the very spirit of the Kauravas.

[20]Arjuna looked at the
Kaurava army arrayed in battle
and lifted his mighty bow,
preparing himself for the clash of weapons
that was about to begin.
[21]Then he told Kṛṣṇa –

"Place my chariot between the two armies
[22]so that I may take a good look

at those with whom I must fight
among these battle-hungry warriors.

The great warriors would choose to fight only with equals.

23"I would also like to see all those
who have eagerly joined the battle
to please the wicked son of Dhṛtarāṣṭra."

24As per Arjuna's request,
Kṛṣṇa placed their magnificent chariot
between the two armies,
25right in front of Bhīṣma, Droṇa
and all the kings of the world.

Then, he said –
"Arjuna, look at the Kurus
who have assembled here!"

26 There, Arjuna saw
grandfathers, teachers,
uncles, cousins, nephews,
sons, grandsons,
27 and friends in both armies.
When he took a closer look at
his relatives ready for battle,
28 Arjuna, the son of Kuntī,
overcome by a sudden burst of pity,
spoke in despair –

"Kṛṣṇa,
when I see my own people
eager to fight us,
29 my limbs grow weak,
my mouth turns dry,
my body trembles,
my hairs stand on end,
30 my bow slips from my hand,
my skin burns,
my mind whirls, and
I can barely stand.

Arjuna's pity was misplaced sympathy that led to the weakening of his mind. Interestingly, Arjuna refers to even his opponents as 'my own people.' Compare this with Dhṛtarāṣṭra's distinction between the two sides in 1.1.

31 "I see only bad omens;
I can't see any good coming from
killing my own people.

32“O herder of cows,
I don’t fancy victory, pleasure, or kingdom.
What is the use of this kingdom,
happiness, or even life?

Kṛṣṇa was the chief of the cowherds and was called ‘Govinda,’ the friend of cows. Arjuna refers to Kṛṣṇa as ‘Govinda’ perhaps to highlight the latter’s simplicity.

33–34“Alas! Teachers, uncles, sons, grandfathers,
nephews, and many relatives –
for whose sake we desire
kingdom, pleasures, and comforts –
the very same ones are standing here in battle,
risking their lives and riches.

35“O Madhusūdana,
I don’t wish to kill them
even if I were to be killed.

‘Madhusūdana’ is a title given to Kṛṣṇa because he (in his original form as Viṣṇu) killed a demon named Madhu.

“I would not kill even for
the lordship of the three worlds,
let alone for this earthly kingdom.

The three worlds or the three ‘realms of existence’ are: earth, *svarga* (loosely, ‘heaven’), and the skies.

36"O protector of men,
what sort of happiness are we going to get
by killing the sons of Dhṛtarāṣṭra?
Although they are eager to kill us,
we will only incur *pāpa* by killing them.

In a war, it is fair to kill the opponents. Arjuna feels that this is immoral because he is blinded by compassion for his relatives and friends.

In fact, it is against the code of a warrior to run away from battle or refuse defending one's honor.

Pāpa can refer to evil, sin, guilt, crime, misfortune, *etc.*

37"Therefore, O kind one,
it is not right to kill our relatives.
How can we ever be happy
after killing our own people?

38"Overcome by greed, they fail to see the evil
in killing one's own family and betraying friends, but
39we can clearly see the wrong in killing our kin.
Isn't it better to stay away from this evil?

40"When a family is destroyed,
time-honored family values are lost.
When family values are destroyed altogether,
chaos reigns in the family.

41 "When chaos reigns,
the women of the family are violated.
When women are violated,
anarchy arises in society,
O Vārṣṇeya!

'Vārṣṇeya' is a name given to Kṛṣṇa because he was born in the Vṛṣṇi clan. Arjuna calls Kṛṣṇa 'Vārṣṇeya,' perhaps to remind him of the importance of a stable social order.

Arjuna's arguments highlighting the aftermath of war are valid – With the men-folk killed in battle, the women are vulnerable to harassment by evil men; children born out of such unions will have a confused lineage and are subjected to hardships. When children have a chaotic life, society will also be chaotic.

The animosity between the cousins was brewing for years and in spite of all efforts to broker for peace, the war became inevitable. Irrespective of Arjuna, the war would take place; whether or not he would fight was his decision.

42 "Anarchy paves the way to *naraka*
for the destroyers of the family
as well as the family itself.
Deprived of post-death rites,
the ancestors of these people
meet their downfall.

The post-death rites include an offering of cooked rice and water to ancestors after invoking their spirits with specific religious chants. To perform the post-death rites, one must know the past three generations of ancestors as well as specified protocol, both of which may be difficult when there is chaos in society. Arjuna laments that the ancestors, bereft of post-death rites, will fall to lower realms (*naraka*).

Some sections of orthodox Hindus accept as authority this flawed logic of Arjuna (that the actions of the current generation can affect the ancestors) and ironically, quote this verse to support their argument.

43 "The age-old practices
of family and community are ruined
by the terrible deeds of these killers
who create anarchy in society.

44 "Further, we have heard that
those who have lost family values
are consigned to *naraka* forever.

This is another fallacy of Arjuna;
there is no such thing as permanent stay in *naraka*.
According to Hindu belief, *naraka* (loosely, 'hell') is a transient place
where people are punished for their immoral deeds; they stay there
until they receive the full course of punishments.

45 "That being the case,
by getting ready to kill our own people,
we are on the verge of
making a terrible mistake
merely out of our greed
for royal pleasures.

46 "It would be better
if the armed Kauravas
were to kill me in battle
while I remain
unresisting and unarmed."

[47]Having said this,
Arjuna cast aside his bow and arrows
and sank down in his chariot,
overwhelmed by grief.

Arjuna was primarily concerned about –
a. Killing relatives and friends,
b. Aftermath of death and destruction caused by war,
c. Purity of bloodline/dynasty, and
d. Fall of ancestors deprived of post-death rites.

Kṛṣṇa addresses all these concerns
through the course of his battlefield counsel.
Straightaway, he mentions that Arjuna's words *appear to be wise*
but are actually incorrect and that the learned ones
grieve neither for the living nor for the dead (see 2.11).

The word '*yoga*' doesn't appear in the first chapter of the *Gītā*
while it appears in each of the remaining seventeen chapters.
Whether or not it was intentional, it serves as a beautiful metaphor
to remind us that despair, tumult, and sorrow are a result of a lack of *yoga*.

Religion is a mix of truth and tradition.
Truth is eternal, and therefore always relevant.
Tradition is contextual, and relevant for a particular place and time.
Arjuna ignored Truth and pursued Tradition,
which was perhaps the cause of his despondency!

2

सञ्जय उवाच ।
तं तथा कृपयाविष्टम्
अश्रुपूर्णाकुलेक्षणम् ।
विषीदन्तमिदं वाक्यम्
उवाच मधुसूदनः ॥ २.१

sañjaya uvāca ।
taṃ tathā kṛpayāviṣṭam
aśrupūrṇākulekṣaṇam ।
viṣīdantamidaṃ vākyam
uvāca madhusūdanaḥ ॥ 2.1

श्रीभगवानुवाच ।
कुतस्त्वा कश्मलमिदं
विषमे समुपस्थितम् ।
अनार्यजुष्टमस्वर्ग्यम्
अकीर्तिकरमर्जुन ॥ २.२

śrībhagavānuvāca ।
kutastvā kaśmalamidaṃ
viṣame samupasthitam ।
anāryajuṣṭamasvargyam
akīrtikaramarjuna ॥ 2.2

क्लैब्यं मा स्म गमः पार्थ
नैतत्त्वय्युपपद्यते ।
क्षुद्रं हृदयदौर्बल्यं
त्यक्त्वोत्तिष्ठ परंतप ॥ २.३

klaibyaṃ mā sma gamaḥ pārtha
naitattvayyupapadyate ।
kṣudraṃ hṛdayadaurbalyaṃ
tyaktvottiṣṭha paraṃtapa ॥ 2.3

अर्जुन उवाच ।
कथं भीष्ममहं संख्ये
द्रोणं च मधुसूदन ।
इषुभिः प्रतियोत्स्यामि
पूजार्हावरिसूदन ॥ २.४

arjuna uvāca ।
kathaṃ bhīṣmamahaṃ saṃkhye
droṇaṃ ca madhusūdana ।
iṣubhiḥ pratiyotsyāmi
pūjārhāvarisūdana ॥ 2.4

गुरूनहत्वा हि महानुभावान्
श्रेयो भोक्तुं भैक्ष्यमपीह लोके ।
हत्वार्थकामांस्तु गुरूनिहैव
भुञ्जीय भोगान्रुधिरप्रदिग्धान् ॥ २.५

gurūnahatvā hi mahānubhāvān
śreyo bhoktuṃ bhaikṣamapīha loke ।
hatvārthakāmāṃstu gurūnihaiva
bhuñjīya bhogānrudhirapradigdhān ॥ 2.5

न चैतद्विद्मः कतरन्नो गरीयो
यद्वा जयेम यदि वा नो जयेयुः ।
यानेव हत्वा न जिजीविषामः
तेऽवस्थिताः प्रमुखे धार्तराष्ट्राः ॥ २.६

na caitadvidmaḥ kataranno garīyo
yadvā jayema yadi vā no jayeyuḥ ।
yāneva hatvā na jijīviṣāmaḥ
te'vasthitāḥ pramukhe dhārtarāṣṭrāḥ ॥ 2.6

कार्पण्यदोषोपहतस्वभावः
पृच्छामि त्वां धर्मसंमूढचेताः ।
यच्छ्रेयः स्यान्निश्चितं ब्रूहि तन्मे
शिष्यस्तेऽहं शाधि मां त्वां प्रपन्नम् ॥ २.७

kārpaṇyadoṣopahatasvabhāvaḥ
pṛcchāmi tvāṃ dharmasaṃmūḍhacetāḥ ।
yacchreyaḥ syānniścitaṃ brūhi tanme
śiṣyaste'haṃ śādhi māṃ tvāṃ prapannam ॥ 2.7

न हि प्रपश्यामि ममापनुद्यात्
यच्छोकमुच्छोषणमिन्द्रियाणाम् ।
अवाप्य भूमावसपत्नमृद्धं
राज्यं सुराणामपि चाधिपत्यम् ॥ २.८

na hi prapaśyāmi mamāpanudyāt
yacchokamucchoṣaṇamindriyāṇām ।
avāpya bhūmāvasapatnamṛddhaṃ
rājyaṃ surāṇāmapi cādhipatyam ॥ 2.8

सञ्जय उवाच ।
एवमुक्त्वा हृषीकेशं
गुडाकेशः परंतप ।
न योत्स्य इति गोविन्दम्
उक्त्वा तूष्णीं बभूव ह ॥ २.९

sañjaya uvāca ।
evamuktvā hṛṣīkeśaṃ
guḍākeśaḥ paraṃtapa ।
na yotsya iti govindam
uktvā tūṣṇīṃ babhūva ha ॥ 2.9

तमुवाच हृषीकेशः
प्रहसन्निव भारत ।
सेनयोरुभयोर्मध्ये
विषीदन्तमिदं वचः ॥ २.१०

tamuvāca hṛṣīkeśaḥ
prahasanniva bhārata ।
senayorubhayormadhye
viṣīdantamidaṃ vacaḥ ॥ 2.10

श्रीभगवानुवाच ।
अशोच्यानन्वशोचस्त्वं
प्रज्ञावादांश्च भाषसे ।
गतासूनगतासूंश्च
नानुशोचन्ति पण्डिताः ॥ २.११

śrībhagavānuvāca ।
aśocyānanvaśocastvaṃ
prajñāvādāṃśca bhāṣase ।
gatāsūnagatāsūṃśca
nānuśocanti paṇḍitāḥ ॥ 2.11

न त्वेवाहं जातु नासं
न त्वं नेमे जनाधिपाः ।
न चैव न भविष्यामः
सर्वे वयमतः परम् ॥ २.१२

na tvevāhaṃ jātu nāsaṃ
na tvaṃ neme janādhipāḥ ।
na caiva na bhaviṣyāmaḥ
sarve vayamataḥ param ॥ 2.12

देहिनोऽस्मिन् यथा देहे
कौमारं यौवनं जरा ।
तथा देहान्तरप्राप्तिः
धीरस्तत्र न मुह्यति ॥ २.१३

dehino'smin yathā dehe
kaumāraṃ yauvanaṃ jarā ।
tathā dehāntaraprāptiḥ
dhīrastatra na muhyati ॥ 2.13

मात्रास्पर्शास्तु कौन्तेय
शीतोष्णसुखदुःखदाः ।

mātrāsparśāstu kaunteya
śītoṣṇasukhaduḥkhadāḥ ।

आगमापायिनोऽनित्याः
तांस्तितिक्षस्व भारत ॥ २.१४

āgamāpāyino'nityāḥ
tāṃstitikṣasva bhārata ॥ 2.14

यं हि न व्यथयन्त्येते
पुरुषं पुरुषर्षभ ।
समदुःखसुखं धीरं
सोऽमृतत्वाय कल्पते ॥ २.१५

yaṃ hi na vyathayantyete
puruṣaṃ puruṣarṣabha ।
samaduḥkhasukhaṃ dhīraṃ
so'mṛtatvāya kalpate ॥ 2.15

नासतो विद्यते भावो
नाभावो विद्यते सतः ।
उभयोरपि दृष्टोऽन्तः
त्वनयोस्तत्त्वदर्शिभिः ॥ २.१६

nāsato vidyate bhāvo
nābhāvo vidyate sataḥ ।
ubhayorapi dṛṣṭo'ntaḥ
tvanayostattvadarśibhiḥ ॥ 2.16

अविनाशि तु तद्विद्धि
येन सर्वमिदं ततम् ।
विनाशमव्ययस्यास्य
न कश्चित् कर्तुमर्हति ॥ २.१७

avināśi tu tadviddhi
yena sarvamidaṃ tatam ।
vināśamavyayasyāsya
na kaścit kartumarhati ॥ 2.17

अन्तवन्त इमे देहा
नित्यस्योक्ताः शरीरिणः ।
अनाशिनोऽप्रमेयस्य
तस्माद्युध्यस्व भारत ॥ २.१८

antavanta ime dehā
nityasyoktāḥ śarīriṇaḥ ।
anāśino'prameyasya
tasmādyudhyasva bhārata ॥ 2.18

य एनं वेत्ति हन्तारं
यश्चैनं मन्यते हतम् ।
उभौ तौ न विजानीतो
नायं हन्ति न हन्यते ॥ २.१९

ya enaṃ vetti hantāraṃ
yaścainaṃ manyate hatam ।
ubhau tau na vijānīto
nāyaṃ hanti na hanyate ॥ 2.19

न जायते म्रियते वा कदाचित्
नायं भूत्वा भविता वा न भूयः ।
अजो नित्यः शाश्वतोऽयं पुराणो
न हन्यते हन्यमाने शरीरे ॥ २.२०

na jāyate mriyate vā kadācit
nāyaṃ bhūtvā bhavitā vā na bhūyaḥ ।
ajo nityaḥ śāśvato'yaṃ purāṇo
na hanyate hanyamāne śarīre ॥ 2.20

वेदाविनाशिनं नित्यं
य एनमजमव्ययम् ।
कथं स पुरुषः पार्थ
कं घातयति हन्ति कम् ॥ २.२१

vedāvināśinaṃ nityaṃ
ya enamajamavyayam ।
kathaṃ sa puruṣaḥ pārtha
kaṃ ghātayati hanti kam ॥ 2.21

वासांसि जीर्णानि यथा विहाय नवानि गृह्णाति नरोऽपराणि । तथा शरीराणि विहाय जीर्णानि अन्यानि संयाति नवानि देही ॥ २.२२	*vāsāṃsi jīrṇāni yathā vihāya* *navāni gṛhṇāti naro'parāṇi* । *tathā śarīrāṇi vihāya jīrṇāni* *anyāni saṃyāti navāni dehī* ॥ 2.22
नैनं छिन्दन्ति शस्त्राणि नैनं दहति पावकः । न चैनं क्लेदयन्त्यापो न शोषयति मारुतः ॥ २.२३	*nainaṃ chindanti śastrāṇi* *nainaṃ dahati pāvakaḥ* । *na cainaṃ kledayantyāpo* *na śoṣayati mārutaḥ* ॥ 2.23
अच्छेद्योऽयमदाह्योऽयम् अक्लेद्योऽशोष्य एव च । नित्यः सर्वगतः स्थाणुः अचलोऽयं सनातनः ॥ २.२४	*acchedyo'yamadāhyo'yam* *akledyo'śoṣya eva ca* । *nityaḥ sarvagataḥ sthāṇuḥ* *acalo'yaṃ sanātanaḥ* ॥ 2.24
अव्यक्तोऽयमचिन्त्योऽयम् अविकार्योऽयमुच्यते । तस्मादेवं विदित्वैनं नानुशोचितुमर्हसि ॥ २.२५	*avyakto'yamacintyo'yam* *avikāryo'yamucyate* । *tasmādevaṃ viditvainaṃ* *nānuśocitumarhasi* ॥ 2.25
अथ चैनं नित्यजातं नित्यं वा मन्यसे मृतम् । तथापि त्वं महाबाहो नैनं शोचितुमर्हसि ॥ २.२६	*atha cainaṃ nityajātaṃ* *nityaṃ vā manyase mṛtam* । *tathāpi tvaṃ mahābāho* *nainaṃ śocitumarhasi* ॥ 2.26
जातस्य हि ध्रुवो मृत्युः ध्रुवं जन्म मृतस्य च । तस्मादपरिहार्येऽर्थे न त्वं शोचितुमर्हसि ॥ २.२७	*jātasya hi dhruvo mṛtyuḥ* *dhruvaṃ janma mṛtasya ca* । *tasmādaparihārye'rthe* *na tvaṃ śocitumarhasi* ॥ 2.27
अव्यक्तादीनि भूतानि व्यक्तमध्यानि भारत । अव्यक्तनिधनान्येव तत्र का परिदेवना ॥ २.२८	*avyaktādīni bhūtāni* *vyaktamadhyāni bhārata* । *avyaktanidhanānyeva* *tatra kā paridevanā* ॥ 2.28
आश्चर्यवत्पश्यति कश्चिदेनम् आश्चर्यवद्वदति तथैव चान्यः । आश्चर्यवच्चैनमन्यः शृणोति श्रुत्वाप्येनं वेद न चैव कश्चित् ॥ २.२९	*āścaryavatpaśyati kaścidenam* *āścaryavadvadati tathaiva cānyaḥ* । *āścaryavaccainamanyaḥ śṛṇoti* *śrutvāpyenaṃ veda na caiva kaścit* ॥ 2.29

देही नित्यमवध्योऽयं
देहे सर्वस्य भारत ।
तस्मात्सर्वाणि भूतानि
न त्वं शोचितुमर्हसि ॥ २.३०

dehī nityamavadhyo'yaṃ
dehe sarvasya bhārata ।
tasmātsarvāṇi bhūtāni
na tvaṃ śocitumarhasi ॥ 2.30

स्वधर्ममपि चावेक्ष्य
न विकम्पितुमर्हसि ।
धर्म्याद्धि युद्धाच्छ्रेयोऽन्यत्
क्षत्रियस्य न विद्यते ॥ २.३१

svadharmamapi cāvekṣya
na vikampitumarhasi ।
dharmyāddhi yuddhācchreyo'nyat
kṣatriyasya na vidyate ॥ 2.31

यदृच्छया चोपपन्नं
स्वर्गद्वारमपावृतम् ।
सुखिनः क्षत्रियाः पार्थ
लभन्ते युद्धमीदृशम् ॥ २.३२

yadṛcchayā copapannaṃ
svargadvāramapāvṛtam ।
sukhinaḥ kṣatriyāḥ pārtha
labhante yuddhamīdṛśam ॥ 2.32

अथ चेत्त्वमिमं धर्म्यं
संग्रामं न करिष्यसि ।
ततः स्वधर्मं कीर्तिं च
हित्वा पापमवाप्स्यसि ॥ २.३३

atha cettvamimaṃ dharmyaṃ
saṃgrāmaṃ na kariṣyasi ।
tataḥ svadharmaṃ kīrtiṃ ca
hitvā pāpamavāpsyasi ॥ 2.33

अकीर्तिं चापि भूतानि
कथयिष्यन्ति तेऽव्ययाम् ।
संभावितस्य चाकीर्तिः
मरणादतिरिच्यते ॥ २.३४

akīrtiṃ cāpi bhūtāni
kathayiṣyanti te'vyayām ।
saṃbhāvitasya cākīrtiḥ
maraṇādatiricyate ॥ 2.34

भयाद्रणादुपरतं
मंस्यन्ते त्वां महारथाः ।
येषां च त्वं बहुमतो
भूत्वा यास्यसि लाघवम् ॥ २.३५

bhayādraṇāduparataṃ
maṃsyante tvāṃ mahārathāḥ ।
yeṣāṃ ca tvaṃ bahumato
bhūtvā yāsyasi lāghavam ॥ 2.35

अवाच्यवादांश्च बहून्
वदिष्यन्ति तवाहिताः ।
निन्दन्तस्तव सामर्थ्यं
ततो दुःखतरं नु किम् ॥ २.३६

avācyavādāṃśca bahūn
vadiṣyanti tavāhitāḥ ।
nindantastava sāmarthyaṃ
tato duḥkhataraṃ nu kim ॥ 2.36

हतो वा प्राप्स्यसि स्वर्गं
जित्वा वा भोक्ष्यसे महीम् ।
तस्मादुत्तिष्ठ कौन्तेय
युद्धाय कृतनिश्चयः ॥ २.३७

hato vā prāpsyasi svargaṃ
jitvā vā bhokṣyase mahīm ।
tasmāduttiṣṭha kaunteya
yuddhāya kṛtaniścayaḥ ॥ 2.37

सुखदुःखे समे कृत्वा
लाभालाभौ जयाजयौ।
ततो युद्धाय युज्यस्व
नैवं पापमवाप्स्यसि ॥ २.३८

sukhaduḥkhe same kṛtvā
lābhālābhau jayājayau ।
tato yuddhāya yujyasva
naivaṃ pāpamavāpsyasi ॥ 2.38

एषा तेऽभिहिता सांख्ये
बुद्धिर्योगे त्विमां शृणु।
बुद्ध्या युक्तो यया पार्थ
कर्मबन्धं प्रहास्यसि ॥ २.३९

eṣā te'bhihitā sāṃkhye
buddhiryoge tvimāṃ śṛṇu ।
buddhyā yukto yayā pārtha
karmabandhaṃ prahāsyasi ॥ 2.39

नेहाभिक्रमनाशोऽस्ति
प्रत्यवायो न विद्यते।
स्वल्पमप्यस्य धर्मस्य
त्रायते महतो भयात् ॥ २.४०

nehābhikramanāśo'sti
pratyavāyo na vidyate ।
svalpamapyasya dharmasya
trāyate mahato bhayāt ॥ 2.40

व्यवसायात्मिका बुद्धिः
एकेह कुरुनन्दन।
बहुशाखा ह्यनन्ताश्च
बुद्धयोऽव्यवसायिनाम् ॥ २.४१

vyavasāyātmikā buddhiḥ
ekeha kurunandana ।
bahuśākhā hyanantāśca
buddhayo'vyavasāyinām ॥ 2.41

यामिमां पुष्पितां वाचं
प्रवदन्त्यविपश्चितः।
वेदवादरताः पार्थ
नान्यदस्तीति वादिनः ॥ २.४२

yāmimāṃ puṣpitāṃ vācaṃ
pravadantyavipaścitaḥ ।
vedavādaratāḥ pārtha
nānyadastīti vādinaḥ ॥ 2.42

कामात्मानः स्वर्गपरा
जन्मकर्मफलप्रदाम्।
क्रियाविशेषबहुलां
भोगैश्वर्यगतिं प्रति ॥ २.४३

kāmātmānaḥ svargaparā
janmakarmaphalapradām ।
kriyāviśeṣabahulāṃ
bhogaiśvaryagatiṃ prati ॥ 2.43

भोगैश्वर्यप्रसक्तानां
तयापहृतचेतसाम्।
व्यवसायात्मिका बुद्धिः
समाधौ न विधीयते ॥ २.४४

bhogaiśvaryaprasaktānāṃ
tayāpahṛtacetasām ।
vyavasāyātmikā buddhiḥ
samādhau na vidhīyate ॥ 2.44

त्रैगुण्यविषया वेदा
निस्त्रैगुण्यो भवार्जुन।

traiguṇyaviṣayā vedā
nistraiguṇyo bhavārjuna ।

निर्द्वन्द्वो नित्यसत्त्वस्थो
निर्योगक्षेम आत्मवान् ॥ २.४५

nirdvandvo nityasattvastho
niryogakṣema ātmavān ॥ 2.45

यावानर्थ उदपाने
सर्वतः सम्प्लुतोदके ।
तावान्सर्वेषु वेदेषु
ब्राह्मणस्य विजानतः ॥ २.४६

yāvānartha udapāne
sarvataḥ samplutodake ।
tāvānsarveṣu vedeṣu
brāhmaṇasya vijānataḥ ॥ 2.46

कर्मण्येवाधिकारस्ते
मा फलेषु कदाचन ।
मा कर्मफलहेतुर्भूः
मा ते सङ्गोऽस्त्वकर्मणि ॥ २.४७

karmaṇyevādhikāraste
mā phaleṣu kadācana ।
mā karmaphalaheturbhūḥ
mā te saṅgo'stvakarmaṇi ॥ 2.47

योगस्थः कुरु कर्माणि
सङ्गं त्यक्त्वा धनञ्जय ।
सिद्ध्यसिद्ध्योः समो भूत्वा
समत्वं योग उच्यते ॥ २.४८

yogasthaḥ kuru karmāṇi
saṅgaṃ tyaktvā dhanañjaya ।
siddhyasiddhyoḥ samo bhūtvā
samatvaṃ yoga ucyate ॥ 2.48

दूरेण ह्यवरं कर्म
बुद्धियोगाद्धनञ्जय ।
बुद्धौ शरणमन्विच्छ
कृपणाः फलहेतवः ॥ २.४९

dūreṇa hyavaraṃ karma
buddhiyogāddhanañjaya ।
buddhau śaraṇamanviccha
kṛpaṇāḥ phalahetavaḥ ॥ 2.49

बुद्धियुक्तो जहातीह
उभे सुकृतदुष्कृते ।
तस्माद्योगाय युज्यस्व
योगः कर्मसु कौशलम् ॥ २.५०

buddhiyukto jahātīha
ubhe sukṛtaduṣkṛte ।
tasmādyogāya yujyasva
yogaḥ karmasu kauśalam ॥ 2.50

कर्मजं बुद्धियुक्ता हि
फलं त्यक्त्वा मनीषिणः ।
जन्मबन्धविनिर्मुक्ताः
पदं गच्छन्त्यनामयम् ॥ २.५१

karmajaṃ buddhiyuktā hi
phalaṃ tyaktvā manīṣiṇaḥ ।
janmabandhavinirmuktāḥ
padaṃ gacchantyanāmayam ॥ 2.51

यदा ते मोहकलिलं
बुद्धिर्व्यतितरिष्यति ।
तदा गन्तासि निर्वेदं
श्रोतव्यस्य श्रुतस्य च ॥ २.५२

yadā te mohakalilaṃ
buddhirvyatitariṣyati ।
tadā gantāsi nirvedaṃ
śrotavyasya śrutasya ca ॥ 2.52

श्रुतिविप्रतिपन्ना ते यदा स्थास्यति निश्चला । समाधावचला बुद्धिः तदा योगमवाप्स्यसि ॥ २.५३	*śrutivipratipannā te* *yadā sthāsyati niścalā* । *samādhāvacalā buddhiḥ* *tadā yogamavāpsyasi* ॥ 2.53
अर्जुन उवाच । स्थितप्रज्ञस्य का भाषा समाधिस्थस्य केशव । स्थितधीः किं प्रभाषेत किमासीत व्रजेत किम् ॥ २.५४	***arjuna uvāca*** । *sthitaprajñasya kā bhāṣā* *samādhisthasya keśava* । *sthitadhīḥ kiṃ prabhāṣeta* *kimāsīta vrajeta kim* ॥ 2.54
श्रीभगवानुवाच । प्रजहाति यदा कामान् सर्वान्पार्थ मनोगतान् । आत्मन्येवात्मना तुष्टः स्थितप्रज्ञस्तदोच्यते ॥ २.५५	***śrībhagavānuvāca*** । *prajahāti yadā kāmān* *sarvānpārtha manogatān* । *ātmanyevātmanā tuṣṭaḥ* *sthitaprajñastadocyate* ॥ 2.55
दुःखेष्वनुद्विग्नमनाः सुखेषु विगतस्पृहः । वीतरागभयक्रोधः स्थितधीर्मुनिरुच्यते ॥ २.५६	*duḥkheṣvanudvignamanāḥ* *sukheṣu vigataspṛhaḥ* । *vītarāgabhayakrodhaḥ* *sthitadhīrmunirucyate* ॥ 2.56
यः सर्वत्रानभिस्नेहः तत् तत् प्राप्य शुभाशुभम् । नाभिनन्दति न द्वेष्टि तस्य प्रज्ञा प्रतिष्ठिता ॥ २.५७	*yaḥ sarvatrānabhisnehaḥ* *tat tat prāpya śubhāśubham* । *nābhinandati na dveṣṭi* *tasya prajñā pratiṣṭhitā* ॥ 2.57
यदा संहरते चायं कूर्मोऽङ्गानीव सर्वशः । इन्द्रियाणीन्द्रियार्थेभ्यः तस्य प्रज्ञा प्रतिष्ठिता ॥ २.५८	*yadā saṃharate cāyaṃ* *kūrmo'ṅgānīva sarvaśaḥ* । *indriyāṇīndriyārthebhyaḥ* *tasya prajñā pratiṣṭhitā* ॥ 2.58
विषया विनिवर्तन्ते निराहारस्य देहिनः । रसवर्जं रसोऽप्यस्य परं दृष्ट्वा निवर्तते ॥ २.५९	*viṣayā vinivartante* *nirāhārasya dehinaḥ* । *rasavarjaṃ raso'pyasya* *paraṃ dṛṣṭvā nivartate* ॥ 2.59
यततो ह्यपि कौन्तेय पुरुषस्य विपश्चितः ।	*yatato hyapi kaunteya* *puruṣasya vipaścitaḥ* ।

इन्द्रियाणि प्रमाथीनि
हरन्ति प्रसभं मनः ॥ २.६०

indriyāṇi pramāthīni
haranti prasabhaṃ manaḥ ॥ 2.60

तानि सर्वाणि संयम्य
युक्त आसीत मत्परः ।
वशे हि यस्येन्द्रियाणि
तस्य प्रज्ञा प्रतिष्ठिता ॥ २.६१

tāni sarvāṇi saṃyamya
yukta āsīta matparaḥ ।
vaśe hi yasyendriyāṇi
tasya prajñā pratiṣṭhitā ॥ 2.61

ध्यायतो विषयान्पुंसः
सङ्गस्तेषूपजायते ।
सङ्गात्सञ्जायते कामः
कामात्क्रोधोऽभिजायते ॥ २.६२

dhyāyato viṣayānpuṃsaḥ
saṅgasteṣūpajāyate ।
saṅgātsañjāyate kāmaḥ
kāmātkrodho'bhijāyate ॥ 2.62

क्रोधाद्भवति संमोहः
संमोहात्स्मृतिविभ्रमः ।
स्मृतिभ्रंशाद्बुद्धिनाशो
बुद्धिनाशात्प्रणश्यति ॥ २.६३

krodhādbhavati saṃmohaḥ
saṃmohātsmṛtivibhramaḥ ।
smṛtibhraṃśādbuddhināśo
buddhināśātpraṇaśyati ॥ 2.63

रागद्वेषवियुक्तैस्तु
विषयानिन्द्रियैश्चरन् ।
आत्मवश्यैर्विधेयात्मा
प्रसादमधिगच्छति ॥ २.६४

rāgadveṣaviyuktaistu
viṣayānindriyaiścaran ।
ātmavaśyairvidheyātmā
prasādamadhigacchati ॥ 2.64

प्रसादे सर्वदुःखानां
हानिरस्योपजायते ।
प्रसन्नचेतसो ह्याशु
बुद्धिः पर्यवतिष्ठते ॥ २.६५

prasāde sarvaduḥkhānāṃ
hānirasyopajāyate ।
prasannacetaso hyāśu
buddhiḥ paryavatiṣṭhate ॥ 2.65

नास्ति बुद्धिरयुक्तस्य
न चायुक्तस्य भावना ।
न चाभावयतः शान्तिः
अशान्तस्य कुतः सुखम् ॥ २.६६

nāsti buddhirayuktasya
na cāyuktasya bhāvanā ।
na cābhāvayataḥ śāntiḥ
aśāntasya kutaḥ sukham ॥ 2.66

इन्द्रियाणां हि चरतां
यन् मनोऽनुविधीयते ।
तदस्य हरति प्रज्ञां
वायुर्नावमिवाम्भसि ॥ २.६७

indriyāṇāṃ hi caratāṃ
yan mano'nuvidhīyate ।
tadasya harati prajñāṃ
vāyurnāvamivāmbhasi ॥ 2.67

तस्माद्यस्य महाबाहो निगृहीतानि सर्वशः । इन्द्रियाणीन्द्रियार्थेभ्यः तस्य प्रज्ञा प्रतिष्ठिता ॥ २.६८	*tasmādyasya mahābāho* *nigṛhītāni sarvaśaḥ* । *indriyāṇīndriyārthebhyaḥ* *tasya prajñā pratiṣṭhitā* ॥ 2.68
या निशा सर्वभूतानां तस्यां जागर्ति संयमी । यस्यां जाग्रति भूतानि सा निशा पश्यतो मुनेः ॥ २.६९	*yā niśā sarvabhūtānām* *tasyām jāgarti saṃyamī* । *yasyāṃ jāgrati bhūtāni* *sā niśā paśyato muneḥ* ॥ 2.69
आपूर्यमाणमचलप्रतिष्ठं समुद्रमापः प्रविशन्ति यद्वत् । तद्वत्कामा यं प्रविशन्ति सर्वे स शान्तिमाप्नोति न कामकामी ॥ २.७०	*āpūryamāṇamacalapratiṣṭhaṃ* *samudramāpaḥ praviśanti yadvat* । *tadvatkāmā yaṃ praviśanti sarve* *sa śāntimāpnoti na kāmakāmī* ॥ 2.70
विहाय कामान्यः सर्वान् पुमांश्चरति निःस्पृहः । निर्ममो निरहंकारः स शान्तिमधिगच्छति ॥ २.७१	*vihāya kāmānyaḥ sarvān* *pumāṃścarati niḥspṛhaḥ* । *nirmamo nirahaṃkāraḥ* *sa śāntimadhigacchati* ॥ 2.71
एषा ब्राह्मी स्थितिः पार्थ नैनां प्राप्य विमुह्यति । स्थित्वास्यामन्तकालेऽपि ब्रह्मनिर्वाणमृच्छति ॥ २.७२	*eṣā brāhmī sthitiḥ pārtha* *naināṃ prāpya vimuhyati* । *sthitvāsyāmantakāle'pi* *brahmanirvāṇamṛcchati* ॥ 2.72

CHAPTER 2

Wisdom and Action

Sañjaya

1 To him, who was thus in despair,
overcome by pity, and in tears,
Kṛṣṇa spoke these words.

Kṛṣṇa

2 **How can you lose heart in this hour of crisis?**
Whence has this weakness arisen in you?

This is disgraceful, ignoble, and
unworthy of higher realms!

3 Don't be a coward, Arjuna –
that's not right for you!

Arise, awake, and abandon your timidity,
O destroyer of enemies!

Arjuna

4 How can I battle Bhīṣma and Droṇa?
How can I shower arrows on them?
They are worthy of my reverence.

5 If I kill these noble elders
for the sake of worldly gains,
my pleasures will be stained with their blood.
I would rather beg for food instead.

6 Dhṛtarāṣṭra's men are standing in front of us.
I don't wish to live at the cost of killing them!

Should ***we*** conquer them?
Should ***they*** conquer us?
I don't know which is better.

[7]I have become very sentimental.
I am totally confused about
what is right and what is wrong.

I surrender at your feet as your disciple.
Please show me the right path and
tell me for certain what is good for me.

[8]I don't see how
gaining absolute control
over this prosperous earth or
even lordship over the heavens
will drive away this grief,
which dampens my spirit.

Sañjaya
[9]Having said this to Kṛṣṇa,
Arjuna—the destroyer of enemies—declared:
"I shall not fight!"
and became silent.

[10]In the midst of the two armies,
Kṛṣṇa, with a subtle smile,
spoke these words
to the grief-stricken one –

Kṛṣṇa

11 You grieve for that which you should not
yet you seem to speak words of wisdom.
The wise neither grieve for the dead nor for the living.

Kṛṣṇa basically tells Arjuna, "Don't cry! Don't fret!"
Neither *weeping* nor *worrying* solves any problem.
It is pointless to mourn for anyone (see 2.28, 2.30).

12 There was never a time when
I or you or these kings did not exist.
There will never be a time when we cease to exist.

Here, 'we' refers to the *ātman* (soul, higher Self).
Kṛṣṇa goes on to explain how the *ātman* is eternal and immortal.

13 The *ātman* that lives in the body
passes through childhood, youth, and old age.
Similarly, it passes through different bodies.
One who is endowed with fortitude
is not disturbed by these changes.

14 When senses come in contact with sensates
we experience cold and heat, pleasure and pain.
These sensations come and go, for they are impermanent.
Patiently endure them, Arjuna.

Senses (or sense organs) are ears, eyes, nose, tongue, and skin.
Sensates are sound, sight, smell, taste, and texture.
Sensations are what we experience when senses come in contact with sensates.

15 One who is not affected by sensations
remains calm in pain and pleasure.
He is firm in his resolve and
he is ready for immortality.

By disconnecting oneself from materials
and by subduing lower instincts,
one gets in touch with the immortal Self.

16 The Unreal doesn't exist.
The Real never ceases to be.
Those who know the Ultimate Truth
have indeed realized the nature of both.

Kṛṣṇa refers to the *ātman* as 'real' since it is imperishable;
he refers to the body as 'unreal' because it is perishable.
Indeed, the body is also real, but it appears unreal
in the face of a higher level of reality, the *ātman*.

17 The imperishable (*ātman*) pervades everything
and no one can destroy the imperishable.

18 The body alone is perishable,
whereas the *ātman* seated within
is eternal, indestructible, and infinite.
Therefore fight, O descendent of Bharata!

Arjuna was a descendent of King Bharata, the founder of the ancient Indian empire.
Kṛṣṇa invokes the name of Arjuna's famous ancestor perhaps as a reminder
that one's character survives long after one is gone.

[19]One who deems it as the killer
and one who thinks it is killed –
both of them do not know,
for it neither kills nor is it killed.

In this verse and in the following few verses, 'it' refers to the *ātman*.

[20]It is never born,
it never dies.

It never came into being
nor will it ever cease to be.

Unborn, eternal, changeless, and primeval,
it is not killed when the body is killed.

The *ātman* is always there – it is not bound by space or time.
The idea of 'birth' and 'death' is only for the body.

[21]One who knows that the *ātman* is
indestructible, infinite, eternal, and unborn,
how can he kill or incite another to kill?

[22]Just as one discards old clothes
and puts on new ones,
the *ātman* discards old bodies
and takes on new ones.

23 Weapons do not cleave it,
fire does not burn it,
water does not wet it, and
wind does not wither it.

24 It cannot be cut or burnt
or drenched or dried.
It is everlasting, all-pervading,
stable, immovable, and primordial.

25 It is beyond form, thought, or change.
Having understood it thus,
why should you grieve?

The *ātman* is free from birth and death,
growth and decay, existence and non-existence.

26 Even if you believe that the *ātman* is
perpetually subject to birth and death,
why should you grieve?

27 Death is certain for those who are born.
Birth is certain for those who have died.
Why worry about the inevitable?

We go through cycles of birth and death
until the *ātman* is redeemed.

28 Beings are formless in their beginnings,
they are formless in their ends, and
they acquire a form only in between.
What is there to lament in this?

Before birth and after death, beings are a part of the Infinite.
It is only during bodily life that beings can be perceived by the senses.

29 One sees it as a wonder,
another speaks of it as a wonder,
yet another hears of it as a wonder
and even having heard it all,
no one really knows.

30 The *ātman* in everyone's body
is eternal and imperishable.
Thus, you should not grieve
for any living being.

31 Even from the point of view of
your own duty as a warrior
you should not hesitate to fight.
There is nothing superior for a warrior
than a war fought for preserving *dharma*.

Here, *dharma* refers to righteousness. The Pāṇḍavas fought the war for the larger good and not merely for their honor or for self-defense.

32 Fortunate are the warriors
who encounter a battle such as this
which comes of its own accord.
Indeed, it is an open door to *svarga*.

According to Hindu belief, *svarga* (loosely 'heaven') is a transient place where people are rewarded for their good deeds; they stay till they receive the full course of rewards.

33 Now if you don't fight in this
battle sanctioned by *dharma*,
you will be making the mistake of
ignoring your own duty and reputation.

34 People will forever talk about your dishonorable act
and for an honorable person,
disgrace is worse than death!

35 The great warriors will think that
you have run away from battle out of fear.
Many who held you in high esteem
will no longer respect you.
36 Your enemies will ridicule your ability
and speak lowly of you, uttering unspeakable words.
What can be more painful than this?

Kṛṣṇa tries to persuade Arjuna by presenting various perspectives on the issue. Earlier he spoke about how Arjuna's fundamental assumptions were wrong and here he speaks about the obvious problems of retreating from war.

37 If you are killed, you will attain *svarga*.
If you are victorious, you will rule over the kingdom.
Therefore arise, Arjuna, with a firm resolve to fight!

38 Gain-loss, victory-defeat, comfort-discomfort –
treat them in the same spirit and fight.
Then you will not incur any guilt.

39 Thus far I revealed to you the way of *Sāṅkhya*.
Now understand the practice of *Yoga*.

'Way of Sāṅkhya' is a cerebral approach based on reasoning.
'Practice of *Yoga*' refers to *Karma-yoga* – doing work without getting attached.

With this insight,
you will break free
from the bondage of action.

'Bondage of action' refers to attachment to the results of an action.

40In this path, no effort is wasted
nor is there any bad outcome.
Even a little effort in this direction
will save you from misery.

41A cultivated intellect
attains single-pointed focus on this path.
But for a wavering intellect
thoughts are multifold and endless.

42Those who lack proper insight
delight in the letter (and not spirit) of the *Vedas*.
They proclaim in flowery words –
"There is nothing else other than this!"

The *Vedas* are the foremost revealed scriptures in Hinduism.

Among many other things, the *Vedas* also discuss
the attainment of material rewards here and hereafter.
Material gains, though tempting, are fleeting.
Those who are engrossed in such pursuits are considered shortsighted
because they are endlessly caught in the cycle of birth and death.
The *Vedas* also contain instructions for those
endowed with the higher aspiration of liberation.

43They are full of desires and
reaching *svarga* is their supreme goal.
They perform many elaborate rituals
to attain pleasure and power.
Their actions eventually result in rebirth.

See 2.49 and 9.20–21.

44Those attached to pleasure and power
are led astray by that flowery language.
They never attain the firm intellect of a contemplative mind.

45The *Veda*s deal with the three inherent tendencies;
free yourself from their influence.

The three inherent tendencies of a human being are:
Sattva (benign goodness), *Rajas* (restless activity), and *Tamas* (deluded lethargy).
These can also be seen as three grades of our attitudes.

Go beyond the dualities and
give up the desire to acquire or hoard.

'Dualities' are relative opposites like hot and cold,
happy and sad, winning and losing, me and other, etc.
'Acquire' refers to pursuing what is yet to be attained.
'Hoard' refers to clinging on to what has already been attained.

Be a master of yourself and be established in *sattva*.

Sattva helps us advance forward, *rajas* is a state of stagnation,
and *tamas* is a downward spiral (see 14.18). 'Being established in *sattva*'
simply means that one is going in the right direction on the path
leading to transcending the *guṇa*s, which is the destination.

46 What is the use of a well when there is a flood
and water is flowing freely everywhere?
What is the use of all the *Vedas*
when one has realized the Ultimate Truth?

47 You can control only your actions;
you can't control the results.
The expected results should not be
the motivation for action.
Also, don't shirk away from your work.

The outcome of an action is governed by multiple factors (see 18.13–14).
You are never in complete control over the outcome of your actions.
It is pointless to worry about something that you cannot control.
Focus on work without fear of failure or greed for success.
At the same time, don't be lazy or aloof.

48 Work with a balanced mind
having given up all attachments.
Such equanimity is called ***Karma-yoga***.

49 Action guided by selfish interests
is far inferior to action guided by wisdom.
Seek refuge in that wisdom.

'Wisdom' refers to working with a balanced mind without attachments.

Pitiable are those
who have their eye on the result!

50 Endowed with that wisdom,
one remains unaffected by both
good and bad outcomes in this life.

Thus, act in the spirit of *karma-yoga*,
which is **a smart approach to work**.

51 With a balanced mind,
the wise ones renounce
their interest in the results.
Freed from the bondage of birth,
they reach a faultless state.

'Bondage of birth' refers to being caught in the cycle of birth and death.

52 When your intellect transcends
the thickets of delusion,
you will go beyond what has been heard
and what is to be heard.

When the intellect becomes free of delusion, it is able to view things objectively and hence is not perturbed by external influences.

53 Unmoved by confusing things
that you may hear,
when your intellect stands still
and is firmly fixed in meditation,
you shall attain ***yoga***.

In this context, *yoga* is 'union with the Supreme.'

ARJUNA

54 How do you describe a man of steady insight?
How does a man of steady intellect speak?
How does he sit?
How does he go about leading his life?

KṚṢṆA

55 When one abandons all selfish desires
and is satisfied within the true Self,
he is said to be of steady intellect.

56 One whose mind is not agitated by adversity,
who does not crave pleasure,
who is free from passion, fear, and anger,
is a sage of steady intellect.

57 He is detached in all matters
and he neither rejoices nor hates
the pleasant and unpleasant situations
that he encounters;
his intellect stands firm.

[58]When he completely withdraws
the senses from the sensates,
just as a tortoise withdraws its limbs,
his intellect stands firm.

A tortoise has four legs, a head, and a tail that it can pull into the shell: this is possibly a reference to the five sense organs and the mind.

[59]Although he abstains from feeding the senses
by turning away from the sensates,
the cravings for sensations still remain.

Even the cravings leave him
once he has realized the Supreme.

[60]The turbulent senses
forcibly distract the mind
even of a wise person
who is sincerely striving
to control them.

[61]Having restrained the senses,
one should sit steady
seeking the Supreme.

When senses are under control
one attains a steady intellect.

62 When one is preoccupied with sensations,
he easily gets attached to them.
From such attachment,
a desire to attain them is born.
Unfulfilled desires
lead to frustration.
63 Frustration
leads to confusion.
Confusion
impairs discretion.
Lack of discretion
destroys reasoning.
Without the power of reasoning,
he is doomed!

64 But a self-disciplined person,
who has subdued his senses and
is devoid of attraction or aversion,
remains peaceful even as
he encounters sensates.

65 In that eternal peace,
all his pains are destroyed
for the intellect of the serene one
soon becomes firmly established in the Self.

66 One who is not disciplined
lacks wisdom and focus.
Without focus,
one cannot attain peace.
Without peace,
how can one be happy?

67 When the mind is led astray
by wandering senses,
then it carries away one's wisdom
just as the wind carries away a ship
off its chartered course.

68 Therefore, O mighty-armed one,
he is of steady intellect
whose senses are completely restrained
from the influence of sensates.

69 The self-restrained person is awake
to which all other beings are asleep.
The seer-sage is asleep
to which all other beings are awake.

The self-restrained person is awake to the Ultimate Truth and the seer-sage is asleep to mundane experiences encountered by sense organs.

70 Just as rivers flow into the ocean
which gets filled up
and yet remains still,
so also, all desires merge in him
and yet he attains peace –
unlike the one who is driven by desires.

71 He attains peace
once he overcomes all desires,
lives without cravings,
and is free from ego
or any sense of ownership.

[72]This is indeed the state of *Brahman*.
He who attains it is never deluded.
Being established in that state,
even barely at the hour of death,
he becomes one with the Supreme.

Brahman is the Supreme Being.

3

अर्जुन उवाच ।	***arjuna uvāca*** ।
ज्यायसी चेत्कर्मणस्ते	*jyāyasī cetkarmaṇaste*
मता बुद्धिर्जनार्दन ।	*matā buddhirjanārdana* ।
तत्किं कर्मणि घोरे मां	*tatkiṃ karmaṇi ghore māṃ*
नियोजयसि केशव ॥ ३.१	*niyojayasi keśava* ॥ 3.1
व्यामिश्रेणैव वाक्येन	*vyāmiśreṇaiva vākyena*
बुद्धिं मोहयसीव मे ।	*buddhiṃ mohayasīva me* ।
तदेकं वद निश्चित्य	*tadekaṃ vada niścitya*
येन श्रेयोऽहम् आप्नुयाम् ॥ ३.२	*yena śreyo'ham āpnuyām* ॥ 3.2
श्रीभगवानुवाच ।	***śrībhagavānuvāca*** ।
लोकेऽस्मिन् द्विविधा निष्ठा	*loke'smin dvividhā niṣṭhā*
पुरा प्रोक्ता मयानघ ।	*purā proktā mayānagha* ।
ज्ञानयोगेन साङ्ख्यानां	*jñānayogena sāṅkhyānāṃ*
कर्मयोगेन योगिनाम् ॥ ३.३	*karmayogena yoginām* ॥ 3.3
न कर्मणामनारम्भात्	*na karmaṇāmanārambhāt*
नैष्कर्म्यं पुरुषोऽश्नुते ।	*naiṣkarmyaṃ puruṣo'śnute* ।
न च संन्यसनादेव	*na ca saṃnyasanādeva*
सिद्धिं समधिगच्छति ॥ ३.४	*siddhiṃ samadhigacchati* ॥ 3.4
न हि कश्चित् क्षणमपि	*na hi kaścit kṣaṇamapi*
जातु तिष्ठत्यकर्मकृत् ।	*jātu tiṣṭhatyakarmakṛt* ।
कार्यते ह्यवशः कर्म	*kāryate hyavaśaḥ karma*
सर्वः प्रकृतिजैर्गुणैः ॥ ३.५	*sarvaḥ prakṛtijairguṇaiḥ* ॥ 3.5
कर्मेन्द्रियाणि संयम्य	*karmendriyāṇi saṃyamya*
य आस्ते मनसा स्मरन् ।	*ya āste manasā smaran* ।
इन्द्रियार्थान्विमूढात्मा	*indriyārthānvimūḍhātmā*
मिथ्याचारः स उच्यते ॥ ३.६	*mithyācāraḥ sa ucyate* ॥ 3.6
यस्त्विन्द्रियाणि मनसा	*yastvindriyāṇi manasā*
नियम्यारभतेऽर्जुन ।	*niyamyārabhate'rjuna* ।
कर्मेन्द्रियैः कर्मयोगम्	*karmendriyaiḥ karmayogam*
असक्तः स विशिष्यते ॥ ३.७	*asaktaḥ sa viśiṣyate* ॥ 3.7

नियतं कुरु कर्म त्वं कर्म ज्यायो ह्यकर्मणः । शरीरयात्रापि च ते न प्रसिध्येदकर्मणः ॥ ३.८	*niyataṃ kuru karma tvaṃ* *karma jyāyo hyakarmaṇaḥ* । *śarīrayātrāpi ca te* *na prasidhyedakarmaṇaḥ* ॥ 3.8
यज्ञार्थात्कर्मणोऽन्यत्र लोकोऽयं कर्मबन्धनः । तदर्थं कर्म कौन्तेय मुक्तसङ्गः समाचर ॥ ३.९	*yajñārthātkarmaṇo'nyatra* *loko'yaṃ karmabandhanaḥ* । *tadarthaṃ karma kaunteya* *muktasaṅgaḥ samācara* ॥ 3.9
सहयज्ञाः प्रजाः सृष्ट्वा पुरोवाच प्रजापतिः । अनेन प्रसविष्यध्वम् एष वोऽस्त्विष्टकामधुक् ॥ ३.१०	*sahayajñāḥ prajāḥ sṛṣṭvā* *purovāca prajāpatiḥ* । *anena prasaviṣyadhvam* *eṣa vo'stviṣṭakāmadhuk* ॥ 3.10
देवान्भावयतानेन ते देवा भावयन्तु वः । परस्परं भावयन्तः श्रेयः परमवाप्स्यथ ॥ ३.११	*devānbhāvayatānena* *te devā bhāvayantu vaḥ* । *parasparaṃ bhāvayantaḥ* *śreyaḥ paramavāpsyatha* ॥ 3.11
इष्टान्भोगान्हि वो देवा दास्यन्ते यज्ञभाविताः । तैर्दत्तानप्रदायैभ्यो यो भुङ्क्ते स्तेन एव सः ॥ ३.१२	*iṣṭānbhogānhi vo devā* *dāsyante yajñabhāvitāḥ* । *tairdattānapradāyaibhyo* *yo bhuṅkte stena eva saḥ* ॥ 3.12
यज्ञशिष्टाशिनः सन्तो मुच्यन्ते सर्वकिल्बिषैः । भुञ्जते ते त्वघं पापा ये पचन्त्यात्मकारणात् ॥ ३.१३	*yajñaśiṣṭāśinaḥ santo* *mucyante sarvakilbiṣaiḥ* । *bhuñjate te tvaghaṃ pāpā* *ye pacantyātmakāraṇāt* ॥ 3.13
अन्नाद्भवन्ति भूतानि पर्जन्यादन्नसम्भवः । यज्ञाद्भवति पर्जन्यो यज्ञः कर्मसमुद्भवः ॥ ३.१४	*annādbhavanti bhūtāni* *parjanyādannasambhavaḥ* । *yajñādbhavati parjanyo* *yajñaḥ karmasamudbhavaḥ* ॥ 3.14
कर्म ब्रह्मोद्भवं विद्धि ब्रह्माक्षरसमुद्भवम् । तस्मात्सर्वगतं ब्रह्म नित्यं यज्ञे प्रतिष्ठितम् ॥ ३.१५	*karma brahmodbhavaṃ viddhi* *brahmākṣarasamudbhavam* । *tasmātsarvagataṃ brahma* *nityaṃ yajñe pratiṣṭhitam* ॥ 3.15

एवं प्रवर्तितं चक्रं
नानुवर्तयतीह यः ।
अघायुरिन्द्रियारामो
मोघं पार्थ स जीवति ॥ ३.१६

evaṃ pravartitaṃ cakraṃ
nānuvartayatīha yaḥ ।
aghāyurindriyārāmo
moghaṃ pārtha sa jīvati ॥ 3.16

यस्त्वात्मरतिरेव स्यात्
आत्मतृप्तश्च मानवः ।
आत्मन्येव च सन्तुष्टः
तस्य कार्यं न विद्यते ॥ ३.१७

yastvātmaratireva syāt
ātmatṛptaśca mānavaḥ ।
ātmanyeva ca santuṣṭaḥ
tasya kāryaṃ na vidyate ॥ 3.17

नैव तस्य कृतेनार्थो
नाकृतेनेह कश्चन ।
न चास्य सर्वभूतेषु
कश्चिद् अर्थव्यपाश्रयः ॥ ३.१८

naiva tasya kṛtenārtho
nākṛteneha kaścana ।
na cāsya sarvabhūteṣu
kaścid arthavyapāśrayaḥ ॥ 3.18

तस्मादसक्तः सततं
कार्यं कर्म समाचर ।
असक्तो ह्याचरन्कर्म
परमाप्नोति पूरुषः ॥ ३.१९

tasmādasaktaḥ satataṃ
kāryaṃ karma samācara ।
asakto hyācarankarma
paramāpnoti pūruṣaḥ ॥ 3.19

कर्मणैव हि संसिद्धिम्
आस्थिता जनकादयः ।
लोकसङ्ग्रहमेवापि
सम्पश्यन्कर्तुमर्हसि ॥ ३.२०

karmaṇaiva hi saṃsiddhim
āsthitā janakādayaḥ ।
lokasaṅgrahamevāpi
sampaśyankartumarhasi ॥ 3.20

यद्यदाचरति श्रेष्ठः
तत्तदेवेतरो जनः ।
स यत्प्रमाणं कुरुते
लोकस्तदनुवर्तते ॥ ३.२१

yadyadācarati śreṣṭhaḥ
tattadevetaro janaḥ ।
sa yatpramāṇaṃ kurute
lokastadanuvartate ॥ 3.21

न मे पार्थास्ति कर्तव्यं
त्रिषु लोकेषु किञ्चन ।
नानवाप्तमवाप्तव्यं
वर्त एव च कर्मणि ॥ ३.२२

na me pārthāsti kartavyaṃ
triṣu lokeṣu kiñcana ।
nānavāptamavāptavyaṃ
varta eva ca karmaṇi ॥ 3.22

यदि ह्यहं न वर्तेयं
जातु कर्मण्यतन्द्रितः ।
मम वर्त्मानुवर्तन्ते
मनुष्याः पार्थ सर्वशः ॥ ३.२३

yadi hyahaṃ na varteyaṃ
jātu karmaṇyatandritaḥ ।
mama vartmānuvartante
manuṣyāḥ pārtha sarvaśaḥ ॥ 3.23

उत्सीदेयुरिमे लोका
न कुर्यां कर्म चेदहम् ।
सङ्करस्य च कर्ता स्याम्
उपहन्यामिमाः प्रजाः ॥ ३.२४

utsīdeyurime lokā
na kuryāṃ karma cedaham ।
saṅkarasya ca kartā syām
upahanyāmimāḥ prajāḥ ॥ 3.24

सक्ताः कर्मण्यविद्वांसो
यथा कुर्वन्ति भारत ।
कुर्याद्विद्वांस्तथासक्तः
चिकीर्षुर्लोकसङ्ग्रहम् ॥ ३.२५

saktāḥ karmaṇyavidvāṃso
yathā kurvanti bhārata ।
kuryādvidvāṃstathāsaktaḥ
cikīrṣurlokasaṅgraham ॥ 3.25

न बुद्धिभेदं जनयेत्
अज्ञानां कर्मसङ्गिनाम् ।
जोषयेत्सर्वकर्माणि
विद्वान्युक्तः समाचरन् ॥ ३.२६

na buddhibhedaṃ janayet
ajñānāṃ karmasaṅginām ।
joṣayetsarvakarmāṇi
vidvānyuktaḥ samācaran ॥ 3.26

प्रकृतेः क्रियमाणानि
गुणैः कर्माणि सर्वशः ।
अहङ्कारविमूढात्मा
कर्ताहमिति मन्यते ॥ ३.२७

prakṛteḥ kriyamāṇāni
guṇaiḥ karmāṇi sarvaśaḥ ।
ahaṅkāravimūḍhātmā
kartāhamiti manyate ॥ 3.27

तत्त्ववित्तु महाबाहो
गुणकर्मविभागयोः ।
गुणा गुणेषु वर्तन्त
इति मत्वा न सज्जते ॥ ३.२८

tattvavittu mahābāho
guṇakarmavibhāgayoḥ ।
guṇā guṇeṣu vartanta
iti matvā na sajjate ॥ 3.28

प्रकृतेर्गुणसंमूढाः
सज्जन्ते गुणकर्मसु ।
तानकृत्स्नविदो मन्दान्
कृत्स्नविन्न विचालयेत् ॥ ३.२९

prakṛterguṇasaṃmūḍhāḥ
sajjante guṇakarmasu ।
tānakṛtsnavido mandān
kṛtsnavinna vicālayet ॥ 3.29

मयि सर्वाणि कर्माणि
संन्यस्याध्यात्मचेतसा ।
निराशीर्निर्ममो भूत्वा
युध्यस्व विगतज्वरः ॥ ३.३०

mayi sarvāṇi karmāṇi
saṃnyasyādhyātmacetasā ।
nirāśīrnirmamo bhūtvā
yudhyasva vigatajvaraḥ ॥ 3.30

ये मे मतमिदं नित्यम्
अनुतिष्ठन्ति मानवाः ।
श्रद्धावन्तोऽनसूयन्तो
मुच्यन्ते तेऽपि कर्मभिः ॥ ३.३१

ye me matamidaṃ nityam
anutiṣṭhanti mānavāḥ ।
śraddhāvanto'nasūyanto
mucyante te'pi karmabhiḥ ॥ 3.31

ये त्वेतदभ्यसूयन्तो	*ye tvetadabhyasūyanto*
नानुतिष्ठन्ति मे मतम् ।	*nānutiṣṭhanti me matam* ।
सर्वज्ञानविमूढांस्तान्	*sarvajñānavimūḍhāṃstān*
विद्धि नष्टानचेतसः ॥ ३.३२	*viddhi naṣṭānacetasaḥ* ॥ 3.32
सदृशं चेष्टते स्वस्याः	*sadṛśaṃ ceṣṭate svasyāḥ*
प्रकृतेर्ज्ञानवानपि ।	*prakṛterjñānavānapi* ।
प्रकृतिं यान्ति भूतानि	*prakṛtiṃ yānti bhūtāni*
निग्रहः किं करिष्यति ॥ ३.३३	*nigrahaḥ kiṃ kariṣyati* ॥ 3.33
इन्द्रियस्येन्द्रियस्यार्थे	*indriyasyendriyasyārthe*
रागद्वेषौ व्यवस्थितौ ।	*rāgadveṣau vyavasthitau* ।
तयोर्न वशमागच्छेत्	*tayorna vaśamāgacchet*
तौ ह्यस्य परिपन्थिनौ ॥ ३.३४	*tau hyasya paripanthinau* ॥ 3.34
श्रेयान्स्वधर्मो विगुणः	*śreyānsvadharmo viguṇaḥ*
परधर्मात्स्वनुष्ठितात् ।	*paradharmātsvanuṣṭhitāt* ।
स्वधर्मे निधनं श्रेयः	*svadharme nidhanaṃ śreyaḥ*
परधर्मो भयावहः ॥ ३.३५	*paradharmo bhayāvahaḥ* ॥ 3.35
अर्जुन उवाच ।	***arjuna uvāca*** ।
अथ केन प्रयुक्तोऽयं	*atha kena prayukto'yaṃ*
पापं चरति पूरुषः ।	*pāpaṃ carati pūruṣaḥ* ।
अनिच्छन्नपि वार्ष्णेय	*anicchannapi vārṣṇeya*
बलादिव नियोजितः ॥ ३.३६	*balādiva niyojitaḥ* ॥ 3.36
श्रीभगवानुवाच ।	***śrībhagavānuvāca*** ।
काम एष क्रोध एष	*kāma eṣa krodha eṣa*
रजोगुणसमुद्भवः ।	*rajoguṇasamudbhavaḥ* ।
महाशनो महापाप्मा	*mahāśano mahāpāpmā*
विद्ध्येनमिह वैरिणम् ॥ ३.३७	*viddhyenamiha vairiṇam* ॥ 3.37
धूमेनाव्रियते वह्निः	*dhūmenāvriyate vahniḥ*
यथादर्शो मलेन च ।	*yathādarśo malena ca* ।
यथोल्बेनावृतो गर्भः	*yatholbenāvṛto garbhaḥ*
तथा तेनेदमावृतम् ॥ ३.३८	*tathā tenedamāvṛtam* ॥ 3.38

आवृतं ज्ञानमेतेन
ज्ञानिनो नित्यवैरिणा ।
कामरूपेण कौन्तेय
दुष्पूरेणानलेन च ॥ ३.३९

āvṛtaṃ jñānametena
jñānino nityavairiṇā ।
kāmarūpeṇa kaunteya
duṣpūreṇānalena ca ॥ 3.39

इन्द्रियाणि मनो बुद्धिः
अस्याधिष्ठानमुच्यते ।
एतैर्विमोहयत्येष
ज्ञानमावृत्य देहिनम् ॥ ३.४०

indriyāṇi mano buddhiḥ
asyādhiṣṭhānamucyate ।
etairvimohayatyeṣa
jñānamāvṛtya dehinam ॥ 3.40

तस्मात्त्वमिन्द्रियाण्यादौ
नियम्य भरतर्षभ ।
पाप्मानं प्रजहिह्येनं
ज्ञानविज्ञाननाशनम् ॥ ३.४१

tasmāttvamindriyāṇyādau
niyamya bharatarṣabha ।
pāpmānaṃ prajahihyenaṃ
jñānavijñānanāśanam ॥ 3.41

इन्द्रियाणि पराण्याहुः
इन्द्रियेभ्यः परं मनः ।
मनसस्तु परा बुद्धिः
यो बुद्धेः परतस्तु सः ॥ ३.४२

indriyāṇi parāṇyāhuḥ
indriyebhyaḥ paraṃ manaḥ ।
manasastu parā buddhiḥ
yo buddheḥ paratastu saḥ ॥ 3.42

एवं बुद्धेः परं बुद्ध्वा
संस्तभ्यात्मानमात्मना ।
जहि शत्रुं महाबाहो
कामरूपं दुरासदम् ॥ ३.४३

evaṃ buddheḥ paraṃ buddhvā
saṃstabhyātmānamātmanā ।
jahi śatruṃ mahābāho
kāmarūpaṃ durāsadam ॥ 3.43

CHAPTER 3

Selfless Action

Arjuna

[1] If you consider knowledge superior to action,
why do you urge me to commit this terrible deed?

[2] You confuse me with this conflicting message.
Tell me for certain just one thing
that will lead me to the greatest good.

Kṛṣṇa

[3] O blameless one!
As I have proclaimed in the past,
there are two ways to lead a fulfilling life –
the **path of knowledge** for adherents of reasoning
and the **path of selfless action** for *yogins*.

The path of knowledge is best suited for the deep thinkers
who like to contemplate and reason.
The path of selfless action is best suited for those
who are active and like to work hard.

4 One cannot achieve freedom from action
by merely staying away from work.

One does not become serene
by merely giving up work.

5 Nobody can remain passive
even for a moment.
Everyone is helplessly drawn into action
by inborn, natural impulses.

6 One who sits idle
restraining the organs of action
yet mentally broods over sensations
is a hypocrite who has fooled himself.

Organs of action are: mouth, hands, feet, genitals, and anus.
One who sits idle fools himself into thinking that he is not acting.

7 A person excels when he
disciplines the senses with the mind and
engages the organs of action in work
without getting attached to sensations.

A recurring idea in this chapter is 'working without attachment.'
It refers to doing one's work merely as a duty and
being detached from the possible outcomes, good or bad.

[8]Do the work you are supposed to do.
Certainly it is better than laziness.
Even the basic maintenance of your body
is impossible without action.

[9]Humans are bound by their actions
except when they are performed
for the sake of *yajña*.
Thus, Arjuna, do your work,
free from attachments,
in the spirit of *yajña*.

Here, *yajña* means 'an act of self-dedication' or 'service above self.' It is also an act of worship; so the message is 'do your work as worship.'

[10]Long ago, Prajāpati, the lord of creatures
brought forth human beings
with the spirit of *yajña* and said,
"By this (spirit of *yajña*), you shall grow!
May this grant you all your desires!
[11]By this, you nourish the *devas* and
they will reward you in return.
By nourishing one another
you shall attain the supreme good.
[12]Pleased with your selfless service,
the *devas* will fulfill your wishes.

"One who enjoys those gifts
without giving back anything in return
is indeed a thief!"

*Deva*s are divine beings that reside in *deva-loka* (higher realm, abode of *deva*s).
The elements and forces of nature such as wind, water, fire, earth,
space, time, sun, moon, stars, planets, rain, oceans, mountains,
plants, animals, *etc.* are also personified as *deva*s.
We have to nourish and respect nature if we want to be nourished by it
and more importantly, for natural goodness to prevail.
*Deva*s are the embodiment of natural infrastructure.
We cannot work without the infrastructure in place,
so we must dedicate a portion of our gains for its maintenance.

13 Wise ones eat the food that remains
after being offered to *yajña*.
Thus, they are released from all evils.
Wicked ones prepare food for their own sake
and indeed live on *pāpa* alone.

In the process of procuring our food, at least to some extent, we cause trouble
to nature and also to other beings. So we purify the food by offering it
to the Supreme and then eating it with a sense of gratitude.
Even if we eat a dry leaf that fell on its own accord,
we must not do so with a sense of entitlement.
That would be nothing short of *pāpa* (evil, sin, guilt, crime, misfortune)!

14 Living beings are sustained by food,
food comes forth from rain,
rain is caused by *yajña*, and
yajña is born out of action.

The idea of '*yajña* causing rain' is perhaps a reference
to the maintenance of the natural cycle.

15 This action originates from *Brahman*,
which is the manifestation of the imperishable.
Therefore the all-pervading *Brahman* is
always established in *yajña*.

Brahman is the Supreme Being.

16 The wheel of life is thus set in motion.
Indulging in sensual pleasures,
those who violate this natural order
live in *pāpa*, thus wasting their lives.

Cosmic order of the universe is rooted in the principle of give and take.

17 But those who find
joy, satisfaction, and fulfillment
solely in the *ātman*
have nothing left to accomplish.

Ātman is the inner, higher self.
'...nothing left to accomplish' indicates that such people
don't work for any gains since they have already found peace within.

18 They have nothing to gain by performing action
and nothing to lose by renouncing action.
They are not dependent on anyone for anything.

19 Therefore, constantly work with a spirit of detachment
and you will attain the highest level.

[20]Janaka and others attained perfection
by just doing their work,
for the welfare of the world.
You too should work like them!

Janaka was a king of Mithilā (a province in Northern India)
who was hailed as a *rājarṣi*, who is both a king and a sage.
He appears in the *Bṛhadāraṇyaka-upaniṣad* and
also in the *Rāmāyaṇa* (as the father of Sītā).

[21]A great man sets an example by his actions.
The whole world follows the standard that he sets.

[22]There is nothing in the three worlds
that I have not yet achieved.
There is nothing to attain
that I have not yet attained.
Yet I continue to do my work.

The three worlds or the three 'realms of existence' are:
earth, *svarga* (loosely, 'heaven'), and the skies.
The three realms may also refer to past, present, and future.

23 Indeed, if I fail to work tirelessly,
humans would blindly follow my example
and sit idle without working.
24 If I did not work, these worlds would perish!
I would be the cause of confusion and chaos,
I would be the one to destroy these beings.

25 Ignorant people work for personal benefit
but wise ones must work for the welfare of the world.

26 The wise should not, however,
discourage the ignorant ones
who are attached to action.
The wise should inspire them
to learn detachment,
while they continue
to work selflessly themselves.

Wise people should not be hasty in trying to correct the ignorant ones but should allow them to relish activities in their own way. Sooner or later, they will realize the joy of working without selfishness, either on their own or from looking at the wise.

27 All actions of material nature
are driven by the *guṇa*s.
One who is deluded by ego thinks –
"I am the one who is doing!"

*Guṇa*s refer to the inherent traits of a person.

28 One who has true insight into
the interplay of *guṇa* and *karma*—
and how they are influenced
by the collective nature of society—
does not get entangled.

Here, '*karma*' refers to the different spheres of action.

The world is always in motion and thus, always changing.
Most of us are a part of society and are influenced by it.
Our customs, mannerisms, and practices adjust themselves
to our surroundings if we let them follow a natural course.
If we are perturbed by changing times and cling to practices that are irrelevant,
we are bound to be confused and frustrated.

29 Those who are fooled by the *guṇas*
are attached to the actions caused by them.
The wise should not disturb such fools.

They are deceived by the physical world into thinking that
the ultimate is what they can perceive through their senses.
The original has: "Those with perfect knowledge should not perturb
the dull-witted ones who have imperfect understanding."

30 Dedicate all your actions to the Supreme.
Focus your mind on the Supreme.
Free yourself from possessions and desire,
cast off your mental fever, and
engage in the battle.

The original has: "...all your actions to me," where 'me' refers to 'the Supreme.'
Dedicating work to the Supreme suggests invoking a higher purpose,
a greater meaning for our seemingly mundane work.

[31]Those who sincerely practise
my teaching without finding fault
are also released from actions.

The teaching here is – "Work with a constant regard for the greater purpose!"

[32]But those who condemn my teaching and don't follow it
are utterly deluded, lost, and mindless.

The original has '*matam*' (literally, 'opinion'), which is translated as 'teaching.' On the one hand, this is a wonderful synthesis of the teachings of the pastmasters and on the other, Kṛṣṇa is presenting it as an opinion rather than an injunction.

[33]People tend to follow their natural instincts.
Even the wise ones act within the
constraints of their natural instincts.
What is the use of superficial restraint?

[34]When senses encounter sensates
indeed Likes and Dislikes arise.
One should not be swayed by them
for they are obstacles in the path.

[35]Excelling in one's own *dharma*—
even if it is less appealing—is better than
trying to excel in another's *dharma*.

'...one's own *dharma*' (*svadharma*) refers to 'work in tune with one's inherent nature.'
One should be natural, free from deceit, and true to oneself.
By staying close to what we are intrinsically good at, we not only attain
personal success but also become valuable to society (see 18.45–48).

It is better to die upholding one's *dharma*!
Following the *dharma* of others is worse than death.

Leading a life doing things against our true nature
and imitating others is worse than death.

ARJUNA

[36]What is that powerful force
which compels a man to commit *pāpa*
though he doesn't want to be sinful?

KṚṢṆA

[37]It is Desire,
leading to anger.
It arises from *rajas*.
Unquenchable and corrupting,
it is an evil enemy indeed!

'Desire' indicates selfishness, lust, and greed.
By their very nature, desires can never be entirely appeased.
Unfulfilled desires naturally lead to frustration and anger.

[38]As fire is enveloped by smoke,
mirror is covered by dust, and
embryo is enclosed in the womb,
wisdom is veiled by Desire.

[39]The insatiable fire of Desire,
indeed a perennial enemy,
veils the wisdom of even the wise.

Also see 2.60.

[40]Desire is seated in
the senses, mind, and intellect.
Through them it deludes people
by eclipsing their wisdom.

Desire leads to delusion and ruin (see 2.62–63).

[41]Thus, control the senses first
and then shatter Desire,
the sinful destroyer of wisdom and reason.

The original has '...destroyer of *jñāna* and *vijñāna*.' The word '*jñāna*' refers to wisdom, ultimate knowledge, or learning in the universal sense while '*vijñāna*' refers to experiential wisdom, domain knowledge, or learning in a contextual sense.

[42]Senses are superior to the body,
mind is superior to the senses,
intellect is superior to the mind,
but This is superior to the intellect.

In light of the previous verses, 'This' can refer to 'desire' in the sense that desire is far more powerful than even the intellect. However, when we consider this verse and the next as a pair, 'This' refers to '*ātman*.' Basically, it alludes to 'inner voice' or 'conscience' – the internal, impartial *dharma*-compass that directs our senses, mind, and intellect inward, away from external influences and desires.

[43]Thus, knowing that
it (*ātman*) is superior to the intellect and
subduing the lower self by the *ātman*,
defeat that formidable foe
appearing in the form of Desire!

'Subduing the lower self' is a recurring motif in the *Gītā* (*e.g.* see 2.64 and 6.7). The lower self is the material aspect of one's being. The self is subjected to the whims and fancies of the body, senses, organs of action, ego, mind, intellect, and conscience. The *ātman* or the higher Self transcends all this.

4

श्रीभगवानुवाच ।	***śrībhagavānuvāca*** ।
इमं विवस्वते योगं	*imaṃ vivasvate yogaṃ*
प्रोक्तवानहमव्ययम् ।	*proktavānahamavyayam* ।
विवस्वान्मनवे प्राह	*vivasvānmanave prāha*
मनुरिक्ष्वाकवेऽब्रवीत् ॥ ४.१	*manurikṣvākave'bravīt* ॥ 4.1
एवं परम्पराप्राप्तम्	*evaṃ paramparāprāptam*
इमं राजर्षयो विदुः ।	*imaṃ rājarṣayo viduḥ* ।
स कालेनेह महता	*sa kāleneha mahatā*
योगो नष्टः परन्तप ॥ ४.२	*yogo naṣṭaḥ parantapa* ॥ 4.2
स एवायं मया तेऽद्य	*sa evāyaṃ mayā te'dya*
योगः प्रोक्तः पुरातनः ।	*yogaḥ proktaḥ purātanaḥ* ।
भक्तोऽसि मे सखा चेति	*bhakto'si me sakhā ceti*
रहस्यं ह्येतदुत्तमम् ॥ ४.३	*rahasyaṃ hyetaduttamam* ॥ 4.3
अर्जुन उवाच ।	***arjuna uvāca*** ।
अपरं भवतो जन्म	*aparaṃ bhavato janma*
परं जन्म विवस्वतः ।	*paraṃ janma vivasvataḥ* ।
कथमेतद्विजानीयां	*kathametadvijānīyāṃ*
त्वमादौ प्रोक्तवानिति ॥ ४.४	*tvamādau proktavāniti* ॥ 4.4
श्रीभगवानुवाच ।	***śrībhagavānuvāca*** ।
बहूनि मे व्यतीतानि	*bahūni me vyatītāni*
जन्मानि तव चार्जुन ।	*janmāni tava cārjuna* ।
तान्यहं वेद सर्वाणि	*tānyahaṃ veda sarvāṇi*
न त्वं वेत्थ परन्तप ॥ ४.५	*na tvaṃ vettha parantapa* ॥ 4.5
अजोऽपि सन्नव्ययात्मा	*ajo'pi sannavyayātmā*
भूतानामीश्वरोऽपि सन् ।	*bhūtānāmīśvaro'pi san* ।
प्रकृतिं स्वामधिष्ठाय	*prakṛtiṃ svāmadhiṣṭhāya*
सम्भवाम्यात्ममायया ॥ ४.६	*sambhavāmyātmamāyayā* ॥ 4.6

यदा यदा हि धर्मस्य
ग्लानिर्भवति भारत ।
अभ्युत्थानमधर्मस्य
तदात्मानं सृजाम्यहम् ॥ ४.७

yadā yadā hi dharmasya
glānirbhavati bhārata ।
abhyutthānamadharmasya
tadātmānaṃ sṛjāmyaham ॥ 4.7

परित्राणाय साधूनां
विनाशाय च दुष्कृताम् ।
धर्मसंस्थापनार्थाय
सम्भवामि युगे युगे ॥ ४.८

paritrāṇāya sādhūnāṃ
vināśāya ca duṣkṛtām ।
dharmasaṃsthāpanārthāya
sambhavāmi yuge yuge ॥ 4.8

जन्म कर्म च मे दिव्यम्
एवं यो वेत्ति तत्त्वतः ।
त्यक्त्वा देहं पुनर्जन्म
नैति मामेति सोऽर्जुन ॥ ४.९

janma karma ca me divyam
evaṃ yo vetti tattvataḥ ।
tyaktvā dehaṃ punarjanma
naiti māmeti so'rjuna ॥ 4.9

वीतरागभयक्रोधा
मन्मया मामुपाश्रिताः ।
बहवो ज्ञानतपसा
पूता मद्भावम् आगताः ॥ ४.१०

vītarāgabhayakrodhā
manmayā māmupāśritāḥ ।
bahavo jñānatapasā
pūtā madbhāvam āgatāḥ ॥ 4.10

ये यथा मां प्रपद्यन्ते
तांस्तथैव भजाम्यहम् ।
मम वर्त्मानुवर्तन्ते
मनुष्याः पार्थ सर्वशः ॥ ४.११

ye yathā māṃ prapadyante
tāṃstathaiva bhajāmyaham ।
mama vartmānuvartante
manuṣyāḥ pārtha sarvaśaḥ ॥ 4.11

काङ्क्षन्तः कर्मणां सिद्धिं
यजन्त इह देवताः ।
क्षिप्रं हि मानुषे लोके
सिद्धिर्भवति कर्मजा ॥ ४.१२

kāṅkṣantaḥ karmaṇāṃ siddhiṃ
yajanta iha devatāḥ ।
kṣipraṃ hi mānuṣe loke
siddhirbhavati karmajā ॥ 4.12

चातुर्वर्ण्यं मया सृष्टं
गुणकर्मविभागशः ।
तस्य कर्तारमपि मां
विद्ध्यकर्तारमव्ययम् ॥ ४.१३

cāturvarṇyaṃ mayā sṛṣṭaṃ
guṇakarmavibhāgaśaḥ ।
tasya kartāramapi māṃ
viddhyakartāramavyayam ॥ 4.13

न मां कर्माणि लिम्पन्ति
न मे कर्मफले स्पृहा ।
इति मां योऽभिजानाति
कर्मभिर्न स बध्यते ॥ ४.१४

na māṃ karmāṇi limpanti
na me karmaphale spṛhā ।
iti māṃ yo'bhijānāti
karmabhirna sa badhyate ॥ 4.14

एवं ज्ञात्वा कृतं कर्म
पूर्वैरपि मुमुक्षुभिः ।
कुरु कर्मैव तस्मात्त्वं
पूर्वैः पूर्वतरं कृतम् ॥ ४.१५

evaṃ jñātvā kṛtaṃ karma
pūrvairapi mumukṣubhiḥ ।
kuru karmaiva tasmāttvaṃ
pūrvaiḥ pūrvataraṃ kṛtam ॥ 4.15

किं कर्म किमकर्मेति
कवयोऽप्यत्र मोहिताः ।
तत्ते कर्म प्रवक्ष्यामि
यज्ज्ञात्वा मोक्ष्यसेऽशुभात् ॥ ४.१६

kiṃ karma kimakarmeti
kavayo'pyatra mohitāḥ ।
tatte karma pravakṣyāmi
yajjñātvā mokṣyase'śubhāt ॥ 4.16

कर्मणो ह्यपि बोद्धव्यं
बोद्धव्यं च विकर्मणः ।
अकर्मणश्च बोद्धव्यं
गहना कर्मणो गतिः ॥ ४.१७

karmaṇo hyapi boddhavyaṃ
boddhavyaṃ ca vikarmaṇaḥ ।
akarmaṇaśca boddhavyaṃ
gahanā karmaṇo gatiḥ ॥ 4.17

कर्मण्यकर्म यः पश्येत्
अकर्मणि च कर्म यः ।
स बुद्धिमान्मनुष्येषु
स युक्तः कृत्स्नकर्मकृत् ॥ ४.१८

karmaṇyakarma yaḥ paśyet
akarmaṇi ca karma yaḥ ।
sa buddhimānmanuṣyeṣu
sa yuktaḥ kṛtsnakarmakṛt ॥ 4.18

यस्य सर्वे समारम्भाः
कामसङ्कल्पवर्जिताः ।
ज्ञानाग्निदग्धकर्माणं
तमाहुः पण्डितं बुधाः ॥ ४.१९

yasya sarve samārambhāḥ
kāmasaṅkalpavarjitāḥ ।
jñānāgnidagdhakarmāṇaṃ
tamāhuḥ paṇḍitaṃ budhāḥ ॥ 4.19

त्यक्त्वा कर्मफलासङ्गं
नित्यतृप्तो निराश्रयः ।
कर्मण्यभिप्रवृत्तोऽपि
नैव किञ्चित्करोति सः ॥ ४.२०

tyaktvā karmaphalāsaṅgaṃ
nityatṛpto nirāśrayaḥ ।
karmaṇyabhipravṛtto'pi
naiva kiñcitkaroti saḥ ॥ 4.20

निराशीर्यतचित्तात्मा
त्यक्तसर्वपरिग्रहः ।
शारीरं केवलं कर्म
कुर्वन्नाप्नोति किल्बिषम् ॥ ४.२१

nirāśīryatacittātmā
tyaktasarvaparigrahaḥ ।
śārīraṃ kevalaṃ karma
kurvannāpnoti kilbiṣam ॥ 4.21

यदृच्छालाभसन्तुष्टो
द्वन्द्वातीतो विमत्सरः ।
समः सिद्धावसिद्धौ च
कृत्वापि न निबध्यते ॥ ४.२२

yadṛcchālābhasantuṣṭo
dvandvātīto vimatsaraḥ ।
samaḥ siddhāvasiddhau ca
kṛtvāpi na nibadhyate ॥ 4.22

गतसङ्गस्य मुक्तस्य
ज्ञानावस्थितचेतसः ।
यज्ञायाचरतः कर्म
समग्रं प्रविलीयते ॥ ४.२३

gatasaṅgasya muktasya
jñānāvasthitacetasaḥ ।
yajñāyācarataḥ karma
samagraṃ pravilīyate ॥ 4.23

ब्रह्मार्पणं ब्रह्महविः
ब्रह्माग्नौ ब्रह्मणा हुतम् ।
ब्रह्मैव तेन गन्तव्यं
ब्रह्मकर्मसमाधिना ॥ ४.२४

brahmārpaṇaṃ brahmahaviḥ
brahmāgnau brahmaṇā hutam ।
brahmaiva tena gantavyaṃ
brahmakarmasamādhinā ॥ 4.24

दैवमेवापरे यज्ञं
योगिनः पर्युपासते ।
ब्रह्माग्नावपरे यज्ञं
यज्ञेनैवोपजुह्वति ॥ ४.२५

daivamevāpare yajñaṃ
yoginaḥ paryupāsate ।
brahmāgnāvapare yajñaṃ
yajñenaivopajuhvati ॥ 4.25

श्रोत्रादीनीन्द्रियाण्यन्ये
संयमाग्निषु जुह्वति ।
शब्दादीन्विषयानन्य
इन्द्रियाग्निषु जुह्वति ॥ ४.२६

śrotrādīnīndriyāṇyanye
saṃyamāgniṣu juhvati ।
śabdādīnviṣayānanya
indriyāgniṣu juhvati ॥ 4.26

सर्वाणीन्द्रियकर्माणि
प्राणकर्माणि चापरे ।
आत्मसंयमयोगाग्नौ
जुह्वति ज्ञानदीपिते ॥ ४.२७

sarvāṇīndriyakarmāṇi
prāṇakarmāṇi cāpare ।
ātmasaṃyamayogāgnau
juhvati jñānadīpite ॥ 4.27

द्रव्ययज्ञास्तपोयज्ञा
योगयज्ञास्तथापरे ।
स्वाध्यायज्ञानयज्ञाश्च
यतयः संशितव्रताः ॥ ४.२८

dravyayajñāstapoyajñā
yogayajñāstathāpare ।
svādhyāyajñānayajñāśca
yatayaḥ saṃśitavratāḥ ॥ 4.28

अपाने जुह्वति प्राणं
प्राणेऽपानं तथापरे ।
प्राणापानगती रुद्ध्वा
प्राणायामपरायणाः ॥ ४.२९

apāne juhvati prāṇaṃ
prāṇe'pānaṃ tathāpare ।
prāṇāpānagatī ruddhvā
prāṇāyāmaparāyaṇāḥ ॥ 4.29

अपरे नियताहाराः
प्राणान्प्राणेषु जुह्वति ।
सर्वेऽप्येते यज्ञविदो
यज्ञक्षपितकल्मषाः ॥ ४.३०

apare niyatāhārāḥ
prāṇānprāṇeṣu juhvati ।
sarve'pyete yajñavido
yajñakṣapitakalmaṣāḥ ॥ 4.30

यज्ञशिष्टामृतभुजो
यान्ति ब्रह्म सनातनम् ।
नायं लोकोऽस्त्ययज्ञस्य
कुतोऽन्यः कुरुसत्तम ॥ ४.३१

yajñaśiṣṭāmṛtabhujo
yānti brahma sanātanam ।
nāyaṃ loko'styayajñasya
kuto'nyaḥ kurusattama ॥ 4.31

एवं बहुविधा यज्ञा
वितता ब्रह्मणो मुखे ।
कर्मजान्विद्धि तान्सर्वान्
एवं ज्ञात्वा विमोक्ष्यसे ॥ ४.३२

evaṃ bahuvidhā yajñā
vitatā brahmaṇo mukhe ।
karmajānviddhi tānsarvān
evaṃ jñātvā vimokṣyase ॥ 4.32

श्रेयान्द्रव्यमयाद्यज्ञात्
ज्ञानयज्ञः परन्तप ।
सर्वं कर्माखिलं पार्थ
ज्ञाने परिसमाप्यते ॥ ४.३३

śreyāndravyamayādyajñāt
jñānayajñaḥ parantapa ।
sarvaṃ karmākhilaṃ pārtha
jñāne parisamāpyate ॥ 4.33

तद्विद्धि प्रणिपातेन
परिप्रश्नेन सेवया ।
उपदेक्ष्यन्ति ते ज्ञानं
ज्ञानिनस्तत्त्वदर्शिनः ॥ ४.३४

tadviddhi praṇipātena
paripraśnena sevayā ।
upadekṣyanti te jñānaṃ
jñāninastattvadarśinaḥ ॥ 4.34

यज्ज्ञात्वा न पुनर्मोहम्
एवं यास्यसि पाण्डव ।
येन भूतान्यशेषेण
द्रक्ष्यस्यात्मन्यथो मयि ॥ ४.३५

yajjñātvā na punarmoham
evaṃ yāsyasi pāṇḍava ।
yena bhūtānyaśeṣeṇa
drakṣyasyātmanyatho mayi ॥ 4.35

अपि चेदसि पापेभ्यः
सर्वेभ्यः पापकृत्तमः ।
सर्वं ज्ञानप्लवेनैव
वृजिनं सन्तरिष्यसि ॥ ४.३६

api cedasi pāpebhyaḥ
sarvebhyaḥ pāpakṛttamaḥ ।
sarvaṃ jñānaplavenaiva
vṛjinaṃ santariṣyasi ॥ 4.36

यथैधांसि समिद्धोऽग्निः
भस्मसात्कुरुतेऽर्जुन ।
ज्ञानाग्निः सर्वकर्माणि
भस्मसात्कुरुते तथा ॥ ४.३७

yathaidhāṃsi samiddho'gniḥ
bhasmasātkurute'rjuna ।
jñānāgniḥ sarvakarmāṇi
bhasmasātkurute tathā ॥ 4.37

न हि ज्ञानेन सदृशं
पवित्रमिह विद्यते ।
तत्स्वयं योगसंसिद्धः
कालेनात्मनि विन्दति ॥ ४.३८

na hi jñānena sadṛśaṃ
pavitramiha vidyate ।
tatsvayaṃ yogasaṃsiddhaḥ
kālenātmani vindati ॥ 4.38

श्रद्धावाँल्लभते ज्ञानं तत्परः संयतेन्द्रियः । ज्ञानं लब्ध्वा परां शान्तिम् अचिरेणाधिगच्छति ॥ ४.३९	*śraddhāvām̐llabhate jñānaṃ* *tatparaḥ saṃyatendriyaḥ* । *jñānaṃ labdhvā parāṃ śāntim* *acireṇādhigacchati* ॥ 4.39
अज्ञश्चाश्रद्दधानश्च संशयात्मा विनश्यति । नायं लोकोऽस्ति न परो न सुखं संशयात्मनः ॥ ४.४०	*ajñaścāśraddadhānaśca* *saṃśayātmā vinaśyati* । *nāyaṃ loko'sti na paro* *na sukhaṃ saṃśayātmanaḥ* ॥ 4.40
योगसंन्यस्तकर्माणं ज्ञानसञ्छिन्नसंशयम् । आत्मवन्तं न कर्माणि निबध्नन्ति धनञ्जय ॥ ४.४१	*yogasaṃnyastakarmāṇaṃ* *jñānasañchinnasaṃśayam* । *ātmavantaṃ na karmāṇi* *nibadhnanti dhanañjaya* ॥ 4.41
तस्मादज्ञानसम्भूतं हृत्स्थं ज्ञानासिनात्मनः । छित्त्वैनं संशयं योगम् आतिष्ठोत्तिष्ठ भारत ॥ ४.४२	*tasmādajñānasambhūtaṃ* *hṛtsthaṃ jñānāsinātmanaḥ* । *chittvainaṃ saṃśayaṃ yogam* *ātiṣṭhottiṣṭha bhārata* ॥ 4.42

CHAPTER 4

Wisdom in Action

Kṛṣṇa

[1]I taught this eternal *yoga* to Vivasvat.
Vivasvat taught Manu and
Manu taught Ikṣvāku.

Vivasvat is the patriarch of the famous *sūrya-vaṃśa* (solar dynasty) to which many Hindus trace their ancestry. Manu and Ikṣvāku are his descendents. Rāma, the hero of the epic *Rāmāyaṇa*, is a descendent of Ikṣvāku.

[2]Thus traditionally handed down
in regular succession,
the *rājarṣis* knew this.

A *rājarṣi* is one who is both a king and a sage.

But over the long course of time
the *yoga* has been lost in the world.

Over time, the eternal *yoga* gets cluttered by tradition and complicated by excessive scholarship. Thus, it is practically lost.

3I have now told you the same ancient *yoga*,
because you are my friend and admirer.
This *yoga* is a supreme secret indeed.

ARJUNA

4Vivasvat was born long before you.
How could you have taught him?

KṚṢṆA

5You and I have passed through many lives, Arjuna.
I remember them all but you do not.

6I am the lord of beings,
unborn and imperishable,
yet restraining my basic nature
I incarnate myself by my own *māyā*.

The Supreme is inherently beyond space and time. Through *māyā*, the divine power of illusion, the Supreme veils its own inherent nature to assume a role and form that is relevant to a particular situation.

[7]Whenever there is a decline of *dharma*
and a rise of *adharma*,
I manifest myself in this world.

Dharma is that which sustains everything. It is the harmony in the universe that sustains the greater good. By definition, *dharma* protects one who protects it. *Adharma* is the opposite of *dharma* – it is that which hinders sustainability.

[8]To protect the good,
to destroy evil, and
to firmly establish *dharma*,
I manifest myself time and again.

Here, 'good' not only refers to sages but also to ordinary, helpless folk, who are exploited by the wicked. History has shown that during a great crisis, someone rises to the occasion, assumes leadership, and brings about change. Here Kṛṣṇa presents the concept of *avatāra* (incarnation) without limitations of space or time.

[9]He who truly knows the scheme of
my divine birth and deeds,
is not reborn when he leaves the body;
he comes to me, Arjuna.

This verse perhaps implies that one who fully comprehends life is liberated.

[10]Freed from passions, fear, and anger,
thinking of me, dedicated to me, and
cleansed by the power of wisdom,
many have attained my state of being.

11 Everywhere, humans pursue a path to attain me.
In whatever manner they approach me,
I reward them accordingly.

12 Those who work craving for worldly success
offer ritualistic worship to the gods.
Indeed, in the world of humans,
one attains material success quickly.

Rituals often arise from the prevailing geographical conditions and culture. They help achieve short-term gains and inculcate basic discipline. Rituals are the *means* to spiritual progress; they should not become the *ends*.

Material success is tangible and is more readily achieved as compared to true knowledge, which is abstract. Without doubt, there is no short-cut to knowledge!

13 I have brought forth the four *varṇas*.
It is a classification based on ***guṇa*** and ***karma***.

Varṇa refers to a categorization of individuals based on their *guṇa* (basic traits, attitudes and aptitudes, inherent qualities) and *karma* (work that is attuned to *guṇa*, chosen profession). The natural disposition of a person makes him/her more suitable to perform a certain set of functions in society. Traditional Hindu society identified four basic traits among humans (see 18.41–44) and on that basis designated individuals to be a member of one of the four *varṇas*.

Although I am their cause,
I am unchanged and beyond all action.

14 I am not bound by actions
because I don't crave for rewards.
One who knows me thus
is also not bound by action.

'One who knows me' refers to identification with the *ātman* within and the relation of the inner self to the Supreme.

15 With this understanding,
ancient seekers of liberation did their work
without being attached to its outcomes.
Therefore, I suggest that you too should act
just as they did in the past.

16 What is action?
What is inaction?
Even the seers are puzzled.
Let me explain the true nature of action.
Once you know this,
you will be liberated from evil.

Here, 'evil' refers to the continued circulation in the cycle of *karma* due to one's attachments (see 9.20–21).

17 The nature of action is hard to grasp.
One should correctly know –
What is right action?
What is not right action?
What is inaction?

18 One who can see Stillness in the midst of Activity
and Action in the midst of Inertia is indeed wise.
He acts sensibly at all times.

'Stillness in the midst of Activity' is explained in the following verses.
'Action in the midst of Inertia' is explained in verse 3.6.

19 The pursuits of the wise
are not motivated by desire.
Their actions are purified
by the fire of wisdom.

The wise don't have any personal agenda.
They work for the welfare of all.

20 They are ever-satisfied and independent.
Even while engaged in action, they do nothing
because they are not attached to the outcome.

The wise realize that they are not *doing* the work,
but rather that the work is *getting done*.

21 Just by doing activities with discipline,
not expecting anything from it,
and free from a sense of possession,
you can stay away from evil.

22 Satisfied with what comes on its own accord,
even-minded in success and failure,
rising above the dualities,
and free from envy,
one is not affected
even when performing action.

'Dualities' are relative opposites like pain and pleasure,
attraction and aversion, gain and loss, me and others, etc.

[23]One who is wise, unattached, and liberated
acts in the spirit of *yajña*.
All his actions are indeed absolved.

'Spirit of *yajña*' refers to a spirit of service or offering.
'Absolved' means that he is not bound by those actions.

Ideally one should perform *all* actions in the spirit of *yajña*.
In other words, one must always work in a dedicated manner.
It might not be possible to do every activity in the spirit of *yajña*
but we should try to do at least some activities in that spirit.
Not doing so is as good as wasting one's life (see 4.31).

The next ten verses describe the various *yajña*s and how every aspect of our life – both voluntary and involuntary activities – is rooted in the Supreme.

[24]*Brahman* is the offering,
Brahman is the fuel, and
Brahman is the fire to which
Brahman makes the offering.
Brahman indeed is attained by
one who is absorbed in action,
which is also *Brahman*.

In this verse, every component of a *yajña* is presented as a metaphor for *Brahman*, the Supreme Being (see 9.16).

Yajña is a *Vedic* ritual in which fire is raised in closed altars
made of bricks, with the top portion open to air.
Agni—the sacred fire—exists in three forms:
gārhapatya, *dakṣiṇa*, and *āhavanīya*,
and fires are raised in three altars, one for each *agni*.
Agni is both a deity as well as the medium
to deliver the offerings made to other deities.
The deities to be worshiped are invoked during the *yajña*.

Clarified butter (fuel for the fire), medicinal herbs, twigs of the pīpal tree (*Ficus religiosa*), and other offerings (milk, grains that are fried and then cooked, juice of the *soma* plant, animals, etc.) are put in the fire, accompanied by reciting specific *mantras* (sacred verses) from the *Vedas*. (*Mantra* also refers to the formative thought behind the recited verses.) Typically, sixteen *ṛtviks* (loosely, 'priests' or 'officiators') preside over the rituals in a *yajña*.

25 Some aspirants perform *yajña*
to the deities and worship them;
others perform *yajña*
in the fire of *Brahman*
offering the *yajña* itself.

When performing a *yajña* dedicated to a certain deity, one can offer something that the deity likes. When performing a *yajña* dedicated to the Supreme *Brahman*, the only thing left to offer is the *yajña* itself. Such aspirants perform every action in the spirit of *yajña*.

26 Some aspirants submit hearing
and other senses
to the fire of restraint.
Some others subdue sound
and other sensations
in the fire of senses.

Some aspirants block their senses to avoid coming in contact with sensates. Others block their sensations, although their senses are in contact with sensates.

27 Some offer the *prāṇa* and
all actions of the senses

in the fire of self-control,
which is kindled by knowledge.

Prāṇa refers to the 'life-force' of an organism, its sustaining energy. It is also known as the 'vital breath,' for without breathing, there is no life.

28 Some aspirants offer their material wealth,
some offer their *yoga* expertise,
some offer austerities, and
others offer learning –
they are true ascetics.

Any action performed with dedication counts as a *yajña*.

29 Others—solely engaged in *prāṇāyāma*,
the art of breathing—
having regulated inward and outward breaths,
offer their inward breath to
their outward breath and *vice-versa*.

Prāṇāyāma (breath control) involves the regulation of the course of inhalations and exhalations.

30 While others, restraining their diet,
offer their *prāṇa* to their *prāṇa*.
They all know the way of *yajña* and
their *pāpas* are cleansed by doing *yajña*.

Ascetics who perform *tapas* gradually consume less and less. When their food intake reduces, their need for oxygen reduces and their bodily functions slow down. They augment it further by mindful breathing and meditation.

31 Relishing the remnants of *yajña*,
which is *amṛta*,
they (performers of *yajña*)
attain the Eternal *Brahman*.

Amṛta refers to divine nectar of immortality.

Those who don't perform any *yajña*
are unfit even for this world.
How can they enter the other world?

Some people devote their life doing what they love
without worrying about any rewards.
One must pursue at least some activities with this spirit of *yajña*;
otherwise, life will be dull and mechanical.
Such dullness never leads to perfection or happiness.

32 Thus, many kinds of *yajña*
are described in the scriptures.
All these *yajñas* are rooted in action.
Know this, and you will be free.

Once we grasp the larger scheme of things,
we begin to do all our actions with a spirit of selflessness.
That breaks all bonds and leads us to true freedom.

33 Pursuing knowledge is superior
to any ritual with material offerings
because all activities
find their fulfillment
only in knowledge.

34 Learn that knowledge from
those who have realized the truth.
Approach them with
a spirit of sincere enquiry
and serve them with humility.
They will impart that knowledge to you.

In ancient India, students lived with a *guru* (teacher) for many years
and over time, learned the path to the Ultimate Truth.
They served the *guru* and attended to all his mundane needs,
which taught them how the *guru* handled daily life situations
and not just the intellectual or spiritual quests.
Just as serving the *guru* with humility was important,
so also was appropriate and incisive questioning
that led to the clarification of all doubts.

35 Having learned it, Arjuna,
you will never be deluded again
because with that knowledge
you will perceive all beings
in yourself and in me.

36Even if you were the gravest of *pāpakṛts*,
you will overcome all evil
with the raft of knowledge.

Pāpa can refer to evil, sin, guilt, crime, misfortune, *etc.* and *pāpakṛt* (loosely, 'sinner' or 'criminal') is one who commits *pāpa*.

37Just as the blazing fire
reduces firewood to ashes,
the fire of knowledge
reduces all *karma* to ashes.

Karma refers to all spheres of action. So it encompasses normal day-to-day work, selfless action, lethargy, inappropriate action, rituals, inevitable action, working for greater good, etc. All *karma* is cleansed by truly understanding the basis of *karma*.

38Nothing is as pure as knowledge in this world.
One who reaches perfection by *yoga*
will eventually find it within.

39A sincere person gains knowledge
through focus and mastery of senses.
Once he has acquired knowledge,
he soon attains supreme peace.

40But a person who is ignorant, insincere,
and ever-skeptical gets destroyed.

One who is overly suspicious and ridden with doubt becomes indecisive.

One who remains hesitant and confused
finds no happiness in this world or beyond.

41 Actions do not bind a person
who has renounced
(the fruit of) action through *yoga*
whose doubts are destroyed through wisdom,
and who is always watchful over himself.

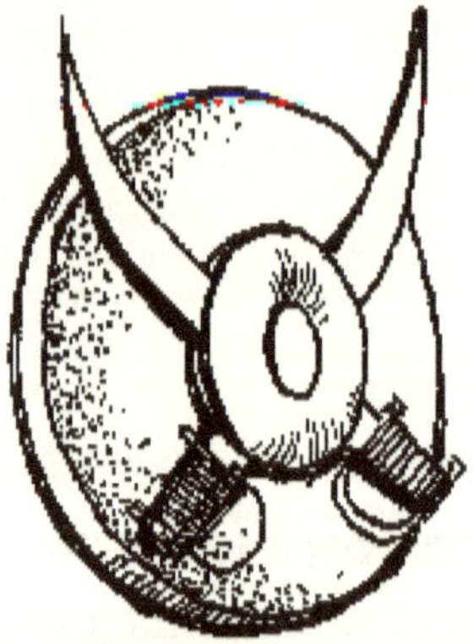

42 Therefore, with the sword of wisdom,
cut through this doubt born of ignorance
residing in your heart.
Arise Arjuna and resort to *yoga*!

5

अर्जुन उवाच ।
संन्यासं कर्मणां कृष्ण
पुनर्योगं च शंससि ।
यच्छ्रेय एतयोरेकं
तन्मे ब्रूहि सुनिश्चितम् ॥ ५.१

arjuna uvāca ।
saṃnyāsaṃ karmaṇāṃ kṛṣṇa
punaryogaṃ ca śaṃsasi ।
yacchreya etayorekaṃ
tanme brūhi suniścitam ॥ 5.1

श्रीभगवानुवाच ।
संन्यासः कर्मयोगश्च
निःश्रेयसकरावुभौ ।
तयोस्तु कर्मसंन्यासात्
कर्मयोगो विशिष्यते ॥ ५.२

śrībhagavānuvāca ।
saṃnyāsaḥ karmayogaśca
niḥśreyasakarāvubhau ।
tayostu karmasaṃnyāsāt
karmayogo viśiṣyate ॥ 5.2

ज्ञेयः स नित्यसंन्यासी
यो न द्वेष्टि न काङ्क्षति ।
निर्द्वन्द्वो हि महाबाहो
सुखं बन्धात्प्रमुच्यते ॥ ५.३

jñeyaḥ sa nityasaṃnyāsī
yo na dveṣṭi na kāṅkṣati ।
nirdvandvo hi mahābāho
sukhaṃ bandhātpramucyate ॥ 5.3

साङ्ख्ययोगौ पृथग्बालाः
प्रवदन्ति न पण्डिताः ।
एकमप्यास्थितः सम्यक्
उभयोर्विन्दते फलम् ॥ ५.४

sāṅkhyayogau pṛthagbālāḥ
pravadanti na paṇḍitāḥ ।
ekamapyāsthitaḥ samyak
ubhayorvindate phalam ॥ 5.4

यत्साङ्ख्यैः प्राप्यते स्थानं
तद्योगैरपि गम्यते ।
एकं सांख्यं च योगं च
यः पश्यति स पश्यति ॥ ५.५

yatsāṅkhyaiḥ prāpyate sthānaṃ
tadyogairapi gamyate ।
ekaṃ sāṃkhyaṃ ca yogaṃ ca
yaḥ paśyati sa paśyati ॥ 5.5

संन्यासस्तु महाबाहो
दुःखमाप्तुमयोगतः ।
योगयुक्तो मुनिर्ब्रह्म
नचिरेणाधिगच्छति ॥ ५.६

saṃnyāsastu mahābāho
duḥkhamāptumayogataḥ ।
yogayukto munirbrahma
nacireṇādhigacchati ॥ 5.6

योगयुक्तो विशुद्धात्मा
विजितात्मा जितेन्द्रियः ।
सर्वभूतात्मभूतात्मा
कुर्वन्नपि न लिप्यते ॥ ५.७

yogayukto viśuddhātmā
vijitātmā jitendriyaḥ ।
sarvabhūtātmabhūtātmā
kurvannapi na lipyate ॥ 5.7

नैव किञ्चित् करोमीति
युक्तो मन्येत तत्त्ववित् ।
पश्यञ्शृण्वन्स्पृशञ्जिघ्रन्
अश्नन्गच्छन्स्वपञ्श्वसन् ॥ ५.८

naiva kiñcit karomīti
yukto manyeta tattvavit ।
paśyañśṛṇvanspṛśañjighran
aśnangacchansvapañśvasan ॥ 5.8

प्रलपन्विसृजन्गृह्णन्
उन्मिषन्निमिषन्नपि ।
इन्द्रियाणीन्द्रियार्थेषु
वर्तन्त इति धारयन् ॥ ५.९

pralapanvisṛjangṛhṇan
unmiṣannimiṣannapi ।
indriyāṇīndriyārtheṣu
vartanta iti dhārayan ॥ 5.9

ब्रह्मण्याधाय कर्माणि
सङ्गं त्यक्त्वा करोति यः ।
लिप्यते न स पापेन
पद्मपत्रमिवाम्भसा ॥ ५.१०

brahmaṇyādhāya karmāṇi
saṅgaṃ tyaktvā karoti yaḥ ।
lipyate na sa pāpena
padmapatramivāmbhasā ॥ 5.10

कायेन मनसा बुद्ध्या
केवलैरिन्द्रियैरपि ।
योगिनः कर्म कुर्वन्ति
सङ्गं त्यक्त्वात्मशुद्धये ॥ ५.११

kāyena manasā buddhyā
kevalairindriyairapi ।
yoginaḥ karma kurvanti
saṅgaṃ tyaktvātmaśuddhaye ॥ 5.11

युक्तः कर्मफलं त्यक्त्वा
शान्तिमाप्नोति नैष्ठिकीम् ।
अयुक्तः कामकारेण
फले सक्तो निबध्यते ॥ ५.१२

yuktaḥ karmaphalaṃ tyaktvā
śāntimāpnoti naiṣṭhikīm ।
ayuktaḥ kāmakāreṇa
phale sakto nibadhyate ॥ 5.12

सर्वकर्माणि मनसा
संन्यस्यास्ते सुखं वशी ।
नवद्वारे पुरे देही
नैव कुर्वन्न कारयन् ॥ ५.१३

sarvakarmāṇi manasā
saṃnyasyāste sukhaṃ vaśī ।
navadvāre pure dehī
naiva kurvanna kārayan ॥ 5.13

न कर्तृत्वं न कर्माणि
लोकस्य सृजति प्रभुः ।
न कर्मफलसंयोगं
स्वभावस्तु प्रवर्तते ॥ ५.१४

na kartṛtvaṃ na karmāṇi
lokasya sṛjati prabhuḥ ।
na karmaphalasaṃyogaṃ
svabhāvastu pravartate ॥ 5.14

नादत्ते कस्यचित् पापं
न चैव सुकृतं विभुः ।
अज्ञानेनावृतं ज्ञानं
तेन मुह्यन्ति जन्तवः ॥ ५.१५

nādatte kasyacit pāpaṃ
na caiva sukṛtaṃ vibhuḥ ।
ajñānenāvṛtaṃ jñānaṃ
tena muhyanti jantavaḥ ॥ 5.15

ज्ञानेन तु तदज्ञानं येषां नाशितमात्मनः । तेषामादित्यवज्ज्ञानं प्रकाशयति तत्परम् ॥ ५.१६	*jñānena tu tadajñānaṃ* *yeṣāṃ nāśitamātmanaḥ* । *teṣāmādityavajjñānaṃ* *prakāśayati tatparam* ॥ 5.16
तद्बुद्धयस्तदात्मानः तन्निष्ठास्तत्परायणाः । गच्छन्त्यपुनरावृत्तिं ज्ञाननिर्धूतकल्मषाः ॥ ५.१७	*tadbuddhayastadātmānaḥ* *tanniṣṭhāstatparāyaṇāḥ* । *gacchantyapunarāvṛttiṃ* *jñānanirdhūtakalmaṣāḥ* ॥ 5.17
विद्याविनयसम्पन्ने ब्राह्मणे गवि हस्तिनि । शुनि चैव श्वपाके च पण्डिताः समदर्शिनः ॥ ५.१८	*vidyāvinayasampanne* *brāhmaṇe gavi hastini* । *śuni caiva śvapāke ca* *paṇḍitāḥ samadarśinaḥ* ॥ 5.18
इहैव तैर्जितः सर्गो येषां साम्ये स्थितं मनः । निर्दोषं हि समं ब्रह्म तस्माद्ब्रह्मणि ते स्थिताः ॥ ५.१९	*ihaiva tairjitaḥ sargo* *yeṣāṃ sāmye sthitaṃ manaḥ* । *nirdoṣaṃ hi samaṃ brahma* *tasmādbrahmaṇi te sthitāḥ* ॥ 5.19
न प्रहृष्येत्प्रियं प्राप्य नोद्विजेत्प्राप्य चाप्रियम् । स्थिरबुद्धिरसंमूढो ब्रह्मविद्ब्रह्मणि स्थितः ॥ ५.२०	*na prahṛṣyetpriyaṃ prāpya* *nodvijetprāpya cāpriyam* । *sthirabuddhirasaṃmūḍho* *brahmavidbrahmaṇi sthitaḥ* ॥ 5.20
बाह्यस्पर्शेष्वसक्तात्मा विन्दत्यात्मनि यत्सुखम् । स ब्रह्मयोगयुक्तात्मा सुखमक्षयमश्नुते ॥ ५.२१	*bāhyasparśeṣvasaktātmā* *vindatyātmani yatsukham* । *sa brahmayogayuktātmā* *sukhamakṣayamaśnute* ॥ 5.21
ये हि संस्पर्शजा भोगा दुःखयोनय एव ते । आद्यन्तवन्तः कौन्तेय न तेषु रमते बुधः ॥ ५.२२	*ye hi saṃsparśajā bhogā* *duḥkhayonaya eva te* । *ādyantavantaḥ kaunteya* *na teṣu ramate budhaḥ* ॥ 5.22
शक्नोतीहैव यः सोढुं प्राक्शरीरविमोक्षणात् । कामक्रोधोद्भवं वेगं स युक्तः स सुखी नरः ॥ ५.२३	*śaknotīhaiva yaḥ soḍhuṃ* *prākśarīravimokṣaṇāt* । *kāmakrodhodbhavaṃ vegaṃ* *sa yuktaḥ sa sukhī naraḥ* ॥ 5.23

योऽन्तःसुखोऽन्तरारामः
तथान्तर्ज्योतिरेव यः ।
स योगी ब्रह्मनिर्वाणं
ब्रह्मभूतोऽधिगच्छति ॥ ५.२४

yo'ntaḥsukho'ntarārāmaḥ
tathāntarjyotireva yaḥ ।
sa yogī brahmanirvāṇaṃ
brahmabhūto'dhigacchati ॥ 5.24

लभन्ते ब्रह्मनिर्वाणम्
ऋषयः क्षीणकल्मषाः ।
छिन्नद्वैधा यतात्मानः
सर्वभूतहिते रताः ॥ ५.२५

labhante brahmanirvāṇam
ṛṣayaḥ kṣīṇakalmaṣāḥ ।
chinnadvaidhā yatātmānaḥ
sarvabhūtahite ratāḥ ॥ 5.25

कामक्रोधवियुक्तानां
यतीनां यतचेतसाम् ।
अभितो ब्रह्मनिर्वाणं
वर्तते विदितात्मनाम् ॥ ५.२६

kāmakrodhaviyuktānāṃ
yatīnāṃ yatacetasām ।
abhito brahmanirvāṇaṃ
vartate viditātmanām ॥ 5.26

स्पर्शान्कृत्वा बहिर्बाह्यान्
चक्षुश्चैवान्तरे भ्रुवोः ।
प्राणापानौ समौ कृत्वा
नासाभ्यन्तरचारिणौ ॥ ५.२७

sparśānkṛtvā bahirbāhyān
cakṣuścaivāntare bhruvoḥ ।
prāṇāpānau samau kṛtvā
nāsābhyantaracāriṇau ॥ 5.27

यतेन्द्रियमनोबुद्धिः
मुनिर्मोक्षपरायणः ।
विगतेच्छाभयक्रोधो
यः सदा मुक्त एव सः ॥ ५.२८

yatendriyamanobuddhiḥ
munirmokṣaparāyaṇaḥ ।
vigatecchābhayakrodho
yaḥ sadā mukta eva saḥ ॥ 5.28

भोक्तारं यज्ञतपसां
सर्वलोकमहेश्वरम् ।
सुहृदं सर्वभूतानां
ज्ञात्वा मां शान्तिमृच्छति ॥ ५.२९

bhoktāraṃ yajñatapasāṃ
sarvalokamaheśvaram ।
suhṛdaṃ sarvabhūtānāṃ
jñātvā māṃ śāntimṛcchati ॥ 5.29

CHAPTER 5

RENUNCIATION

ARJUNA

[1]Kṛṣṇa, you praise *saṃnyāsa*
and also *karma-yoga*.
Tell me for certain,
which of the two is better?

While *saṃnyāsa* means 'giving up action' or 'renunciation,' in this context it refers to *sāṅkhya*, the path of reasoning and knowledge (see 5.4). *Karma-yoga* refers to the path of selfless action (see 3.3).

KṚṢṆA

[2]Both *saṃnyāsa* and *karma-yoga*
lead to matchless bliss.
Of the two, however,
***karma-yoga* is superior.**

Work is the prerequisite for *karma-yoga*.
Detachment is the prerequisite for *saṃnyāsa*.
It is easier to work and progress on the path of *karma-yoga*.
The path of detachment easily drifts towards laziness rather than realization.

[3]A true *saṃnyāsin* harbors no hate or desire.
Free from duality, he is free from bondage.

A *saṃnyāsin* is a person who is on the path of *saṃnyāsa*.
'Duality' refers to relative opposites like success and failure, hot and cold, *etc*.
'Bondage' refers to any sort of clinging or attachment.

[4]Only the novice, not the wise,
speaks of *sāṅkhya* and *yoga* as different.
One who earnestly pursues either
will reap the benefits of both.

Sāṅkhya is the 'path of knowledge' and *yoga* is the 'path of action.'

[5]A *sāṅkhya-yogin* and a *karma-yogin*
reach the same state.
He truly sees, who sees
sāṅkhya and *yoga* as the same!

A *yogin* is one who is steadfast on the path of *yoga*.

[6]It is difficult to achieve *saṃnyāsa*
by simply avoiding *yoga*.
But the sage who
diligently practises *karma-yoga*
readily attains *Brahman*.

[7]One who controls his senses
and masters himself
is steadfast in *yoga*.
He relates to everyone
as he relates to himself.
He is pure within and is not tainted
even as he engages in action.

[8–9]For even while
seeing, hearing, touching, eating, or smelling;
walking, sleeping, breathing, or speaking;
letting go or grasping; opening or closing the eyes –
one who knows the truth, thinks:

"It is not **I** who is performing action;
it is simply the Interplay of
the senses with the sensates."

[10]Just as water doesn't stick to a lotus leaf,
pāpa doesn't stick to a person
who works unattached and
dedicates the work to the Supreme.

One who works without selfish motives and has true humility has a lesser chance of committing *pāpa* (evil, sin, guilt, crime).

[11]Giving up attachments,
a *yogin* engages in action
with his body, senses, mind, and intellect
merely for purifying himself.

When there is absolute focus on work, there is no craving for rewards. This is self purification of the highest order and also the ideal of *karma-yoga*.

[12]Endowed with determination,
a man of poise doesn't care for rewards
and attains lasting peace.

Driven by selfish desires,
a man who lacks self-control,
craves for rewards, and lives in bondage.

5. *Renunciation*

[13]Mentally renouncing all actions,
the inner master lives happily
in the city of nine gates,
neither acting nor causing action.

The body is considered as a city of nine gates (the nine gates being: two eyes, two ears, two nostrils, a mouth, a genital organ, and an anus).

14 God does not command people to act.
God does not create activities
or its associated rewards.
All these arise from Nature.

15 **God is not responsible**
for good or evil in this world.

Beings are deluded because
their knowledge is clouded by ignorance.

Good and evil are merely results of actions that people perform.
It is foolish to think that god is responsible for this.

16 For those who have
destroyed ignorance using Knowledge,
that Knowledge, like the shining sun,
illuminates the Supreme within.

17 With thoughts absorbed in that,
with the self immersed in that,
with faith in that, and
finding fulfillment in that,
a self-realized person
attains liberation.

Here, 'that' refers to the Supreme within.

[18]A wise person treats everyone equally –
a *brāhmaṇa* endowed with wisdom and modesty, a cow,
an elephant, a dog, and one who eats a dog.

A *brāhmaṇa* endowed with scholarship and humility was held in high esteem in society while a person who ate dogs was considered to be at the lowest level. The wise ones see the same inner spirit in all these beings irrespective of their external characteristics (see 4.35 and 6.29–30).

[19]Those who are always impartial
overcome rebirth in this world.
Brahman is flawless and impartial;
so are those established in *Brahman*.

Brahman is the Supreme Being.

[20]They are not overjoyed when good things happen.
They are not dismayed when bad things happen.

With stability of mind and freedom from delusion,
those who know *Brahman* are established in *Brahman*.

[21]One who is not attached to external objects
finds happiness in one's own self.

One whose self is united with *Brahman*
attains a state of everlasting bliss.

[22]Sensory pleasures are the cause of sorrow
as they are short-lived.
The wise do not rejoice in them.

In the original, the expression for 'sensory pleasures' is 'pleasures that are born from contact (of senses and sensates).' All sensations of pleasure are short-lived and often one is disappointed when they come to an end.

[23]**In the midst of daily life**,
if one can endure the turmoil
caused by selfish desire and anger,
then he is truly happy.
Indeed, he is a *yogin*!

24 A *yogin* finds comfort, joy, and radiance within himself.
He is liberated and becomes one with *Brahman*.

25 He has cleared his doubts,
he is free from flaws, and
he has subdued his senses.
Involved in the welfare of all,
the seer attains supreme bliss.

26 Even among sages, those who are self-controlled,
liberated from desire and anger, and
established in the knowledge of the Self
are assuredly close to ultimate release!

27–28 Keeping away all external contacts;
fixing the gaze between the two eyebrows;
having made equal the inward and outward breaths;
having controlled the senses, mind, and intellect;
free from desire, fear, and anger;
with liberation as the highest goal
the sage is free from all bondages.

'...fixing the gaze between the two eyebrows' denotes concentration at one point,
which helps us elevate our focus to a greater objective.
To get the bigger picture, we cannot just look at something,
but rather we have to look beyond everything.

[29]One attains peace
when he realizes that
the purpose and the beneficiary
of all forms of worship
is the Supreme,
the sole lord of the universe,
and the true friend of all beings.

6

श्रीभगवानुवाच ।
अनाश्रितः कर्मफलं
कार्यं कर्म करोति यः ।
स संन्यासी च योगी च
न निरग्निर्न चाक्रियः ॥ ६.१

śrībhagavānuvāca ।
anāśritaḥ karmaphalaṃ
kāryaṃ karma karoti yaḥ ।
sa saṃnyāsī ca yogī ca
na niragnirna cākriyaḥ ॥ 6.1

यं संन्यासमिति प्राहुः
योगं तं विद्धि पाण्डव ।
न ह्यसंन्यस्तसङ्कल्पो
योगी भवति कश्चन ॥ ६.२

yaṃ saṃnyāsamiti prāhuḥ
yogaṃ taṃ viddhi pāṇḍava ।
na hyasaṃnyastasaṅkalpo
yogī bhavati kaścana ॥ 6.2

आरुरुक्षोर्मुनेर्योगं
कर्म कारणमुच्यते ।
योगारूढस्य तस्यैव
शमः कारणमुच्यते ॥ ६.३

ārurukṣormuneryogaṃ
karma kāraṇamucyate ।
yogārūḍhasya tasyaiva
śamaḥ kāraṇamucyate ॥ 6.3

यदा हि नेन्द्रियार्थेषु
न कर्मस्वनुषज्जते ।
सर्वसङ्कल्पसंन्यासी
योगारूढस्तदोच्यते ॥ ६.४

yadā hi nendriyārtheṣu
na karmasvanuṣajjate ।
sarvasaṅkalpasaṃnyāsī
yogārūḍhastadocyate ॥ 6.4

उद्धरेदात्मनात्मानं
नात्मानमवसादयेत् ।
आत्मैव ह्यात्मनो बन्धुः
आत्मैव रिपुरात्मनः ॥ ६.५

uddharedātmanātmānaṃ
nātmānamavasādayet ।
ātmaiva hyātmano bandhuḥ
ātmaiva ripurātmanaḥ ॥ 6.5

बन्धुरात्मात्मनस्तस्य
येनात्मैवात्मना जितः ।
अनात्मनस्तु शत्रुत्वे
वर्तेतात्मैव शत्रुवत् ॥ ६.६

bandhurātmātmanastasya
yenātmaivātmanā jitaḥ ।
anātmanastu śatrutve
vartetātmaiva śatruvat ॥ 6.6

जितात्मनः प्रशान्तस्य
परमात्मा समाहितः ।
शीतोष्णसुखदुःखेषु
तथा मानावमानयोः ॥ ६.७

jitātmanaḥ praśāntasya
paramātmā samāhitaḥ ।
śītoṣṇasukhaduḥkheṣu
tathā mānāvamānayoḥ ॥ 6.7

ज्ञानविज्ञानतृप्तात्मा कूटस्थो विजितेन्द्रियः । युक्त इत्युच्यते योगी समलोष्टाश्मकाञ्चनः ॥ ६.८	*jñānavijñānatṛptātmā* *kūṭastho vijitendriyaḥ* । *yukta ityucyate yogī* *samaloṣṭāśmakāñcanaḥ* ॥ 6.8
सुहृन्मित्रार्युदासीन- मध्यस्थद्वेष्यबन्धुषु । साधुष्वपि च पापेषु समबुद्धिर्विशिष्यते ॥ ६.९	*suhṛnmitrāryudāsīna-* *madhyasthadveṣyabandhuṣu* । *sādhuṣvapi ca pāpeṣu* *samabuddhirviśiṣyate* ॥ 6.9
योगी युञ्जीत सततम् आत्मानं रहसि स्थितः । एकाकी यतचित्तात्मा निराशीरपरिग्रहः ॥ ६.१०	*yogī yuñjīta satatam* *ātmānaṃ rahasi sthitaḥ* । *ekākī yatacittātmā* *nirāśīraparigrahaḥ* ॥ 6.10
शुचौ देशे प्रतिष्ठाप्य स्थिरमासनमात्मनः । नात्युच्छ्रितं नातिनीचं चैलाजिनकुशोत्तरम् ॥ ६.११	*śucau deśe pratiṣṭhāpya* *sthiramāsanamātmanaḥ* । *nātyucchritaṃ nātinīcaṃ* *cailājinakuśottaram* ॥ 6.11
तत्रैकाग्रं मनः कृत्वा यतचित्तेन्द्रियक्रियः । उपविश्यासने युञ्ज्यात् योगमात्मविशुद्धये ॥ ६.१२	*tatraikāgraṃ manaḥ kṛtvā* *yatacittendriyakriyaḥ* । *upaviśyāsane yuñjyāt* *yogamātmaviśuddhaye* ॥ 6.12
समं कायशिरोग्रीवं धारयन्नचलं स्थिरः । सम्प्रेक्ष्य नासिकाग्रं स्वं दिशश्चानवलोकयन् ॥ ६.१३	*samaṃ kāyaśirogrīvaṃ* *dhārayannacalaṃ sthiraḥ* । *samprekṣya nāsikāgraṃ svaṃ* *diśaścānavalokayan* ॥ 6.13
प्रशान्तात्मा विगतभीः ब्रह्मचारिव्रते स्थितः । मनः संयम्य मच्चित्तो युक्त आसीत मत्परः ॥ ६.१४	*praśāntātmā vigatabhīḥ* *brahmacārivrate sthitaḥ* । *manaḥ saṃyamya maccitto* *yukta āsīta matparaḥ* ॥ 6.14
युञ्जन्नेवं सदात्मानं योगी नियतमानसः । शान्तिं निर्वाणपरमां मत्संस्थामधिगच्छति ॥ ६.१५	*yuñjannevaṃ sadātmānaṃ* *yogī niyatamānasaḥ* । *śāntiṃ nirvāṇaparamāṃ* *matsaṃsthāmadhigacchati* ॥ 6.15
नात्यश्नतस्तु योगोऽस्ति न चैकान्तमनश्नतः ।	*nātyaśnatastu yogo'sti* *na caikāntamanaśnataḥ* ।

न चातिस्वप्नशीलस्य
जाग्रतो नैव चार्जुन ॥ ६.१६

na cātisvapnaśīlasya
jāgrato naiva cārjuna ॥ 6.16

युक्ताहारविहारस्य
युक्तचेष्टस्य कर्मसु ।
युक्तस्वप्नावबोधस्य
योगो भवति दुःखहा ॥ ६.१७

yuktāhāravihārasya
yuktaceṣṭasya karmasu ।
yuktasvapnāvabodhasya
yogo bhavati duḥkhahā ॥ 6.17

यदा विनियतं चित्तम्
आत्मन्येवावतिष्ठते ।
निःस्पृहः सर्वकामेभ्यो
युक्त इत्युच्यते तदा ॥ ६.१८

yadā viniyataṃ cittam
ātmanyevāvatiṣṭhate ।
niḥspṛhaḥ sarvakāmebhyo
yukta ityucyate tadā ॥ 6.18

यथा दीपो निवातस्थो
नेङ्गते सोपमा स्मृता ।
योगिनो यतचित्तस्य
युञ्जतो योगमात्मनः ॥ ६.१९

yathā dīpo nivātastho
neṅgate sopamā smṛtā ।
yogino yatacittasya
yuñjato yogamātmanaḥ ॥ 6.19

यत्रोपरमते चित्तं
निरुद्धं योगसेवया ।
यत्र चैवात्मनात्मानं
पश्यन्नात्मनि तुष्यति ॥ ६.२०

yatroparamate cittaṃ
niruddhaṃ yogasevayā ।
yatra caivātmanātmānaṃ
paśyannātmani tuṣyati ॥ 6.20

सुखमात्यन्तिकं यत्तत्
बुद्धिग्राह्यम् अतीन्द्रियम् ।
वेत्ति यत्र न चैवायं
स्थितश्चलति तत्त्वतः ॥ ६.२१

sukhamātyantikaṃ yattat
buddhigrāhyam atīndriyam ।
vetti yatra na caivāyaṃ
sthitaścalati tattvataḥ ॥ 6.21

यं लब्ध्वा चापरं लाभं
मन्यते नाधिकं ततः ।
यस्मिन्स्थितो न दुःखेन
गुरुणापि विचाल्यते ॥ ६.२२

yaṃ labdhvā cāparaṃ lābhaṃ
manyate nādhikaṃ tataḥ ।
yasminsthito na duḥkhena
guruṇāpi vicālyate ॥ 6.22

तं विद्याद्दुःखसंयोग-
वियोगं योगसञ्ज्ञितम् ।
स निश्चयेन योक्तव्यो
योगोऽनिर्विण्णचेतसा ॥ ६.२३

taṃ vidyādduḥkhasaṃyoga-
viyogaṃ yogasañjñitam ।
sa niścayena yoktavyo
yogo'nirviṇṇacetasā ॥ 6.23

सङ्कल्पप्रभवान्कामान्
त्यक्त्वा सर्वानशेषतः ।
मनसैवेन्द्रियग्रामं
विनियम्य समन्ततः ॥ ६.२४

saṅkalpaprabhavānkāmān
tyaktvā sarvānaśeṣataḥ ।
manasaivendriyagrāmaṃ
viniyamya samantataḥ ॥ 6.24

शनैः शनैरुपरमेत्
बुद्ध्या धृतिगृहीतया ।
आत्मसंस्थं मनः कृत्वा
न किञ्चिदपि चिन्तयेत् ॥ ६.२५

śanaiḥ śanairuparamet
buddhyā dhṛtigṛhītayā ।
ātmasaṃsthaṃ manaḥ kṛtvā
na kiñcidapi cintayet ॥ 6.25

यतो यतो निश्चरति
मनश्चञ्चलमस्थिरम् ।
ततस्ततो नियम्यैतत्
आत्मन्येव वशं नयेत् ॥ ६.२६

yato yato niścarati
manaścañcalamasthiram ।
tatastato niyamyaitat
ātmanyeva vaśaṃ nayet ॥ 6.26

प्रशान्तमनसं ह्येनं
योगिनं सुखमुत्तमम् ।
उपैति शान्तरजसं
ब्रह्मभूतमकल्मषम् ॥ ६.२७

praśāntamanasaṃ hyenaṃ
yoginaṃ sukhamuttamam ।
upaiti śāntarajasaṃ
brahmabhūtamakalmaṣam ॥ 6.27

युञ्जन्नेवं सदात्मानं
योगी विगतकल्मषः ।
सुखेन ब्रह्मसंस्पर्शम्
अत्यन्तं सुखमश्नुते ॥ ६.२८

yuñjannevaṃ sadātmānaṃ
yogī vigatakalmaṣaḥ ।
sukhena brahmasaṃsparśam
atyantaṃ sukhamaśnute ॥ 6.28

सर्वभूतस्थमात्मानं
सर्वभूतानि चात्मनि ।
ईक्षते योगयुक्तात्मा
सर्वत्र समदर्शनः ॥ ६.२९

sarvabhūtasthamātmānaṃ
sarvabhūtāni cātmani ।
īkṣate yogayuktātmā
sarvatra samadarśanaḥ ॥ 6.29

यो मां पश्यति सर्वत्र
सर्वं च मयि पश्यति ।
तस्याहं न प्रणश्यामि
स च मे न प्रणश्यति ॥ ६.३०

yo māṃ paśyati sarvatra
sarvaṃ ca mayi paśyati ।
tasyāhaṃ na praṇaśyāmi
sa ca me na praṇaśyati ॥ 6.30

सर्वभूतस्थितं यो मां
भजत्येकत्वमास्थितः ।
सर्वथा वर्तमानोऽपि
स योगी मयि वर्तते ॥ ६.३१

sarvabhūtasthitaṃ yo māṃ
bhajatyekatvamāsthitaḥ ।
sarvathā vartamāno'pi
sa yogī mayi vartate ॥ 6.31

आत्मौपम्येन सर्वत्र
समं पश्यति योऽर्जुन ।
सुखं वा यदि वा दुःखं
स योगी परमो मतः ॥ ६.३२

ātmaupamyena sarvatra
samaṃ paśyati yo'rjuna ।
sukhaṃ vā yadi vā duḥkhaṃ
sa yogī paramo mataḥ ॥ 6.32

अर्जुन उवाच ।
योऽयं योगस्त्वया प्रोक्तः
साम्येन मधुसूदन ।
एतस्याहं न पश्यामि
चञ्चलत्वात्स्थितिं स्थिराम् ॥ ६.३३

arjuna uvāca ।
yo'yaṃ yogastvayā proktaḥ
sāmyena madhusūdana ।
etasyāhaṃ na paśyāmi
cañcalatvātsthitiṃ sthirām ॥ 6.33

चञ्चलं हि मनः कृष्ण
प्रमाथि बलवद्दृढम् ।
तस्याहं निग्रहं मन्ये
वायोरिव सुदुष्करम् ॥ ६.३४

cañcalaṃ hi manaḥ kṛṣṇa
pramāthi balavaddṛḍham ।
tasyāhaṃ nigrahaṃ manye
vāyoriva suduṣkaram ॥ 6.34

श्रीभगवानुवाच ।
असंशयं महाबाहो
मनो दुर्निग्रहं चलम् ।
अभ्यासेन तु कौन्तेय
वैराग्येण च गृह्यते ॥ ६.३५

śrībhagavānuvāca ।
asaṃśayaṃ mahābāho
mano durnigrahaṃ calam ।
abhyāsena tu kaunteya
vairāgyeṇa ca gṛhyate ॥ 6.35

असंयतात्मना योगो
दुष्प्राप इति मे मतिः ।
वश्यात्मना तु यतता
शक्योऽवाप्तुम् उपायतः ॥ ६.३६

asaṃyatātmanā yogo
duṣprāpa iti me matiḥ ।
vaśyātmanā tu yatatā
śakyo'vāptum upāyataḥ ॥ 6.36

अर्जुन उवाच ।
अयतिः श्रद्धयोपेतो
योगाच्चलितमानसः ।
अप्राप्य योगसंसिद्धिं
कां गतिं कृष्ण गच्छति ॥ ६.३७

arjuna uvāca ।
ayatiḥ śraddhayopeto
yogāccalitamānasaḥ ।
aprāpya yogasaṃsiddhiṃ
kāṃ gatiṃ kṛṣṇa gacchati ॥ 6.37

कच्चिन्नोभयविभ्रष्टः
छिन्नाभ्रमिव नश्यति ।
अप्रतिष्ठो महाबाहो
विमूढो ब्रह्मणः पथि ॥ ६.३८

kaccinnobhayavibhraṣṭaḥ
chinnābhramiva naśyati ।
apratiṣṭho mahābāho
vimūḍho brahmaṇaḥ pathi ॥ 6.38

एतन्मे संशयं कृष्ण
छेत्तुमर्हस्यशेषतः ।
त्वदन्यः संशयस्यास्य
छेत्ता न ह्युपपद्यते ॥ ६.३९

etanme saṃśayaṃ kṛṣṇa
chettumarhasyaśeṣataḥ ।
tvadanyaḥ saṃśayasyāsya
chettā na hyupapadyate ॥ 6.39

श्रीभगवानुवाच ।
पार्थ नैवेह नामुत्र
विनाशस्तस्य विद्यते ।
न हि कल्याणकृत् कश्चित्
दुर्गतिं तात गच्छति ॥ ६.४०

śrībhagavānuvāca ।
pārtha naiveha nāmutra
vināśastasya vidyate ।
na hi kalyāṇakṛt kaścit
durgatiṃ tāta gacchati ॥ 6.40

प्राप्य पुण्यकृताँल्लोकान्
उषित्वा शाश्वतीः समाः ।
शुचीनां श्रीमतां गेहे
योगभ्रष्टोऽभिजायते ॥ ६.४१

prāpya puṇyakṛtāṁllokān
uṣitvā śāśvatīḥ samāḥ ।
śucīnāṃ śrīmatāṃ gehe
yogabhraṣṭo'bhijāyate ॥ 6.41

अथ वा योगिनामेव
कुले भवति धीमताम् ।
एतद्धि दुर्लभतरं
लोके जन्म यदीदृशम् ॥ ६.४२

atha vā yogināmeva
kule bhavati dhīmatām ।
etaddhi durlabhataraṃ
loke janma yadīdṛśam ॥ 6.42

तत्र तं बुद्धिसंयोगं
लभते पौर्वदेहिकम् ।
यतते च ततो भूयः
संसिद्धौ कुरुनन्दन ॥ ६.४३

tatra taṃ buddhisaṃyogaṃ
labhate paurvadehikam ।
yatate ca tato bhūyaḥ
saṃsiddhau kurunandana ॥ 6.43

पूर्वाभ्यासेन तेनैव
ह्रियते ह्यवशोऽपि सः ।
जिज्ञासुरपि योगस्य
शब्दब्रह्मातिवर्तते ॥ ६.४४

pūrvābhyāsena tenaiva
hriyate hyavaśo'pi saḥ ।
jijñāsurapi yogasya
śabdabrahmātivartate ॥ 6.44

प्रयत्नाद्यतमानस्तु
योगी संशुद्धकिल्बिषः ।
अनेकजन्मसंसिद्धः
ततो याति परां गतिम् ॥ ६.४५

prayatnādyatamānastu
yogī saṃśuddhakilbiṣaḥ ।
anekajanmasaṃsiddhaḥ
tato yāti parāṃ gatim ॥ 6.45

तपस्विभ्योऽधिको योगी
ज्ञानिभ्योऽपि मतोऽधिकः ।
कर्मिभ्यश्चाधिको योगी
तस्माद्योगी भवार्जुन ॥ ६.४६

tapasvibhyo'dhiko yogī
jñānibhyo'pi mato'dhikaḥ ।
karmibhyaścādhiko yogī
tasmādyogī bhavārjuna ॥ 6.46

योगिनामपि सर्वेषां
मद्गतेनान्तरात्मना ।
श्रद्धावान्भजते यो मां
स मे युक्ततमो मतः ॥ ६.४७

yogināmapi sarveṣāṃ
madgatenāntarātmanā ।
śraddhāvānbhajate yo māṃ
sa me yuktatamo mataḥ ॥ 6.47

CHAPTER 6

Meditation

Kṛṣṇa

[1]One who works without seeking rewards
is both a *saṃnyāsin* and a *karma-yogin*.
One who merely avoids work is neither.

In the original, the expression for avoiding work is:
"One who lights no fire and does nothing,"
indicating someone who neglects his responsibilities.

A *saṃnyāsin* is one who renounces the
rewards of action and not the action itself.
The idea of a *saṃnyāsin* here is different from
the typical image of an old man who has given up everything
and has fully retired from active life.

A *karma-yogin* is one who works without attachment to results.

[2]Arjuna, *saṃnyāsa* is indeed *yoga*.
Nobody can become a *yogin*
without giving up selfish motives!

Saṃnyāsa refers to 'renunciation of rewards'
and *yoga* refers to 'selfless action.'

3 Work is the path for one
who wants to advance in *yoga*.
Serenity is the path for one
who has already attained *yoga*.

If we want to climb to a high level, we have to work hard.
Once we reach the top, we have to remain calm.

4 When you renounce selfish thoughts
and are no longer attached to sensations and actions
you will ascend to *yoga*.

5 One should advance by one's own efforts;
one should not degrade oneself;
for **the self alone is**
one's true friend or enemy.

6 When one has self-control
one's own self becomes a friend.
When one lacks self-control
one's own self becomes a hostile foe.

7 One who has conquered the self
is united with the Supreme.
He is always at peace – in cold or heat,
in pleasure or pain, and in honor or dishonor.

[8]A *yogin* is one who is steadfast in *yoga*.

He has attained fulfillment
through knowledge and wisdom.

He has conquered his senses and
his mind doesn't waver.

He has equal regard for
gold, mud, or stone.

[9]He behaves in the same way
with his family, friends, foes,
a mediator, a bystander,
a saint, or a sinner.
Thus, he attains excellence.

[10]With mind and body under control,
free from ownerships and desires,
a seeker of *yoga*
should go to a secluded place and
steadily meditate on the *ātman* in solitude.

'...free from ownerships and desires' indicates
a reasoned disregard towards possessions.

Ātman is the inner, higher self.

11 One should set up a firm seat of
Kuśa grass, deerskin, and a cloth –
one over the other, in a clean place
neither too high nor too low.

Kuśa grass is a kind of Bermuda grass;
it is a sacred grass for the Hindus.
The cloth is put above the deerskin,
which in turn is placed over the grass.

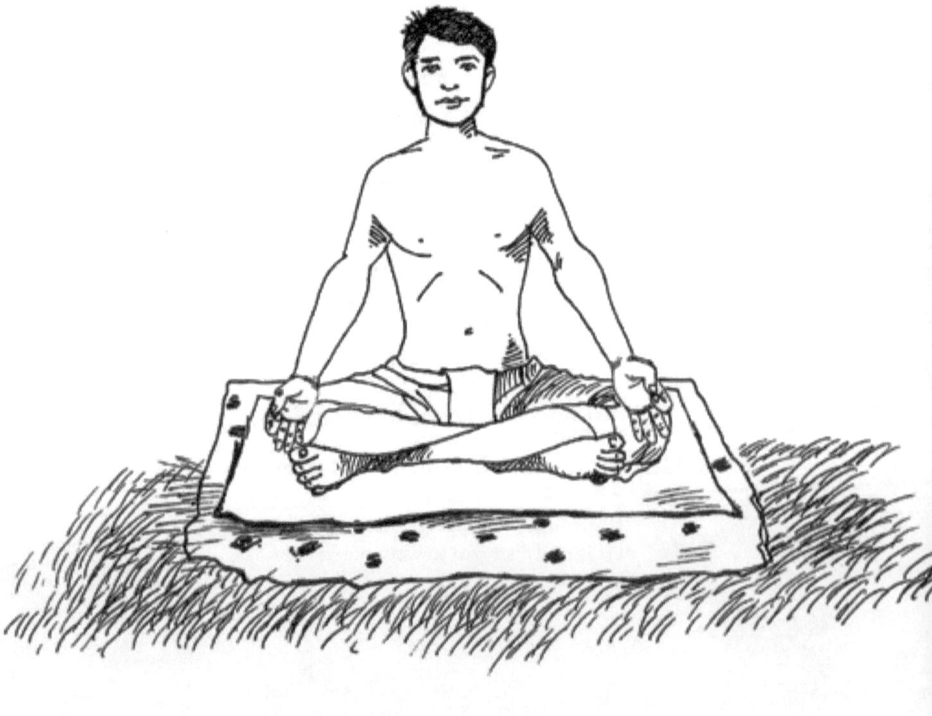

[12]One should sit on that seat,
control the senses and thoughts,
direct the mind to a single object, and
practice meditation for self-purification.

[13]Keeping the body, head, and neck
straight, steady, and still,
looking at the tip of the nose,
not letting the eyes wander,
[14]remaining calm and fearless,
sticking to principles of *brahmacarya*,
with the mind under control,
one should sit resolute,
thinking of me
as the Supreme Goal.

We cannot see the tip of our nose however wide we keep our eyes open, so the idea is possible to look at no external thing in particular but rather look inward.

Brahmacarya (following the path of *Brahman*) refers to leading a life of purity and not letting the mind wander around trivial things.

[15]Thus, a seeker of *yoga* –
constantly disciplining himself
with a steady mind –
attains the supreme blissful peace
that abides in me.

16 Indeed *yoga* is not for one
who eats too much or too little.
It is also not for one
who sleeps too much or
stays awake for too long.

Yoga is not for those indulging in excesses.
It is of little value for those who have not learnt moderation.

17 Whereas, for one who
takes the right measure of food,
is moderate in sleep and in staying awake,
works in a disciplined manner, and
enjoys moments of recreation,
yoga destroys all sorrows.

18 With the mind under control,
free from all cravings, and
absorbed in the *ātman*,
one attains *yoga*.

19 A *yogin* who has mastered **thought**
by meditating on the *ātman*
is like a lamp that does not flicker
when sheltered from the wind.

[20]With thoughts restrained and mind silenced
by the regular practice of *yoga*,
the *yogin* sees the *ātman* through the *ātman*
and rejoices in the *ātman*.

See 2.55.

[21]A *yogin* will never stray from Truth
once he attains infinite Bliss
that transcends the senses and
can be perceived only by intuition.

[22]Upon gaining infinite Bliss,
he knows that there is no greater attainment.
Once he is established thus,
he is not moved by even the deepest sorrow.

[23]He should practise *yoga*
with undaunted determination
for it is a blissful state of being.

[24]He should renounce, without the slightest remnant,
all desires born of selfish motives.

He should completely control his senses
with the power of the mind.

25 Little by little,
thinking of nothing else,
he should attain stillness of mind
and focus it firmly on the *ātman*.

26 Whenever and wherever
the unsteady, restless mind
tends to stray away,
then and there
he should pull it back
and bring it under his control.

27 A *yogin* attains supreme Joy
once he overcomes restlessness,
keeps his mind calm,
breaks free from evil, and
tunes himself to *Brahman*.

28 Free from all *pāpa* and ever in unison with the Self,
a *yogin* at once feels boundless Joy
that comes from merging with *Brahman*.

Pāpa can refer to evil, sin, guilt, crime, misfortune, *etc.*

29 In that state,
the *yogin* sees the *ātman* in all beings

and all beings in the *ātman* –
everywhere he sees the same *ātman*!

30He who sees me everywhere
and sees everything in me,
I am never lost to him
nor is he ever lost to me.

Here, 'me' is a reference to *ātman* (see 10.20).
Also see 5.18.

[31]The *yogin* who is aware of this oneness
worships me as the one who lives in all beings.
He abides in me, regardless of his way of living.

Such a person is always connected with the Supreme,
regardless of where he is, what he does, or how he is treated by society.

[32]He is indeed a *yogin*, Arjuna,
who sees true equality of all beings and
thus relates to the joy and sorrow of others
just as he relates to his own.

A true *yogin* doesn't discriminate between himself and others.
He knows that he is one with the rest and feels their joys and sorrows.

ARJUNA

[33]You have taught me that *yoga* is,
in essence, **equanimity of the mind**.
I'm unable to perceive how one can attain
this state of steadiness,
given that the mind is so fickle.

[34]The mind is restless, Kṛṣṇa.
It is turbulent, powerful, and unyielding!

Controlling the mind
seems as difficult as
controlling the wind.

Kṛṣṇa

[35]Without doubt, O mighty one,
the mind is restless and tough to restrain.
But the mind can be controlled
by **practice** and by **detachment**.

[36]In my opinion, *yoga* is hard to attain
for one who lacks self-restraint.
But one who has self-control
can attain it by proper practice.

Arjuna

[37]What happens to him
who is sincere but lacks self-control,
when he strays from the right path and
fails to attain perfection in *yoga*?
[38]Having fallen from both,
gone astray on the path to *Brahman*,
with no place to stand,
will he not perish like a cloud
that is scattered and lost in the sky?

Here, 'both' refers to 'self-control' and 'proper practice.'
It may also refer to 'the material' and 'the spiritual' – "By giving up the material and improperly following the spiritual, won't he miss out on both?"

Alternatively, 'both' can refer to 'the path of action' and 'the path of wisdom.'

39Only you can completely dispel my doubt, Kṛṣṇa!
Who else is better suited to answer my question?

Kṛṣṇa

40**One who strives to do good**
never ends up in misery.
Whether in this world or beyond,
he never perishes, my son.

Liberation is the ultimate goal but those who fall short are not condemned.
There is no urgency for liberation either. Each can work at his own pace.
What truly matters is one's sincerity of purpose and constancy of practice.

41One who falls short of perfection in *yoga*
reaches the world of the righteous,
dwells there for a very long time, and
is reborn in the house of the pious and the wealthy;
42or he may be born into a family of *yogins*
who are endowed with wisdom;
but such a birth is rare in this world.

Those who fall short of liberation are reborn in this world. Similarly, those who have exhausted their period of enjoyment in *svarga* (loosely, 'heaven') are reborn. Rebirth bears imprints from previous life, and this influences not only the inherent tendencies and aptitudes but also the lineage or the family in which one is born.

'...the house of the pious and the wealthy' refers to a good home that provides a healthy atmosphere to enable spiritual growth.

After all, birth and death are happening all the time:
the previous moment is dead, the next one is born;
what we did in the previous moment impacts what we do in the next.

[43]In the family of *yogins*,
he regains the knowledge that he had in his previous life.
From there, he strives once again for perfection.

We are not born with a clean slate. The *ātman* carries experiences from previous births, which to some extent influence the present life – for better or worse, depending on the nature of the experiences. Birth is a new opportunity but has roots in the past (see 15.8).

[44]All that past experience
guides him on the path of *yoga*.
He transcends the rewards
gained by performing rituals
by just desiring to tread this path of *yoga*.
[45]Striving with great effort over many births,
a *yogin* cleanses himself of his defects
and attains the ultimate goal.

The ultimate goal is to attain *Brahman*, which is the same as liberation from the cycles of birth and death.

46 A *yogin* is superior to an ascetic,
he is also superior to the learned,
and is superior to a ritualist.
Therefore (aim to) be a *yogin*, Arjuna!

An 'ascetic' is one who practices severe *tapas* (penance, meditation),
'learned' refers to one who is well-versed in the scriptures, and
'ritualist' is one who performs religious rites merely seeking favors.
All these people are entangled to some extent,
so Kṛṣṇa advises Arjuna to be a *yogin*.

47 Among all *yogins*,
the most dedicated ones
sincerely worship the Supreme
with their minds immersed in the Supreme.

The most superior among the ascetics are those
whose thoughts are merged in *Brahman*.
They think of nothing but the Supreme.

7

श्रीभगवानुवाच ।
मय्यासक्तमनाः पार्थ
योगं युञ्जन्मदाश्रयः ।
असंशयं समग्रं मां
यथा ज्ञास्यसि तच्छृणु ॥ ७.१

śrībhagavānuvāca ।
mayyāsaktamanāḥ pārtha
yogaṃ yuñjanmadāśrayaḥ ।
asaṃśayaṃ samagraṃ māṃ
yathā jñāsyasi tacchṛṇu ॥ 7.1

ज्ञानं तेऽहं सविज्ञानम्
इदं वक्ष्याम्यशेषतः ।
यज्ज्ञात्वा नेह भूयोऽन्यत्
ज्ञातव्यमवशिष्यते ॥ ७.२

jñānaṃ te'haṃ savijñānam
idaṃ vakṣyāmyaśeṣataḥ ।
yajjñātvā neha bhūyo'nyat
jñātavyamavaśiṣyate ॥ 7.2

मनुष्याणां सहस्रेषु
कश्चिद् यतति सिद्धये ।
यततामपि सिद्धानां
कश्चिन्मां वेत्ति तत्त्वतः ॥ ७.३

manuṣyāṇāṃ sahasreṣu
kaścid yatati siddhaye ।
yatatāmapi siddhānāṃ
kaścinmāṃ vetti tattvataḥ ॥ 7.3

भूमिरापोऽनलो वायुः
खं मनो बुद्धिरेव च ।
अहङ्कार इतीयं मे
भिन्ना प्रकृतिरष्टधा ॥ ७.४

bhūmirāpo'nalo vāyuḥ
khaṃ mano buddhireva ca ।
ahaṅkāra itīyaṃ me
bhinnā prakṛtiraṣṭadhā ॥ 7.4

अपरेयमितस्त्वन्यां
प्रकृतिं विद्धि मे पराम् ।
जीवभूतां महाबाहो
ययेदं धार्यते जगत् ॥ ७.५

apareyamitastvanyāṃ
prakṛtiṃ viddhi me parām ।
jīvabhūtāṃ mahābāho
yayedaṃ dhāryate jagat ॥ 7.5

एतद्योनीनि भूतानि
सर्वाणीत्युपधारय ।
अहं कृत्स्नस्य जगतः
प्रभवः प्रलयस्तथा ॥ ७.६

etadyonīni bhūtāni
sarvāṇītyupadhāraya ।
ahaṃ kṛtsnasya jagataḥ
prabhavaḥ pralayastathā ॥ 7.6

मत्तः परतरं नान्यत्
किञ्चिदस्ति धनञ्जय ।
मयि सर्वमिदं प्रोतं
सूत्रे मणिगणा इव ॥ ७.७

mattaḥ parataraṃ nānyat
kiñcidasti dhanañjaya ।
mayi sarvamidaṃ protaṃ
sūtre maṇigaṇā iva ॥ 7.7

रसोऽहमप्सु कौन्तेय प्रभास्मि शशिसूर्ययोः । प्रणवः सर्ववेदेषु शब्दः खे पौरुषं नृषु ॥ ७.८	*raso'hamapsu kaunteya* *prabhāsmi śaśisūryayoḥ* । *praṇavaḥ sarvavedeṣu* *śabdaḥ khe pauruṣaṃ nṛṣu* ॥ 7.8
पुण्यो गन्धः पृथिव्यां च तेजश्चास्मि विभावसौ । जीवनं सर्वभूतेषु तपश्चास्मि तपस्विषु ॥ ७.९	*puṇyo gandhaḥ pṛthivyāṃ ca* *tejaścāsmi vibhāvasau* । *jīvanaṃ sarvabhūteṣu* *tapaścāsmi tapasviṣu* ॥ 7.9
बीजं मां सर्वभूतानां विद्धि पार्थ सनातनम् । बुद्धिर्बुद्धिमतामस्मि तेजस्तेजस्विनामहम् ॥ ७.१०	*bījaṃ māṃ sarvabhūtānāṃ* *viddhi pārtha sanātanam* । *buddhirbuddhimatāmasmi* *tejastejasvināmaham* ॥ 7.10
बलं बलवतां चाहं कामरागविवर्जितम् । धर्माविरुद्धो भूतेषु कामोऽस्मि भरतर्षभ ॥ ७.११	*balaṃ balavatāṃ cāhaṃ* *kāmarāgavivarjitam* । *dharmāviruddho bhūteṣu* *kāmo'smi bharatarṣabha* ॥ 7.11
ये चैव सात्त्विका भावा राजसास्तामसाश्च ये । मत्त एवेति तान्विद्धि न त्वहं तेषु ते मयि ॥ ७.१२	*ye caiva sāttvikā bhāvā* *rājasāstāmasāśca ye* । *matta eveti tānviddhi* *na tvahaṃ teṣu te mayi* ॥ 7.12
त्रिभिर्गुणमयैर्भावैः एभिः सर्वमिदं जगत् । मोहितं नाभिजानाति मामेभ्यः परमव्ययम् ॥ ७.१३	*tribhirguṇamayairbhāvaiḥ* *ebhiḥ sarvamidaṃ jagat* । *mohitaṃ nābhijānāti* *māmebhyaḥ paramavyayam* ॥ 7.13
दैवी ह्येषा गुणमयी मम माया दुरत्यया । मामेव ये प्रपद्यन्ते मायामेतां तरन्ति ते ॥ ७.१४	*daivī hyeṣā guṇamayī* *mama māyā duratyayā* । *māmeva ye prapadyante* *māyāmetāṃ taranti te* ॥ 7.14
न मां दुष्कृतिनो मूढाः प्रपद्यन्ते नराधमाः । माययापहृतज्ञाना आसुरं भावमाश्रिताः ॥ ७.१५	*na māṃ duṣkṛtino mūḍhāḥ* *prapadyante narādhamāḥ* । *māyayāpahṛtajñānā* *āsuraṃ bhāvamāśritāḥ* ॥ 7.15

चतुर्विधा भजन्ते मां
जनाः सुकृतिनोऽर्जुन
आर्तो जिज्ञासुरर्थार्थी
ज्ञानी च भरतर्षभ ॥ ७.१६

caturvidhā bhajante māṃ
janāḥ sukṛtino'rjuna
ārto jijñāsurarthārthī
jñānī ca bharatarṣabha ॥ 7.16

तेषां ज्ञानी नित्ययुक्त
एकभक्तिर्विशिष्यते ।
प्रियो हि ज्ञानिनोऽत्यर्थम्
अहं स च मम प्रियः ॥ ७.१७

teṣāṃ jñānī nityayukta
ekabhaktirviśiṣyate ।
priyo hi jñānino'tyartham
ahaṃ sa ca mama priyaḥ ॥ 7.17

उदाराः सर्व एवैते
ज्ञानी त्वात्मैव मे मतम् ।
आस्थितः स हि युक्तात्मा
मामेवानुत्तमां गतिम् ॥ ७.१८

udārāḥ sarva evaite
jñānī tvātmaiva me matam ।
āsthitaḥ sa hi yuktātmā
māmevānuttamāṃ gatim ॥ 7.18

बहूनां जन्मनामन्ते
ज्ञानवान्मां प्रपद्यते ।
वासुदेवः सर्वमिति
स महात्मा सुदुर्लभः ॥ ७.१९

bahūnāṃ janmanāmante
jñānavānmāṃ prapadyate ।
vāsudevaḥ sarvamiti
sa mahātmā sudurlabhaḥ ॥ 7.19

कामैस्तैस्तैर्हृतज्ञानाः
प्रपद्यन्तेऽन्यदेवताः ।
तं तं नियममास्थाय
प्रकृत्या नियताः स्वया ॥ ७.२०

kāmaistaistairhṛtajñānāḥ
prapadyante'nyadevatāḥ ।
taṃ taṃ niyamamāsthāya
prakṛtyā niyatāḥ svayā ॥ 7.20

यो यो यां यां तनुं भक्तः
श्रद्धयार्चितुमिच्छति ।
तस्य तस्याचलां श्रद्धां
तामेव विदधाम्यहम् ॥ ७.२१

yo yo yāṃ yāṃ tanuṃ bhaktaḥ
śraddhayārcitumicchati ।
tasya tasyācalāṃ śraddhāṃ
tāmeva vidadhāmyaham ॥ 7.21

स तया श्रद्धया युक्तः
तस्या राधनमीहते ।
लभते च ततः कामान्
मयैव विहितान्हि तान् ॥ ७.२२

sa tayā śraddhayā yuktaḥ
tasyā rādhanamīhate ।
labhate ca tataḥ kāmān
mayaiva vihitānhi tān ॥ 7.22

अन्तवत्तु फलं तेषां
तद्भवत्यल्पमेधसाम् ।
देवान्देवयजो यान्ति
मद्भक्ता यान्ति मामपि ॥ ७.२३

antavattu phalaṃ teṣāṃ
tadbhavatyalpamedhasām ।
devāndevayajo yānti
madbhaktā yānti māmapi ॥ 7.23

अव्यक्तं व्यक्तिमापन्नं
मन्यन्ते मामबुद्धयः ।
परं भावमजानन्तो
ममाव्ययमनुत्तमम् ॥ ७.२४

avyaktaṃ vyaktimāpannaṃ
manyante māmabuddhayaḥ ।
paraṃ bhāvamajānanto
mamāvyayamanuttamam ॥ 7.24

नाहं प्रकाशः सर्वस्य
योगमायासमावृतः ।
मूढोऽयं नाभिजानाति
लोको मामजमव्ययम् ॥ ७.२५

nāhaṃ prakāśaḥ sarvasya
yogamāyāsamāvṛtaḥ ।
mūḍho'yaṃ nābhijānāti
loko māmajamavyayam ॥ 7.25

वेदाहं समतीतानि
वर्तमानानि चार्जुन ।
भविष्याणि च भूतानि
मां तु वेद न कश्चन ॥ ७.२६

vedāhaṃ samatītāni
vartamānāni cārjuna ।
bhaviṣyāṇi ca bhūtāni
māṃ tu veda na kaścana ॥ 7.26

इच्छाद्वेषसमुत्थेन
द्वन्द्वमोहेन भारत ।
सर्वभूतानि संमोहं
सर्गे यान्ति परन्तप ॥ ७.२७

icchādveṣasamutthena
dvandvamohena bhārata ।
sarvabhūtāni saṃmohaṃ
sarge yānti parantapa ॥ 7.27

येषां त्वन्तगतं पापं
जनानां पुण्यकर्मणाम् ।
ते द्वन्द्वमोहनिर्मुक्ता
भजन्ते मां दृढव्रताः ॥ ७.२८

yeṣāṃ tvantagataṃ pāpaṃ
janānāṃ puṇyakarmaṇām ।
te dvandvamohanirmuktā
bhajante māṃ dṛḍhavratāḥ ॥ 7.28

जरामरणमोक्षाय
मामाश्रित्य यतन्ति ये ।
ते ब्रह्म तद्विदुः कृत्स्नम्
अध्यात्मं कर्म चाखिलम् ॥ ७.२९

jarāmaraṇamokṣāya
māmāśritya yatanti ye ।
te brahma tadviduḥ kṛtsnam
adhyātmaṃ karma cākhilam ॥ 7.29

साधिभूताधिदैवं मां
साधियज्ञं च ये विदुः ।
प्रयाणकालेऽपि च मां
ते विदुर्युक्तचेतसः ॥ ७.३०

sādhibhūtādhidaivaṃ māṃ
sādhiyajñaṃ ca ye viduḥ ।
prayāṇakāle'pi ca māṃ
te viduryuktacetasaḥ ॥ 7.30

CHAPTER 7

Knowledge and Wisdom

Kṛṣṇa

[1]Listen, Arjuna:
Practise *yoga* with focus,
fix your mind on me,
and take refuge in me.
Without doubt you will
know me completely.

Here, *yoga* refers to 'contemplation'
and 'me' refers to 'the Supreme.'

[2]I will fully teach you
this knowledge
as well as
how you may apply it.

Once you know this,
nothing remains to be known.

3 Among thousands of humans,
hardly a few strive for perfection.
Among the few striving for perfection
barely one will realize the Supreme.

4 Earth, fire, wind, water, space,
mind, intellect, and ego –
such is the eightfold division of my nature.

[5]But this is just my lower nature.
Beyond this, I have a higher nature,
which is the life-force
that sustains the universe.

Here, 'this' refers to the eightfold divisions.

[6]All beings originate from
my higher and lower states.
I am the source and the dissolution
of the entire universe.

[7]There is nothing beyond me!
Everything in the universe is strung on me
like a row of pearls on a string.

The Supreme One sustains everything in the universe, like a string that holds together pearls in a necklace.

[8]Know me as the essence in the waters,
the light of the sun and moon,
the '*om*' in all the *Vedas*,
the sound in space, and
the manliness of men.

Om is a single syllable word that denotes *Brahman*, the Supreme Being. It is the most sacred sound according to Hindu belief.

Here, 'manliness' refers to courage, heroism, effort, and free will.

[9]I am the sacred scent of earth,
the radiance in fire,
the life in the living, and
the austerity of the austere.

[10]I am the eternal seed of all beings,
the wisdom of the wise, and
the splendor of the splendid.

[11]In those who are strong
I am pure strength,
devoid of lust and passion.
In all beings
I am the desire
that doesn't violate *dharma*.

Dharma refers to a moral law or principle that sustains natural goodness.

[12]The traits of
Sattva, *Rajas*, and *Tamas*
come from me alone.
They are in me
but I am beyond them.

Typically, humans have three *guṇas* (inherent tendencies) –
sattva (benign goodness),
rajas (relentless activity), and
tamas (deluded lethargy).

[13]The whole world is governed by
the interplay of these *guṇas*.
People are fooled by the *guṇas* and
fail to recognize my true nature.

The Supreme is imperishable and above the *guṇas*.

[14]It is indeed difficult to overcome
the influence of my divine *māyā*,
which is pervaded by the *guṇas*.
But those who submit to me
overcome the influence of *māyā*.

Māyā is the divine power of illusion.
Recognizing that a greater force governs the cosmic order
in the universe helps overcome this illusion.
In essence, 'submit to me' refers to realizing the Self.

[15]The wicked, the foolish, and the demonic,
languishing at the lowest level of humanity
are not endowed with that humility
as their minds are carried away by illusion.

[16]Four kinds of sincere people worship me:
a person in distress,
a seeker of wisdom,
a seeker of wealth,
and a wise person.

17 Among the four,
the wise one is ever-steady.
He is devoted to the Supreme
and he excels.
I am dear to him
and he is dear to me.

18 While all these devotees are noble,
I consider the wise one to be my very self.
Having realized his true Self
he looks upon me as the Supreme Goal
and abides in me.

19 At the end of many cycles of birth and death,
the wise one realizes that Vāsudeva is everything
and connects with the Supreme.
Indeed, such great souls are hard to find.

Vāsudeva refers to the soul of the universe, which pervades everything.
Vāsudeva—'the son of Vasudeva'—is another name for Kṛṣṇa.

At the end of many births, the wise man exhausts all options
and comes to realize that there is nothing beyond the Supreme.

20 One whose knowledge is abducted (by ignorance)
gets distracted by desires for this or that
and turns to other deities,
following this or that rule of his own making.

[21]But, **in whatever form** one chooses
to **worship the Supreme** in good faith,
I strengthen his faith further.
[22]Endowed with that steady faith,
he gets his desires fulfilled.
Those desires are indeed granted by me.

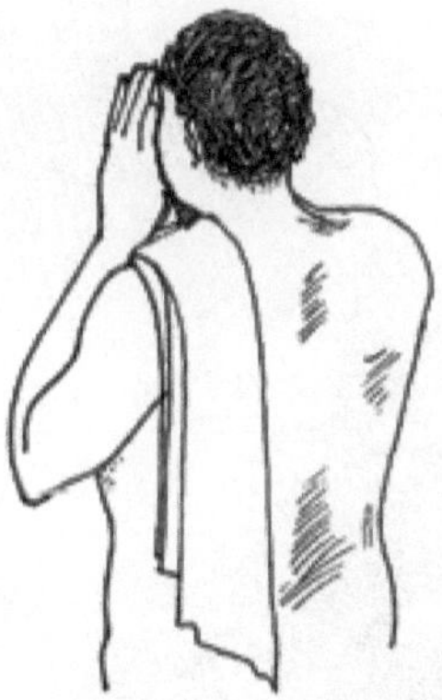

[23]But these are men of limited learning;
the rewards that they get are temporary.
People who worship other deities
go to the deities they worship
but my devotees surely come to me.

We become what we think we will become.
People who worship a particular deity will attain that state of being.
Those who worship the Supreme will attain the Supreme
and those who pursue the *ātman* will realise the *ātman*.

24 Ignorant people think of me only as having a form.
They are unaware of my mysterious higher existence,
eternal and incomparable.

25 Hidden by my own *yoga-māyā*,
my glory is not revealed to all.

The deluded ones do not know me
as the unborn and the unending.

26 Arjuna, I know all the beings
of the past, present, and future
but no one knows me!

27 All beings are born ignorant
due to the illusion caused by duality,
arising from love and hate.

At a basic level, our thinking is dualistic –
it is governed by likes and dislikes.
Due to these opposing emotions,
we fail to examine things objectively.

28 But as people do good and put an end to evil,
they are freed from the illusion caused by duality.
They worship the Supreme with intense devotion.

29 Those who take refuge in the Supreme and
strive for freedom from old age and death –
they will know all there is to know about
Brahman, *adhyātma*, and *karma*.

30 Those who know me as the
adhibhūta, *adhidaiva*, and *adhiyajña*,
truly know me.
They are controlled in their thoughts.
They are aware of me
even at the moment of their death.

In the next chapter, Kṛṣṇa goes on to explain the terms *Brahman*, *adhyātma*, *karma*, *adhibhūta*, *adhidaiva*, and *adhiyajña*.

8

अर्जुन उवाच ।
किं तद्ब्रह्म किमध्यात्मं
किं कर्म पुरुषोत्तम ।
अधिभूतं च किं प्रोक्तम्
अधिदैवं किमुच्यते ॥ ८.१

arjuna uvāca ।
kiṃ tadbrahma kimadhyātmaṃ
kiṃ karma puruṣottama ।
adhibhūtaṃ ca kiṃ proktam
adhidaivaṃ kimucyate ॥ 8.1

अधियज्ञः कथं कोऽत्र
देहेऽस्मिन्मधुसूदन ।
प्रयाणकाले च कथं
ज्ञेयोऽसि नियतात्मभिः ॥ ८.२

adhiyajñaḥ kathaṃ ko'tra
dehe'sminmadhusūdana ।
prayāṇakāle ca kathaṃ
jñeyo'si niyatātmabhiḥ ॥ 8.2

श्रीभगवानुवाच ।
अक्षरं ब्रह्म परमं
स्वभावोऽध्यात्ममुच्यते ।
भूतभावोद्भवकरो
विसर्गः कर्मसञ्ज्ञितः ॥ ८.३

śrībhagavānuvāca ।
akṣaraṃ brahma paramaṃ
svabhāvo'dhyātmamucyate ।
bhūtabhāvodbhavakaro
visargaḥ karmasañjñitaḥ ॥ 8.3

अधिभूतं क्षरो भावः
पुरुषश्चाधिदैवतम् ।
अधियज्ञोऽहमेवात्र
देहे देहभृतां वर ॥ ८.४

adhibhūtaṃ kṣaro bhāvaḥ
puruṣaścādhidaivatam ।
adhiyajño'hamevātra
dehe dehabhṛtāṃ vara ॥ 8.4

अन्तकाले च मामेव
स्मरन्मुक्त्वा कलेवरम् ।
यः प्रयाति स मद्भावं
याति नास्त्यत्र संशयः ॥ ८.५

antakāle ca māmeva
smaranmuktvā kalevaram ।
yaḥ prayāti sa madbhāvaṃ
yāti nāstyatra saṃśayaḥ ॥ 8.5

यं यं वापि स्मरन्भावं
त्यजत्यन्ते कलेवरम् ।
तं तमेवैति कौन्तेय
सदा तद्भावभावितः ॥ ८.६

yaṃ yaṃ vāpi smaranbhāvaṃ
tyajatyante kalevaram ।
taṃ tamevaiti kaunteya
sadā tadbhāvabhāvitaḥ ॥ 8.6

तस्मात्सर्वेषु कालेषु
मामनुस्मर युध्य च ।
मय्यर्पितमनोबुद्धिः
मामेवैष्यस्यसंशयः ॥ ८.७

tasmātsarveṣu kāleṣu
māmanusmara yudhya ca ।
mayyarpitamanobuddhiḥ
māmevaiṣyasyasaṃśayaḥ ॥ 8.7

अभ्यासयोगयुक्तेन
चेतसा नान्यगामिना ।
परमं पुरुषं दिव्यं
याति पार्थानुचिन्तयन् ॥ ८.८

abhyāsayogayuktena
cetasā nānyagāminā ।
paramaṃ puruṣaṃ divyaṃ
yāti pārthānucintayan ॥ 8.8

कविं पुराणमनुशासितारम्
अणोरणीयांसमनुस्मरेद्यः ।
सर्वस्य धातारमचिन्त्यरूपम्
आदित्यवर्णं तमसः परस्तात् ॥ ८.९

kaviṃ purāṇamanuśāsitāram
aṇoraṇīyāṃsamanusmaredyaḥ ।
sarvasya dhātāramacintyarūpam
ādityavarṇaṃ tamasaḥ parastāt ॥ 8.9

प्रयाणकाले मनसाचलेन
भक्त्या युक्तो योगबलेन चैव ।
भ्रुवोर्मध्ये प्राणमावेश्य सम्यक्
स तं परं पुरुषमुपैति दिव्यम् ॥ ८.१०

prayāṇakāle manasācalena
bhaktyā yukto yogabalena caiva ।
bhruvormadhye prāṇamāveśya samyak
sa taṃ paraṃ puruṣamupaiti divyam ॥ 8.10

यदक्षरं वेदविदो वदन्ति
विशन्ति यद्यतयो वीतरागाः ।
यदिच्छन्तो ब्रह्मचर्यं चरन्ति
तत्ते पदं सङ्ग्रहेण प्रवक्ष्ये ॥ ८.११

yadakṣaraṃ vedavido vadanti
viśanti yadyatayo vītarāgāḥ ।
yadicchanto brahmacaryaṃ caranti
tatte padaṃ saṅgraheṇa pravakṣye ॥ 8.11

सर्वद्वाराणि संयम्य
मनो हृदि निरुध्य च ।
मूर्ध्न्याधायात्मनः प्राणम्
आस्थितो योगधारणाम् ॥ ८.१२

sarvadvārāṇi saṃyamya
mano hṛdi nirudhya ca ।
mūrdhnyādhāyātmanaḥ prāṇam
āsthito yogadhāraṇām ॥ 8.12

ओम् इत्येकाक्षरं ब्रह्म
व्याहरन्मामनुस्मरन् ।
यः प्रयाति त्यजन्देहं
स याति परमां गतिम् ॥ ८.१३

om ityekākṣaraṃ brahma
vyāharanmāmanusmaran ।
yaḥ prayāti tyajandehaṃ
sa yāti paramāṃ gatim ॥ 8.13

अनन्यचेताः सततं
यो मां स्मरति नित्यशः ।
तस्याहं सुलभः पार्थ
नित्ययुक्तस्य योगिनः ॥ ८.१४

ananyacetāḥ satataṃ
yo māṃ smarati nityaśaḥ ।
tasyāhaṃ sulabhaḥ pārtha
nityayuktasya yoginaḥ ॥ 8.14

मामुपेत्य पुनर्जन्म
दुःखालयमशाश्वतम् ।
नाप्नुवन्ति महात्मानः
संसिद्धिं परमां गताः ॥ ८.१५

māmupetya punarjanma
duḥkhālayamaśāśvatam ।
nāpnuvanti mahātmānaḥ
saṃsiddhiṃ paramāṃ gatāḥ ॥ 8.15

आ ब्रह्मभुवनाल्लोकाः पुनरावर्तिनोऽर्जुन । मामुपेत्य तु कौन्तेय पुनर्जन्म न विद्यते ॥ ८.१६	*ā brahmabhuvanāllokāḥ* *punarāvartino'rjuna* । *māmupetya tu kaunteya* *punarjanma na vidyate* ॥ 8.16
सहस्रयुगपर्यन्तम् अहर्यद्ब्रह्मणो विदुः । रात्रिं युगसहस्रान्तां तेऽहोरात्रविदो जनाः ॥ ८.१७	*sahasrayugaparyantam* *aharyadbrahmaṇo viduḥ* । *rātriṃ yugasahasrāntāṃ* *te'horātravido janāḥ* ॥ 8.17
अव्यक्ताद्व्यक्तयः सर्वाः प्रभवन्त्यहरागमे । रात्र्यागमे प्रलीयन्ते तत्रैवाव्यक्तसञ्ज्ञके ॥ ८.१८	*avyaktādvyaktayaḥ sarvāḥ* *prabhavantyaharāgame* । *rātryāgame pralīyante* *tatraivāvyaktasañjñake* ॥ 8.18
भूतग्रामः स एवायं भूत्वा भूत्वा प्रलीयते । रात्र्यागमेऽवशः पार्थ प्रभवत्यहरागमे ॥ ८.१९	*bhūtagrāmaḥ sa evāyaṃ* *bhūtvā bhūtvā pralīyate* । *rātryāgame'vaśaḥ pārtha* *prabhavatyaharāgame* ॥ 8.19
परस्तस्मात्तु भावोऽन्यः अव्यक्तोऽव्यक्तात्सनातनः । यः स सर्वेषु भूतेषु नश्यत्सु न विनश्यति ॥ ८.२०	*parastasmāttu bhāvo'nyaḥ* *avyakto'vyaktātsanātanaḥ* । *yaḥ sa sarveṣu bhūteṣu* *naśyatsu na vinaśyati* ॥ 8.20
अव्यक्तोऽक्षर इत्युक्तः तमाहुः परमां गतिम् । यं प्राप्य न निवर्तन्ते तद्धाम परमं मम ॥ ८.२१	*avyakto'kṣara ityuktaḥ* *tamāhuḥ paramāṃ gatim* । *yaṃ prāpya na nivartante* *taddhāma paramaṃ mama* ॥ 8.21
पुरुषः स परः पार्थ भक्त्या लभ्यस्त्वनन्यया । यस्यान्तःस्थानि भूतानि येन सर्वमिदं ततम् ॥ ८.२२	*puruṣaḥ sa paraḥ pārtha* *bhaktyā labhyastvananyayā* । *yasyāntaḥsthāni bhūtāni* *yena sarvamidaṃ tatam* ॥ 8.22
यत्र काले त्वनावृत्तिम् आवृत्तिं चैव योगिनः । प्रयाता यान्ति तं कालं वक्ष्यामि भरतर्षभ ॥ ८.२३	*yatra kāle tvanāvṛttim* *āvṛttiṃ caiva yoginaḥ* । *prayātā yānti taṃ kālaṃ* *vakṣyāmi bharatarṣabha* ॥ 8.23

अग्निर्ज्योतिरहः शुक्लः	*agnirjyotirahaḥ śuklaḥ*
षण्मासा उत्तरायणम् ।	*ṣaṇmāsā uttarāyaṇam* ।
तत्र प्रयाता गच्छन्ति	*tatra prayātā gacchanti*
ब्रह्म ब्रह्मविदो जनाः ॥ ८.२४	*brahma brahmavido janāḥ* ॥ 8.24
धूमो रात्रिस्तथा कृष्णः	*dhūmo rātristathā kṛṣṇaḥ*
षण्मासा दक्षिणायनम् ।	*ṣaṇmāsā dakṣiṇāyanam* ।
तत्र चान्द्रमसं ज्योतिः	*tatra cāndramasaṃ jyotiḥ*
योगी प्राप्य निवर्तते ॥ ८.२५	*yogī prāpya nivartate* ॥ 8.25
शुक्लकृष्णे गती ह्येते	*śuklakṛṣṇe gatī hyete*
जगतः शाश्वते मते ।	*jagataḥ śāśvate mate* ।
एकया यात्यनावृत्तिम्	*ekayā yātyanāvṛttim*
अन्ययावर्तते पुनः ॥ ८.२६	*anyayāvartate punaḥ* ॥ 8.26
नैते सृती पार्थ जानन्	*naite sṛtī pārtha jānan*
योगी मुह्यति कश्चन ।	*yogī muhyati kaścana* ।
तस्मात्सर्वेषु कालेषु	*tasmātsarveṣu kāleṣu*
योगयुक्तो भवार्जुन ॥ ८.२७	*yogayukto bhavārjuna* ॥ 8.27
वेदेषु यज्ञेषु तपःसु चैव	*vedeṣu yajñeṣu tapaḥsu caiva*
दानेषु यत्पुण्यफलं प्रदिष्टम् ।	*dāneṣu yatpuṇyaphalaṃ pradiṣṭam* ।
अत्येति तत्सर्वमिदं विदित्वा	*atyeti tatsarvamidaṃ viditvā*
योगी परं स्थानमुपैति चाद्यम् ॥ ८.२८	*yogī paraṃ sthānamupaiti cādyam* ॥ 8.28

CHAPTER 8

The Imperishable

Arjuna

[1]What is *Brahman*?
What is *adhyātma*?
What is *karma*?
What is *adhibhūta*?
Who is the *adhidaiva*?

[2]Who is the *adhiyajña*?
Who resides in this body?

In a *yajña* (traditional fire ritual) many deities are invoked,
like Indra, Soma, Varuṇa, Rudra, and Mitra.
Arjuna wishes to know the real recipient
of the prayers and offerings.
In other words, he is asking:
"Who is truly venerated in a *yajña*?"

How does a man of self-restraint
attain the supreme state of mind
at the time of his death?

KṚṢṆA

[3]*Brahman* is the imperishable and the supreme.

Adhyātma is the essence of one's unique qualities;
it is an individual's real identity.
Karma is every activity associated with origin, sustenance, and destruction.

Karma refers to all activities, including the creative impulse that brought all creation into existence and keeps it going.

[4]*Adhibhūta* refers to the body,
the perishable aspect of all beings.

he *adhidaiva* is *puruṣa*, the Supreme Spirit.

Indeed, I am the *adhiyajña* and
I am the one who resides in the body.

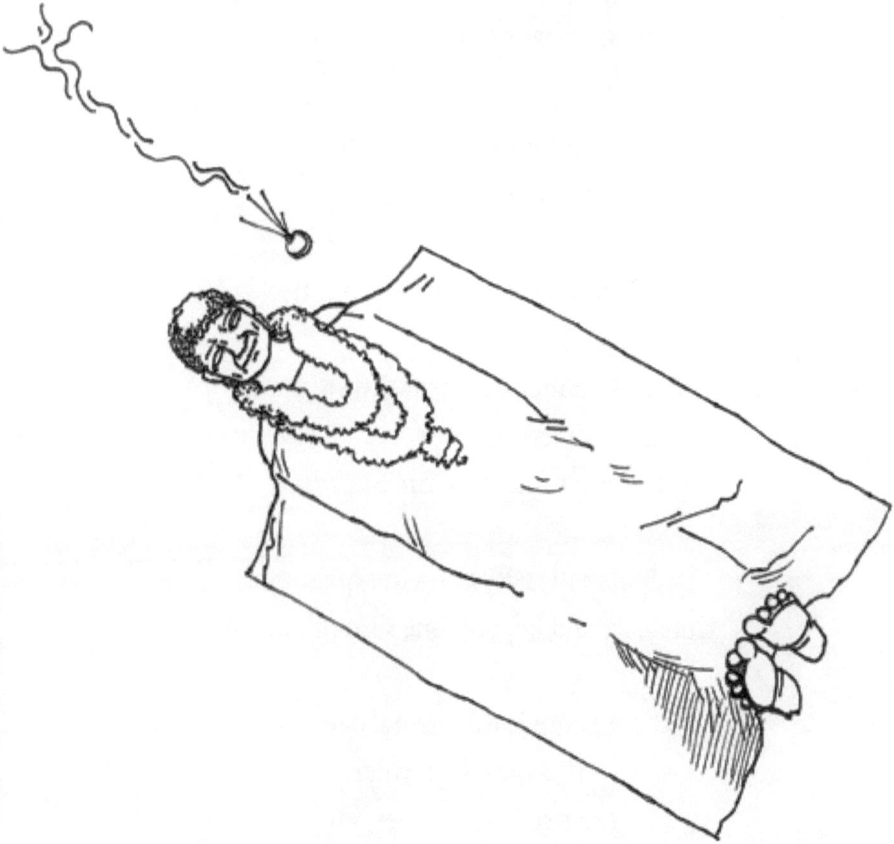

[5]At the moment of death,
those who depart from their body
thinking of me alone,
will surely be united with me.

[6]The state of mind prevailing at the time of one's death
is the very state one will attain
because those thoughts are a true reflection
of the kind of life one has led.

7 So remember me at all times,
even during combat.
Fix your mind and intellect on me
and you will surely come to me.

8 One who meditates on the Supreme
with unwavering focus and discipline
becomes one with the Supreme.

9–10 *Brahman* is all-knowing, primeval,
timeless, and beyond one's imagination.

Brahman is the primal cause,
the sovereign ruler,
the primordial poet, and
the supporter of all.

Brahman is subtler than the subtlest
and mightier than the mightiest.

Brahman is radiant like the sun
and beyond all darkness.

At the time of death,
one who fixes the *prāṇa*
in the middle of the eyebrows

with the power of *yoga*
and meditates on the
magnificent *Brahman*
with sincerity and steadiness,
certainly attains *Brahman*.

Prāṇa refers to 'vital breath' or 'life force.'
It is the essential component of our energy.

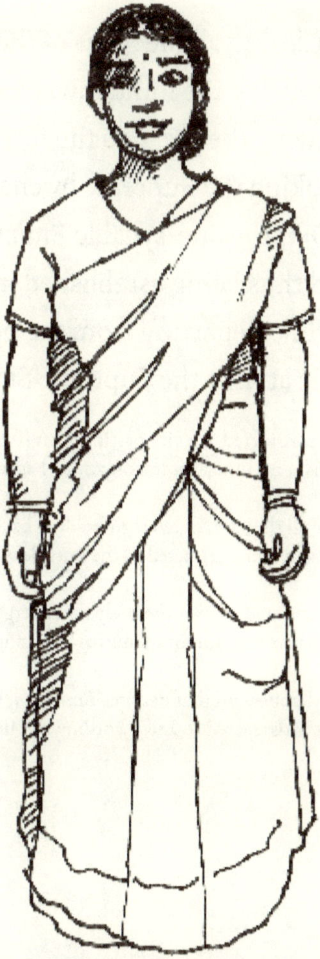

[11]The seers call it the Imperishable.
Those who hope to reach that state
lead a life of *brahmacarya* and
sages who are rid of passions attain it.
I will tell you in essence
how one reaches there.

Brahmacarya is following the path of *brahman*, leading a life of purity, and not letting the mind wander around trivial things.

[12–13]Closing all the gates of the body,
focusing the mind inward, and
drawing the *prāṇa* to the forehead;
invoking the Supreme by chanting
'*Om*,' the one-syllable *Brahman*;
and thus being established in *yoga*
while departing from the body,
he attains the Supreme State.

The body is considered as a city of nine gates (two eyes, two ears, two nostrils, a mouth, a genital organ, and an anus; see 5.13).

'Closing all the gates...' refers to holding back the senses from being attracted to the outside world.

Prāṇa is distributed all over the body as it energizes all the cells. '...drawing the *prāṇa* to the forehead' means 'focusing all energy upward.'

Om is a single-syllable word that denotes *Brahman*, the Supreme Being. It is the most sacred sound according to Hindu belief.

[14]Arjuna, the *yogin* who is steadfast,
never distracted by other things, and
constantly contemplates on the Supreme
easily attains the Supreme State.

A *yogin* is one who is steadfast on the path of *yoga*.

[15]Great souls who have attained the Supreme
have reached the state of highest perfection.
They are spared from rebirth,
which is sorrowful and impermanent.

[16]All the realms from the earth
up to that of lord Brahmā
are subject to rebirth.
But on reaching the Supreme,
there is no rebirth.

According to the Hindu belief of afterlife, there are many intermediate abodes between earth and the supreme state like *Pitṛ-loka*, *Deva-loka*, *Yama-loka*, *Brahma-loka*, and so on. All these in-between realms are impermanent while the Supreme State of no return is eternal.
Lord Brahmā has a life span of 100 Brahmā years (~300 trillion human years)
He arises from *Brahman* and performs the function of creation.
At the end of his tenure, he is absolved and another Brahmā emanates.

Note that Brahmā (lord of creation) is different from *Brahman* (Supreme Being).

[17]A day of lord Brahmā spans a thousand *yugas* and
a night of lord Brahmā also spans a thousand *yugas*.

Only those who know this fact truly understand
the cosmic meaning of day and night.

A *yuga* is equal to 4.32 million years.
A day or night of Brahmā spans 4.32 billion years.
See the *Introduction* (*pp.* 22–23) for an overview of the Hindu timelines.

18When the day of Brahmā begins,
all forms emerge from the hidden state.

When the night of Brahmā begins,
all forms disappear from the visible state.

19Indeed, the countless beings
that come into existence again and again
are inevitably dissolved at the arrival of night.
They come forth again at the arrival of day.

This process goes on throughout the life of Brahmā,
spanning a hundred Brahmā years.
After that, Brahmā also dies, and is born again.

20But higher than this,
there is a formless, eternal state of being
that remains untouched by cosmic cycles.

A cosmic cycle, spanning 8.64 billion years,
equals a day and a night of Brahmā.
The Eternal state of being doesn't get destroyed
even when all beings perish.

DRESS

21 What is spoken of as
the unseen and the indestructible
is considered the highest state.
Those who reach it, stay on forever
for that is the supreme domain.

22 *Puruṣa* is the supreme spirit
that pervades the entire universe
and in whom all beings abide.
One can attain the state of *Puruṣa*
by wholehearted devotion.

23 When a *yogin* dies,
either he comes back
or he stays on forever.
Let me explain.

When a *yogin* dies, either he returns to earthly existence
or he lives forever in the supreme domain.

24 The *yogin* who dies during *uttarāyaṇa*,
the symbol of dazzling white daylight
goes forth to reach *Brahman*.

This verse refers to the path of brightness, invoking the terms –
Fire, Light, Day, Bright Fortnight, and *Uttarāyaṇa*,
which is the period of six months following winter solstice.
The days grow longer during *uttarāyaṇa*—northward movement of the sun—
and so it is regarded as the 'bright-half' of the year.

[25]The *yogin* who dies during *dakṣiṇāyana*,
the symbol of hazy dark night
attains the lunar light
and is born again.

This verse refers to the path of darkness, invoking the terms – Smoke, Moonlight, Night, Dark Fortnight, and *Dakṣiṇāyana*, which is the period of six months following summer solstice. The nights grow longer during *dakṣiṇāyana*—southward movement of the sun—and so it is regarded as the 'dark-half' of the year.

The period of *uttarāyaṇa* is equal to one day for the *deva*s and the period of *dakṣiṇāyana* equals one night.

This suggests that only some of the realized people get liberated. The rest of them are perhaps among us, guiding us towards liberation.

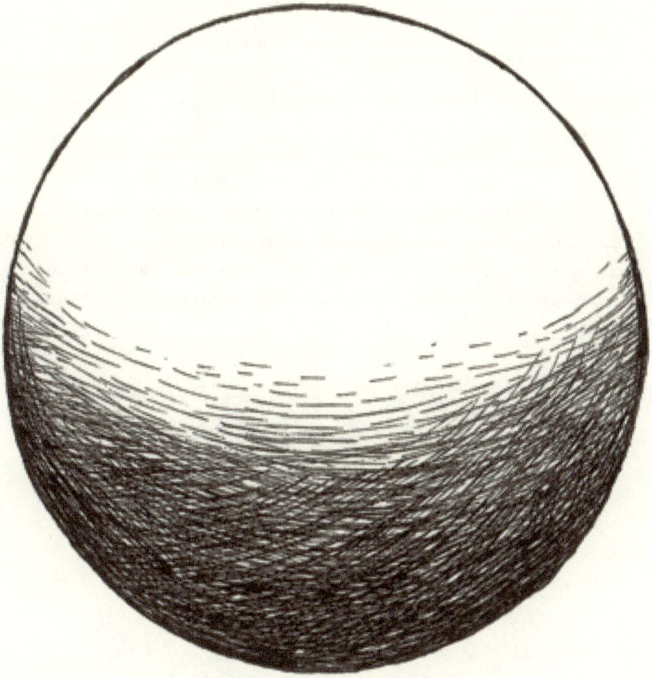

[26]Indeed, the bright and the dark
have always been the two paths of this world.

By one, the *yogin* goes to stay on forever,
whereas by the other, the *yogin* returns again.

[27]Knowing these two paths,
a true *yogin* is never deluded.
Thus, be established in *yoga* at all times.

[28]Knowing this truth,
a *yogin* goes beyond all the merits
of studying the *Vedas* or
yajña, *dāna*, and *tapas*.
He truly attains that
foremost Supreme State.

Yajña is the *Vedic* fire ritual, which inolves
worship of the divine, interaction, and sharing.
In a broader sense, it refers to a sense of dedication to work.
Dāna is charity that is undertaken with a feeling that it is one's duty to give
and includes offering the right gift to the deserving person at an appropriate time.
Tapas refers to austerity, penance, and single-minded focus on work.
Also see 17.11–22.

9

श्रीभगवानुवाच ।
इदं तु ते गुह्यतमं
प्रवक्ष्याम्यनसूयवे ।
ज्ञानं विज्ञानसहितं
यज्ज्ञात्वा मोक्ष्यसेऽशुभात् ॥ ९.१

śrībhagavānuvāca ।
idaṃ tu te guhyatamaṃ
pravakṣyāmyanasūyave ।
jñānaṃ vijñānasahitaṃ
yajjñātvā mokṣyase'śubhāt ॥ 9.1

राजविद्या राजगुह्यं
पवित्रमिदमुत्तमम् ।
प्रत्यक्षावगमं धर्म्यं
सुसुखं कर्तुमव्ययम् ॥ ९.२

rājavidyā rājaguhyaṃ
pavitramidamuttamam ।
pratyakṣāvagamaṃ dharmyaṃ
susukhaṃ kartumavyayam ॥ 9.2

अश्रद्दधानाः पुरुषा
धर्मस्यास्य परन्तप ।
अप्राप्य मां निवर्तन्ते
मृत्युसंसारवर्त्मनि ॥ ९.३

aśraddadhānāḥ puruṣā
dharmasyāsya parantapa ।
aprāpya māṃ nivartante
mṛtyusaṃsāravartmani ॥ 9.3

मया ततमिदं सर्वं
जगदव्यक्तमूर्तिना ।
मत्स्थानि सर्वभूतानि
न चाहं तेष्ववस्थितः ॥ ९.४

mayā tatamidaṃ sarvaṃ
jagadavyaktamūrtinā ।
matsthāni sarvabhūtāni
na cāhaṃ teṣvavasthitaḥ ॥ 9.4

न च मत्स्थानि भूतानि
पश्य मे योगमैश्वरम् ।
भूतभृन्न च भूतस्थो
ममात्मा भूतभावनः ॥ ९.५

na ca matsthāni bhūtāni
paśya me yogamaiśvaram ।
bhūtabhṛnna ca bhūtastho
mamātmā bhūtabhāvanaḥ ॥ 9.5

यथाकाशस्थितो नित्यं
वायुः सर्वत्रगो महान् ।
तथा सर्वाणि भूतानि
मत्स्थानीत्युपधारय ॥ ९.६

yathākāśasthito nityaṃ
vāyuḥ sarvatrago mahān ।
tathā sarvāṇi bhūtāni
matsthānītyupadhāraya ॥ 9.6

सर्वभूतानि कौन्तेय
प्रकृतिं यान्ति मामिकाम् ।
कल्पक्षये पुनस्तानि
कल्पादौ विसृजाम्यहम् ॥ ९.७

sarvabhūtāni kaunteya
prakṛtiṃ yānti māmikām ।
kalpakṣaye punastāni
kalpādau visṛjāmyaham ॥ 9.7

प्रकृतिं स्वामवष्टभ्य
विसृजामि पुनः पुनः ।
भूतग्राममिमं कृत्स्नम्
अवशं प्रकृतेर्वशात् ॥ ९.८

prakṛtiṃ svāmavaṣṭabhya
visṛjāmi punaḥ punaḥ ।
bhūtagrāmamimaṃ kṛtsnam
avaśaṃ prakṛtervaśāt ॥ 9.8

न च मां तानि कर्माणि
निबध्नन्ति धनञ्जय ।
उदासीनवदासीनम्
असक्तं तेषु कर्मसु ॥ ९.९

na ca māṃ tāni karmāṇi
nibadhnanti dhanañjaya ।
udāsīnavadāsīnam
asaktaṃ teṣu karmasu ॥ 9.9

मयाध्यक्षेण प्रकृतिः
सूयते सचराचरम् ।
हेतुनानेन कौन्तेय
जगद्विपरिवर्तते ॥ ९.१०

mayādhyakṣeṇa prakṛtiḥ
sūyate sacarācaram ।
hetunānena kaunteya
jagadviparivartate ॥ 9.10

अवजानन्ति मां मूढा
मानुषीं तनुमाश्रितम् ।
परं भावमजानन्तो
मम भूतमहेश्वरम् ॥ ९.११

avajānanti māṃ mūḍhā
mānuṣīṃ tanumāśritam ।
paraṃ bhāvamajānanto
mama bhūtamaheśvaram ॥ 9.11

मोघाशा मोघकर्माणो
मोघज्ञाना विचेतसः ।
राक्षसीमासुरीं चैव
प्रकृतिं मोहिनीं श्रिताः ॥ ९.१२

moghāśā moghakarmāṇo
moghajñānā vicetasaḥ ।
rākṣasīmāsurīṃ caiva
prakṛtiṃ mohinīṃ śritāḥ ॥ 9.12

महात्मानस्तु मां पार्थ
दैवीं प्रकृतिमाश्रिताः ।
भजन्त्यनन्यमनसो
ज्ञात्वा भूतादिमव्ययम् ॥ ९.१३

mahātmānastu māṃ pārtha
daivīṃ prakṛtimāśritāḥ ।
bhajantyananyamanaso
jñātvā bhūtādimavyayam ॥ 9.13

सततं कीर्तयन्तो मां
यतन्तश्च दृढव्रताः ।
नमस्यन्तश्च मां भक्त्या
नित्ययुक्ता उपासते ॥ ९.१४

satataṃ kīrtayanto māṃ
yatantaśca dṛḍhavratāḥ ।
namasyantaśca māṃ bhaktyā
nityayuktā upāsate ॥ 9.14

ज्ञानयज्ञेन चाप्यन्ये
यजन्तो मामुपासते ।
एकत्वेन पृथक्त्वेन
बहुधा विश्वतोमुखम् ॥ ९.१५

jñānayajñena cāpyanye
yajanto māmupāsate ।
ekatvena pṛthaktvena
bahudhā viśvatomukham ॥ 9.15

अहं क्रतुरहं यज्ञः
स्वधाहमहम् औषधम् ।
मन्त्रोऽहमहमेवाज्यम्
अहमग्निरहं हुतम् ॥ ९.१६

ahaṃ kraturahaṃ yajñaḥ
svadhāhamaham auṣadham ।
mantro'hamahamevājyam
ahamagniraham hutam ॥ 9.16

पिताहमस्य जगतो
माता धाता पितामहः ।
वेद्यं पवित्रम् ओंकार
ऋक्सामयजुरेव च ॥ ९.१७

pitāhamasya jagato
mātā dhātā pitāmahaḥ ।
vedyaṃ pavitram oṃkāra
ṛksāmayajureva ca ॥ 9.17

गतिर्भर्ता प्रभुः साक्षी
निवासः शरणं सुहृत् ।
प्रभवः प्रलयः स्थानं
निधानं बीजमव्ययम् ॥ ९.१८

gatirbhartā prabhuḥ sākṣī
nivāsaḥ śaraṇaṃ suhṛt ।
prabhavaḥ pralayaḥ sthānaṃ
nidhānaṃ bījamavyayam ॥ 9.18

तपाम्यहम् अहं वर्षं
निगृह्णाम्युत्सृजामि च ।
अमृतं चैव मृत्युश्च
सदसच्चाहमर्जुन ॥ ९.१९

tapāmyaham ahaṃ varṣaṃ
nigṛhṇāmyutsṛjāmi ca ।
amṛtaṃ caiva mṛtyuśca
sadasaccāhamarjuna ॥ 9.19

त्रैविद्या मां सोमपाः पूतपापा
यज्ञैरिष्ट्वा स्वर्गतिं प्रार्थयन्ते ।
ते पुण्यमासाद्य सुरेन्द्रलोकम्
अश्नन्ति दिव्यान्दिवि देवभोगान् ॥ ९.२०

traividyā māṃ somapāḥ pūtapāpā
yajñairiṣṭvā svargatiṃ prārthayante ।
te puṇyamāsādya surendralokam
aśnanti divyāndivi devabhogān ॥ 9.20

ते तं भुक्त्वा स्वर्गलोकं विशालं
क्षीणे पुण्ये मर्त्यलोकं विशन्ति ।
एवं त्रयीधर्मम् अनुप्रपन्ना
गतागतं कामकामा लभन्ते ॥ ९.२१

te taṃ bhuktvā svargalokaṃ viśālaṃ
kṣīṇe puṇye martyalokaṃ viśanti ।
evaṃ trayīdharmam anuprapannā
gatāgataṃ kāmakāmā labhante ॥ 9.21

अनन्याश्चिन्तयन्तो मां
ये जनाः पर्युपासते ।
तेषां नित्याभियुक्तानां
योगक्षेमं वहाम्यहम् ॥ ९.२२

ananyāścintayanto māṃ
ye janāḥ paryupāsate ।
teṣāṃ nityābhiyuktānāṃ
yogakṣemaṃ vahāmyaham ॥ 9.22

येऽप्यन्यदेवता भक्ता
यजन्ते श्रद्धयान्विताः ।
तेऽपि मामेव कौन्तेय
यजन्त्यविधिपूर्वकम् ॥ ९.२३

ye'pyanyadevatā bhaktā
yajante śraddhayānvitāḥ ।
te'pi māmeva kaunteya
yajantyavidhipūrvakam ॥ 9.23

अहं हि सर्वयज्ञानां भोक्ता च प्रभुरेव च । न तु मामभिजानन्ति तत्त्वेनातश्च्यवन्ति ते ॥ ९.२४	*ahaṃ hi sarvayajñānāṃ* *bhoktā ca prabhureva ca* । *na tu māmabhijānanti* *tattvenātaścyavanti te* ॥ 9.24
यान्ति देवव्रता देवान् पितृन्यान्ति पितृव्रताः । भूतानि यान्ति भूतेज्या यान्ति मद्याजिनोऽपि माम् ॥ ९.२५	*yānti devavratā devān* *pitṝnyānti pitṛvratāḥ* । *bhūtāni yānti bhūtejyā* *yānti madyājino'pi mām* ॥ 9.25
पत्रं पुष्पं फलं तोयं यो मे भक्त्या प्रयच्छति । तदहं भक्त्युपहृतम् अश्नामि प्रयतात्मनः ॥ ९.२६	*patraṃ puṣpaṃ phalaṃ toyaṃ* *yo me bhaktyā prayacchati* । *tadahaṃ bhaktyupahṛtam* *aśnāmi prayatātmanaḥ* ॥ 9.26
यत्करोषि यदश्नासि यज्जुहोषि ददासि यत् । यत्तपस्यसि कौन्तेय तत्कुरुष्व मदर्पणम् ॥ ९.२७	*yatkaroṣi yadaśnāsi* *yajjuhoṣi dadāsi yat* । *yattapasyasi kaunteya* *tatkuruṣva madarpaṇam* ॥ 9.27
शुभाशुभफलैरेवं मोक्ष्यसे कर्मबन्धनैः । संन्यासयोगयुक्तात्मा विमुक्तो मामुपैष्यसि ॥ ९.२८	*śubhāśubhaphalairevaṃ* *mokṣyase karmabandhanaiḥ* । *saṃnyāsayogayuktātmā* *vimukto māmupaiṣyasi* ॥ 9.28
समोऽहं सर्वभूतेषु न मे द्वेष्योऽस्ति न प्रियः । ये भजन्ति तु मां भक्त्या मयि ते तेषु चाप्यहम् ॥ ९.२९	*samo'haṃ sarvabhūteṣu* *na me dveṣyo'sti na priyaḥ* । *ye bhajanti tu māṃ bhaktyā* *mayi te teṣu cāpyaham* ॥ 9.29
अपि चेत्सुदुराचारो भजते मामनन्यभाक् । साधुरेव स मन्तव्यः सम्यग्व्यवसितो हि सः ॥ ९.३०	*api cetsudurācāro* *bhajate māmananyabhāk* । *sādhureva sa mantavyaḥ* *samyagvyavasito hi saḥ* ॥ 9.30
क्षिप्रं भवति धर्मात्मा शश्वच्छान्तिं निगच्छति । कौन्तेय प्रतिजानीहि न मे भक्तः प्रणश्यति ॥ ९.३१	*kṣipraṃ bhavati dharmātmā* *śaśvacchāntiṃ nigacchati* । *kaunteya pratijānīhi* *na me bhaktaḥ praṇaśyati* ॥ 9.31

मां हि पार्थ व्यपाश्रित्य
येऽपि स्युः पापयोनयः ।
स्त्रियो वैश्यास्तथा शूद्राः
तेऽपि यान्ति परां गतिम् ॥ ९.३२

māṃ hi pārtha vyapāśritya
ye'pi syuḥ pāpayonayaḥ ।
striyo vaiśyāstathā śūdrāḥ
te'pi yānti parāṃ gatim ॥ 9.32

किं पुनर्ब्राह्मणाः पुण्या
भक्ता राजर्षयस्तथा ।
अनित्यमसुखं लोकम्
इमं प्राप्य भजस्व माम् ॥ ९.३३

kiṃ punarbrāhmaṇāḥ puṇyā
bhaktā rājarṣayastathā ।
anityamasukhaṃ lokam
imaṃ prāpya bhajasva mām ॥ 9.33

मन्मना भव मद्भक्तो
मद्याजी मां नमस्कुरु ।
मामेवैष्यसि युक्त्वैवम्
आत्मानं मत्परायणः ॥ ९.३४

manmanā bhava madbhakto
madyājī māṃ namaskuru ।
māmevaiṣyasi yuktvaivam
ātmānaṃ matparāyaṇaḥ ॥ 9.34

CHAPTER 9

Best of Secrets

Kṛṣṇa

[1]Arjuna, you value my words
so I shall reveal to you the best of secrets:
it is practical knowledge guided by wisdom.

Know this and you will be free from sorrow.

[2]This is the deepest of all mysteries
and the greatest of all studies.

It is the purest of the pure
and the best of the best.

It follows the rules of *dharma*.
It is easy to practice and
one can experience it directly.

Dharma refers to a moral law or principle that sustains natural goodness.

3 Those who reject *dharma* fail to attain the Supreme.
They are born again and again
in the endless cycle of death and rebirth.

4 I pervade the entire universe but I am invisible.
All beings depend on me
but I don't depend on them.

Here, 'I' is a reference to *Brahman*, the Supreme Being that is the source and the sustainer of the entire universe; there is nothing beyond *Brahman*.

5 Though I bring forth and sustain all beings,
I am not dependent on them.

In a way,
even they don't depend on me.
Behold the grandeur
of my *yoga*, O Arjuna!

The previous verse refers to
the indispensable aspect of dependency
and this verse hints at the dispensable aspect.
While matter is inevitable,
spirit is not compulsory!

6 The mighty wind arises in space and
moves freely in all directions,
yet it is always confined to the space.

In the same way,
all creatures
arise from me
yet they always
remain within me.

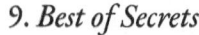

[7]At the end of a cosmic day,
all beings return to my unmanifest state.
Again, I bring them forth
at the beginning of the next cosmic day.

A cosmic day spans 4.32 billion years and is followed by a cosmic night that spans another 4.32 billion years; this together forms a cosmic cycle (see 8.17–19).

8 Again and again,
controlling my own nature,
I bring forth these myriads of beings
and subject them to the laws of nature.

9 These actions don't bind me because
I remain unconcerned and unattached.

10 Under my supervision,
nature brings forth all beings –
animate and inanimate –
and sets the universe in motion.

11 When I appear in human form,
the foolish people disregard me,
for they don't recognize my higher state
as the great lord of all beings.

They fail to look beyond physical appearances.

12 They lack insight
and are utterly confused.
With unreal hopes,
trivial knowledge, and
insignificant deeds,
they resort to wicked ways.

13But the great souls who abide in divinity
are aware that I am the eternal source of all beings.
They worship me with singular focus.

14Further, those great souls glorify me,
honor me with intense devotion, and
worship me with firm resolve.

15There are some others, engaged in
jñāna-yajña (cultivation of knowledge),
who worship me as the One, the distinct, and
the Supreme Presence manifested everywhere.

16 I am the ritual, I am the *yajña*, I am the *mantra*,
I am the offering that nourishes and heals,
I am the fuel and I am the fire.

Yajña is a *Vedic* ritual in which fire is raised
in closed altars made of bricks, with the top portion open to air.
Agni—the sacred fire—exists in three forms:
gārhapatya, *dakṣiṇa*, and *āhavanīya*,
and fires are raised in three altars, one for each *agni*.
Agni is both a deity as well as the medium
to deliver the offerings made to other deities.
The deities to be worshiped are invoked during the *yajña*.
Clarified butter (fuel for the fire), medicinal herbs, twigs of the
pīpal tree (*Ficus religiosa*), and other offerings (milk, grains that are fried
and then cooked, juice of the *soma* plant, animals, etc.) are put in the fire,
accompanied by reciting specific *mantras* (sacred verses) from the *Vedas*.
(*Mantra* also refers to the formative thought behind the recited verses.)
Typically, sixteen *ṛtviks* (loosely, 'priests' or 'officiators')
preside over the rituals in a *yajña*.

All the distinct elements of a *yajña* are recognized here
as embodiments of the Supreme (see 4.24).

17 I am also the father, the mother, the grandfather,
and the protector of this universe.
I am the purpose of knowledge,
I am the one who purifies,
I am the sacred syllable '*Om*,' and
I am the *Ṛg-*, *Sāma-*, and *Yajur-vedas*.

Ṛk, *Sāma*, and *Yajus* are the three principal *Veda*s.
The *Ṛg-veda* is the foremost one and the other *Veda*s were developed from it.
A wholesome *Vedic yajña* involves the three principal *Veda*s.

18 I am the lord, friend, and witness.
I am creation, dissolution, and existence.
I am the everlasting seed and the sustainer.
I am the goal, the abode, the refuge,
and the final resting place.

19 I radiate warmth.
I send forth and also hold back rain.
I am both immortality and death.
I am *Sat* (what is) and *Asat* (what is not).

See 17.26–28.

20 Those well-versed in the three (principal) *Veda*s,
who relish *soma* and are cleansed of *pāpa*
honor me through *yajña*
with the desire to go to *svarga*.

By the *puṇya* gained they reach *svarga*—
the domain of Indra—and enjoy celestial pleasures.

Soma is the brew of the *soma* plant, which the *Vedic ṛṣi*s
drank as an instant reward of performing a *yajña*.
In general *puṇya* refers to 'righteous,' 'just,' 'auspicious,' *etc.*
but here it means 'religious merit' or 'virtuous action.'
Svarga loosely translates into 'heaven' – and it is attained by people
who sincerely follow *Vedic* rituals and refrain from doing bad deeds.

21 Having enjoyed the wide world of *svarga*,
they return to earth once their *puṇya* is exhausted.
Again impelled by desire for the pleasures of *svarga*,
they resort to meritorious rites prescribed in the *Veda*s
and are thus caught in the cycle of birth and death.

The duration and level of enjoyment in *svarga* is proportional to the *puṇya* earned
in one's life; once the *puṇya* is exhausted, one returns to earth. See 1.44 and 2.43.

22 But those who are eternally devoted to me
and think of me alone,
I provide them with what they desire and
preserve what they already possess.
I will completely look after their welfare.

In this verse and the following verses, 'I' and 'me' are references to the Supreme.
The original uses the terms '*yoga*' (acquring or obtaining new things)
and '*kṣema*' (preserving what has been acquired).

23 Arjuna, even those who faithfully worship other gods
in essence, are worshipping me, though unaware of it.

24 I am the recipient and the overseer of all worships.
But those who are unaware of my true nature
are trapped in the cycle of birth and death.

25 Those who worship *devas*
go to the *devas* they seek.
Those who worship the *pitṛs* go to the *pitṛs*.
Those who worship elemental spirits
attain those spirits.
Those who worship me, attain me!

Devas are divine beings. *Pitṛs* are the spirits of dead ancestors (see 8.16).

26 I happily accept whatever one offers me –
a leaf, a flower, a fruit or just water –
with love, devotion, and a pure heart.

27 Whatever you do,
whatever you eat,
whatever you
offer in worship
or give as charity
or give up in austerity –
dedicate that to me.

28 Living in the spirit of dedication to me,
you will be freed from the bondages of actions.
Then the results of your action – good or bad –
will not impact you in any way.
Thus, you will be liberated
and will come to me.

29 I am equally present in all beings;
none is hateful or dear to me.

But those who worship me with devotion –
I am in them and they are in me.

30 Even if a man steeped in evil
takes on to my worship with undivided devotion,
he must be considered as noble
because he has taken the right decision.

31 Readily, he becomes righteous and
attains everlasting peace.
Arjuna, know this:
no devotee of mine is ever lost.

32 Whoever takes refuge in me –
even men who are deemed to be of sinful birth,
women, traders, or laborers –
will attain the Supreme Goal.

Societies typically look down upon certain sections of people. Kṛṣṇa clarifies that whoever submits to the Supreme—*irrespective of their birth, gender, or occupation*—attains liberation.

When Kṛṣṇa lists out noble traits in 12.13–20, 13.7–11, or 16.1–3, he doesn't link them to men or women nor to any social or economic class. Also see 10.34.

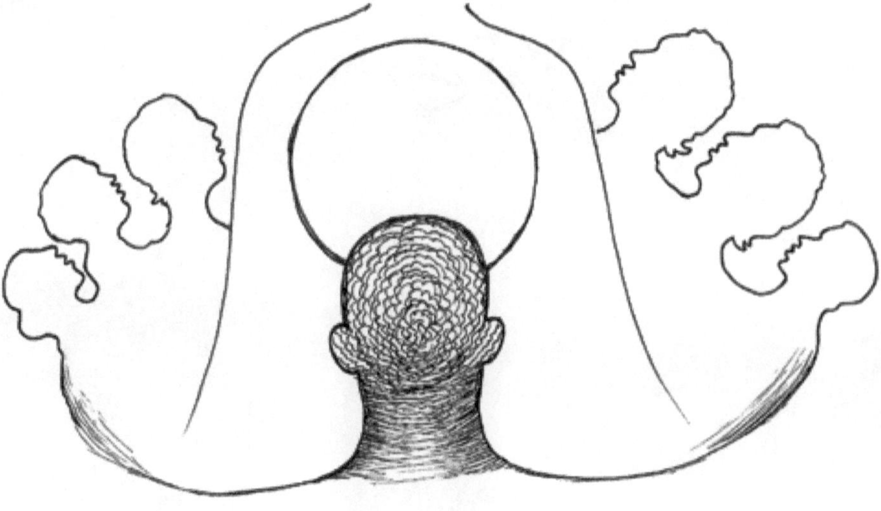

[33]What more to say of
the pure and wise ones,
the devotees, and *rājarṣis*,
who take refuge in me?

Having come into this fleeting
and unhappy world,
engage yourself in my worship.

[34]Fix your mind on me, be devoted to me,
worship me, bow down to me.
Seek me as the Supreme Goal with all your heart,
and you shall certainly be united with me!

In verses 30–34, Kṛṣṇa explains the path of devotion leading to liberation.
Even an evil person can instantly attain goodness and peace.
One can be liberated regardless of birth, gender,
learning, occupation, or position in society.

10

श्रीभगवानुवाच ।
भूय एव महाबाहो
शृणु मे परमं वचः ।
यत् तेऽहं प्रीयमाणाय
वक्ष्यामि हितकाम्यया ॥ १०.१

śrībhagavānuvāca ।
bhūya eva mahābāho
śṛṇu me paramaṃ vacaḥ ।
yat te'haṃ prīyamāṇāya
vakṣyāmi hitakāmyayā ॥ 10.1

न मे विदुः सुरगणाः
प्रभवं न महर्षयः ।
अहमादिर्हि देवानां
महर्षीणां च सर्वशः ॥ १०.२

na me viduḥ suragaṇāḥ
prabhavaṃ na maharṣayaḥ ।
ahamādirhi devānāṃ
maharṣīṇāṃ ca sarvaśaḥ ॥ 10.2

यो मामजमनादिं च
वेत्ति लोकमहेश्वरम् ।
असंमूढः स मर्त्येषु
सर्वपापैः प्रमुच्यते ॥ १०.३

yo māmajamanādiṃ ca
vetti lokamaheśvaram ।
asaṃmūḍhaḥ sa martyeṣu
sarvapāpaiḥ pramucyate ॥ 10.3

बुद्धिर्ज्ञानमसंमोहः
क्षमा सत्यं दमः शमः ।
सुखं दुःखं भवोऽभावो
भयं चाभयम् एव च ॥ १०.४

buddhirjñānamasaṃmohaḥ
kṣamā satyaṃ damaḥ śamaḥ ।
sukhaṃ duḥkhaṃ bhavo'bhāvo
bhayaṃ cābhayam eva ca ॥ 10.4

अहिंसा समता तुष्टिः
तपो दानं यशोऽयशः ।
भवन्ति भावा भूतानां
मत्त एव पृथग्विधाः ॥ १०.५

ahiṃsā samatā tuṣṭiḥ
tapo dānaṃ yaśo'yaśaḥ ।
bhavanti bhāvā bhūtānāṃ
matta eva pṛthagvidhāḥ ॥ 10.5

महर्षयः सप्त पूर्वे
चत्वारो मनवस्तथा ।
मद्भावा मानसा जाता
येषां लोक इमाः प्रजाः ॥ १०.६

maharṣayaḥ sapta pūrve
catvāro manavastathā ।
madbhāvā mānasā jātā
yeṣāṃ loka imāḥ prajāḥ ॥ 10.6

एतां विभूतिं योगं च
मम यो वेत्ति तत्त्वतः ।
सोऽविकम्पेन योगेन
युज्यते नात्र संशयः ॥ १०.७

etāṃ vibhūtiṃ yogaṃ ca
mama yo vetti tattvataḥ ।
so'vikampena yogena
yujyate nātra saṃśayaḥ ॥ 10.7

अहं सर्वस्य प्रभवो मत्तः सर्वं प्रवर्तते । इति मत्वा भजन्ते मां बुधा भावसमन्विताः ॥ १०.८	*ahaṃ sarvasya prabhavo* *mattaḥ sarvaṃ pravartate* । *iti matvā bhajante māṃ* *budhā bhāvasamanvitāḥ* ॥ 10.8
मच्चित्ता मद्गतप्राणा बोधयन्तः परस्परम् । कथयन्तश्च मां नित्यं तुष्यन्ति च रमन्ति च ॥ १०.९	*maccittā madgataprāṇā* *bodhayantaḥ parasparam* । *kathayantaśca māṃ nityaṃ* *tuṣyanti ca ramanti ca* ॥ 10.9
तेषां सततयुक्तानां भजतां प्रीतिपूर्वकम् । ददामि बुद्धियोगं तं येन मामुपयान्ति ते ॥ १०.१०	*teṣāṃ satatayuktānāṃ* *bhajatāṃ prītipūrvakam* । *dadāmi buddhiyogaṃ taṃ* *yena māmupayānti te* ॥ 10.10
तेषामेवानुकम्पार्थम् अहमज्ञानजं तमः । नाशयाम्यात्मभावस्थो ज्ञानदीपेन भास्वता ॥ १०.११	*teṣāmevānukampārtham* *ahamajñānajaṃ tamaḥ* । *nāśayāmyātmabhāvastho* *jñānadīpena bhāsvatā* ॥ 10.11
अर्जुन उवाच । परं ब्रह्म परं धाम पवित्रं परमं भवान् । पुरुषं शाश्वतं दिव्यम् आदिदेवमजं विभुम् ॥ १०.१२	***arjuna uvāca*** । *paraṃ brahma paraṃ dhāma* *pavitraṃ paramaṃ bhavān* । *puruṣaṃ śāśvataṃ divyam* *ādidevamajaṃ vibhum* ॥ 10.12
आहुस्त्वाम् ऋषयः सर्वे देवर्षिर्नारदस्तथा । असितो देवलो व्यासः स्वयं चैव ब्रवीषि मे ॥ १०.१३	*āhustvām ṛṣayaḥ sarve* *devarṣirnāradastathā* । *asito devalo vyāsaḥ* *svayaṃ caiva bravīṣi me* ॥ 10.13
सर्वमेतदृतं मन्ये यन्मां वदसि केशव । न हि ते भगवन् व्यक्तिं विदुर्देवा न दानवाः ॥ १०.१४	*sarvametadṛtaṃ manye* *yanmāṃ vadasi keśava* । *na hi te bhagavan vyaktiṃ* *vidurdevā na dānavāḥ* ॥ 10.14

स्वयमेवात्मनात्मानं
वेत्थ त्वं पुरुषोत्तम ।
भूतभावन भूतेश
देवदेव जगत्पते ॥ १०.१५

svayamevātmanātmānaṃ
vettha tvaṃ puruṣottama ।
bhūtabhāvana bhūteśa
devadeva jagatpate ॥ 10.15

वक्तुम् अर्हस्यशेषेण
दिव्या ह्यात्मविभूतयः ।
याभिर्विभूतिभिर्लोकान्
इमांस्त्वं व्याप्य तिष्ठसि ॥ १०.१६

vaktum arhasyaśeṣeṇa
divyā hyātmavibhūtayaḥ ।
yābhirvibhūtibhirlokān
imāṃstvaṃ vyāpya tiṣṭhasi ॥ 10.16

कथं विद्यामहं योगिन्
त्वां सदा परिचिन्तयन् ।
केषु केषु च भावेषु
चिन्त्योऽसि भगवन् मया ॥ १०.१७

kathaṃ vidyāmahaṃ yogin
tvāṃ sadā paricintayan ।
keṣu keṣu ca bhāveṣu
cintyo'si bhagavan mayā ॥ 10.17

विस्तरेणात्मनो योगं
विभूतिं च जनार्दन ।
भूयः कथय तृप्तिर्हि
शृण्वतो नास्ति मेऽमृतम् ॥ १०.१८

vistareṇātmano yogaṃ
vibhūtiṃ ca janārdana ।
bhūyaḥ kathaya tṛptirhi
śṛṇvato nāsti me'mṛtam ॥ 10.18

श्रीभगवानुवाच ।
हन्त ते कथयिष्यामि
दिव्या ह्यात्मविभूतयः ।
प्राधान्यतः कुरुश्रेष्ठ
नास्त्यन्तो विस्तरस्य मे ॥ १०.१९

śrībhagavānuvāca ।
hanta te kathayiṣyāmi
divyā hyātmavibhūtayaḥ ।
prādhānyataḥ kuruśreṣṭha
nāstyanto vistarasya me ॥ 10.19

अहमात्मा गुडाकेश
सर्वभूताशयस्थितः ।
अहमादिश्च मध्यं च
भूतानामन्त एव च ॥ १०.२०

ahamātmā guḍākeśa
sarvabhūtāśayasthitaḥ ।
ahamādiśca madhyaṃ ca
bhūtānāmanta eva ca ॥ 10.20

आदित्यानामहं विष्णुः
ज्योतिषां रविरंशुमान् ।
मरीचिर्मरुतामस्मि
नक्षत्राणामहं शशी ॥ १०.२१

ādityānāmahaṃ viṣṇuḥ
jyotiṣāṃ raviraṃśumān ।
marīcirmarutāmasmi
nakṣatrāṇāmahaṃ śaśī ॥ 10.21

वेदानां सामवेदोऽस्मि देवानामस्मि वासवः । इन्द्रियाणां मनश्चास्मि भूतानामस्मि चेतना ॥ १०.२२	*vedānāṃ sāmavedo'smi* *devānāmasmi vāsavaḥ* । *indriyāṇāṃ manaścāsmi* *bhūtānāmasmi cetanā* ॥ 10.22
रुद्राणां शङ्करश्चास्मि वित्तेशो यक्षरक्षसाम् । वसूनां पावकश्चास्मि मेरुः शिखरिणामहम् ॥ १०.२३	*rudrāṇāṃ śaṅkaraścāsmi* *vitteśo yakṣarakṣasām* । *vasūnāṃ pāvakaścāsmi* *meruḥ śikhariṇāmaham* ॥ 10.23
पुरोधसां च मुख्यं मां विद्धि पार्थ बृहस्पतिम् । सेनानीनामहं स्कन्दः सरसामस्मि सागरः ॥ १०.२४	*purodhasāṃ ca mukhyaṃ māṃ* *viddhi pārtha bṛhaspatim* । *senānīnāmahaṃ skandaḥ* *sarasāmasmi sāgaraḥ* ॥ 10.24
महर्षीणां भृगुरहं गिरामस्म्येकमक्षरम् । यज्ञानां जपयज्ञोऽस्मि स्थावराणां हिमालयः ॥ १०.२५	*maharṣīṇāṃ bhṛguraham* *girāmasmyekamakṣaram* । *yajñānāṃ japayajño'smi* *sthāvarāṇāṃ himālayaḥ* ॥ 10.25
अश्वत्थः सर्ववृक्षाणां देवर्षीणां च नारदः । गन्धर्वाणां चित्ररथः सिद्धानां कपिलो मुनिः ॥ १०.२६	*aśvatthaḥ sarvavṛkṣāṇāṃ* *devarṣīṇāṃ ca nāradaḥ* । *gandharvāṇāṃ citrarathaḥ* *siddhānāṃ kapilo muniḥ* ॥ 10.26
उच्चैःश्रवसमश्वानां विद्धि माममृतोद्भवम् । ऐरावतं गजेन्द्राणां नराणां च नराधिपम् ॥ १०.२७	*uccaiḥśravasamaśvānāṃ* *viddhi māmamṛtodbhavam* । *airāvataṃ gajendrāṇāṃ* *narāṇāṃ ca narādhipam* ॥ 10.27
आयुधानामहं वज्रं धेनूनामस्मि कामधुक् । प्रजनश्चास्मि कन्दर्पः सर्पाणामस्मि वासुकिः ॥ १०.२८	*āyudhānāmahaṃ vajraṃ* *dhenūnāmasmi kāmadhuk* । *prajanaścāsmi kandarpaḥ* *sarpāṇāmasmi vāsukiḥ* ॥ 10.28
अनन्तश्चास्मि नागानां वरुणो यादसामहम् । पितॄणामर्यमा चास्मि यमः संयमतामहम् ॥ १०.२९	*anantaścāsmi nāgānāṃ* *varuṇo yādasāmaham* । *pitṝṇāmaryamā cāsmi* *yamaḥ saṃyamatāmaham* ॥ 10.29

प्रह्लादश्चास्मि दैत्यानां
कालः कलयतामहम् ।
मृगाणां च मृगेन्द्रोऽहं
वैनतेयश्च पक्षिणाम् ॥ १०.३०

prahlādaścāsmi daityānāṃ
kālaḥ kalayatāmaham ।
mṛgāṇāṃ ca mṛgendro'haṃ
vainateyaśca pakṣiṇām ॥ 10.30

पवनः पवतामस्मि
रामः शस्त्रभृतामहम् ।
झषाणां मकरश्चास्मि
स्रोतसामस्मि जाह्नवी ॥ १०.३१

pavanaḥ pavatāmasmi
rāmaḥ śastrabhṛtāmaham ।
jhaṣāṇāṃ makaraścāsmi
srotasāmasmi jāhnavī ॥ 10.31

सर्गाणामादिरन्तश्च
मध्यं चैवाहमर्जुन ।
अध्यात्मविद्या विद्यानां
वादः प्रवदतामहम् ॥ १०.३२

sargāṇāmādirantaśca
madhyaṃ caivāhamarjuna ।
adhyātmavidyā vidyānāṃ
vādaḥ pravadatāmaham ॥ 10.32

अक्षराणामकारोऽस्मि
द्वन्द्वः सामासिकस्य च ।
अहमेवाक्षयः कालो
धाताहं विश्वतोमुखः ॥ १०.३३

akṣarāṇāmakāro'smi
dvandvaḥ sāmāsikasya ca ।
ahamevākṣayaḥ kālo
dhātāhaṃ viśvatomukhaḥ ॥ 10.33

मृत्युः सर्वहरश्चाहम्
उद्भवश्च भविष्यताम् ।
कीर्तिः श्रीर्वाक्च नारीणां
स्मृतिर्मेधा धृतिः क्षमा ॥ १०.३४

mṛtyuḥ sarvaharaścāham
udbhavaśca bhaviṣyatām ।
kīrtiḥ śrīrvākca nārīṇāṃ
smṛtirmedhā dhṛtiḥ kṣamā ॥ 10.34

बृहत्साम तथा साम्नां
गायत्री छन्दसामहम् ।
मासानां मार्गशीर्षोऽहम्
ऋतूनां कुसुमाकरः ॥ १०.३५

bṛhatsāma tathā sāmnāṃ
gāyatrī chandasāmaham ।
māsānāṃ mārgaśīrṣo'ham
ṛtūnāṃ kusumākaraḥ ॥ 10.35

द्यूतं छलयतामस्मि
तेजस्तेजस्विनामहम् ।
जयोऽस्मि व्यवसायोऽस्मि
सत्त्वं सत्त्ववतामहम् ॥ १०.३६

dyūtaṃ chalayatāmasmi
tejastejasvināmaham ।
jayo'smi vyavasāyo'smi
sattvaṃ sattvavatāmaham ॥ 10.36

वृष्णीनां वासुदेवोऽस्मि
पाण्डवानां धनञ्जयः ।
मुनीनामप्यहं व्यासः
कवीनामुशना कविः ॥ १०.३७

vṛṣṇīnāṃ vāsudevo'smi
pāṇḍavānāṃ dhanañjayaḥ ।
munīnāmapyahaṃ vyāsaḥ
kavīnāmuśanā kaviḥ ॥ 10.37

दण्डो दमयतामस्मि
नीतिरस्मि जिगीषताम् ।
मौनं चैवास्मि गुह्यानां
ज्ञानं ज्ञानवतामहम् ॥ १०.३८

daṇḍo damayatāmasmi
nītirasmi jigīṣatām ।
maunaṃ caivāsmi guhyānāṃ
jñānaṃ jñānavatāmaham ॥ 10.38

यच्चापि सर्वभूतानां
बीजं तदहमर्जुन ।
न तदस्ति विना यत्स्यात्
मया भूतं चराचरम् ॥ १०.३९

yaccāpi sarvabhūtānāṃ
bījaṃ tadahamarjuna ।
na tadasti vinā yatsyāt
mayā bhūtaṃ carācaram ॥ 10.39

नान्तोऽस्ति मम दिव्यानां
विभूतीनां परन्तप ।
एष तूद्देशतः प्रोक्तो
विभूतेर्विस्तरो मया ॥ १०.४०

nānto'sti mama divyānāṃ
vibhūtīnāṃ parantapa ।
eṣa tūddeśataḥ prokto
vibhūter vistāro mayā ॥ 10.40

यद्यद्विभूतिमत्सत्त्वं
श्रीमदूर्जितमेव वा ।
तत्तदेवावगच्छ त्वं
मम तेजोंऽशसम्भवम् ॥ १०.४१

yadyadvibhūtimatsattvaṃ
śrīmadūrjitameva vā ।
tattadevāvagaccha tvaṃ
mama tejoṃśasambhavam ॥ 10.41

अथ वा बहुनैतेन
किं ज्ञातेन तवार्जुन ।
विष्टभ्याहमिदं कृत्स्नम्
एकांशेन स्थितो जगत् ॥ १०.४२

atha vā bahunaitena
kiṃ jñātena tavārjuna ।
viṣṭabhyāhamidaṃ kṛtsnam
ekāṃśena sthito jagat ॥ 10.42

CHAPTER 10

Divine Splendor

Kṛṣṇa

[1]O mighty one,
listen to more
of my supreme words,
which I speak for your good
because you are dear to me
and you are interested
in what I have to say.

[2]Even the *devas* and *maharṣis*
do not know my origin
because in every way,
I am the source of them all!

Devas are divine beings.
Maharṣis are great seers.

[3]I am the Supreme Lord of the universe
without birth or beginning.

One who knows this
has understood me correctly
and is free from evil.

People who recognize a greater force
that governs the cosmic order in the universe
attain true humility and are thus freed from evil.

[4]Intellect, wisdom, clarity,
forgiveness, truth, self-control,
calmness, joy, sorrow,
birth, death, fear, courage,
[5]benevolence, equanimity,
fulfillment, austerity,
generosity, fame, infamy –
all these traits of beings
arise from me alone.

[6]The seven *maharṣis*,
the four ancient ones, and the *manus*
are projections of my thought
and have powers like mine.
The creatures of the world
came forth from them.

The seven great seers (Atri, Bhṛgu, Vasiṣṭha, *etc.*), the four ancient ones
(Sanaka-, Sanandana-, Sanātana- and Sanat-kumāras), and
the fourteen *manus* (Svayambhuva, Svarociṣa, Uttama, *etc.*)
are the ancestors of the human race.

7 One who understands my *yogic* powers
and my manifold manifestations
becomes steadily established in *yoga*.
There is no doubt about this!

Here, *yoga* means 'union with the Supreme.'
When one perceives the cosmos as divine force at work,
he can no longer distance himself from the Supreme –
just as the waves have no independent existence from the ocean;
they arise from ocean and merge into ocean.

8 I am the origin of all and
everything evolves out of me.
Knowing this, the wise worship me
with all their heart.

9 Their focus is totally on me.
With their senses absorbed in me,
they enlighten one another.
Forever they speak of my glory
and find immense peace and joy.

10 I grant the power of discretion to those
who love me and are always devoted to me,
so that they may unite with me.

Buddhi-yoga—'the power of discretion'—is the ability to
discriminate between right and wrong,
between the higher and lower states of truth.

[11]Out of my kindness, I,
residing in their hearts,
destroy the darkness of ignorance
by lighting the lamp of wisdom.

ARJUNA

[12–14]Kṛṣṇa! All the *ṛṣis*
including Asita, Devala, Vyāsa, and
the divine seer Nārada,
describe you as
the Supreme *Brahman*,

the Ultimate Refuge,
the Greatest Purifier,
the Supreme Spirit,
the Lord of Lords,
the Eternal, the Divine,
the Unborn, and
the All-pervading one.

The 'unborn' refers to something that is always there. The idea of 'birth' and 'death' is only for mortals (see 4.6).

Besides, you have confirmed it yourself.
I take this as true.

Neither the gods nor their enemies
can truly know your infinite grandeur,
15 because only you know
your true self,
O Lord of Lords,
O Supreme Person,
O Lord of the beings,
O Source of all beings,
O Master of the universe!

16 You are the only one who can tell me in detail
about your boundless divine manifestations
with which you pervade the universe.

17 O master of *yoga*,
how may I know you?

O blessed lord,
which of your forms
should I meditate upon
so that I will always be aware of you?

18 Tell me more about your power and glory!
I feel that I can never hear enough
of your immortal words.

KṚṢṆA

19 There's no end to my divine manifestations
so I will share with you
just a few prominent ones.

20 I am the true Self,
seated in the heart of all beings.
I am the beginning, the middle,
and the end of all creatures.

Here, the 'beginning, middle, and end' refers to 'birth, growth, and decay.'

21 I am Viṣṇu among *ādityas*;
of the lights, I am the radiant sun.

I am Marīci among *maruts*;
amidst stars, I am the moon.

The *ādityas* are the twelve children of Sage Kaśyapa and his first wife Aditi.
Viṣṇu is one of the *ādityas* (not to be confused with Lord Viṣṇu).
The five lights (or luminaries) are – sun, moon, stars, fire, and lightening.
The *maruts* are a group of wind gods;
Marīci, the breeze in the vicinity, is the chief of *maruts*.
'...amidst stars, I am the moon' indicates that
the moon is the most prominent object in the night sky.

22 I am *Sāma-veda* among *Vedas*;
I am Indra among *devas*;
of the senses, I am the mind and
in living beings, I am consciousness.

Vedas are the foremost revealed scriptures in Hinduism.
They are four in number – *Ṛg-*, *Sāma-*, *Yajur-*, and *Atharva-vedas*.
Indra is the king of the *devas*.

[23]I am Śaṅkara among *rudras*;
among *yakṣas* and *rākṣasas*, I am Kubera;
I am *pāvaka* (fire) among *vasus*;
among mountain peaks, I am Meru.

The *rudras* are a group of storm gods, Śaṅkara being the foremost among them.
The *yakṣas* and *rākṣasas* are spirits with special powers;
while *yakṣas* are semi-divine and benevolent,
rākṣasas are notorious and often disturb the harmony.
Kubera is the deity of wealth and the king of the *yakṣas*.
The *vasus* are divinities presiding over the elements of nature.
Meru is the golden mountain at the center of the cosmos.

24 Of high priests,
I am their chief, Bṛhaspati;
of war generals, I am Skanda;
among the waters, I am the ocean.

Bṛhaspati is the *purodhas* (loosely 'principal priest') of the *devas*.
Skanda is the general of the army of gods.

25 Of *maharṣis*,
I am Bhṛgu;
among words,
I am the syllable '*Om*;'
among *yajñas*,
I am *japa*;
among stationary objects,
I am the Himālayas.

Om is a single-syllable word that denotes *Brahman*, the Supreme Being.
It is the most sacred sound according to Hindu belief.
Japa is the chanting of divine names or sacred verses mentally or in a low voice.
It is the simplest and the best form of all *yajñas* (worships).

26 Of trees, I am Aśvattha;
I am Nārada among divine seers;
of *gandharvas*, I am Citraratha;
I am sage Kapila among *siddhas*.

Aśvattha is the sacred fig tree (*Ficus religiosa*).
'*Devarṣi*' Nārada is the seer among gods.
The *gandharvas* are a group of divine artists and musicians; Citraratha is their king.
Siddhas are people who have attained a high degree of perfection.

[27]Among horses,
I am Uccaiśravas, born of *amṛta*;
of mighty elephants, I am Airāvata;
among men, I am the king.

Uccaiśravas is the great horse of Indra and
Airāvata is his famous white-colored elephant.
The legendary cosmic ocean was churned for *amṛta*, the nectar of immortality,
and it was during that time both these animals arose.

[28]I am Vajra among weapons;
I am Kāmadhenu among cows;
of instincts for procreation, I am Kandarpa;
of *sarpas*, I am Vāsuki.

Vajra is the thunderbolt weapon of Indra.
Kāmadhenu is the cosmic cow that fulfills all wishes.
Kandarpa is the god of love; perhaps the best way to fulfill the instinct of procreation
is through mutual love rather than mere physical interaction.
Vāsuki is the king of the *sarpa*s, a group of serpents that live on land.

[29]I am Ananta among *nāgas*;
I am Varuṇa among water creatures;
I am Aryaman among ancestors;
I am Yama among the enforcers of law.

The *nāga*s are a group of multi-hooded snakes.
Ananta is the infinite snake on which Lord Viṣṇu reclines.
Varuṇa is the water god (and the deity of cosmic order).
Aryaman is the noblest of all ancestors.
Yama is the god of death. He accords punishments to people during afterlife
for the *pāpa* (evil, sin, crime) they committed in their lives.

[30]Among *daityas*, I am Prahlāda,
of all measures, I am time;
among animals, I am the lion;
among birds, I am Garuḍa.

The *daitya*s are the children of Sage Kaśyapa and his second wife Diti (who was the sister of Aditi); they are typically of demonic nature. Prahlāda was born in a family of *daitya*s but was very virtuous. The lion is the king of the jungle. The eagle Garuḍa is the king of birds.

31 Among things that purify, I am the wind;
of the wielders of weapons, I am Rāma;
among the fish, I am the crocodile;
and of rivers, I am Gaṅgā.

Rāma is the hero of the epic *Rāmāyaṇa*.
'...among the fish, I am the crocodile' indicates that the crocodile,
which lives among the fish, is more powerful than them.
Gaṅgā is a river that flows in Northern India; it is a sacred river for Hindus.

32 I am the beginning, middle, and end of all manifestations;
among all the branches of knowledge,
I am the knowledge of the Supreme Self;
among all arguments, I am *vāda*.

Among the various types of debates, *vāda* is a discussion between two people —without the need for a mediator—with the sole intention of getting closer to the truth with their joint intellect.

33 I am 'a' among letters,
I am *dvandva* among *samāsas*,
I am the ever-lasting time,
I am the omnipresent sustainer.

Samāsa is a system for formation of compound words.
The three primary *samāsa*s are *tatpuruṣa*, *bahuvrīhi*, and *dvandva*.
The *dvandva-samāsa* elegantly combines two words and both words have equal importance (whereas in other *samāsa*s, one word dominates the other).

34 I am Death that destroys all and
I am the origin of beings yet to be born!

Of women, I am fame, fortune, eloquence,
memory, intelligence, firmness, and forgiveness.

35 Of *mantras* of the *Sāma-veda*,
I am those that uniquely govern the mind;
among poetic meters, I am the Gāyatrī;
I am Mārgaśīrṣa among months;
I am spring among seasons.

Gāyatrī is a popular poetic meter found in *mantras* (sacred verses, prayers)
of the *Vedas*; it has three lines with eight syllables per line.
Mārgaśīrṣa is the month just before winter solstice.
Early on, the Hindu calendar used to start with Mārgaśīrṣa.
The season of spring is colourful; there is music in nature,
enthusiasm everywhere, and a new lease of life in the world.

36 Among all deceptions, I am gambling;
I am the splendor of the splendid;
of success, I am the effort;
I am goodness of the good.

Among deceptions, gambling is the most honest
since everyone has an equal chance at winning.
It offers the highest material gain depending on one's luck.

37 I am Kṛṣṇa among Vṛṣṇis;
I am Arjuna among Pāṇḍavas;
I am Vyāsa among sages;
I am Uśanas among poet-seers.

The Vṛṣṇis were an ancient clan. Pāṇḍavas were the sons of King Pāṇḍu.
Sage Vyāsa organized the *Vedas* and composed the *Mahā-bhārata*.
Uśanas (Śukrācārya) was the teacher of the *daityas*.

38 Of law enforcements, I am punishment;
of the paths to victory, I am statesmanship;
of secrets, I am silence;
of the wise, I am wisdom.

The traditional methods of law enforcement are: *sāma* (gentle persuasion), *dāna* (offering incentives), *bheda* (manipulating behavior), and if all fails, *daṇḍa* (punishment). Of these, *daṇḍa* is perhaps the one that is sure to work for all! A secret is best kept when silence is maintained.

39 Whatever is the source of all beings, I am that.
Nothing animate or inanimate can exist without me.

40 Arjuna, what I have told you
is simply a brief illustration of my countless attributes,
because there is no end to my divine manifestations.
41 All that is endowed with glory, grace, and grandeur,
has sprung from a mere flare of my radiance.

42 But what is the use of all this information, Arjuna?
Just remember that I stand holding the entire cosmos
with a fraction of my divine splendor.

Kṛṣṇa mentions all these things because Arjuna asked him for the ways in which he could relate to the Supreme. It is evident that Kṛṣṇa uses the examples already known to Arjuna. Finally, he reminds Arjuna that the focus should be on the sublime and not the mundane.

11

अर्जुन उवाच ।
मदनुग्रहाय परमं
गुह्यमध्यात्मसञ्ज्ञितम् ।
यत्त्वयोक्तं वचस्तेन
मोहोऽयं विगतो मम ॥ ११.१

arjuna uvāca |
madanugrahāya paramaṃ
guhyamadhyātmasañjñitam |
yattvayoktaṃ vacastena
moho'yaṃ vigato mama || 11.1

भवाप्ययौ हि भूतानां
श्रुतौ विस्तरशो मया ।
त्वत्तः कमलपत्राक्ष
माहात्म्यमपि चाव्ययम् ॥ ११.२

bhavāpyayau hi bhūtānāṃ
śrutau vistaraśo mayā |
tvattaḥ kamalapatrākṣa
māhātmyamapi cāvyayam || 11.2

एवमेतद् यथात्थ त्वम्
आत्मानं परमेश्वर ।
द्रष्टुमिच्छामि ते रूपम्
ऐश्वरं पुरुषोत्तम ॥ ११.३

evametad yathāttha tvam
ātmānaṃ parameśvara |
draṣṭumicchāmi te rūpam
aiśvaraṃ puruṣottama || 11.3

मन्यसे यदि तच्छक्यं
मया द्रष्टुमिति प्रभो ।
योगेश्वर ततो मे त्वं
दर्शयात्मानमव्ययम् ॥ ११.४

manyase yadi tacchakyaṃ
mayā draṣṭumiti prabho |
yogeśvara tato me tvaṃ
darśayātmānamavyayam || 11.4

श्रीभगवानुवाच ।
पश्य मे पार्थ रूपाणि
शतशोऽथ सहस्रशः ।
नानाविधानि दिव्यानि
नानावर्णाकृतीनि च ॥ ११.५

śrībhagavānuvāca |
paśya me pārtha rūpāṇi
śataśo'tha sahasraśaḥ |
nānāvidhāni divyāni
nānāvarṇākṛtīni ca || 11.5

पश्यादित्यान्वसून्रुद्रान्
अश्विनौ मरुतस्तथा ।
बहून्यदृष्टपूर्वाणि
पश्याश्चर्याणि भारत ॥ ११.६

paśyādityānvasūnrudrān
aśvinau marutastathā |
bahūnyadṛṣṭapūrvāṇi
paśyāścaryāṇi bhārata || 11.6

इहैकस्थं जगत्कृत्स्नं
पश्याद्य सचराचरम् ।
मम देहे गुडाकेश
यच्चान्यद्द्रष्टुमिच्छसि ॥ ११.७

ihaikasthaṃ jagatkṛtsnaṃ
paśyādya sacarācaram |
mama dehe guḍākeśa
yaccānyaddraṣṭumicchasi || 11.7

न तु मां शक्यसे द्रष्टुम्
अनेनैव स्वचक्षुषा ।
दिव्यं ददामि ते चक्षुः
पश्य मे योगमैश्वरम् ॥ ११.८

na tu māṃ śakyase draṣṭum
anenaiva svacakṣuṣā ।
divyaṃ dadāmi te cakṣuḥ
paśya me yogamaiśvaram ॥ 11.8

सञ्जय उवाच ।
एवमुक्त्वा ततो राजन्
महायोगेश्वरो हरिः ।
दर्शयामास पार्थाय
परमं रूपमैश्वरम् ॥ ११.९

sañjaya uvāca ।
evamuktvā tato rājan
mahāyogeśvaro hariḥ ।
darśayāmāsa pārthāya
paramaṃ rūpamaiśvaram ॥ 11.9

अनेकवक्त्रनयनम्
अनेकाद्भुतदर्शनम् ।
अनेकदिव्याभरणं
दिव्यानेकोद्यतायुधम् ॥ ११.१०

anekavaktranayanam
anekādbhutadarśanam ।
anekadivyābharaṇaṃ
divyānekodyatāyudham ॥ 11.10

दिव्यमाल्याम्बरधरं
दिव्यगन्धानुलेपनम् ।
सर्वाश्चर्यमयं देवम्
अनन्तं विश्वतोमुखम् ॥ ११.११

divyamālyāmbaradharaṃ
divyagandhānulepanam ।
sarvāścaryamayaṃ devam
anantaṃ viśvatomukham ॥ 11.11

दिवि सूर्यसहस्रस्य
भवेद्युगपदुत्थिता ।
यदि भाः सदृशी सा स्यात्
भासस्तस्य महात्मनः ॥ ११.१२

divi sūryasahasrasya
bhavedyugapadutthitā ।
yadi bhāḥ sadṛśī sā syāt
bhāsastasya mahātmanaḥ ॥ 11.12

तत्रैकस्थं जगत्कृत्स्नं
प्रविभक्तमनेकधा ।
अपश्यद्देवदेवस्य
शरीरे पाण्डवस्तदा ॥ ११.१३

tatraikasthaṃ jagatkṛtsnaṃ
pravibhaktamanekadhā ।
apaśyaddevadevasya
śarīre pāṇḍavastadā ॥ 11.13

ततः स विस्मयाविष्टो
हृष्टरोमा धनञ्जयः ।
प्रणम्य शिरसा देवं
कृताञ्जलिरभाषत ॥ ११.१४

tataḥ sa vismayāviṣṭo
hṛṣṭaromā dhanañjayaḥ ।
praṇamya śirasā devaṃ
kṛtāñjalirabhāṣata ॥ 11.14

अर्जुन उवाच ।
पश्यामि देवांस्तव देव देहे
सर्वांस्तथा भूतविशेषसङ्घान् ।
ब्रह्माणमीशं कमलासनस्थम्
ऋषींश्च सर्वानुरगांश्च दिव्यान् ॥ ११.१५

arjuna uvāca ।
paśyāmi devāṃstava deva dehe
sarvāṃstathā bhūtaviśeṣasaṅghān ।
brahmāṇamīśaṃ kamalāsanastham
ṛṣīṃśca sarvānuragāṃśca divyān ॥ 11.15

अनेकबाहूदरवक्त्रनेत्रं
पश्यामि त्वा सर्वतोऽनन्तरूपम् ।
नान्तं न मध्यं न पुनस्तवादिं
पश्यामि विश्वेश्वर विश्वरूप ॥ ११.१६

anekabāhūdaravaktranetraṃ
paśyāmi tvā sarvato'nantarūpam ।
nāntaṃ na madhyaṃ na punastavādiṃ
paśyāmi viśveśvara viśvarūpa ॥ 11.16

किरीटिनं गदिनं चक्रिणं च
तेजोराशिं सर्वतो दीप्तिमन्तम् ।
पश्यामि त्वां दुर्निरीक्ष्यं समन्ताद्
दीप्तानलार्कद्युतिमप्रमेयम् ॥ ११.१७

kirīṭinaṃ gadinaṃ cakriṇaṃ ca
tejorāśiṃ sarvato dīptimantam ।
paśyāmi tvāṃ durnirīkṣyaṃ samantād
dīptānalārkadyutimaprameyam ॥ 11.17

त्वमक्षरं परमं वेदितव्यं
त्वमस्य विश्वस्य परं निधानम् ।
त्वमव्ययः शाश्वतधर्मगोप्ता
सनातनस्त्वं पुरुषो मतो मे ॥ ११.१८

tvamakṣaraṃ paramaṃ veditavyaṃ
tvamasya viśvasya paraṃ nidhānam ।
tvamavyayaḥ śāśvatadharmagoptā
sanātanastvaṃ puruṣo mato me ॥ 11.18

अनादिमध्यान्तमनन्तवीर्यम्
अनन्तबाहुं शशिसूर्यनेत्रम् ।
पश्यामि त्वां दीप्तहुताशवक्त्रं
स्वतेजसा विश्वमिदं तपन्तम् ॥ ११.१९

anādimadhyāntamanantavīryam
anantabāhuṃ śaśisūryanetram ।
paśyāmi tvāṃ dīptahutāśavaktraṃ
svatejasā viśvamidaṃ tapantam ॥ 11.19

द्यावापृथिव्योरिदमन्तरं हि
व्याप्तं त्वयैकेन दिशश्च सर्वाः ।
दृष्ट्वाद्भुतं रूपमिदं तवोग्रं
लोकत्रयं प्रव्यथितं महात्मन् ॥ ११.२०

dyāvāpṛthivyoridamantaraṃ hi
vyāptaṃ tvayaikena diśaśca sarvāḥ ।
dṛṣṭvādbhutaṃ rūpamidaṃ tavograṃ
lokatrayaṃ pravyathitaṃ mahātman ॥ 11.20

अमी हि त्वा सुरसङ्घा विशन्ति
केचिद्भीताः प्राञ्जलयो गृणन्ति ।
स्वस्तीत्युक्त्वा महर्षिसिद्धसङ्घाः
स्तुवन्ति त्वां स्तुतिभिः पुष्कलाभिः ॥ ११.२१

amī hi tvā surasaṅghā viśanti
kecidbhītāḥ prāñjalayo gṛṇanti ।
svastītyuktvā maharṣisiddhasaṅghāḥ
stuvanti tvāṃ stutibhiḥ puṣkalābhiḥ ॥ 11.21

रुद्रादित्या वसवो ये च साध्या	*rudrādityā vasavo ye ca sādhyā*
विश्वेऽश्विनौ मरुतश्चोष्मपाश्च ।	*viśve'śvinau marutaścoṣmapāśca* ।
गन्धर्वयक्षासुरसिद्धसङ्घा	*gandharvayakṣāsurasiddhasaṅghā*
वीक्षन्ते त्वा विस्मिताश्चैव सर्वे ॥ ११.२२	*vīkṣante tvā vismitāścaiva sarve* ॥ 11.22
रूपं महत्ते बहुवक्त्रनेत्रं	*rūpaṃ mahatte bahuvaktranetraṃ*
महाबाहो बहुबाहूरुपादम् ।	*mahābāho bahubāhūrupādam* ।
बहूदरं बहुदंष्ट्राकरालं	*bahūdaraṃ bahudaṃṣṭrākarālaṃ*
दृष्ट्वा लोकाः प्रव्यथितास्तथाहम् ॥ ११.२३	*dṛṣṭvā lokāḥ pravyathitāstathāham* ॥ 11.23
नभःस्पृशं दीप्तमनेकवर्णं	*nabhaḥspṛśaṃ dīptamanekavarṇaṃ*
व्यात्ताननं दीप्तविशालनेत्रम् ।	*vyāttānanaṃ dīptaviśālanetram* ।
दृष्ट्वा हि त्वां प्रव्यथितान्तरात्मा	*dṛṣṭvā hi tvāṃ pravyathitāntarātmā*
धृतिं न विन्दामि शमं च विष्णो ॥ ११.२४	*dhṛtiṃ na vindāmi śamaṃ ca viṣṇo* ॥ 11.24
दंष्ट्राकरालानि च ते मुखानि	*daṃṣṭrākarālāni ca te mukhāni*
दृष्ट्वैव कालानलसंनिभानि ।	*dṛṣṭvaiva kālānalasaṃnibhāni* ।
दिशो न जाने न लभे च शर्म	*diśo na jāne na labhe ca śarma*
प्रसीद देवेश जगन्निवास ॥ ११.२५	*prasīda deveśa jagannivāsa* ॥ 11.25
अमी च त्वां धृतराष्ट्रस्य पुत्राः	*amī ca tvāṃ dhṛtarāṣṭrasya putrāḥ*
सर्वे सहैवावनिपालसङ्घैः ।	*sarve sahaivāvanipālasaṅghaiḥ* ।
भीष्मो द्रोणः सूतपुत्रस्तथासौ	*bhīṣmo droṇaḥ sūtaputrastathāsau*
सहास्मदीयैरपि योधमुख्यैः ॥ ११.२६	*sahāsmadīyairapi yodhamukhyaiḥ* ॥ 11.26
वक्त्राणि ते त्वरमाणा विशन्ति	*vaktrāṇi te tvaramāṇā viśanti*
दंष्ट्राकरालानि भयानकानि ।	*daṃṣṭrākarālāni bhayānakāni* ।
केचिद् विलग्ना दशनान्तरेषु	*kecid vilagnā daśanāntareṣu*
सन्दृश्यन्ते चूर्णितैरुत्तमाङ्गैः ॥ ११.२७	*sandṛśyante cūrṇitairuttamāṅgaiḥ* ॥ 11.27
यथा नदीनां बहवोऽम्बुवेगाः	*yathā nadīnāṃ bahavo'mbuvegāḥ*
समुद्रमेवाभिमुखा द्रवन्ति ।	*samudramevābhimukhā dravanti* ।
तथा तवामी नरलोकवीरा	*tathā tavāmī naralokavīrā*
विशन्ति वक्त्राण्यभिविज्वलन्ति ॥ ११.२८	*viśanti vaktrāṇyabhivijvalanti* ॥ 11.28
यथा प्रदीप्तं ज्वलनं पतङ्गा	*yathā pradīptaṃ jvalanaṃ pataṅgā*
विशन्ति नाशाय समृद्धवेगाः ।	*viśanti nāśāya samṛddhavegāḥ* ।
तथैव नाशाय विशन्ति लोकाः	*tathaiva nāśāya viśanti lokāḥ*
तवापि वक्त्राणि समृद्धवेगाः ॥ ११.२९	*tavāpi vaktrāṇi samṛddhavegāḥ* ॥ 11.29

लेलिह्यसे ग्रसमानः समन्तात्
लोकान्समग्रान्वदनैर्ज्वलद्भिः ।
तेजोभिरापूर्य जगत्समग्रं
भासस्तवोग्राः प्रतपन्ति विष्णो ॥ ११.३०

lelihyase grasamānaḥ samantāt
lokānsamagrānvadanairjvaladbhiḥ ।
tejobhirāpūrya jagatsamagraṃ
bhāsastavogrāḥ pratapanti viṣṇo ॥ 11.30

आख्याहि मे को भवानुग्ररूपो
नमोऽस्तु ते देववर प्रसीद ।
विज्ञातुमिच्छामि भवन्तमाद्यं
न हि प्रजानामि तव प्रवृत्तिम् ॥ ११.३१

ākhyāhi me ko bhavānugrarūpo
namo'stu te devavara prasīda ।
vijñātumicchāmi bhavantamādyaṃ
na hi prajānāmi tava pravṛttim ॥ 11.31

श्रीभगवानुवाच ।
कालोऽस्मि लोकक्षयकृत् प्रवृद्धो
लोकान्समाहर्तुमिह प्रवृत्तः ।
ऋतेऽपि त्वा न भविष्यन्ति सर्वे
येऽवस्थिताः प्रत्यनीकेषु योधाः ॥ ११.३२

śrībhagavānuvāca ।
kālo'smi lokakṣayakṛt pravṛddho
lokānsamāhartumiha pravṛttaḥ ।
ṛte'pi tvā na bhaviṣyanti sarve
ye'vasthitāḥ pratyanīkeṣu yodhāḥ ॥ 11.32

तस्मात्त्वमुत्तिष्ठ यशो लभस्व
जित्वा शत्रून्भुङ्क्ष्व राज्यं समृद्धम् ।
मयैवैते निहताः पूर्वमेव
निमित्तमात्रं भव सव्यसाचिन् ॥ ११.३३

tasmāttvamuttiṣṭha yaśo labhasva
jitvā śatrūnbhuṅkṣva rājyaṃ samṛddham ।
mayaivaite nihatāḥ pūrvameva
nimittamātraṃ bhava savyasācin ॥ 11.33

द्रोणं च भीष्मं च जयद्रथं च
कर्णं तथान्यानपि योधवीरान् ।
मया हतांस्त्वं जहि मा व्यथिष्ठा
युध्यस्व जेतासि रणे सपत्नान् ॥ ११.३४

droṇaṃ ca bhīṣmaṃ ca jayadrathaṃ ca
karṇaṃ tathānyānapi yodhavīrān ।
mayā hatāṃstvaṃ jahi mā vyathiṣṭhā
yudhyasva jetāsi raṇe sapatnān ॥ 11.34

सञ्जय उवाच ।
एतच्छ्रुत्वा वचनं केशवस्य
कृताञ्जलिर्वेपमानः किरीटी ।
नमस्कृत्वा भूय एवाह कृष्णं
सगद्गदं भीतभीतः प्रणम्य ॥ ११.३५

sañjaya uvāca ।
etacchrutvā vacanaṃ keśavasya
kṛtāñjalirvepamānaḥ kirīṭī ।
namaskṛtvā bhūya evāha kṛṣṇaṃ
sagadgadaṃ bhītabhītaḥ praṇamya ॥ 11.35

अर्जुन उवाच ।
स्थाने हृषीकेश तव प्रकीर्त्या
जगत्प्रहृष्यत्यनुरज्यते च ।
रक्षांसि भीतानि दिशो द्रवन्ति
सर्वे नमस्यन्ति च सिद्धसङ्घाः ॥ ११.३६

arjuna uvāca ।
sthāne hṛṣīkeśa tava prakīrtyā
jagatprahṛṣyatyanurajyate ca ।
rakṣāṃsi bhītāni diśo dravanti
sarve namasyanti ca siddhasaṅghāḥ ॥ 11.36

कस्माच्च ते न नमेरन्महात्मन्	*kasmācca te na nameranmahātman*
गरीयसे ब्रह्मणोऽप्य् आदिकर्त्रे ।	*garīyase brahmaṇo'py ādikartre* ।
अनन्त देवेश जगन्निवास	*ananta deveśa jagannivāsa*
त्वमक्षरं सदसत्तत्परं यत् ॥ ११.३७	*tvamakṣaraṃ sadasattatparaṃ yat* ॥ 11.37
त्वमादिदेवः पुरुषः पुराणः	*tvamādidevaḥ puruṣaḥ purāṇaḥ*
त्वमस्य विश्वस्य परं निधानम् ।	*tvamasya viśvasya paraṃ nidhānam* ।
वेत्तासि वेद्यं च परं च धाम	*vettāsi vedyaṃ ca paraṃ ca dhāma*
त्वया ततं विश्वमनन्तरूप ॥ ११.३८	*tvayā tataṃ viśvamanantarūpa* ॥ 11.38
वायुर्यमोऽग्निर्वरुणः शशाङ्कः	*vāyuryamo'gnirvaruṇaḥ śaśāṅkaḥ*
प्रजापतिस्त्वं प्रपितामहश्च ।	*prajāpatistvaṃ prapitāmahaśca* ।
नमो नमस्तेऽस्तु सहस्रकृत्वः	*namo namaste'stu sahasrakṛtvaḥ*
पुनश्च भूयोऽपि नमो नमस्ते ॥ ११.३९	*punaśca bhūyo'pi namo namaste* ॥ 11.39
नमः पुरस्तादथ पृष्ठतस्ते	*namaḥ purastādatha pṛṣṭhataste*
नमोऽस्तु ते सर्वत एव सर्व ।	*namo'stu te sarvata eva sarva* ।
अनन्तवीर्यामितविक्रमस्त्वं	*anantavīryāmitavikramastvaṃ*
सर्वं समाप्नोषि ततोऽसि सर्वः ॥ ११.४०	*sarvaṃ samāpnoṣi tato'si sarvaḥ* ॥ 11.40
सखेति मत्वा प्रसभं यदुक्तं	*sakheti matvā prasabhaṃ yaduktaṃ*
हे कृष्ण हे यादव हे सखेति ।	*he kṛṣṇa he yādava he sakheti* ।
अजानता महिमानं तवेदं	*ajānatā mahimānaṃ tavedaṃ*
मया प्रमादात्प्रणयेन वापि ॥ ११.४१	*mayā pramādātpraṇayena vāpi* ॥ 11.41
यच्चावहासार्थमसत्कृतोऽसि	*yaccāvahāsārthamasatkṛto'si*
विहारशय्यासनभोजनेषु ।	*vihāraśayyāsanabhojaneṣu* ।
एकोऽथ वाप्यच्युत तत्समक्षं	*eko'tha vāpyacyuta tatsamakṣaṃ*
तत्क्षामये त्वामहमप्रमेयम् ॥ ११.४२	*tatkṣāmaye tvāmahamaprameyam* ॥ 11.42
पितासि लोकस्य चराचरस्य	*pitāsi lokasya carācarasya*
त्वमस्य पूज्यश्च गुरुर्गरीयान् ।	*tvamasya pūjyaśca gururgarīyān* ।
न त्वत्समोऽस्त्यभ्यधिकः कुतोऽन्यो	*na tvatsamo'styabhyadhikaḥ kuto'nyo*
लोकत्रयेऽप्यप्रतिमप्रभाव ॥ ११.४३	*lokatraye'pyapratimaprabhāva* ॥ 11.43
तस्मात्प्रणम्य प्रणिधाय कायं	*tasmātpraṇamya praṇidhāya kāyaṃ*
प्रसादये त्वामहमीशमीड्यम् ।	*prasādaye tvāmahamīśamīḍyam* ।
पितेव पुत्रस्य सखेव सख्युः	*piteva putrasya sakheva sakhyuḥ*
प्रियः प्रियायार्हसि देव सोढुम् ॥ ११.४४	*priyaḥ priyāyārhasi deva soḍhum* ॥ 11.44

अदृष्टपूर्वं हृषितोऽस्मि दृष्ट्वा भयेन च प्रव्यथितं मनो मे । तदेव मे दर्शय देव रूपं प्रसीद देवेश जगन्निवास ॥ ११.४५	*adṛṣṭapūrvaṃ hṛṣito'smi dṛṣṭvā* *bhayena ca pravyathitaṃ mano me* । *tadeva me darśaya deva rūpaṃ* *prasīda deveśa jagannivāsa* ॥ 11.45
किरीटिनं गदिनं चक्रहस्तम् इच्छामि त्वां द्रष्टुमहं तथैव । तेनैव रूपेण चतुर्भुजेन सहस्रबाहो भव विश्वमूर्ते ॥ ११.४६	*kirīṭinaṃ gadinaṃ cakrahastam* *icchāmi tvāṃ draṣṭumahaṃ tathaiva* । *tenaiva rūpeṇa caturbhujena* *sahasrabāho bhava viśvamūrte* ॥ 11.46
श्रीभगवानुवाच । मया प्रसन्नेन तवार्जुनेदं रूपं परं दर्शितमात्मयोगात् । तेजोमयं विश्वमनन्तमाद्यं यन्मे त्वदन्येन न दृष्टपूर्वम् ॥ ११.४७	***śrībhagavānuvāca*** । *mayā prasannena tavārjunedaṃ* *rūpaṃ paraṃ darśitamātmayogāt* । *tejomayaṃ viśvamanantamādyaṃ* *yanme tvadanyena na dṛṣṭapūrvam* ॥ 11.47
न वेदयज्ञाध्ययनैर्न दानैर् न च क्रियाभिर्न तपोभिरुग्रैः । एवंरूपः शक्य अहं नृलोके द्रष्टुं त्वदन्येन कुरुप्रवीर ॥ ११.४८	*na vedayajñādhyayanairna dānair* *na ca kriyābhirna tapobhirugraiḥ* । *evaṃrūpaḥ śakya ahaṃ nṛloke* *draṣṭuṃ tvadanyena kurupravīra* ॥ 11.48
मा ते व्यथा मा च विमूढभावो दृष्ट्वा रूपं घोरमीदृङ्ममेदम् । व्यपेतभीः प्रीतमनाः पुनस्त्वं तदेव मे रूपमिदं प्रपश्य ॥ ११.४९	*mā te vyathā mā ca vimūḍhabhāvo* *dṛṣṭvā rūpaṃ ghoramīdṛṅmamedam* । *vyapetabhīḥ prītamanāḥ punastvaṃ* *tadeva me rūpamidaṃ prapaśya* ॥ 11.49
सञ्जय उवाच । इत्यर्जुनं वासुदेवस्तथोक्त्वा स्वकं रूपं दर्शयामास भूयः । आश्वासयामास च भीतमेनं भूत्वा पुनः सौम्यवपुर्महात्मा ॥ ११.५०	***sañjaya uvāca*** । *ityarjunaṃ vāsudevastathoktvā* *svakaṃ rūpaṃ darśayāmāsa bhūyaḥ* । *āśvāsayāmāsa ca bhītamenaṃ* *bhūtvā punaḥ saumyavapurmahātmā* ॥ 11.50
अर्जुन उवाच । दृष्ट्वेदं मानुषं रूपं तव सौम्यं जनार्दन । इदानीमस्मि संवृत्तः सचेताः प्रकृतिं गतः ॥ ११.५१	***arjuna uvāca*** । *dṛṣṭvedaṃ mānuṣaṃ rūpaṃ* *tava saumyaṃ janārdana* । *idānīmasmi saṃvṛttaḥ* *sacetāḥ prakṛtiṃ gataḥ* ॥ 11.51

श्रीभगवानुवाच ।
सुदुर्दर्शमिदं रूपं
दृष्टवानसि यन्मम ।
देवा अप्यस्य रूपस्य
नित्यं दर्शनकाङ्क्षिणः ॥ ११.५२

śrībhagavānuvāca ।
sudurdarśamidaṃ rūpaṃ
dṛṣṭavānasi yanmama ।
devā apyasya rūpasya
nityaṃ darśanakāṅkṣiṇaḥ ॥ 11.52

नाहं वेदैर्न तपसा
न दानेन न चेज्यया ।
शक्य एवंविधो द्रष्टुं
दृष्टवानसि मां यथा ॥ ११.५३

nāhaṃ vedairna tapasā
na dānena na cejyayā ।
śakya evaṃvidho draṣṭuṃ
dṛṣṭavānasi māṃ yathā ॥ 11.53

भक्त्या त्वनन्यया शक्य
अहमेवंविधोऽर्जुन ।
ज्ञातुं द्रष्टुं च तत्त्वेन
प्रवेष्टुं च परन्तप ॥ ११.५४

bhaktyā tvananyayā śakya
ahamevaṃvidho'rjuna ।
jñātuṃ draṣṭuṃ ca tattvena
praveṣṭuṃ ca parantapa ॥ 11.54

मत्कर्मकृन्मत्परमो
मद्भक्तः सङ्गवर्जितः ।
निर्वैरः सर्वभूतेषु
यः स मामेति पाण्डव ॥ ११.५५

matkarmakṛnmatparamo
madbhaktaḥ saṅgavarjitaḥ ।
nirvairaḥ sarvabhūteṣu
yaḥ sa māmeti pāṇḍava ॥ 11.55

CHAPTER 11

Universal Form

Arjuna

[1]You have graciously taught me
the grand spiritual truth
of the Supreme Self.
Your words have cleared my delusion.

[2]You have taught me in detail
about the origin and dissolution of everything
and also about your own imperishable majesty.

[3–4]O magnificent lord and master of *yoga*!
Now I wish to see you with all your divine splendor
just the way you have described it.

If you think that it is possible for me
to see your divine form,
then please show it to me.

Kṛṣṇa

5 Arjuna see my divine forms
by the hundreds or by the thousands
of many colors and shapes.
6 Behold many marvels never seen before!
Look at all the *ādityas*, the *vasus*, the *rudras*,
the Aśvins, and the *maruts*.

The *ādityas* are the twelve children of Sage Kaśyapa and his first wife Aditi.
The *vasus* are divinities presiding over the elements of nature.
The *rudras* are a group of storm gods.
Aśvins are the divine twins who are the physicians of the gods
and are believed to witness all religious ceremonies.
The *maruts* are a group of wind gods.

7 Now, you can see in my body
the assembly of the entire universe,
with every animate and inanimate being
and whatever else you wish to see.

8 I grant you divine vision;
else, you won't be able to see
my universal form.

Sañjaya

9 Having said this, O king,
the great master of *yoga* revealed
his majestic universal form to Arjuna.

[10–11]With countless mouths and eyes,
sporting many divine ornaments, garlands, and garments;
anointed with heavenly fragrances and
armed with divine weapons ready to strike,
the infinite and all-pervading god is full of wonder.

[12]If a thousand suns were to appear in the sky all at once,
the brilliance of their light would perhaps
resemble the splendor of this glorious being.

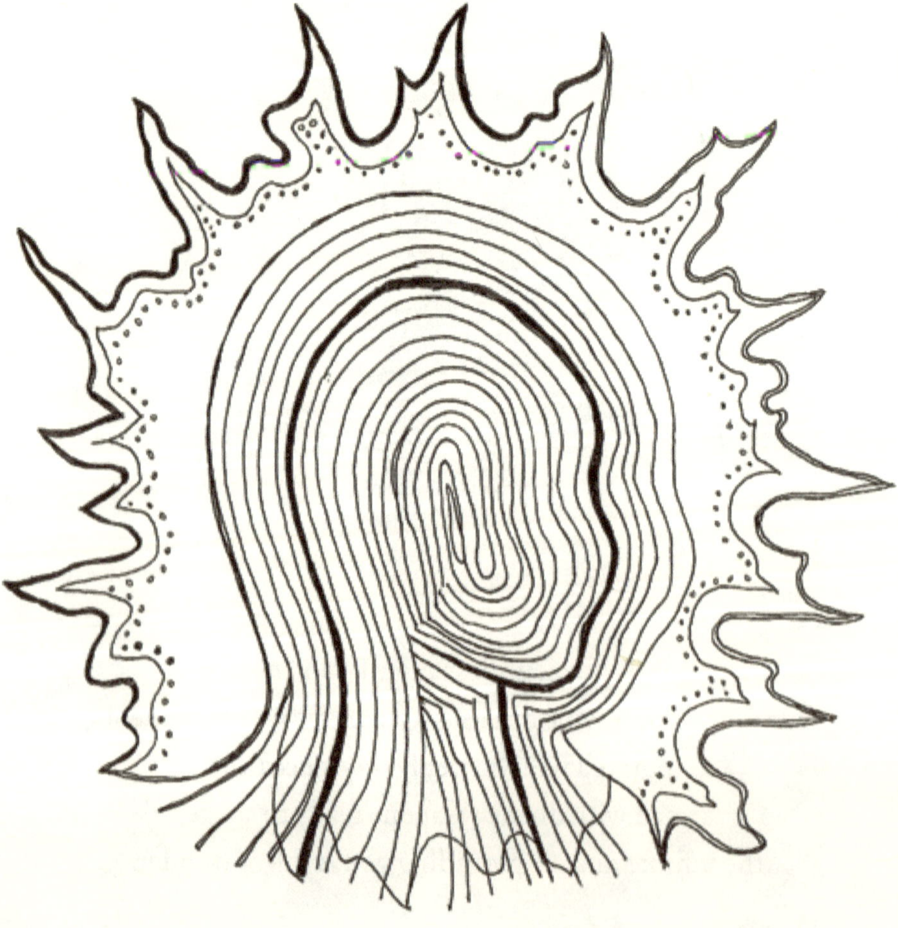

[13]Within the body of the lord of lords,
Arjuna saw the entire universe
with its countless elements
gathered together as one.

[14]Wonderstruck, with his hair standing on end
and hands folded in salutation,
Arjuna bowed down to the lord, and said –

Arjuna

[15–16]O lord of the universe
and essence of the cosmos!
In your body, I see the *devas*,
the *ṛṣis*, the divine snakes,
Lord Brahmā seated on his lotus throne,
and beings of all forms and shapes.

*Deva*s are divine beings, *ṛṣi*s are seer-sages, and divine snakes refer to serpents with special powers.

I see you everywhere,
with countless arms, bellies, mouths and eyes;
but I see neither your beginning nor middle nor end.

The universal form is a seamless joining of space-time pieces; due to the sheer magnitude of the universal form, Arjuna is unable to see any boundaries.

17 I see you wearing a crown
and holding a mace and a discus.

The mace and the discus are two of Kṛṣṇa's divine weapons.

Your brilliance spreads in all directions
with the radiance of the sun and a blazing fire.

It is difficult to fathom
your immeasurable form.

18 You are the imperishable, supreme being
worthy to be known.
You are the purpose of all knowledge.
You are the ultimate abode
of the universe.
You are the guardian
of the eternal law and order.
You are the primeval spirit.

19 You are without beginning, middle, or end.
You have countless arms with infinite power,
with the sun and the moon as your eyes.

Your face glows like the burning fire,
whose radiance burns the whole world.

[20]You pervade the entire space
between *svarga* and earth
and all the quarters.
The three worlds tremble
upon seeing your intimidating form.

The three worlds or the three 'realms of existence' are:
earth, *svarga* (loosely, 'heavens'), and the skies.
The three realms may also refer to past, present, and future.

[21]Hordes of deities are entering your body;
some of them, out of fear, are greeting you reverently.

Many great *ṛṣis* and *siddhas*
are singing your glory
with lofty verses of praise,
chanting: "May all be well!"

Siddhas are people who have attained a high degree of perfection.

[22]The *rudras*, *ādityas*, *vasus*, *sādhyas*,
viśvedevas, Aśvins, *maruts*, *uṣmapas*, and
several *gandharvas*, *yakṣas*, *asuras*, and *siddhas*–
all of them are looking at you with awe.

The *sādhyas* are a group of accomplished ancient seers who are not bound by time.
Viśvedevas are the group of *Vedic* deities taken as a whole. *Uṣmapas* are ancestors.
The *gandharvas* are a group of divine artists and musicians.
Yakṣas are spirits with special powers; they are semi-divine and benevolent.
The *asuras* are a demonic group, opposed to the *devas*.

[23]O mighty-armed one!
Seeing your immense form
with countless mouths and eyes,
with numerous arms, feet, and thighs, and
with several bellies and dreadful tusks,
the whole world is terrified, and so am I.

[24]I shudder
seeing your body
glow in different colors,
stretched as far as the sky,
with wide-open mouths
and large fiery eyes;
I am terrified when I look at it.
I find neither courage nor calm.

[25]Seeing your mouths with terrible tusks
blazing like the fire at the end of time.
I lose sense of direction and find no peace.
Have mercy on me, O refuge of the universe!

[26–27]I see all the sons of Dhṛtarāṣṭra,
Bhīṣma, Droṇa, Karṇa, and various various kings;
I see our own chief warriors and hosts of others
rushing into your dreadful mouths with fearful teeth.

Many of them are getting stuck between your teeth
and their heads are getting crushed to powder.

[28–29]Just as rivers having many torrents
swiftly flow into ocean and
as moths are drawn into the blazing fire
only to be burnt,
so do these heroes of the world
rush into your mouths
for their own destruction.

[30]You are hungrily licking up and devouring
all the worlds from every side
with your fiery mouths.
Your brilliance is scorching
the entire universe!

[31]I bow to you,
O foremost among gods!

Have mercy on me and
tell me who you are,
in this dreadful form.

I don't understand your true nature or purpose!

Kṛṣṇa

32–34 I am Time, the mighty destroyer of the world!
I am engaged now in the destruction of all creation.
With or without you, all these warriors shall die,
for I have already killed them.
Therefore, arise and be victorious!
Fight merely to show the world your skill in archery.

Do not hesitate; kill Droṇa, Bhīṣma, Karṇa,
Jayadratha, and other brave warriors,
whom I have already killed.
Conquer your enemies and
enjoy the bountiful kingdom.
Be fearless! Fight!
You will win!

SAÑJAYA

35 Hearing Kṛṣṇa's words, Arjuna, trembling
and with palms joined in prayer, offered salutations.
Overwhelmed with fear,
he prostrated over and over again,
and spoke in a choked, faltering voice.

ARJUNA

36 *Rākṣasa*s run away from you in all directions,
while the rest of the world
is truly delighted to sing your glory and
hoards of *siddha*s are bowing to you with respect.

37 And why would they not bow to you,
O great one?
You are the primeval cause,
greater than even Lord Brahmā.

You are infinite and imperishable,
the abode of the universe and the lord of gods.
You are what all there is, what there isn't, and beyond that.

38 You are the primal god, the primordial person;
you are the ultimate refuge of the universe.

You are the knower and the goal of knowledge.

You are the supreme abode and
you pervade the universe
with your infinite form.

39 You are Yama, Vāyu, Agni, Varuṇa,
Śaśāṅka, and the grandsire Prajāpati.
I salute you a thousand times,
and over and over again.

Yama is the god of death. He accords punishments to people during afterlife for the *pāpa* (evil, sin, crime) they committed in their lives. Vāyu is the wind god. Agni is the deity of fire. Varuṇa is the water god (and the deity of cosmic order). Śaśāṅka is the moon deity. Prajāpati is the lord of the creatures and the progenitor of the universe.

40 I salute you from every direction!
You have unfathomable energy
and immeasurable courage.
You pervade everything;
therefore you are everything.

41–42 Taking you for granted as a mere friend
and unaware of your greatness,
I have arrogantly addressed you as:
"Hey Kṛṣṇa," "Hey Yādava," and "Hey companion!"
perhaps out familiarity or sheer carelessness.

In whatever other ways
I may have jokingly offended you,
while at play or at rest,
during conversations or at meals,
either alone or in the company of others –
please forgive me for everything.

43 You are the father of the universe,
of the animate and the inanimate;
you are the object of worship and the greatest teacher;
there is no one equal to you in the three worlds.
You are of incomparable greatness!
How can any other be greater than you?

44 Therefore, I offer my respects and
plead you to have mercy on me;
just as a father pardons his son,
a friend forgives another,
or a lover is kind to his beloved,
you be merciful to me!

45–46 O thousand-armed one!
I am delighted to have seen this rare form,
never seen before and yet I am trembling.
I wish to see you as before!

Please assume that four-armed form,
wearing a crown and holding a mace and discus.
Be kind to me and show me your familiar form!

Kṛṣṇa

47 With my *yogic* power and grace
I have revealed to you my universal form –
infinite, unique, and full of splendor.
Apart from you, no one has seen this form before.
48 Neither by worship nor by scholarship
nor through charitable or pious activities
and not even by severe austerities
can anyone else see me in this form.

This form was shown for the sake of Arjuna; Sañjaya saw it by default.

49 Don't be afraid having seen my dreadful form.
Free from fear and with a light heart,
see my gentle form, which is familiar to you.

Sañjaya

50 Saying thus, Kṛṣṇa revealed his previous form.
The terrified Arjuna was reassured
once Kṛṣṇa took on his pleasant form.

Arjuna

51 I now feel at ease, having seen your human form.

Kṛṣṇa

52 The universal form of mine
that you have seen is very rare.
Even the *devas* are always longing
to see me in that form.
53 Neither by study of the *Vedas*
nor by *yajña*, *dāna*, and *tapas*
can anyone see me the way you have.

Yajña is the *Vedic* fire ritual, which inolves
worship of the divine, interaction, and sharing.
In a broader sense, it refers to a sense of dedication to work.
Dāna is charity that is undertaken with a feeling that it is one's duty to give
and includes offering the right gift to the deserving person at an appropriate time.
Tapas refers to austerity, penance, and single-minded focus on work.

54 But I may be known, seen, and attained
through single-minded devotion.

55 One who is truly devoted to me
dedicates all actions to me
and looks upon me as Supreme;
he is free from attachments
and he does not hate anyone.
Without doubt, he attains me.

12

अर्जुन उवाच ।
एवं सततयुक्ता ये
भक्तास्त्वां पर्युपासते ।
ये चाप्यक्षरमव्यक्तं
तेषां के योगवित्तमाः ॥ १२.१

arjuna uvāca ।
evaṃ satatayuktā ye
bhaktāstvāṃ paryupāsate ।
ye cāpyakṣaramavyaktaṃ
teṣāṃ ke yogavittamāḥ ॥ 12.1

श्रीभगवानुवाच ।
मय्यावेश्य मनो ये मां
नित्ययुक्ता उपासते ।
श्रद्धया परयोपेताः
ते मे युक्ततमा मताः ॥ १२.२

śrībhagavānuvāca ।
mayyāveśya mano ye māṃ
nityayuktā upāsate ।
śraddhayā parayopetāḥ
te me yuktatamā matāḥ ॥ 12.2

ये त्वक्षरमनिर्देश्यम्
अव्यक्तं पर्युपासते ।
सर्वत्रगमचिन्त्यं च
कूटस्थमचलं ध्रुवम् ॥ १२.३

ye tvakṣaramanirdeśyam
avyaktaṃ paryupāsate ।
sarvatragamacintyaṃ ca
kūṭasthamacalaṃ dhruvam ॥ 12.3

संनियम्येन्द्रियग्रामं
सर्वत्र समबुद्धयः ।
ते प्राप्नुवन्ति मामेव
सर्वभूतहिते रताः ॥ १२.४

saṃniyamyendriyagrāmaṃ
sarvatra samabuddhayaḥ ।
te prāpnuvanti māmeva
sarvabhūtahite ratāḥ ॥ 12.4

क्लेशोऽधिकतरस्तेषाम्
अव्यक्तासक्तचेतसाम् ।
अव्यक्ता हि गतिर्दुःखं
देहवद्भिरवाप्यते ॥ १२.५

kleśo'dhikatarasteṣām
avyaktāsaktacetasām ।
avyaktā hi gatirduḥkhaṃ
dehavadbhiravāpyate ॥ 12.5

ये तु सर्वाणि कर्माणि
मयि संन्यस्य मत्पराः ।
अनन्येनैव योगेन मां
ध्यायन्त उपासते ॥ १२.६

ye tu sarvāṇi karmāṇi
mayi saṃnyasya matparāḥ ।
ananyenaiva yogena māṃ
dhyāyanta upāsate ॥ 12.6

तेषामहं समुद्धर्ता
मृत्युसंसारसागरात् ।
भवामि नचिरात् पार्थ
मय्यावेशितचेतसाम् ॥ १२.७

teṣāmahaṃ samuddhartā
mṛtyusaṃsārasāgarāt ।
bhavāmi nacirāt pārtha
mayyāveśitacetasām ॥ 12.7

मय्येव मन आधत्स्व मयि बुद्धिं निवेशय। निवसिष्यसि मय्येव अत ऊर्ध्वं न संशयः॥ १२.८	*mayyeva mana ādhatsva* *mayi buddhiṃ niveśaya* । *nivasiṣyasi mayyeva* *ata ūrdhvaṃ na saṃśayaḥ* ॥ 12.8
अथ चित्तं समाधातुं न शक्नोषि मयि स्थिरम्। अभ्यासयोगेन ततो मामिच्छाप्तुं धनञ्जय॥ १२.९	*atha cittaṃ samādhātuṃ* *na śaknoṣi mayi sthiram* । *abhyāsayogena tato* *māmicchāptuṃ dhanañjaya* ॥ 12.9
अभ्यासेऽप्यसमर्थोऽसि मत्कर्मपरमो भव। मदर्थमपि कर्माणि कुर्वन्सिद्धिमवाप्स्यसि॥ १२.१०	*abhyāse'pyasamartho'si* *matkarmaparamo bhava* । *madarthamapi karmāṇi* *kurvansiddhimavāpsyasi* ॥ 12.10
अथैतदप्यशक्तोऽसि कर्तुं मद्योगमाश्रितः। सर्वकर्मफलत्यागं ततः कुरु यतात्मवान्॥ १२.११	*athaitadapyaśakto'si* *kartuṃ madyogamāśritaḥ* । *sarvakarmaphalatyāgaṃ* *tataḥ kuru yatātmavān* ॥ 12.11
श्रेयो हि ज्ञानमभ्यासात् ज्ञानाद्ध्यानं विशिष्यते। ध्यानात्कर्मफलत्यागः त्यागाच्छान्तिरनन्तरम्॥ १२.१२	*śreyo hi jñānamabhyāsāt* *jñānāddhyānaṃ viśiṣyate* । *dhyānātkarmaphalatyāgaḥ* *tyāgācchāntiranantaram* ॥ 12.12
अद्वेष्टा सर्वभूतानां मैत्रः करुण एव च। निर्ममो निरहङ्कारः समदुःखसुखः क्षमी॥ १२.१३	*adveṣṭā sarvabhūtānāṃ* *maitraḥ karuṇa eva ca* । *nirmamo nirahaṅkāraḥ* *samaduḥkhasukhaḥ kṣamī* ॥ 12.13
सन्तुष्टः सततं योगी यतात्मा दृढनिश्चयः। मय्यर्पितमनोबुद्धिः यो मद्भक्तः स मे प्रियः॥ १२.१४	*santuṣṭaḥ satataṃ yogī* *yatātmā dṛḍhaniścayaḥ* । *mayyarpitamanobuddhiḥ* *yo madbhaktaḥ sa me priyaḥ* ॥ 12.14
यस्मान्नोद्विजते लोको लोकान्नोद्विजते च यः। हर्षामर्षभयोद्वेगैः मुक्तो यः स च मे प्रियः॥ १२.१५	*yasmānnodvijate loko* *lokānnodvijate ca yaḥ* । *harṣāmarṣabhayodvegaiḥ* *mukto yaḥ sa ca me priyaḥ* ॥ 12.15

अनपेक्षः शुचिर्दक्ष	*anapekṣaḥ śucirdakṣa*
उदासीनो गतव्यथः ।	*udāsīno gatavyathaḥ* ।
सर्वारम्भपरित्यागी	*sarvārambhaparityāgī*
यो मद्भक्तः स मे प्रियः ॥ १२.१६	*yo madbhaktaḥ sa me priyaḥ* ॥ 12.16
यो न हृष्यति न द्वेष्टि	*yo na hṛṣyati na dveṣṭi*
न शोचति न काङ्क्षति ।	*na śocati na kāṅkṣati* ।
शुभाशुभपरित्यागी	*śubhāśubhaparityāgī*
भक्तिमान्यः स मे प्रियः ॥ १२.१७	*bhaktimānyaḥ sa me priyaḥ* ॥ 12.17
समः शत्रौ च मित्रे च	*samaḥ śatrau ca mitre ca*
तथा मानावमानयोः ।	*tathā mānāvamānayoḥ* ।
शीतोष्णसुखदुःखेषु	*śītoṣṇasukhaduḥkheṣu*
समः सङ्गविवर्जितः ॥ १२.१८	*samaḥ saṅgavivarjitaḥ* ॥ 12.18
तुल्यनिन्दास्तुतिर्मौनी	*tulyanindāstutirmaunī*
सन्तुष्टो येन केनचित् ।	*santuṣṭo yena kenacit* ।
अनिकेतः स्थिरमतिः	*aniketaḥ sthiramatiḥ*
भक्तिमान्मे प्रियो नरः ॥ १२.१९	*bhaktimānme priyo naraḥ* ॥ 12.19
ये तु धर्म्यामृतमिदं	*ye tu dharmyāmṛtamidaṃ*
यथोक्तं पर्युपासते ।	*yathoktaṃ paryupāsate* ।
श्रद्दधाना मत्परमा	*śraddadhānā matparamā*
भक्तास्तेऽतीव मे प्रियाः ॥ १२.२०	*bhaktāste'tīva me priyāḥ* ॥ 12.20

CHAPTER 12

Devotion

Arjuna

[1]There are people who worship you
(as a personal god with form and attributes)
with their mind fixed on you.
There are others who contemplate on
the eternal and formless.
Who among them knows *yoga* better?

Arjuna wishes to know who is better established
in *yoga* (union with Supreme) –
those who worship Kṛṣṇa as he just described (11.55)
or those who follow his earlier statement (7.24).

Kṛṣṇa

[2]In my opinion,
those who always worship me
(as a personal god with form and attributes)
with focus and faith
are better established in *yoga*.

3 Yet those who worship
the all-pervading,
the eternal, the formless,
the changeless, the inconceivable,
and the immovable,
4 with complete control over their senses,
balanced in all situations, and
rejoicing in the welfare of all,
also reach me.

5 Greater is the trouble
for those who contemplate
on the formless
for it is only through much pain
that they succeed in the path
to the invisible, formless god.

6–7 Those who worship me
by dedicating their actions to me,
considering me as the Supreme Goal,
and meditating upon me
with single-minded concentration,
I liberate them at once, O Arjuna,
from the deadly ocean of worldly life.

8 If you fix your mind and intellect on the Supreme
you will certainly reach the Supreme.
There is no doubt about this!

9 If you can't focus on the Supreme,
then try to reach the Supreme
through diligent practice.

It is easier to focus on our work than to meditate on an unseen, supreme being.

10 If you are incapable of regular practice,
try to dedicate all your actions to the Supreme.
This way, you will attain perfection.

If we realize that our work is part of the grand cosmic design,
it brings a greater purpose to the activities that we look upon as mundane.

11 But if you are unable to dedicate
all your actions to the Supreme,
act with self-restraint,
giving up the fruits of your actions.

'Fruits' of action are the rewards or results of our work.
One should ideally focus on the work and not on the result.

12 Knowledge is better than
blindly following routines.

'Routines' refers to mechanically performing an action
without understanding the underlying principles.

Contemplation is better than knowledge.

Renouncing the fruits of one's actions
is better than contemplation
because soon after this,
one attains peace.

13 One who harbors no hatred,
who is gentle and friendly to all,
who is beyond the feeling of 'I' or 'mine,'
who is poised in pain or pleasure
and is endowed with forgiveness
(is dear to me).

14 The *yogin* who is self-controlled,
always content, and of firm resolve,
with single-minded devotion to me,
is dear to me!

A *yogin* is one who is steadfast on the path of *yoga*.

15 He is dear to me
whose peace is not shaken by anyone,
who agitates not another, and
who is free from fear, restlessness,
envy, and reckless joy.

[16]One who is pure
and expects nothing,
one who is diligent,
impartial, and calm,
one who works
without selfish motives
and is devoted to me,
is dear to me!

[17]He neither revels nor hates
nor complains nor craves,
he has given up
fortune and misfortune,
and he is truly devoted.
He is dear to me!

The outcome of a process may be favorable or unfavorable; but it makes no difference to such a person because he has given up reacting to both. We tend to enjoy good fortune and complain about misfortune but such a person does neither; he just does his work.

[18]He is the same to friend and foe,
in honor and disgrace,
to heat and cold,
in pleasure and pain;
he is free from attachments!

19 Praise and criticism are the same to him,
he is contemplative and contented,
he does not care for a home,
he is steady-minded, and
he is full of devotion.
He is dear to me!

‘He does not care for a home’ indicates that
he doesn’t consider any place as home,
yet he feels at home everywhere.

20 Those who regard me as the highest goal
and practice with sincerity and faith
the immortal wisdom that I have declared
are indeed very dear to me!

13

श्रीभगवानुवाच ।
इदं शरीरं कौन्तेय
क्षेत्रमित्यभिधीयते ।
एतद्यो वेत्ति तं प्राहुः
क्षेत्रज्ञ इति तद्विदः ॥ १३.१

śrībhagavānuvāca ।
idaṃ śarīraṃ kaunteya
kṣetramityabhidhīyate ।
etadyo vetti taṃ prāhuḥ
kṣetrajña iti tadvidaḥ ॥ 13.1

क्षेत्रज्ञं चापि मां विद्धि
सर्वक्षेत्रेषु भारत ।
क्षेत्रक्षेत्रज्ञयोर्ज्ञानं
यत्तज्ज्ञानं मतं मम ॥ १३.२

kṣetrajñaṃ cāpi māṃ viddhi
sarvakṣetreṣu bhārata ।
kṣetrakṣetrajñayorjñānaṃ
yattajjñānaṃ mataṃ mama ॥ 13.2

तत् क्षेत्रं यच्च यादृक्च
यद्विकारि यतश्च यत् ।
स च यो यत्प्रभावश्च
तत् समासेन मे शृणु ॥ १३.३

tat kṣetraṃ yacca yādṛkca
yadvikāri yataśca yat ।
sa ca yo yatprabhāvaśca
tat samāsena me śṛṇu ॥ 13.3

ऋषिभिर्बहुधा गीतं
छन्दोभिर्विविधैः पृथक् ।
ब्रह्मसूत्रपदैश्चैव
हेतुमद्भिर्विनिश्चितैः ॥ १३.४

ṛṣibhirbahudhā gītaṃ
chandobhirvividhaiḥ pṛthak ।
brahmasūtrapadaiścaiva
hetumadbhirviniścitaiḥ ॥ 13.4

महाभूतान्यहङ्कारो
बुद्धिरव्यक्तमेव च ।
इन्द्रियाणि दशैकं च
पञ्च चेन्द्रियगोचराः ॥ १३.५

mahābhūtānyahaṅkāro
buddhiravyaktameva ca ।
indriyāṇi daśaikaṃ ca
pañca cendriyagocarāḥ ॥ 13.5

इच्छा द्वेषः सुखं दुःखं
सङ्घातश्चेतना धृतिः ।
एतत्क्षेत्रं समासेन
सविकारमुदाहृतम् ॥ १३.६

icchā dveṣaḥ sukhaṃ duḥkhaṃ
saṅghātaścetanā dhṛtiḥ ।
etatkṣetraṃ samāsena
savikāramudāhṛtam ॥ 13.6

अमानित्वमदम्भित्वम्
अहिंसा क्षान्तिरार्जवम् ।
आचार्योपासनं शौचं
स्थैर्यमात्मविनिग्रहः ॥ १३.७

amānitvamadambhitvam
ahiṃsā kṣāntirārjavam ।
ācāryopāsanaṃ śaucaṃ
sthairyamātmavinigrahaḥ ॥ 13.7

इन्द्रियार्थेषु वैराग्यम् अनहङ्कार एव च । जन्ममृत्युजराव्याधि- दुःखदोषानुदर्शनम् ॥ १३.८	*indriyārtheṣu vairāgyam* *anahaṅkāra eva ca* । *janmamṛtyujarāvyādhi-* *duḥkhadoṣānudarśanam* ॥ 13.8
असक्तिरनभिष्वङ्गः पुत्रदारगृहादिषु । नित्यं च समचित्तत्वम् इष्टानिष्टोपपत्तिषु ॥ १३.९	*asaktiranabhiṣvaṅgaḥ* *putradāragṛhādiṣu* । *nityaṃ ca samacittatvam* *iṣṭāniṣṭopapattiṣu* ॥ 13.9
मयि चानन्ययोगेन भक्तिरव्यभिचारिणी । विविक्तदेशसेवित्वम् अरतिर्जनसंसदि ॥ १३.१०	*mayi cānanyayogena* *bhaktiravyabhicāriṇī* । *viviktadeśasevitvam* *aratirjanasaṃsadi* ॥ 13.10
अध्यात्मज्ञाननित्यत्वं तत्त्वज्ञानार्थदर्शनम् । एतज्ज्ञानमिति प्रोक्तम् अज्ञानं यदतोऽन्यथा ॥ १३.११	*adhyātmajñānanityatvaṃ* *tattvajñānārthadarśanam* । *etajjñānamiti proktam* *ajñānaṃ yadato'nyathā* ॥ 13.11
ज्ञेयं यत्तत् प्रवक्ष्यामि यज्ज्ञात्वामृतमश्नुते । अनादिमत्परं ब्रह्म न सत्तन्नासदुच्यते ॥ १३.१२	*jñeyaṃ yattat pravakṣyāmi* *yajjñātvāmṛtamaśnute* । *anādimatparaṃ brahma* *na sattannāsaducyate* ॥ 13.12
सर्वतःपाणिपादं तत् सर्वतोक्षिशिरोमुखम् । सर्वतःश्रुतिमल्लोके सर्वमावृत्य तिष्ठति ॥ १३.१३	*sarvataḥpāṇipādaṃ tat* *sarvatokṣiśiromukham* । *sarvataḥśrutimalloke* *sarvamāvṛtya tiṣṭhati* ॥ 13.13
सर्वेन्द्रियगुणाभासं सर्वेन्द्रियविवर्जितम् । असक्तं सर्वभृच्चैव निर्गुणं गुणभोक्तृ च ॥ १३.१४	*sarvendriyaguṇābhāsaṃ* *sarvendriyavivarjitam* । *asaktaṃ sarvabhṛccaiva* *nirguṇaṃ guṇabhoktṛ ca* ॥ 13.14
बहिरन्तश्च भूतानाम् अचरं चरमेव च । सूक्ष्मत्वात्तदविज्ञेयं दूरस्थं चान्तिके च तत् ॥ १३.१५	*bahirantaśca bhūtānām* *acaraṃ carameva ca* । *sūkṣmatvāttadavijñeyaṃ* *dūrasthaṃ cāntike ca tat* ॥ 13.15

अविभक्तं च भूतेषु विभक्तमिव च स्थितम् । भूतभर्तृ च तज्ज्ञेयं ग्रसिष्णु प्रभविष्णु च ॥ १३.१६	*avibhaktaṃ ca bhūteṣu* *vibhaktamiva ca sthitam* । *bhūtabhartṛ ca tajjñeyaṃ* *grasiṣṇu prabhaviṣṇu ca* ॥ 13.16
ज्योतिषामपि तज्ज्योतिः तमसः परमुच्यते । ज्ञानं ज्ञेयं ज्ञानगम्यं हृदि सर्वस्य विष्ठितम् ॥ १३.१७	*jyotiṣāmapi tajjyotiḥ* *tamasaḥ paramucyate* । *jñānaṃ jñeyaṃ jñānagamyaṃ* *hṛdi sarvasya viṣṭhitam* ॥ 13.17
इति क्षेत्रं तथा ज्ञानं ज्ञेयं चोक्तं समासतः । मद्भक्त एतद्विज्ञाय मद्भावायोपपद्यते ॥ १३.१८	*iti kṣetraṃ tathā jñānaṃ* *jñeyaṃ coktaṃ samāsataḥ* । *madbhakta etadvijñāya* *madbhāvāyopapadyate* ॥ 13.18
प्रकृतिं पुरुषं चैव विद्ध्यनादी उभावपि । विकारांश्च गुणांश्चैव विद्धि प्रकृतिसम्भवान् ॥ १३.१९	*prakṛtiṃ puruṣaṃ caiva* *viddhyanādī ubhāvapi* । *vikārāṃśca guṇāṃścaiva* *viddhi prakṛtisambhavān* ॥ 13.19
कार्यकारणकर्तृत्वे हेतुः प्रकृतिरुच्यते । पुरुषः सुखदुःखानां भोक्तृत्वे हेतुरुच्यते ॥ १३.२०	*kāryakāraṇakartṛtve* *hetuḥ prakṛtirucyate* । *puruṣaḥ sukhaduḥkhānāṃ* *bhoktṛtve heturucyate* ॥ 13.20
पुरुषः प्रकृतिस्थो हि भुङ्क्ते प्रकृतिजान्गुणान् । कारणं गुणसङ्गोऽस्य सदसद्योनिजन्मसु ॥ १३.२१	*puruṣaḥ prakṛtistho hi* *bhuṅkte prakṛtijānguṇān* । *kāraṇaṃ guṇasaṅgo'sya* *sadasadyonijanmasu* ॥ 13.21
उपद्रष्टानुमन्ता च भर्ता भोक्ता महेश्वरः । परमात्मेति चाप्युक्तो देहेऽस्मिन्पुरुषः परः ॥ १३.२२	*upadraṣṭānumantā ca* *bhartā bhoktā maheśvaraḥ* । *paramātmeti cāpyukto* *dehe'sminpuruṣaḥ paraḥ* ॥ 13.22
य एवं वेत्ति पुरुषं प्रकृतिं च गुणैः सह । सर्वथा वर्तमानोऽपि न स भूयोऽभिजायते ॥ १३.२३	*ya evaṃ vetti puruṣaṃ* *prakṛtiṃ ca guṇaiḥ saha* । *sarvathā vartamāno'pi* *na sa bhūyo'bhijāyate* ॥ 13.23

ध्यानेनात्मनि पश्यन्ति
केचिदात्मानमात्मना ।
अन्ये साङ्ख्येन योगेन
कर्मयोगेन चापरे ॥ १३.२४

dhyānenātmani paśyanti
kecidātmānamātmanā ।
anye sāṅkhyena yogena
karmayogena cāpare ॥ 13.24

अन्ये त्वेवमजानन्तः
श्रुत्वान्येभ्य उपासते ।
तेऽपि चातितरन्त्येव
मृत्युं श्रुतिपरायणाः ॥ १३.२५

anye tvevamajānantaḥ
śrutvānyebhya upāsate ।
te'pi cātitarantyeva
mṛtyuṃ śrutiparāyaṇāḥ ॥ 13.25

यावत्सञ्जायते किञ्चित्
सत्त्वं स्थावरजङ्गमम् ।
क्षेत्रक्षेत्रज्ञसंयोगात्
तद्विद्धि भरतर्षभ ॥ १३.२६

yāvatsañjāyate kiñcit
sattvaṃ sthāvarajaṅgamam ।
kṣetrakṣetrajñasaṃyogāt
tadviddhi bharatarṣabha ॥ 13.26

समं सर्वेषु भूतेषु
तिष्ठन्तं परमेश्वरम् ।
विनश्यत्स्वविनश्यन्तं
यः पश्यति स पश्यति ॥ १३.२७

samaṃ sarveṣu bhūteṣu
tiṣṭhantaṃ parameśvaram ।
vinaśyatsvavinaśyantaṃ
yaḥ paśyati sa paśyati ॥ 13.27

समं पश्यन्हि सर्वत्र
समवस्थितमीश्वरम् ।
न हिनस्त्यात्मनात्मानं
ततो याति परां गतिम् ॥ १३.२८

samaṃ paśyanhi sarvatra
samavasthitamīśvaram ।
na hinastyātmanātmānaṃ
tato yāti parāṃ gatim ॥ 13.28

प्रकृत्यैव च कर्माणि
क्रियमाणानि सर्वशः ।
यः पश्यति तथात्मानम्
अकर्तारं स पश्यति ॥ १३.२९

prakṛtyaiva ca karmāṇi
kriyamāṇāni sarvaśaḥ ।
yaḥ paśyati tathātmānam
akartāraṃ sa paśyati ॥ 13.29

यदा भूतपृथग्भावम्
एकस्थमनुपश्यति ।
तत एव च विस्तारं
ब्रह्म सम्पद्यते तदा ॥ १३.३०

yadā bhūtapṛthagbhāvam
ekasthamanupaśyati ।
tata eva ca vistāraṃ
brahma sampadyate tadā ॥ 13.30

अनादित्वान्निर्गुणत्वात्
परमात्मायमव्ययः ।
शरीरस्थोऽपि कौन्तेय
न करोति न लिप्यते ॥ १३.३१

anāditvānnirguṇatvāt
paramātmāyamavyayaḥ ।
śarīrastho'pi kaunteya
na karoti na lipyate ॥ 13.31

यथा सर्वगतं सौक्ष्म्यात्	*yathā sarvagataṃ saukṣmyāt*
आकाशं नोपलिप्यते ।	*ākāśaṃ nopalipyate* ।
सर्वत्रावस्थितो देहे	*sarvatrāvasthito dehe*
तथात्मा नोपलिप्यते ॥ १३.३२	*tathātmā nopalipyate* ॥ 13.32
यथा प्रकाशयत्येकः	*yathā prakāśayatyekaḥ*
कृत्स्नं लोकमिमं रविः ।	*kṛtsnaṃ lokamimaṃ raviḥ* ।
क्षेत्रं क्षेत्री तथा कृत्स्नं	*kṣetraṃ kṣetrī tathā kṛtsnaṃ*
प्रकाशयति भारत ॥ १३.३३	*prakāśayati bhārata* ॥ 13.33
क्षेत्रक्षेत्रज्ञयोरेवम्	*kṣetrakṣetrajñayorevam*
अन्तरं ज्ञानचक्षुषा ।	*antaraṃ jñānacakṣuṣā* ।
भूतप्रकृतिमोक्षं च	*bhūtaprakṛtimokṣaṃ ca*
ये विदुर्यान्ति ते परम् ॥ १३.३४	*ye viduryānti te param* ॥ 13.34

CHAPTER 13

Matter and Spirit

Kṛṣṇa

[1]The wise refer to this body as the *kṣetra*.
One who knows the *kṣetra*
is called *kṣetrajña*.

Kṣetra means 'field,' 'domain,' or 'realm.'
It can also mean 'body,' 'matter,' or 'world.'
Kṣetrajña is 'one who knows the field' or 'domain expert.'
It can also mean 'soul,' 'spirit,' 'lord,' or 'one who knows the Self.'

[2]I am the *kṣetrajña* in every *kṣetra*.
In my opinion, true knowledge is
knowledge of the *kṣetra* and the *kṣetrajña*.

True knowledge comprises knowledge of
Matter (organic and inorganic) and Spirit.

[3]In summary, I shall explain
about the *kṣetra*,
its attributes, its origins,
and how it changes.

I will also tell you about
the *kṣetrajña* and his powers.

[4]Seers have revealed this in many distinct ways
in the *mantras* (sacred verses) of the *Vedas*.
It is also conclusively stated
in the *Brahma-sūtra*.

Here, 'this' refers to knowledge of matter and spirit.
Brahma-sūtra is a collection of aphorisms that was compiled,
drawing from the *Vedic* philosophy. It is an authoritative text that presents
the nature of *Brahman* (Supreme Being) and how to attain *Brahman*.

[5]The five great elements,
ego, intellect,
the unseen,
five sense organs and
five organs of action,
five sensations,
[6]desire, hatred,
pleasure, pain,
awareness, and courage—
along with various modifications—
together constitute the *kṣetra*.

The five great elements are earth, fire, water, air and space/ether.
The five sense organs are ears, eyes, nose, tongue, and skin;
the five sensations are sound, sight, smell, taste, and touch.
The five organs of action are mouth, hands, feet, genitals, and anus.

[7] Humility,
freedom from hypocrisy,
not causing harm or injury,
forbearance,
uprightness,
reverence towards one's teacher,
purity (in thought, speech, and deed),
steadiness and fortitude,
self-control;
[8] reasoned disregard towards sensates,
absence of egoism,
deep insight into
the limitations and tribulations
of birth, death, old-age, sickness, and pain;
[9] freedom from selfishness,
devoid of undue love for
family and community,
constant equanimity towards
desirable and undesirable events;
[10] unwavering and single-minded devotion to the Supreme,
seeking solitude and avoiding sordid crowds;
[11] sincere persistence in knowing the Supreme,
and the quest for the vision of Truth –
these numerous factors constitute true knowledge;
anything contrary to these is ignorance.

12 Next, I shall explain about that
which ought to be known.
Once you know it,
you will be immortal.
It is the Supreme *Brahman*
that is without beginning;
it is spoken of as neither real nor unreal.

Brahman—the Supreme Being—transcends existence and non-existence.

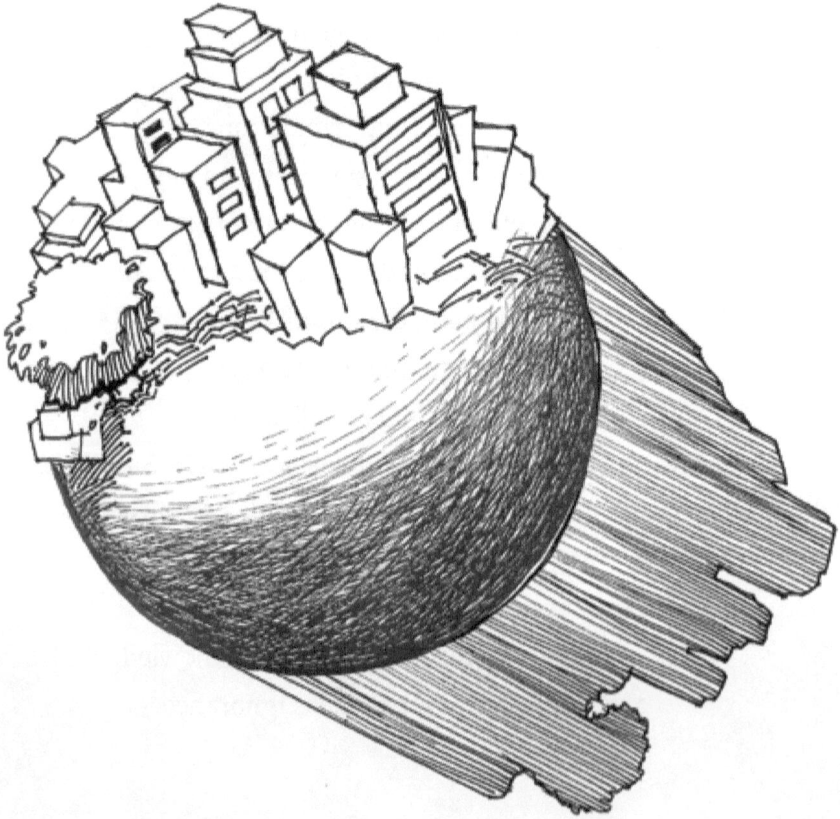

[13]With heads, hands, legs,
eyes, ears, and mouths everywhere,
Brahman abides in the universe
encompassing everything.
[14]It is free from the influence of the senses.
It sets illuminates the senses yet is devoid of them.
It supports everything but remains unattached.
It is free from *guṇa*s and yet enjoys them all.

Here, 'it' refers to *Brahman*.
*Guṇa*s are inherent tendencies of a human being.

[15]It is outside and within all beings,
motionless and always moving,
far away and nearby –
it is too subtle to grasp.
[16]It is the undivided whole and
it appears divided among beings.
It supports all the creatures,
consuming them as well as creating them.

[17]It is the knowledge,
it is the knowable subject,
it is the purpose of knowledge;
it is seated in the heart of all beings.
It is the light of lights, beyond all darkness.

18 I have summarily told you about the *kṣetra* and
also about Knowledge and its purpose.
Having learned this,
my devotee is united with me.

19 *Prakṛti* and *puruṣa*
are both without beginning.
Change arises from *prakṛti*
and so do the *guṇas*.

Everything in the universe constantly undergoes change because everything arises from *prakṛti* (material nature), which is always changing whereas *puruṣa* (indwelling spirit) is beyond change.

20 *Prakṛti* is the material basis
of the body and
associated activities.
Puruṣa is the cause
of the experiences of
pleasure and pain.

Prakṛti is the source of the five elements and the body, including the five senses, mind, ego, and intellect. *Puruṣa* is the cause of one's feeling of being alive and the associated experiences of pleasures and pains.

21 When associated with *prakṛti*,
puruṣa experiences the *guṇas*
that arise from *prakṛti*.

Attachment to the *guṇa*s is the cause of one's rebirth,
for the better or for the worse.

Any attachment, good or bad, leads to bondage (rebirth).
The type of experiences to which one is most attached in this life
determines the type of person one is going to be in the next.

22 The indwelling *puruṣa* is said to be
the witness, the approver, the supporter, the enjoyer,
the Supreme Lord, and the Supreme Self.

23 One who thus understands
puruṣa, *prakṛti*, and the *guṇas*,
although engaged in worldly activities,
will not be born again.

24 Some people perceive the *ātman*
through meditation,
some others through the *ātman*;
some people realize it through wisdom
while others through selfless action.

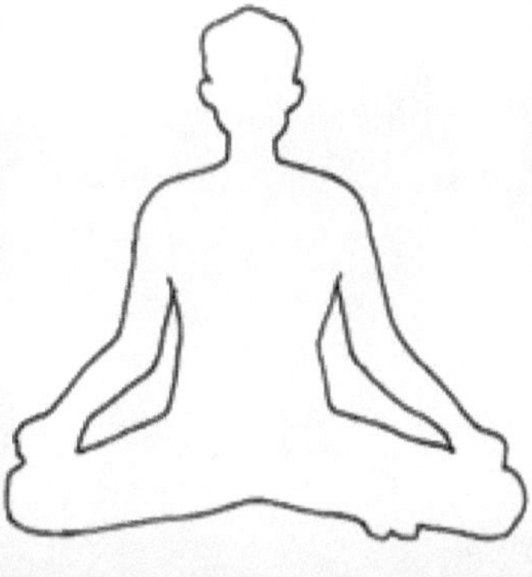

[25]Those who don't know these paths
pursue the *ātman* by hearing it from others.
They too transcend death by faithfully following
what they have learned from others.

[26]Every being that exists—
fixed or moving—
is born as a result of the interaction
between *kṣetra* and *kṣetrajña*.

[27]He truly sees who sees
the same Supreme
living in all beings and
undying within the dying.

[28]He doesn't degrade himself
for he sees the same lord
established everywhere.
He attains the supreme state.

He recognizes the same Supreme Spirit in himself and in others (see 6.29–30).

[29]He truly sees who sees that
all actions are performed by *prakṛti* alone
and the *puruṣa* is a mere witness.

30 When one observes the **diversity of existence as having a common source** in the Supreme and
all manifestations arising from that alone,
then he becomes one with *Brahman*.

31–32 Arjuna, the Supreme Self is imperishable,
without beginning, and beyond attributes.
Though it resides in the body,
it does not act and it is not tainted;
just as the all-pervading space
remains pure because of its subtlety.

Space is the unlimited expanse that is within and outside everything. Though all events occur in space, nothing happens to it because it is far too subtle and ethereal.

[33]Just as a single sun illuminates the whole world,
so also the *kṣetrajña* illumines every *kṣetra*.

In the original, the word '*kṣetrin*' – 'owner of the field'
or 'the Supreme' – has been used instead of '*kṣetrajña*.'

[34]Those with spiritual insight
recognize the difference between
kṣetra and *kṣetrajña*;
they know how all beings are liberated
from the bondages of *prakṛti*;
they reach the Supreme!

The wise see a distinction between the lower (*kṣetra/prakṛti*)
and higher (*kṣetrajña/puruṣa*) levels of reality.

Kṛṣṇa starts with, 'true knowledge is knowledge of *kṣetra* and *kṣetrajña*.'
He concludes by pointing out the difference between the two.

It is important for us to learn in total and
then distinguish the important from the trivial.
There is no short cut to true knowledge.

14

श्रीभगवानुवाच।
परं भूयः प्रवक्ष्यामि
ज्ञानानां ज्ञानमुत्तमम्।
यज्ज्ञात्वा मुनयः सर्वे
परां सिद्धिमितो गताः॥ १४.१

śrībhagavānuvāca ।
paraṃ bhūyaḥ pravakṣyāmi
jñānānāṃ jñānamuttamam ।
yajjñātvā munayaḥ sarve
parāṃ siddhimito gatāḥ ॥ 14.1

इदं ज्ञानमुपाश्रित्य
मम साधर्म्यमागताः।
सर्गेऽपि नोपजायन्ते
प्रलये न व्यथन्ति च॥ १४.२

idaṃ jñānamupāśritya
mama sādharmyamāgatāḥ ।
sarge'pi nopajāyante
pralaye na vyathanti ca ॥ 14.2

मम योनिर्महद्ब्रह्म
तस्मिन्गर्भं दधाम्यहम्।
सम्भवः सर्वभूतानां
ततो भवति भारत॥ १४.३

mama yonirmahadbrahma
tasmingarbhaṃ dadhāmyaham ।
sambhavaḥ sarvabhūtānāṃ
tato bhavati bhārata ॥ 14.3

सर्वयोनिषु कौन्तेय
मूर्तयः सम्भवन्ति याः।
तासां ब्रह्म महद्योनिः
अहं बीजप्रदः पिता॥ १४.४

sarvayoniṣu kaunteya
mūrtayaḥ sambhavanti yāḥ ।
tāsāṃ brahma mahadyoniḥ
ahaṃ bījapradaḥ pitā ॥ 14.4

सत्त्वं रजस्तम इति
गुणाः प्रकृतिसम्भवाः।
निबध्नन्ति महाबाहो
देहे देहिनमव्ययम्॥ १४.५

sattvaṃ rajastama iti
guṇāḥ prakṛtisambhavāḥ ।
nibadhnanti mahābāho
dehe dehinamavyayam ॥ 14.5

तत्र सत्त्वं निर्मलत्वात्
प्रकाशकमनामयम्।
सुखसङ्गेन बध्नाति
ज्ञानसङ्गेन चानघ॥ १४.६

tatra sattvaṃ nirmalatvāt
prakāśakamanāmayam ।
sukhasaṅgena badhnāti
jñānasaṅgena cānagha ॥ 14.6

रजो रागात्मकं विद्धि
तृष्णासङ्गसमुद्भवम्।
तन्निबध्नाति कौन्तेय
कर्मसङ्गेन देहिनम्॥ १४.७

rajo rāgātmakaṃ viddhi
tṛṣṇāsaṅgasamudbhavam ।
tannibadhnāti kaunteya
karmasaṅgena dehinam ॥ 14.7

तमस्त्वज्ञानजं विद्धि मोहनं सर्वदेहिनाम् । प्रमादालस्यनिद्राभिः तन्निबध्नाति भारत ॥ १४.८	*tamastvajñānajaṃ viddhi* *mohanaṃ sarvadehinām* । *pramādālasyanidrābhiḥ* *tannibadhnāti bhārata* ॥ 14.8
सत्त्वं सुखे सञ्जयति रजः कर्मणि भारत । ज्ञानमावृत्य तु तमः प्रमादे सञ्जयत्युत ॥ १४.९	*sattvaṃ sukhe sañjayati* *rajaḥ karmaṇi bhārata* । *jñānamāvṛtya tu tamaḥ* *pramāde sañjayatyuta* ॥ 14.9
रजस्तमश्चाभिभूय सत्त्वं भवति भारत । रजः सत्त्वं तमश्चैव तमः सत्त्वं रजस्तथा ॥ १४.१०	*rajastamaścābhibhūya* *sattvaṃ bhavati bhārata* । *rajaḥ sattvaṃ tamaścaiva* *tamaḥ sattvaṃ rajastathā* ॥ 14.10
सर्वद्वारेषु देहेऽस्मिन् प्रकाश उपजायते । ज्ञानं यदा तदा विद्यात् विवृद्धं सत्त्वमित्युत ॥ १४.११	*sarvadvāreṣu dehe'smin* *prakāśa upajāyate* । *jñānaṃ yadā tadā vidyāt* *vivṛddhaṃ sattvamityuta* ॥ 14.11
लोभः प्रवृत्तिरारम्भः कर्मणामशमः स्पृहा । रजस्येतानि जायन्ते विवृद्धे भरतर्षभ ॥ १४.१२	*lobhaḥ pravṛttirārambhaḥ* *karmaṇāmaśamaḥ spṛhā* । *rajasyetāni jāyante* *vivṛddhe bharatarṣabha* ॥ 14.12
अप्रकाशोऽप्रवृत्तिश्च प्रमादो मोह एव च । तमस्येतानि जायन्ते विवृद्धे कुरुनन्दन ॥ १४.१३	*aprakāśo'pravṛttiśca* *pramādo moha eva ca* । *tamasyetāni jāyante* *vivṛddhe kurunandana* ॥ 14.13
यदा सत्त्वे प्रवृद्धे तु प्रलयं याति देहभृत् । तदोत्तमविदां लोकान् अमलान्प्रतिपद्यते ॥ १४.१४	*yadā sattve pravṛddhe tu* *pralayaṃ yāti dehabhṛt* । *tadottamavidāṃ lokān* *amalānpratipadyate* ॥ 14.14
रजसि प्रलयं गत्वा कर्मसङ्गिषु जायते । तथा प्रलीनस्तमसि मूढयोनिषु जायते ॥ १४.१५	*rajasi pralayaṃ gatvā* *karmasaṅgiṣu jāyate* । *tathā pralīnastamasi* *mūḍhayoniṣu jāyate* ॥ 14.15

कर्मणः सुकृतस्याहुः
सात्त्विकं निर्मलं फलम् ।
रजसस्तु फलं दुःखम्
अज्ञानं तमसः फलम् ॥ १४.१६

karmaṇaḥ sukṛtasyāhuḥ
sāttvikaṃ nirmalaṃ phalam ।
rajasastu phalaṃ duḥkham
ajñānaṃ tamasaḥ phalam ॥ 14.16

सत्त्वात्सञ्जायते ज्ञानं
रजसो लोभ एव च ।
प्रमादमोहौ तमसो
भवतोऽज्ञानमेव च ॥ १४.१७

sattvātsañjāyate jñānaṃ
rajaso lobha eva ca ।
pramādamohau tamaso
bhavato'jñānameva ca ॥ 14.17

ऊर्ध्वं गच्छन्ति सत्त्वस्था
मध्ये तिष्ठन्ति राजसाः ।
जघन्यगुणवृत्तस्था
अधो गच्छन्ति तामसाः ॥ १४.१८

ūrdhvaṃ gacchanti sattvasthā
madhye tiṣṭhanti rājasāḥ ।
jaghanyaguṇavṛttasthā
adho gacchanti tāmasāḥ ॥ 14.18

नान्यं गुणेभ्यः कर्तारं
यदा द्रष्टानुपश्यति ।
गुणेभ्यश्च परं वेत्ति
मद्भावं सोऽधिगच्छति ॥ १४.१९

nānyaṃ guṇebhyaḥ kartāraṃ
yadā draṣṭānupaśyati ।
guṇebhyaśca paraṃ vetti
madbhāvaṃ so'dhigacchati ॥ 14.19

गुणानेतानतीत्य त्रीन्
देही देहसमुद्भवान् ।
जन्ममृत्युजरादुःखैः
विमुक्तोऽमृतमश्नुते ॥ १४.२०

guṇānetānatītya trīn
dehī dehasamudbhavān ।
janmamṛtyujarāduḥkhaiḥ
vimukto'mṛtamaśnute ॥ 14.20

अर्जुन उवाच ।
कैर्लिङ्गैस्त्रीन्गुणान्
एतानतीतो भवति प्रभो ।
किमाचारः कथं चैतान्
त्रीन् गुणानतिवर्तते ॥ १४.२१

arjuna uvāca ।
kairliṅgaistrīnguṇān
etānatīto bhavati prabho ।
kimācāraḥ kathaṃ caitān
trīn guṇānativartate ॥ 14.21

श्रीभगवानुवाच ।
प्रकाशं च प्रवृत्तिं च
मोहमेव च पाण्डव ।
न द्वेष्टि सम्प्रवृत्तानि
न निवृत्तानि काङ्क्षति ॥ १४.२२

śrībhagavānuvāca ।
prakāśaṃ ca pravṛttiṃ ca
mohameva ca pāṇḍava ।
na dveṣṭi sampravṛttāni
na nivṛttāni kāṅkṣati ॥ 14.22

उदासीनवदासीनो गुणैर्यो न विचाल्यते । गुणा वर्तन्त इत्येव योऽवतिष्ठति नेङ्गते ॥ १४.२३	*udāsīnavadāsīno* *guṇairyo na vicālyate* । *guṇā vartanta ityeva* *yo'vatiṣṭhati neṅgate* ॥ 14.23
समदुःखसुखः स्वस्थः समलोष्टाश्मकाञ्चनः । तुल्यप्रियाप्रियो धीरः तुल्यनिन्दात्मसंस्तुतिः ॥ १४.२४	*samaduḥkhasukhaḥ svasthaḥ* *samaloṣṭāśmakāñcanaḥ* । *tulyapriyāpriyo dhīraḥ* *tulyanindātmasaṃstutiḥ* ॥ 14.24
मानावमानयोस्तुल्यः तुल्यो मित्रारिपक्षयोः । सर्वारम्भपरित्यागी गुणातीतः स उच्यते ॥ १४.२५	*mānāvamānayostulyaḥ* *tulyo mitrāripakṣayoḥ* । *sarvārambhaparityāgī* *guṇātītaḥ sa ucyate* ॥ 14.25
मां च योऽव्यभिचारेण भक्तियोगेन सेवते । स गुणान्समतीत्यैतान् ब्रह्मभूयाय कल्पते ॥ १४.२६	*māṃ ca yo'vyabhicāreṇa* *bhaktiyogena sevate* । *sa guṇānsamatītyaitān* *brahmabhūyāya kalpate* ॥ 14.26
ब्रह्मणो हि प्रतिष्ठाहम् अमृतस्याव्ययस्य च । शाश्वतस्य च धर्मस्य सुखस्यैकान्तिकस्य च ॥ १४.२७	*brahmaṇo hi pratiṣṭhāham* *amṛtasyāvyayasya ca* । *śāśvatasya ca dharmasya* *sukhasyaikāntikasya ca* ॥ 14.27

CHAPTER 14

The Attitudes

Kṛṣṇa

1 I shall tell you more
about this Supreme Wisdom,
which transcends all knowledge.
By knowing this, the sages have
attained the highest perfection.

2 Contemplating on this wisdom,
they have reached the Supreme State.
They remain unaffected
by creation or destruction.

Having reached the Supreme State,
they are not born again at the time of creation
nor are they disturbed at the time of dissolution.

3 Primordial nature is my womb,
in which I plant my seed;
all creatures are born from that.

[4]Whatever life forms develop in any womb,
primordial nature is their mother
and I am their seed-giving father.

[5]***Sattva*, *rajas*,** and ***tamas***
are the three ***guṇas***.
These *guṇas* are born out of *prakṛti* and
they bind the imperishable *ātman* to the body.

Guṇa refers to the inherent tendency of a person.
Prakṛti refers to nature or environment.

[6]*Sattva*, which is pure, luminous, and free from distress
binds one by attachment to knowledge and serenity.

[7]*Rajas*, marked by passion,
the source of thirst and anxiety,
binds one to indulge in activity.

[8]*Tamas*, born of ignorance and delusion,
makes one careless, lethargic, and sleepy.

The states of *sattva*, *rajas*, and *tamas* are temporary.
All of them are merely different kinds of bondages of the *ātman*.
The objective is to go beyond the *guṇas* and realize the true Self.

Interestingly, in 2.23–25, there is no mention of 'the *ātman* can't be bound.'
Perhaps, attachment is the one thing that affects the *ātman*!

9 *Sattva* brings happiness.
Rajas gives rise to action.
Tamas shrouds knowledge and
binds one to delusion.

10 *Sattva* predominates,
subduing *rajas* and *tamas*;
or *rajas* prevails,
overpowering *sattva* and *tamas*;
or *tamas* sets in,
masking *sattva* and *rajas*.

Among the three *guṇas*, one dominates over the other two.

11 When the glow of wisdom
emanates from all the gates of the body,
indeed *sattva* is dominant.

The body is considered as a city of nine gates (two eyes, two ears, two nostrils, a mouth, a genital organ, and an anus; see 5.13).

12 When *rajas* predominates,
one is governed by greed, vigor, desire,
unrest, and constant activity.

Such a person takes up many activities out of greed and with an eye on the rewards.

13 Darkness, delusion, lethargy, and negligence arise
when *tamas* is predominant.

14 When the soul departs a body
while *sattva* is predominant,
the *soul* attains the pure worlds of the wise.

15 Departing in the state of *rajas*,
one takes birth among those attached to action.
Likewise, dying in the state of *tamas*,
one is born among the deluded.

The state of mind that prevails at the time of one's death
is often a reflection of the kind of life one has lived (see 8.6).

16 The fruit of *sattva* is purity and goodness;
the fruit of *rajas* is pain;
the fruit of *tamas* is ignorance.

17 Wisdom is born from *sattva*.
Greed is born from *rajas*.
Distraction, ignorance, and delusion
are born from *tamas*.

18 Those who live in *sattva* advance upwards.
Those in *rajas* are stuck in the middle.

Those in *tamas*,
the lowest quality of activity,
sink downward.

The 'upward,' 'middle,' and 'downward'
are references to spiritual advancement.

[19]One who has realized that the three *guṇas*
are the driving force (in every activity)
and also knows what exists beyond *guṇas*,
attains the Supreme State.

He realizes that the Self is not the cause of action and activities, but it is *guṇa*.

[20]When one has risen above these *guṇas*,
which are associated with the body,
he is liberated from birth, death, old age, and pain
and becomes immortal!

ARJUNA

[21]What are the traits of one
who has gone beyond the three *guṇas*?
What is his way of life?
How does he go beyond the *guṇas*?

Arjuna raises a similar question before (see 2.54) and
Kṛṣṇa gives a detailed response (see 2.55–71).
The following verses may be seen in the backdrop of the earlier verses
that explains the nature of one who is ever-balanced.

KṚṢṆA

22 One who has gone beyond the influence of the *guṇas*
is not moved by the illumination of *sattva*,
the activity arising from *rajas*,
or the delusion caused by *tamas*.
He neither dislikes them when they are present
nor desires for them when they are absent.

23 He is never distracted and he stands firm;
he remains calm and unaffected by the *guṇas*
for he understands how the *guṇas* work.

24 He is the same towards pleasure and pain;
gold, mud, or stone make no difference to him;

with the same courage he faces
reward and punishment or
the pleasant and the unpleasant;
[25]he regards alike:
praise and criticism,
friend and foe, and
honor and dishonor;
he is above selfish pursuits.
He has truly gone beyond the *guṇas*.

'Established in the *ātman*' refers to a sense of self-satisfaction and self-sufficiency.

[26]One who sincerely worships me
through the path of devotion,
crosses the barriers of *guṇa* and
is ready to attain *Brahman*.

[27]For I am the *Brahman* –
the immortal, the imperishable,
the eternal *dharma*, and the absolute Bliss.

The 'eternal *dharma*' refers to the natural law that governs universal welfare.

15

श्रीभगवानुवाच ।
ऊर्ध्वमूलमधःशाखम्
अश्वत्थं प्राहुरव्ययम् ।
छन्दांसि यस्य पर्णानि
यस्तं वेद स वेदवित् ॥ १५.१

śrībhagavānuvāca ।
ūrdhvamūlamadhaḥśākham
aśvatthaṃ prāhuravyayam ।
chandāṃsi yasya parṇāni
yastaṃ veda sa vedavit ॥ 15.1

अधश्चोर्ध्वं प्रसृतास्तस्य शाखा
गुणप्रवृद्धा विषयप्रवालाः ।
अधश्च मूलान्यनुसन्ततानि
कर्मानुबन्धीनि मनुष्यलोके ॥ १५.२

adhaścordhvaṃ prasṛtāstasya śākhā
guṇapravṛddhā viṣayapravālāḥ ।
adhaśca mūlānyanusantatāni
karmānubandhīni manuṣyaloke ॥ 15.2

न रूपमस्येह तथोपलभ्यते
नान्तो न चादिर्न च सम्प्रतिष्ठा ।
अश्वत्थमेनं सुविरूढमूलम्
असङ्गशस्त्रेण दृढेन छित्त्वा ॥ १५.३

na rūpamasyeha tathopalabhyate
nānto na cādirna ca sampratiṣṭhā ।
aśvatthamenaṃ suvirūḍhamūlam
asaṅgaśastreṇa dṛḍhena chittvā ॥ 15.3

ततः पदं तत्परिमार्गितव्यं
यस्मिन्गता न निवर्तन्ति भूयः ।
तमेव चाद्यं पुरुषं प्रपद्ये
यतः प्रवृत्तिः प्रसृता पुराणी ॥ १५.४

tataḥ padaṃ tatparimārgitavyaṃ
yasmingatā na nivartanti bhūyaḥ ।
tameva cādyaṃ puruṣaṃ prapadye
yataḥ pravṛttiḥ prasṛtā purāṇī ॥ 15.4

निर्मानमोहा जितसङ्गदोषा
अध्यात्मनित्या विनिवृत्तकामाः ।
द्वन्द्वैर्विमुक्ताः सुखदुःखसञ्ज्ञैः
गच्छन्त्यमूढाः पदमव्ययं तत् ॥ १५.५

nirmānamohā jitasaṅgadoṣā
adhyātmanityā vinivṛttakāmāḥ ।
dvandvairvimuktāḥ sukhaduḥkhasañjñaiḥ
gacchantyamūḍhāḥ padamavyayaṃ tat ॥ 15.5

न तद्भासयते सूर्यो
न शशाङ्को न पावकः ।
यद्गत्वा न निवर्तन्ते
तद्धाम परमं मम ॥ १५.६

na tadbhāsayate sūryo
na śaśāṅko na pāvakaḥ ।
yadgatvā na nivartante
taddhāma paramaṃ mama ॥ 15.6

ममैवांशो जीवलोके
जीवभूतः सनातनः ।
मनःषष्ठानीन्द्रियाणि
प्रकृतिस्थानि कर्षति ॥ १५.७

mamaivāṃśo jīvaloke
jīvabhūtaḥ sanātanaḥ ।
manaḥṣaṣṭhānīndriyāṇi
prakṛtisthāni karṣati ॥ 15.7

शरीरं यदवाप्नोति
यच्चाप्युत्क्रामतीश्वरः ।
गृहीत्वैतानि संयाति
वायुर्गन्धानिवाशयात् ॥ १५.८

śarīraṃ yadavāpnoti
yaccāpyutkrāmatīśvaraḥ ।
gṛhītvaitāni saṃyāti
vāyurgandhānivāśayāt ॥ 15.8

श्रोत्रं चक्षुः स्पर्शनं च
रसनं घ्राणमेव च ।
अधिष्ठाय मनश्चायं
विषयानुपसेवते ॥ १५.९

śrotraṃ cakṣuḥ sparśanaṃ ca
rasanaṃ ghrāṇameva ca ।
adhiṣṭhāya manaścāyaṃ
viṣayānupasevate ॥ 15.9

उत्क्रामन्तं स्थितं वापि
भुञ्जानं वा गुणान्वितम् ।
विमूढा नानुपश्यन्ति
पश्यन्ति ज्ञानचक्षुषः ॥ १५.१०

utkrāmantaṃ sthitaṃ vāpi
bhuñjānaṃ vā guṇānvitam ।
vimūḍhā nānupaśyanti
paśyanti jñānacakṣuṣaḥ ॥ 15.10

यतन्तो योगिनश्चैनं
पश्यन्त्यात्मन्यवस्थितम् ।
यतन्तोऽप्यकृतात्मानो
नैनं पश्यन्त्यचेतसः ॥ १५.११

yatanto yoginaścainaṃ
paśyantyātmanyavasthitam ।
yatanto'pyakṛtātmāno
nainaṃ paśyantyacetasaḥ ॥ 15.11

यदादित्यगतं तेजो
जगद्भासयतेऽखिलम् ।
यच्चन्द्रमसि यच्चाग्नौ
तत्तेजो विद्धि मामकम् ॥ १५.१२

yadādityagataṃ tejo
jagadbhāsayate'khilam ।
yaccandramasi yaccāgnau
tattejo viddhi māmakam ॥ 15.12

गामाविश्य च भूतानि
धारयाम्यहमोजसा ।
पुष्णामि चौषधीः सर्वाः
सोमो भूत्वा रसात्मकः ॥ १५.१३

gāmāviśya ca bhūtāni
dhārayāmyahamojasā ।
puṣṇāmi cauṣadhīḥ sarvāḥ
somo bhūtvā rasātmakaḥ ॥ 15.13

अहं वैश्वानरो भूत्वा
प्राणिनां देहमाश्रितः ।
प्राणापानसमायुक्तः
पचाम्यन्नं चतुर्विधम् ॥ १५.१४

ahaṃ vaiśvānaro bhūtvā
prāṇināṃ dehamāśritaḥ ।
prāṇāpānasamāyuktaḥ
pacāmyannaṃ caturvidham ॥ 15.14

सर्वस्य चाहं हृदि संनिविष्टो
मत्तः स्मृतिर्ज्ञानमपोहनं च ।
वेदैश्च सर्वैरहमेव वेद्यो
वेदान्तकृद्वेदविदेव चाहम् ॥ १५.१५

sarvasya cāhaṃ hṛdi saṃniviṣṭo
mattaḥ smṛtirjñānamapohanaṃ ca ।
vedaiśca sarvairahameva vedyo
vedāntakṛdvedavideva cāham ॥ 15.15

द्वाविमौ पुरुषौ लोके
क्षरश्चाक्षर एव च ।
क्षरः सर्वाणि भूतानि
कूटस्थोऽक्षर उच्यते ॥ १५.१६

dvāvimau puruṣau loke
kṣaraścākṣara eva ca ।
kṣaraḥ sarvāṇi bhūtāni
kūṭastho'kṣara ucyate ॥ 15.16

उत्तमः पुरुषस्त्वन्यः
परमात्मेत्युदाहृतः ।
यो लोकत्रयमाविश्य
बिभर्त्यव्यय ईश्वरः ॥ १५.१७

uttamaḥ puruṣastvanyaḥ
paramātmetyudāhṛtaḥ ।
yo lokatrayamāviśya
bibhartyavyaya īśvaraḥ ॥ 15.17

यस्मात्क्षरमतीतोऽहम्
अक्षरादपि चोत्तमः ।
अतोऽस्मि लोके वेदे च
प्रथितः पुरुषोत्तमः ॥ १५.१८

yasmātkṣaramatīto'ham
akṣarādapi cottamaḥ ।
ato'smi loke vede ca
prathitaḥ puruṣottamaḥ ॥ 15.18

यो मामेवमसंमूढो
जानाति पुरुषोत्तमम् ।
स सर्वविद्भजति मां
सर्वभावेन भारत ॥ १५.१९

yo māmevamasaṃmūḍho
jānāti puruṣottamam ।
sa sarvavidbhajati māṃ
sarvabhāvena bhārata ॥ 15.19

इति गुह्यतमं शास्त्रम्
इदमुक्तं मयानघ ।
एतद्बुद्ध्वा बुद्धिमान्स्यात्
कृतकृत्यश्च भारत ॥ १५.२०

iti guhyatamaṃ śāstram
idamuktaṃ mayānagha ।
etadbuddhvā buddhimānsyāt
kṛtakṛtyaśca bhārata ॥ 15.20

CHAPTER 15

The Supreme Path

Kṛṣṇa

[1]The wise speak of the perennial Aśvattha tree,
which has roots above and branches below.
The leaves protecting it are the *Vedas*.
One who knows this tree, truly knows.

Aśvattha is the sacred fig tree (*Ficus religiosa*). It is used as a metaphor for existence. The roots above show our infinite, immeasurable, spiritual dimension whereas the branches below depict our limited, measurable, material dimension. Material existence (the branches *below*) is rooted in the spiritual (the roots *above*). The perennial nature of the tree represents cycles of birth and death. Just as the leaves nourish the tree, knowledge (the *Vedas*) nourishes human life. One who understands this metaphor truly understands both the spiritual and material dimensions of life.

[2]The tender sprouts of this mighty tree
are the senses nourished by the *guṇas*.
The branches extend both above and below.
The secondary roots going downward represent actions
that bind the individual soul to earthly existence.

Guṇa refers to the inherent tendency of a person.

3 The true nature of this tree –
its basis, beginning, or end –
is not readily perceived.

It is difficult for us mortals to be a part of life and understand it too. The only thing we know for certain is that life goes on.

Cut down this firmly-rooted Aśvattha tree
with the sharp axe of Detachment.
4 Then seek that eternal goal –
attaining which one is liberated –

by submitting yourself
to the Supreme *Puruṣa*,
the primal cause of
this ancient universe
and its activity.

[5]Free from false pride and delusion,
overcoming the taint of attachment,
always conscious of the *ātman*,
renouncing desires entirely, and
unaffected by pairs of opposites
such as pleasure and pain,
the wise reach that Eternal Goal.

Ātman is the inner, higher self.

[6]Neither sun nor moon nor fire
can illuminate that state.
It is verily my Supreme Abode.
Having gone there,
you will not return.

Here, 'that state' refers to the state of *Brahman*, the Supreme Being.
The Supreme Abode is self-luminous and beyond all light.
'...you will not return' indicates that no force can dislodge you from there.

[7]A fraction of my Eternal Self exists
as the individual soul in this world of living beings.

Abiding in *prakṛti*, it attracts towards itself
the five senses and the mind.

Prakṛti refers to 'nature' or 'environment.'

8When one acquires a body or departs from it,
the master within carries these senses,
just as the wind carries scents
from one place to another.

We acquire a body when we are born; we depart from it when we die.
Here, 'the master within' refers to the *ātman*, the eternal witness
that carries the *vāsanas* (past baggage from earlier births).

9Through the mind,
the ear, the eye, and
organs of touch, smell, and taste,
the *ātman* experiences the sensations.

'Sensations' are the experiences of sound, sight, smell, taste, and touch
but in a broader sense, it refers to the worldly pleasures and pains that one feels.

10The deluded ones fail to perceive the *ātman*
residing, entering, or departing the body.
They also fail to see the *ātman*
enjoying the sensations
as well as being impacted by *guṇas*.

See 13.21.

But those with
the eye of wisdom
perceive this.

They sense the *ātman* at all times.

[11]Those who strive with discipline
can see the fraction of the Supreme
situated in their own self.
But those who are selfish
and insensitive
fail to see it,
however hard they try.

The selfish ones are too full of themselves and fail to see anything else. Preoccupied with lower motives, they miss out on the higher ideals.

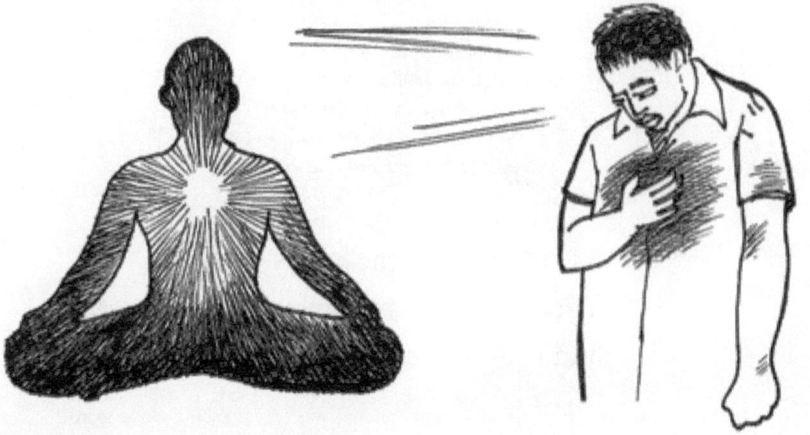

[12]The radiance of the sun which lights up the world,
the radiance in the moon and in fire –
I am the source of all that radiance.

[13]Entering the earth,
I support all creatures with my energy;
becoming the life-giving sap,
I nourish all plants and herbs.

[14]Having entered the bodies of creatures as the digestive fire
and working along with inward and outward breaths,
I digest the four kinds of food.

The four kinds of food are:
foods that are swallowed (*bhakṣyam*),
foods that are chewed (*bhojyam*),
foods that are licked (*lehyam*), and
foods that are sucked (*coṣyam*).

[15]I am seated in the hearts of all.
I grant memory and knowledge,
and I also make them disappear!

The original has the word '*apohanam*' and if we take it as a stand-alone word, we get the meaning of 'disappear,' 'denial,' 'reasoning,' *etc.*

Perhaps a part of our memory and knowledge should recede
if we want to function coherently. For example, we know death is certain,
yet we are able to live without being troubled by that idea every day.

If we, however, take the word '*apohanam*' as '*apa + ūhanam*'
we get the meaning of 'conjecture,' 'guesswork,' *etc.*, thus giving –
"I grant memory as well as conjecture."

I know all the *Vedas* and
I am the author of the *Upaniṣads*
I am the one who is to be known in them.

Upaniṣads are the concluding portion of the *Vedas*,
which are the foremost revealed scriptures in Hinduism.

The initial portions of the *Vedas* largely comprise contextual knowledge
while the *Upaniṣads* mainly contain universal wisdom.

One needs to know both and use them appropriately.

16 There are two entities in this world:
kṣaram and *akṣaram*.
Kṣaram consists of all beings
(yet to be liberated).
Akṣaram refers to those
that are immutable
(the liberated beings).

Kṣaram refers to something that is changing.
Akṣaram refers to something that is beyond change.

Another way of looking at this verse is by considering
kṣaram as a reference to all beings, and
akṣaram as a reference to the individual soul.

[17]But above these two entities,
there is a higher principle:
the Supreme Soul, the Ultimate Person,
known as the Eternal God
who sustains and pervades the universe.
[18]I am beyond *kṣaram* and
I am superior to *akṣaram*.
So I am respected as the Supreme Spirit
by the people and in the *Veda*s alike.

The idea of a higher power is shared by the laity and the learned.

[19]One who is free from delusion
knows me as the Supreme Spirit.
Indeed, he knows all there is to know
and he wholeheartedly worships me.

[20]Arjuna, I have taught you a great truth.
He who learns this
will become enlightened and
will have accomplished everything.

16

श्रीभगवानुवाच ।
अभयं सत्त्वसंशुद्धिः
ज्ञानयोगव्यवस्थितिः ।
दानं दमश्च यज्ञश्च
स्वाध्यायस्तप आर्जवम् ॥ १६.१

śrībhagavānuvāca ।
abhayaṃ sattvasaṃśuddhiḥ
jñānayogavyavasthitiḥ ।
dānaṃ damaśca yajñaśca
svādhyāyastapa ārjavam ॥ 16.1

अहिंसा सत्यमक्रोधः
त्यागः शान्तिरपैशुनम् ।
दया भूतेष्वलोलुप्त्वं
मार्दवं ह्रीरचापलम् ॥ १६.२

ahiṃsā satyamakrodhaḥ
tyāgaḥ śāntirapaiśunam ।
dayā bhūteṣvaloluptvaṃ
mārdavaṃ hrīracāpalam ॥ 16.2

तेजः क्षमा धृतिः शौचम्
अद्रोहो नातिमानिता ।
भवन्ति सम्पदं दैवीम्
अभिजातस्य भारत ॥ १६.३

tejaḥ kṣamā dhṛtiḥ śaucam
adroho nātimānitā ।
bhavanti sampadaṃ daivīm
abhijātasya bhārata ॥ 16.3

दम्भो दर्पोऽतिमानश्च
क्रोधः पारुष्यमेव च ।
अज्ञानं चाभिजातस्य
पार्थ सम्पदमासुरीम् ॥ १६.४

dambho darpo'timānaśca
krodhaḥ pāruṣyameva ca ।
ajñānaṃ cābhijātasya
pārtha sampadamāsurīm ॥ 16.4

दैवी सम्पद्विमोक्षाय
निबन्धायासुरी मता ।
मा शुचः सम्पदं दैवीम्
अभिजातोऽसि पाण्डव ॥ १६.५

daivī sampadvimokṣāya
nibandhāyāsurī matā ।
mā śucaḥ sampadaṃ daivīm
abhijāto'si pāṇḍava ॥ 16.5

द्वौ भूतसर्गौ लोकेऽस्मिन्
दैव आसुर एव च ।
दैवो विस्तरशः प्रोक्त
आसुरं पार्थ मे शृणु ॥ १६.६

dvau bhūtasargau loke'smin
daiva āsura eva ca ।
daivo vistaraśaḥ prokta
āsuraṃ pārtha me śṛṇu ॥ 16.6

प्रवृत्तिं च निवृत्तिं च
जना न विदुरासुराः ।
न शौचं नापि चाचारो
न सत्यं तेषु विद्यते ॥ १६.७

pravṛttiṃ ca nivṛttiṃ ca
janā na vidurāsurāḥ ।
na śaucaṃ nāpi cācāro
na satyaṃ teṣu vidyate ॥ 16.7

असत्यमप्रतिष्ठं ते	*asatyamapratiṣṭhaṃ te*
जगदाहुरनीश्वरम् ।	*jagadāhuranīśvaram* ׀
अपरस्परसम्भूतं	*aparasparasambhūtaṃ*
किमन्यत्कामहैतुकम् ॥ १६.८	*kimanyatkāmahaitukam* ॥ 16.8
एतां दृष्टिमवष्टभ्य	*etāṃ dṛṣṭimavaṣṭabhya*
नष्टात्मानोऽल्पबुद्धयः ।	*naṣṭātmāno'lpabuddhayaḥ* ׀
प्रभवन्त्युग्रकर्माणः	*prabhavantyugrakarmāṇaḥ*
क्षयाय जगतोऽहिताः ॥ १६.९	*kṣayāya jagato'hitāḥ* ॥ 16.9
काममाश्रित्य दुष्पूरं	*kāmamāśritya duṣpūraṃ*
दम्भमानमदान्विताः ।	*dambhamānamadānvitāḥ* ׀
मोहाद्गृहीत्वासद्ग्राहान्	*mohādgṛhītvāsadgrāhān*
प्रवर्तन्तेऽशुचिव्रताः ॥ १६.१०	*pravartante'śucivratāḥ* ॥ 16.10
चिन्तामपरिमेयां च	*cintāmaparimeyāṃ ca*
प्रलयान्तामुपाश्रिताः ।	*pralayāntāmupāśritāḥ* ׀
कामोपभोगपरमा	*kāmopabhogaparamā*
एतावदिति निश्चिताः ॥ १६.११	*etāvaditi niścitāḥ* ॥ 16.11
आशापाशशतैर्बद्धाः	*āśāpāśaśatairbaddhāḥ*
कामक्रोधपरायणाः ।	*kāmakrodhaparāyaṇāḥ* ׀
ईहन्ते कामभोगार्थम्	*īhante kāmabhogārtham*
अन्यायेनार्थसञ्चयान् ॥ १६.१२	*anyāyenārthasañcayān* ॥ 16.12
इदमद्य मया लब्धम्	*idamadya mayā labdham*
इदं प्राप्स्ये मनोरथम् ।	*idaṃ prāpsye manoratham* ׀
इदमस्तीदमपि मे	*idamastīdamapi me*
भविष्यति पुनर्धनम् ॥ १६.१३	*bhaviṣyati punardhanam* ॥ 16.13
असौ मया हतः शत्रुः	*asau mayā hataḥ śatruḥ*
हनिष्ये चापरानपि ।	*haniṣye cāparānapi* ׀
ईश्वरोऽहमहं भोगी	*īśvaro'hamahaṃ bhogī*
सिद्धोऽहं बलवान्सुखी ॥ १६.१४	*siddho'haṃ balavānsukhī* ॥ 16.14

आढ्योऽभिजनवानस्मि
कोऽन्योऽस्ति सदृशो मया ।
यक्ष्ये दास्यामि मोदिष्य
इत्यज्ञानविमोहिताः ॥ १६.१५

āḍhyo'bhijanavānasmi
ko'nyo'sti sadṛśo mayā ।
yakṣye dāsyāmi modiṣya
ityajñānavimohitāḥ ॥ 16.15

अनेकचित्तविभ्रान्ता
मोहजालसमावृताः ।
प्रसक्ताः कामभोगेषु
पतन्ति नरकेऽशुचौ ॥ १६.१६

anekacittavibhrāntā
mohajālasamāvṛtāḥ ।
prasaktāḥ kāmabhogeṣu
patanti narake'śucau ॥ 16.16

आत्मसम्भाविताः स्तब्धा
धनमानमदान्विताः ।
यजन्ते नामयज्ञैस्ते
दम्भेनाविधिपूर्वकम् ॥ १६.१७

ātmasambhāvitāḥ stabdhā
dhanamānamadānvitāḥ ।
yajante nāmayajñaiste
dambhenāvidhipūrvakam ॥ 16.17

अहङ्कारं बलं दर्पं
कामं क्रोधं च संश्रिताः ।
मामात्मपरदेहेषु
प्रद्विषन्तोऽभ्यसूयकाः ॥ १६.१८

ahaṅkāraṃ balaṃ darpaṃ
kāmaṃ krodhaṃ ca saṃśritāḥ ।
māmātmaparadeheṣu
pradviṣanto'bhyasūyakāḥ ॥ 16.18

तानहं द्विषतः क्रूरान्
संसारेषु नराधमान् ।
क्षिपाम्यजस्रमशुभान्
आसुरीष्वेव योनिषु ॥ १६.१९

tānahaṃ dviṣataḥ krūrān
saṃsāreṣu narādhamān ।
kṣipāmyajasramaśubhān
āsurīṣveva yoniṣu ॥ 16.19

आसुरीं योनिमापन्ना
मूढा जन्मनि जन्मनि ।
मामप्राप्यैव कौन्तेय
ततो यान्त्यधमां गतिम् ॥ १६.२०

āsurīṃ yonimāpannā
mūḍhā janmani janmani ।
māmaprāpyaiva kaunteya
tato yāntyadhamāṃ gatim ॥ 16.20

त्रिविधं नरकस्येदं
द्वारं नाशनमात्मनः ।
कामः क्रोधस्तथा लोभः
तस्मादेतत्त्रयं त्यजेत् ॥ १६.२१

trividhaṃ narakasyedaṃ
dvāraṃ nāśanamātmanaḥ ।
kāmaḥ krodhastathā lobhaḥ
tasmādetattrayaṃ tyajet ॥ 16.21

एतैर्विमुक्तः कौन्तेय तमोद्वारैस्त्रिभिर्नरः । आचरत्यात्मनः श्रेयः ततो याति परां गतिम् ॥ १६.२२	*etairvimuktaḥ kaunteya* *tamodvāraistribhirnaraḥ* । *ācaratyātmanaḥ śreyaḥ* *tato yāti parāṃ gatim* ॥ 16.22
यः शास्त्रविधिमुत्सृज्य वर्तते कामकारतः । न स सिद्धिमवाप्नोति न सुखं न परां गतिम् ॥ १६.२३	*yaḥ śāstravidhimutsṛjya* *vartate kāmakārataḥ* । *na sa siddhimavāpnoti* *na sukhaṃ na parāṃ gatim* ॥ 16.23
तस्माच्छास्त्रं प्रमाणं ते कार्याकार्यव्यवस्थितौ । ज्ञात्वा शास्त्रविधानोक्तं कर्म कर्तुमिहार्हसि ॥ १६.२४	*tasmācchāstraṃ pramāṇaṃ te* *kāryākāryavyavasthitau* । *jñātvā śāstravidhānoktaṃ* *karma kartumihārhasi* ॥ 16.24

CHAPTER 16

Divine and Demonic

Kṛṣṇa

[1]Courage, purity of heart,
pursuit of knowledge and wisdom,
generosity, self-control,
spirit of sacrifice, study of scriptures,
austerity, simplicity, righteousness,
[2]benevolence, honesty, freedom from anger,
a sense of renunciation, serenity,
not finding fault with others,
kindness to all beings,
gentleness, modesty,
absence of greed and fickleness,
[3]radiance, patience,
strength, cleanliness, and
absence of malice and false pride –
these are the qualities of a person
of divine nature.

4 Hypocrisy, arrogance, vanity, anger, cruelty, and ignorance
are the traits of a person with demonic nature.

Here, 'ignorance' refers to lack of perseverance in the path of knowledge.

In a strict traditional sense, divine and demonic qualities belong to one who is 'born with' a divine or demonic nature. However, a person with demonic traits can readily become noble by undivided devotion to the Supreme (see 9.30–32).

5 The divine qualities lead to liberation.
The demonic qualities lead to bondage.
But don't worry Arjuna,
you are endowed with divine qualities.

6 There are two types of people in the world:
the divine and the demonic.
I have spoken about the divine ones in detail.
Now hear from me about the demonic ones.

Kṛṣṇa has explained divine attributes in 12.13–20, 13.7–11, and in other instances.

7Demonic people don't understand
what should be done and what shouldn't.
They are neither pure nor honest;
even their behavior is not good.

8They proclaim:
"The universe has no basis and no abiding truth.
There is no greater force governing it.
Life is merely a product of mutual union, driven by lust!"

Here, 'basis' refers to *dharma*, that which supports and sustains everything. Such people claim that the universe has no meaningful order; they also fail to see a larger purpose for any activity. Since they don't recognize the cosmic order they don't realize how much they owe to the world around them.

9Rigidly holding on to such views,
these lost souls of limited understanding
commit many cruel deeds.
They are indeed enemies of the world,
bent upon its destruction.

These people neither perceive a grander cosmic order of the universe nor recognize a greater social order of the world and disturb the overall harmony for satisfying momentary pleasures.

10Clinging on to unquenchable passions,
drunk with pride and hypocrisy,
they live in delusion with false notions,
and act with impure motives.

11 Till their last breath
they are lost in
boundless wishes and anxieties.
Gratification of desire is their highest aim,
as if that is all there is to one's life!

12 Bound by a hundred chains of vain hope and
driven by lust and anger,
they amass wealth by unjust means
for sensual enjoyment.

13 "I have gained this today and
I shall attain that tomorrow.
All these riches are mine, and
soon I shall have more!
14 I am the lord.
I have killed this enemy and
I will also destroy all other enemies.
I am successful and I am powerful;
I am healthy and I enjoy life.
15 I am noble and I am rich.
Who is my equal?
I will perform elaborate rituals,
I will give alms and
I will rejoice as per my will" –
thus they boast out of sheer ignorance.

16 Carried away
by countless fanciful thoughts,
they get caught in the web of illusion
and are addicted to
gratification of the senses.

Thus they plunge into the hell
of their own making.

17 They are arrogant and stubborn.
Intoxicated by wealth and pride,
they engage in worship
only in name (and not in spirit)
focusing more on pomp and show,
without regard for rules or regulations.

18 Clinging on to egoism and vanity,
exhibiting force, lust, and rage,
these malicious people
undermine the Divine Presence
in their own bodies and in the bodies of others.

19 I constantly throw these cruel, hateful, and worst of men,
into demonic wombs in the vast cycles of birth and death.

Here 'demonic womb' signifies rebirth with demonic qualities.

[20]Again and again, these deluded people
are born with demonic traits
and fail to attain the Supreme;
they sink to the lowest state.

There is always an option to come out of the demonic state and tread the path of goodness but those who choose not to adhere to the wisdom (as laid out in the following verses) are subjected to rebirth with demonic traits, time and again.

[21]**Lust, anger, and greed**
are the three gates to *naraka*
that degrade the self.
One should renounce them!

Lust, anger, and greed are impediments in the path of self-realization.
In this context, '*naraka*' is a confused state of mind that degrades the self.
In the literal sense, *naraka*—loosely, 'hell'—is a transient, after-death abode where one is punished for the *pāpa* (evil, sin, guilt, crime) he has committed.

[22]One who is liberated from these three gates of darkness
elevates his inner self and attains the ultimate goal.

[23]One who ignores the established rules
and follows his own preferences
driven by selfish desires does not attain
perfection, happiness, or liberation.

The wise have given us practical guides and principles to lead a good life.
While Kṛṣṇa advises Arjuna to engage in battle, Arjuna has to use
his own knowledge and skill of warfare.
Texts like the *Bhagavad-gītā* suffice for eternal aspects,
but we still have to know the rules for the roles we play in daily life.

[24]Therefore, let the words of the wise
be your guide in determining
what should be done and what should not.
Having understood the mandate of the scriptures,
you should act accordingly.

17

अर्जुन उवाच।
ये शास्त्रविधिमुत्सृज्य
यजन्ते श्रद्धयान्विताः।
तेषां निष्ठा तु का कृष्ण
सत्त्वमाहो रजस्तमः॥ १७.१

arjuna uvāca ।
ye śāstravidhimutsṛjya
yajante śraddhayānvitāḥ ।
teṣāṃ niṣṭhā tu kā kṛṣṇa
sattvamāho rajastamaḥ ॥ 17.1

श्रीभगवानुवाच।
त्रिविधा भवति श्रद्धा
देहिनां सा स्वभावजा।
सात्त्विकी राजसी चैव
तामसी चेति तां शृणु॥ १७.२

śrībhagavānuvāca ।
trividhā bhavati śraddhā
dehināṃ sā svabhāvajā ।
sāttvikī rājasī caiva
tāmasī ceti tāṃ śṛṇu ॥ 17.2

सत्त्वानुरूपा सर्वस्य
श्रद्धा भवति भारत।
श्रद्धामयोऽयं पुरुषो
यो यच्छ्रद्धः स एव सः॥ १७.३

sattvānurūpā sarvasya
śraddhā bhavati bhārata ।
śraddhāmayo'yaṃ puruṣo
yo yacchraddhaḥ sa eva saḥ ॥ 17.3

यजन्ते सात्त्विका देवान्
यक्षरक्षांसि राजसाः।
प्रेतान्भूतगणांश्चान्ये
यजन्ते तामसा जनाः॥ १७.४

yajante sāttvikā devān
yakṣarakṣāṃsi rājasāḥ ।
pretānbhūtagaṇāṃścānye
yajante tāmasā janāḥ ॥ 17.4

अशास्त्रविहितं घोरं
तप्यन्ते ये तपो जनाः।
दम्भाहङ्कारसंयुक्ताः
कामरागबलान्विताः॥ १७.५

aśāstravihitaṃ ghoraṃ
tapyante ye tapo janāḥ ।
dambhāhaṅkārasaṃyuktāḥ
kāmarāgabalānvitāḥ ॥ 17.5

कर्शयन्तः शरीरस्थं
भूतग्राममचेतसः।
मां चैवान्तःशरीरस्थं
तान्विद्ध्यासुरनिश्चयान्॥ १७.६

karśayantaḥ śarīrasthaṃ
bhūtagrāmamacetasaḥ ।
māṃ caivāntaḥśarīrasthaṃ
tānviddhyāsuraniścayān ॥ 17.6

आहारस्त्वपि सर्वस्य
त्रिविधो भवति प्रियः।
यज्ञस्तपस्तथा दानं
तेषां भेदमिमं शृणु॥ १७.७

āhārastvapi sarvasya
trividho bhavati priyaḥ ।
yajñastapastathā dānaṃ
teṣāṃ bhedamimaṃ śṛṇu ॥ 17.7

आयुःसत्त्वबलारोग्य-
सुखप्रीतिविवर्धनाः ।
रस्याः स्निग्धाः स्थिरा हृद्या
आहाराः सात्त्विकप्रियाः ॥ १७.८

āyuḥsattvabalārogya-
sukhaprītivivardhanāḥ ।
rasyāḥ snigdhāḥ sthirā hṛdyā
āhārāḥ sāttvikapriyāḥ ॥ 17.8

कट्वम्ललवणात्युष्ण-
तीक्ष्णरूक्षविदाहिनः ।
आहारा राजसस्येष्टा
दुःखशोकामयप्रदाः ॥ १७.९

kaṭvamlalavaṇātyuṣṇa-
tīkṣṇarūkṣavidāhinaḥ ।
āhārā rājasasyeṣṭā
duḥkhaśokāmayapradāḥ ॥ 17.9

यातयामं गतरसं
पूति पर्युषितं च यत् ।
उच्छिष्टमपि चामेध्यं
भोजनं तामसप्रियम् ॥ १७.१०

yātayāmaṃ gatarasaṃ
pūti paryuṣitaṃ ca yat ।
ucchiṣṭamapi cāmedhyaṃ
bhojanaṃ tāmasapriyam ॥ 17.10

अफलाकाङ्क्षिभिर्यज्ञो
विधिदृष्टो य इज्यते ।
यष्टव्यमेवेति मनः
समाधाय स सात्त्विकः ॥ १७.११

aphalākāṅkṣibhiryajño
vidhidṛṣṭo ya ijyate ।
yaṣṭavyameveti manaḥ
samādhāya sa sāttvikaḥ ॥ 17.11

अभिसन्धाय तु फलं
दम्भार्थमपि चैव यत् ।
इज्यते भरतश्रेष्ठ
तं यज्ञं विद्धि राजसम् ॥ १७.१२

abhisandhāya tu phalaṃ
dambhārthamapi caiva yat ।
ijyate bharataśreṣṭha
taṃ yajñaṃ viddhi rājasam ॥ 17.12

विधिहीनमसृष्टान्नं
मन्त्रहीनमदक्षिणम् ।
श्रद्धाविरहितं यज्ञं
तामसं परिचक्षते ॥ १७.१३

vidhihīnamasṛṣṭānnaṃ
mantrahīnamadakṣiṇam ।
śraddhāvirahitaṃ yajñaṃ
tāmasaṃ paricakṣate ॥ 17.13

देवद्विजगुरुप्राज्ञ-
पूजनं शौचमार्जवम् ।
ब्रह्मचर्यमहिंसा च
शारीरं तप उच्यते ॥ १७.१४

devadvijaguruprājña-
pūjanaṃ śaucamārjavam ।
brahmacaryamahiṃsā ca
śārīraṃ tapa ucyate ॥ 17.14

अनुद्वेगकरं वाक्यं सत्यं प्रियहितं च यत्। स्वाध्यायाभ्यसनं चैव वाङ्मयं तप उच्यते ॥ १७.१५	*anudvegakaraṃ vākyaṃ* *satyaṃ priyahitaṃ ca yat* । *svādhyāyābhyasanaṃ caiva* *vāṅmayaṃ tapa ucyate* ॥ 17.15
मनःप्रसादः सौम्यत्वं मौनमात्मविनिग्रहः। भावसंशुद्धिरित्येतत् तपो मानसमुच्यते ॥ १७.१६	*manaḥprasādaḥ saumyatvaṃ* *maunamātmavinigrahaḥ* । *bhāvasaṃśuddhirityetat* *tapo mānasamucyate* ॥ 17.16
श्रद्धया परया तप्तं तपस्तत्त्रिविधं नरैः। अफलाकाङ्क्षिभिर्युक्तैः सात्त्विकं परिचक्षते ॥ १७.१७	*śraddhayā parayā taptaṃ* *tapastattrividhaṃ naraiḥ* । *aphalākāṅkṣibhiryuktaiḥ* *sāttvikaṃ paricakṣate* ॥ 17.17
सत्कारमानपूजार्थं तपो दम्भेन चैव यत्। क्रियते तदिह प्रोक्तं राजसं चलमध्रुवम् ॥ १७.१८	*satkāramānapūjārthaṃ* *tapo dambhena caiva yat* । *kriyate tadiha proktaṃ* *rājasaṃ calamadhruvam* ॥ 17.18
मूढग्राहेणात्मनो यत् पीडया क्रियते तपः। परस्योत्सादनार्थं वा तत्तामसमुदाहृतम् ॥ १७.१९	*mūḍhagrāheṇātmano yat* *pīḍayā kriyate tapaḥ* । *parasyotsādanārthaṃ vā* *tattāmasamudāhṛtam* ॥ 17.19
दातव्यमिति यद्दानं दीयतेऽनुपकारिणे। देशे काले च पात्रे च तद्दानं सात्त्विकं स्मृतम् ॥ १७.२०	*dātavyamiti yaddānaṃ* *dīyate'nupakāriṇe* । *deśe kāle ca pātre ca* *taddānaṃ sāttvikaṃ smṛtam* ॥ 17.20
यत्तु प्रत्युपकारार्थं फलमुद्दिश्य वा पुनः। दीयते च परिक्लिष्टं तद्दानं राजसं स्मृतम् ॥ १७.२१	*yattu pratyupakārārthaṃ* *phalamuddiśya vā punaḥ* । *dīyate ca parikliṣṭaṃ* *taddānaṃ rājasaṃ smṛtam* ॥ 17.21

अदेशकाले यद्दानम्
अपात्रेभ्यश्च दीयते।
असत्कृतमवज्ञातं
तत्तामसमुदाहृतम् ॥ १७.२२

adeśakāle yaddānam
apātrebhyaśca dīyate ।
asatkṛtamavajñātaṃ
tattāmasamudāhṛtam ॥ 17.22

ॐ तत्सदिति निर्देशो
ब्रह्मणस्त्रिविधः स्मृतः।
ब्राह्मणास्तेन वेदाश्च
यज्ञाश्च विहिताः पुरा ॥ १७.२३

oṃ tatsaditi nirdeśo
brahmaṇastrividhaḥ smṛtaḥ ।
brāhmaṇāstena vedāśca
yajñāśca vihitāḥ purā ॥ 17.23

तस्मादोमित्युदाहृत्य
यज्ञदानतपःक्रियाः।
प्रवर्तन्ते विधानोक्ताः
सततं ब्रह्मवादिनाम् ॥ १७.२४

tasmādomityudāhṛtya
yajñadānatapaḥkriyāḥ ।
pravartante vidhānoktāḥ
satataṃ brahmavādinām ॥ 17.24

तदित्यनभिसन्धाय
फलं यज्ञतपःक्रियाः।
दानक्रियाश्च विविधाः
क्रियन्ते मोक्षकाङ्क्षिभिः ॥ १७.२५

tadityanabhisandhāya
phalaṃ yajñatapaḥkriyāḥ ।
dānakriyāśca vividhāḥ
kriyante mokṣakāṅkṣibhiḥ ॥ 17.25

सद्भावे साधुभावे च
सदित्येतत्प्रयुज्यते।
प्रशस्ते कर्मणि तथा
सच्छब्दः पार्थ युज्यते ॥ १७.२६

sadbhāve sādhubhāve ca
sadityetatprayujyate ।
praśaste karmaṇi tathā
sacchabdaḥ pārtha yujyate ॥ 17.26

यज्ञे तपसि दाने च
स्थितिः सदिति चोच्यते।
कर्म चैव तदर्थीयं
सदित्येवाभिधीयते ॥ १७.२७

yajñe tapasi dāne ca
sthitiḥ saditi cocyate ।
karma caiva tadarthīyaṃ
sadityevābhidhīyate ॥ 17.27

अश्रद्धया हुतं दत्तं
तपस्तप्तं कृतं च यत्।
असदित्युच्यते पार्थ
न च तत्प्रेत्य नो इह ॥ १७.२८

aśraddhayā hutaṃ dattaṃ
tapastaptaṃ kṛtaṃ ca yat ।
asadityucyate pārtha
na ca tatpretya no iha ॥ 17.28

CHAPTER 17

Attitudes at Work

Arjuna

[1]When a person sincerely engages in worship
but fails to follow the prescribed rules,
is that an act of
sattva, *rajas*, or *tamas*?

The three *guṇas* (inherent tendencies) are –
sattva (benign goodness),
rajas (relentless activity), and
tamas (deluded lethargy).

Kṛṣṇa

[2]Human attitudes
are of three kinds –
sattva, *rajas*, or *tamas*.
They are born of one's own nature.
Listen, as I explain further.

In any individual, the three *guṇas* prevail to varying extents.
'...one's own nature' refers to the innate and untutored aspect of the personality.

3Each one's temperament conforms with his inborn nature.
A man is made up of his attitude.
He is what his attitude is.

4People with the nature of *sattva* worship the *devas*,
those of *rajas* worship *yakṣas* and *rākṣasas*, and
those of *tamas* worship evil spirits and ghosts.

Devas are divine beings.
Yakṣas and *rākṣasas* are spirits with special powers;
while *yakṣas* are semi-divine and benevolent,
rākṣasas are notorious and often disturb the harmony.

5Those who perform austerities
motivated by false pride and ego,
driven by the force of lust and passion
indeed violate the sayings of the scriptures.

[6]They foolishly torture the body
and also the divine spirit within.
Know them to be of a demonic resolve!

Some people feel that it is a noble thing to subject oneself or others to torture in the name of religion. Kṛṣṇa reminds Arjuna that exaggerated austerities or mortifications of the body are unwarranted, to the point of being demonic.

[7]Food that is dear to a person
is also of three kinds,
just as with the ways of
yajña, *dāna*, and *tapas*.
Let me explain the differences to you.

Yajña is the *Vedic* fire ritual, which inolves
worship of the divine, interaction, and sharing.
In a broader sense, it refers to a sense of dedication to work.
Dāna is charity that is undertaken with a feeling that it is one's duty to give
and includes offering the right gift to the deserving person at an appropriate time.
Tapas refers to austerity, penance, and single-minded focus on work.

[8]Foods that promote longevity, vitality, stamina,
health, happiness, and contentment and
foods that are tasty, mild, nourishing, and pleasant
are dear to those of the nature of *sattva*.

[9]Foods that cause pain, sorrow, and sickness,
and foods that are bitter, sour, salty,
excessively hot, spicy, dry, and pungent
are dear to those of the nature of *rajas*.

10 Foods which are insipid, stale, rotten,
left-over, filthy, and unhygienic
are dear to those of the nature of *tamas*.

The above verses (17.7–10) describe the kinds of food that people like.
Here, '...dear to those of the nature of *sattva* (or *rajas* or *tamas*)'
is perhaps just an indication of *what they don't mind eating*.
It is likely that a person who relishes stale food
will also relish fresh food, but not the other way round!

11 The *yajña* that is carefully performed,
according to the scriptures,
without any thought of reward, and
with the sense that it must be performed
is of the nature of *sattva*.

12 The *yajña* that is performed
for the sake of reward
or merely to show off
is of the nature of *rajas*.

[13]The *yajña* that is performed
contrary to the scriptures –
without sincerity,
without offering food,
with no sacred texts recited,
without respect to guests, and
without paying the officiator of the ritual –
is of the nature of *tamas*.

[14]Simplicity, self-restraint, purity, benevolence, and
respect for gods, *brāhmaṇas*, *gurus*, and the wise –
this is austerity of body.

This leads to the refinement of the body.
A *brāhmaṇa* is one who has traits of serenity, austerity, forgiveness, *etc.* (see 18.42).

[15]Speaking words that are truthful, pleasant,
beneficial, and not causing distress or anxiety,
as well as the study and recitation of scriptures –
this is austerity of speech.

This leads to the refinement of speech.

[16]Silence, serenity of mind, self-control,
gentleness, and purity of thought and being –
this is austerity of mind.

This leads to the refinement of the mind.

[17]This threefold austerity, diligently practiced
with utmost commitment and without desire for reward
is of the nature of *sattva*.

[18]This threefold austerity practiced
merely out of pride and hypocrisy
for the sake of gaining temporary rewards
such as praise, respect, and special treatment,
are of the nature of *rajas*.

[19]This threefold austerity performed with foolish notions
by torturing oneself or by injuring others,
are of the nature of *tamas*.

[20]Giving with the feeling that it is one's duty to give,
without expectation of anything in return, and
offering it at the right place and at the right time
to a worthy person
who cannot return the favor,
is of the nature of *sattva*.

[21]Giving something reluctantly or
with the aim of getting something in return or
with some other ulterior motive
is of the nature of *rajas*.

[22]Giving with contempt and disrespect,
offering it at the wrong place
and at the wrong time
to an unworthy person,
is of the nature of *tamas*.

[23]'*Om*,' '*Tat*,' and '*Sat*' –
each word is a reference to *Brahman*.
The *Vedas*, *yajñas*, and *brāhmaṇas*
were established in them
from ancient times.

Brahman is the Supreme Being.
The *Vedas* are the foremost revealed scriptures in Hinduism.

Performing *yajña*, *dāna*, and *tapas* with the attitude of *sattva* is best
but even so, there is a tinge of impurity associated with them.
Invoking '*om*,' '*tat*,' and '*sat*' helps cleanse those activities.

Om is a single syllable word that denotes *Brahman*.
It is the most sacred sound according to Hindu belief.

Tat means 'that' or 'it' and refers to *Brahman*.
It reminds us that 'we are not doing the work' and helps overcome our ego.

Sat means 'existence,' 'real,' or 'good' and refers to *Brahman*.
It inspires an overall attitude of goodness in action.

24 Therefore, as a rule,
students of the scriptures
always chant '*om*' before
yajña, *dāna*, or *tapas*.

25 The seekers of liberation
say '*tat*' prior to
yajña, *dāna*, and *tapas*,
with no desire for rewards.

26 '*Sat*' refers to goodness and reality.
Thus, the word '*sat*' is also used
to denote any act worthy of praise.

27 Doing *yajña*, *dāna*, and *tapas*
with dedication is *sat*.
Any action we perform
to support that is also *sat*.

28 Doing *yajña*, *dāna*, or *tapas*
without dedication is *asat*
and has no value in this world or beyond.

Asat means 'unreal,' the opposite of reality and goodness.
Compare this verse with verse 6.40.

18

अर्जुन उवाच ।
संन्यासस्य महाबाहो
तत्त्वमिच्छामि वेदितुम् ।
त्यागस्य च हृषीकेश
पृथक्केशिनिषूदन ॥ १८.१

arjuna uvāca ।
saṃnyāsasya mahābāho
tattvamicchāmi veditum ।
tyāgasya ca hṛṣīkeśa
pṛthakkeśiniṣūdana ॥ 18.1

श्रीभगवानुवाच ।
काम्यानां कर्मणां न्यासं
संन्यासं कवयो विदुः ।
सर्वकर्मफलत्यागं
प्राहुस्त्यागं विचक्षणाः ॥ १८.२

śrībhagavānuvāca ।
kāmyānāṃ karmaṇāṃ nyāsaṃ
saṃnyāsaṃ kavayo viduḥ ।
sarvakarmaphalatyāgaṃ
prāhustyāgaṃ vicakṣaṇāḥ ॥ 18.2

त्याज्यं दोषवदित्येके
कर्म प्राहुर्मनीषिणः ।
यज्ञदानतपःकर्म
न त्याज्यमिति चापरे ॥ १८.३

tyājyaṃ doṣavadityeke
karma prāhurmanīṣiṇaḥ ।
yajñadānatapaḥkarma
na tyājyamiti cāpare ॥ 18.3

निश्चयं शृणु मे तत्र
त्यागे भरतसत्तम ।
त्यागो हि पुरुषव्याघ्र
त्रिविधः सम्प्रकीर्तितः ॥ १८.४

niścayaṃ śṛṇu me tatra
tyāge bharatasattama ।
tyāgo hi puruṣavyāghra
trividhaḥ samprakīrtitaḥ ॥ 18.4

यज्ञदानतपःकर्म
न त्याज्यं कार्यमेव तत् ।
यज्ञो दानं तपश्चैव
पावनानि मनीषिणाम् ॥ १८.५

yajñadānatapaḥkarma
na tyājyaṃ kāryameva tat ।
yajño dānaṃ tapaścaiva
pāvanāni manīṣiṇām ॥ 18.5

एतान्यपि तु कर्माणि
सङ्गं त्यक्त्वा फलानि च ।
कर्तव्यानीति मे पार्थ
निश्चितं मतमुत्तमम् ॥ १८.६

etānyapi tu karmāṇi
saṅgaṃ tyaktvā phalāni ca ।
kartavyānīti me pārtha
niścitaṃ matamuttamam ॥ 18.6

नियतस्य तु संन्यासः
कर्मणो नोपपद्यते ।
मोहात्तस्य परित्यागः
तामसः परिकीर्तितः ॥ १८.७

niyatasya tu saṃnyāsaḥ
karmaṇo nopapadyate ।
mohāttasya parityāgaḥ
tāmasaḥ parikīrtitaḥ ॥ 18.7

दुःखमित्येव यत्कर्म
कायक्लेशभयात्त्यजेत् ।
स कृत्वा राजसं त्यागं
नैव त्यागफलं लभेत् ॥ १८.८

duḥkhamityeva yatkarma
kāyakleśabhayāttyajet ।
sa kṛtvā rājasaṃ tyāgaṃ
naiva tyāgaphalaṃ labhet ॥ 18.8

कार्यमित्येव यत्कर्म
नियतं क्रियतेऽर्जुन ।
सङ्गं त्यक्त्वा फलं चैव
स त्यागः सात्त्विको मतः ॥ १८.९

kāryamityeva yatkarma
niyataṃ kriyate'rjuna ।
saṅgaṃ tyaktvā phalaṃ caiva
sa tyāgaḥ sāttviko mataḥ ॥ 18.9

न द्वेष्ट्यकुशलं कर्म
कुशले नानुषज्जते ।
त्यागी सत्त्वसमाविष्टो
मेधावी छिन्नसंशयः ॥ १८.१०

na dveṣṭyakuśalaṃ karma
kuśale nānuṣajjate ।
tyāgī sattvasamāviṣṭo
medhāvī chinnasaṃśayaḥ ॥ 18.10

न हि देहभृता शक्यं
त्यक्तुं कर्माण्यशेषतः ।
यस्तु कर्मफलत्यागी
स त्यागीत्यभिधीयते ॥ १८.११

na hi dehabhṛtā śakyaṃ
tyaktuṃ karmāṇyaśeṣataḥ ।
yastu karmaphalatyāgī
sa tyāgītyabhidhīyate ॥ 18.11

अनिष्टमिष्टं मिश्रं च
त्रिविधं कर्मणः फलम् ।
भवत्यत्यागिनां प्रेत्य
न तु संन्यासिनां क्वचित् ॥ १८.१२

aniṣṭamiṣṭaṃ miśraṃ ca
trividhaṃ karmaṇaḥ phalam ।
bhavatyatyāgināṃ pretya
na tu saṃnyāsināṃ kvacit ॥ 18.12

पञ्चैतानि महाबाहो
कारणानि निबोध मे ।
साङ्ख्ये कृतान्ते प्रोक्तानि
सिद्धये सर्वकर्मणाम् ॥ १८.१३

pañcaitāni mahābāho
kāraṇāni nibodha me ।
sāṅkhye kṛtānte proktāni
siddhaye sarvakarmaṇām ॥ 18.13

अधिष्ठानं तथा कर्ता
करणं च पृथग्विधम् ।
विविधाश्च पृथक्चेष्टा
दैवं चैवात्र पञ्चमम् ॥ १८.१४

adhiṣṭhānaṃ tathā kartā
karaṇaṃ ca pṛthagvidham ।
vividhāśca pṛthakceṣṭā
daivaṃ caivātra pañcamam ॥ 18.14

शरीरवाङ्मनोभिर्यत्
कर्म प्रारभते नरः ।
न्याय्यं वा विपरीतं वा
पञ्चैते तस्य हेतवः ॥ १८.१५

śarīravāṅmanobhiryat
karma prārabhate naraḥ ।
nyāyyaṃ vā viparītaṃ vā
pañcaite tasya hetavaḥ ॥ 18.15

तत्रैवं सति कर्तारम्
आत्मानं केवलं तु यः ।
पश्यत्यकृतबुद्धित्वान्
न स पश्यति दुर्मतिः ॥ १८.१६

tatraivaṃ sati kartāram
ātmānaṃ kevalaṃ tu yaḥ ।
paśyatyakṛtabuddhitvān
na sa paśyati durmatiḥ ॥ 18.16

यस्य नाहङ्कृतो भावो
बुद्धिर्यस्य न लिप्यते ।
हत्वापि स इमाँल्लोकान्
न हन्ति न निबध्यते ॥ १८.१७

yasya nāhaṅkṛto bhāvo
buddhiryasya na lipyate ।
hatvāpi sa imām̐llokān
na hanti na nibadhyate ॥ 18.17

ज्ञानं ज्ञेयं परिज्ञाता
त्रिविधा कर्मचोदना ।
करणं कर्म कर्तेति
त्रिविधः कर्मसङ्ग्रहः ॥ १८.१८

jñānaṃ jñeyaṃ parijñātā
trividhā karmacodanā ।
karaṇaṃ karma karteti
trividhaḥ karmasaṅgrahaḥ ॥ 18.18

ज्ञानं कर्म च कर्ता च
त्रिधैव गुणभेदतः ।
प्रोच्यते गुणसङ्ख्याने
यथावच्छृणु तान्यपि ॥ १८.१९

jñānaṃ karma ca kartā ca
tridhaiva guṇabhedataḥ ।
procyate guṇasaṅkhyāne
yathāvacchṛṇu tānyapi ॥ 18.19

सर्वभूतेषु येनैकं
भावमव्ययमीक्षते ।
अविभक्तं विभक्तेषु
तज्ज्ञानं विद्धि सात्त्विकम् ॥ १८.२०

sarvabhūteṣu yenaikaṃ
bhāvamavyayamīkṣate ।
avibhaktaṃ vibhakteṣu
tajjñānaṃ viddhi sāttvikam ॥ 18.20

पृथक्त्वेन तु यज्ज्ञानं
नानाभावान्पृथग्विधान् ।
वेत्ति सर्वेषु भूतेषु
तज्ज्ञानं विद्धि राजसम् ॥ १८.२१

pṛthaktvena tu yajjñānaṃ
nānābhāvānpṛthagvidhān ।
vetti sarveṣu bhūteṣu
tajjñānaṃ viddhi rājasam ॥ 18.21

यत्तु कृत्स्नवदेकस्मिन्
कार्ये सक्तमहैतुकम् ।
अतत्त्वार्थवदल्पं च
तत्तामसमुदाहृतम् ॥ १८.२२

yattu kṛtsnavadekasmin
kārye saktamahaitukam ।
atattvārthavadalpaṃ ca
tattāmasamudāhṛtam ॥ 18.22

नियतं सङ्गरहितम्
अरागद्वेषतः कृतम् ।
अफलप्रेप्सुना कर्म
यत्तत्सात्त्विकमुच्यते ॥ १८.२३

niyataṃ saṅgarahitam
arāgadveṣataḥ kṛtam ।
aphalaprepsunā karma
yattatsāttvikamucyate ॥ 18.23

यत्तु कामेप्सुना कर्म
साहङ्कारेण वा पुनः ।
क्रियते बहुलायासं
तद्राजसमुदाहृतम् ॥ १८.२४

yattu kāmepsunā karma
sāhaṅkāreṇa vā punaḥ ।
kriyate bahulāyāsaṃ
tadrājasamudāhṛtam ॥ 18.24

अनुबन्धं क्षयं हिंसाम्
अनपेक्ष्य च पौरुषम् ।
मोहादारभ्यते कर्म
यत्तत्तामसमुच्यते ॥ १८.२५

anubandhaṃ kṣayaṃ hiṃsām
anapekṣya ca pauruṣam ।
mohādārabhyate karma
yattattāmasamucyate ॥ 18.25

मुक्तसङ्गोऽनहंवादी
धृत्युत्साहसमन्वितः ।
सिद्ध्यसिद्ध्योर्निर्विकारः
कर्ता सात्त्विक उच्यते ॥ १८.२६

muktasaṅgo'nahaṃvādī
dhṛtyutsāhasamanvitaḥ ।
siddhyasiddhyornirvikāraḥ
kartā sāttvika ucyate ॥ 18.26

रागी कर्मफलप्रेप्सुः
लुब्धो हिंसात्मकोऽशुचिः ।
हर्षशोकान्वितः कर्ता
राजसः परिकीर्तितः ॥ १८.२७

rāgī karmaphalaprepsuḥ
lubdho hiṃsātmako'śuciḥ ।
harṣaśokānvitaḥ kartā
rājasaḥ parikīrtitaḥ ॥ 18.27

अयुक्तः प्राकृतः स्तब्धः
शठो नैकृतिकोऽलसः ।
विषादी दीर्घसूत्री च
कर्ता तामस उच्यते ॥ १८.२८

ayuktaḥ prākṛtaḥ stabdhaḥ
śaṭho naikṛtiko'lasaḥ ।
viṣādī dīrghasūtrī ca
kartā tāmasa ucyate ॥ 18.28

बुद्धेर्भेदं धृतेश्चैव
गुणतस्त्रिविधं शृणु ।
प्रोच्यमानमशेषेण
पृथक्त्वेन धनञ्जय ॥ १८.२९

buddherbhedaṃ dhṛteścaiva
guṇatastrividhaṃ śṛṇu ।
procyamānamaśeṣeṇa
pṛthaktvena dhanañjaya ॥ 18.29

प्रवृत्तिं च निवृत्तिं च
कार्याकार्ये भयाभये ।
बन्धं मोक्षं च या वेत्ति
बुद्धिः सा पार्थ सात्त्विकी ॥ १८.३०

pravṛttiṃ ca nivṛttiṃ ca
kāryākārye bhayābhaye ।
bandhaṃ mokṣaṃ ca yā vetti
buddhiḥ sā pārtha sāttvikī ॥ 18.30

यया धर्ममधर्मं च
कार्यं चाकार्यम् एव च ।
अयथावत्प्रजानाति
बुद्धिः सा पार्थ राजसी ॥ १८.३१

yayā dharmamadharmaṃ ca
kāryaṃ cākāryam eva ca ।
ayathāvatprajānāti
buddhiḥ sā pārtha rājasī ॥ 18.31

अधर्मं धर्ममिति या
मन्यते तमसावृता ।
सर्वार्थान्विपरीतांश्च
बुद्धिः सा पार्थ तामसी ॥ १८.३२

adharmaṃ dharmamiti yā
manyate tamasāvṛtā ।
sarvārthānviparītāṃśca
buddhiḥ sā pārtha tāmasī ॥ 18.32

धृत्या यया धारयते
मनःप्राणेन्द्रियक्रियाः ।
योगेनाव्यभिचारिण्या
धृतिः सा पार्थ सात्त्विकी ॥ १८.३३

dhṛtyā yayā dhārayate
manaḥprāṇendriyakriyāḥ ।
yogenāvyabhicāriṇyā
dhṛtiḥ sā pārtha sāttvikī ॥ 18.33

यया तु धर्मकामार्थान्
धृत्या धारयतेऽर्जुन ।
प्रसङ्गेन फलाकाङ्क्षी
धृतिः सा पार्थ राजसी ॥ १८.३४

yayā tu dharmakāmārthān
dhṛtyā dhārayate'rjuna ।
prasaṅgena phalākāṅkṣī
dhṛtiḥ sā pārtha rājasī ॥ 18.34

यया स्वप्नं भयं शोकं
विषादं मदमेव च ।
न विमुञ्चति दुर्मेधा
धृतिः सा पार्थ तामसी ॥ १८.३५

yayā svapnaṃ bhayaṃ śokaṃ
viṣādaṃ madameva ca ।
na vimuñcati durmedhā
dhṛtiḥ sā pārtha tāmasī ॥ 18.35

सुखं त्विदानीं त्रिविधं
शृणु मे भरतर्षभ ।
अभ्यासाद्रमते यत्र
दुःखान्तं च निगच्छति ॥ १८.३६

sukhaṃ tvidānīṃ trividhaṃ
śṛṇu me bharatarṣabha ।
abhyāsādramate yatra
duḥkhāntaṃ ca nigacchati ॥ 18.36

यत्तदग्रे विषमिव
परिणामेऽमृतोपमम् ।
तत्सुखं सात्त्विकं प्रोक्तम्
आत्मबुद्धिप्रसादजम् ॥ १८.३७

yattadagre viṣamiva
pariṇāme'mṛtopamam ।
tatsukhaṃ sāttvikaṃ proktam
ātmabuddhiprasādajam ॥ 18.37

विषयेन्द्रियसंयोगात्
यत्तदग्रेऽमृतोपमम् ।
परिणामे विषमिव
तत्सुखं राजसं स्मृतम् ॥ १८.३८

viṣayendriyasaṃyogāt
yattadagre'mṛtopamam ।
pariṇāme viṣamiva
tatsukhaṃ rājasaṃ smṛtam ॥ 18.38

यदग्रे चानुबन्धे च
सुखं मोहनमात्मनः ।
निद्रालस्यप्रमादोत्थं
तत्तामसमुदाहृतम् ॥ १८.३९

yadagre cānubandhe ca
sukhaṃ mohanamātmanaḥ ।
nidrālasyapramādotthaṃ
tattāmasamudāhṛtam ॥ 18.39

न तदस्ति पृथिव्यां वा
दिवि देवेषु वा पुनः ।
सत्त्वं प्रकृतिजैर्मुक्तं
यदेभिः स्यात्त्रिभिर्गुणैः ॥ १८.४०

na tadasti pṛthivyāṃ vā
divi deveṣu vā punaḥ ।
sattvaṃ prakṛtijairmuktaṃ
yadebhiḥ syāttribhirguṇaiḥ ॥ 18.40

ब्राह्मणक्षत्रियविशां
शूद्राणां च परन्तप ।
कर्माणि प्रविभक्तानि
स्वभावप्रभवैर्गुणैः ॥ १८.४१

brāhmaṇakṣatriyaviśāṃ
śūdrāṇāṃ ca parantapa ।
karmāṇi pravibhaktāni
svabhāvaprabhavairguṇaiḥ ॥ 18.41

शमो दमस्तपः शौचं
क्षान्तिरार्जवमेव च ।
ज्ञानं विज्ञानमास्तिक्यं
ब्रह्मकर्म स्वभावजम् ॥ १८.४२

śamo damastapaḥ śaucaṃ
kṣāntirārjavameva ca ।
jñānaṃ vijñānamāstikyaṃ
brahmakarma svabhāvajam ॥ 18.42

शौर्यं तेजो धृतिर्दाक्ष्यं
युद्धे चाप्यपलायनम् ।
दानमीश्वरभावश्च
क्षत्रकर्म स्वभावजम् ॥ १८.४३

śauryaṃ tejo dhṛtirdākṣyaṃ
yuddhe cāpyapalāyanam ।
dānamīśvarabhāvaśca
kṣatrakarma svabhāvajam ॥ 18.43

कृषिगोरक्ष्यवाणिज्यं
वैश्यकर्म स्वभावजम् ।
परिचर्यात्मकं कर्म
शूद्रस्यापि स्वभावजम् ॥ १८.४४

kṛṣigorakṣyavāṇijyaṃ
vaiśyakarma svabhāvajam ।
paricaryātmakaṃ karma
śūdrasyāpi svabhāvajam ॥ 18.44

स्वे स्वे कर्मण्यभिरतः
संसिद्धिं लभते नरः ।
स्वकर्मनिरतः सिद्धिं
यथा विन्दति तच्छृणु ॥ १८.४५

sve sve karmaṇyabhirataḥ
saṃsiddhiṃ labhate naraḥ ।
svakarmanirataḥ siddhiṃ
yathā vindati tacchṛṇu ॥ 18.45

यतः प्रवृत्तिर्भूतानां
येन सर्वमिदं ततम् ।
स्वकर्मणा तमभ्यर्च्य
सिद्धिं विन्दति मानवः ॥ १८.४६

yataḥ pravṛttirbhūtānāṃ
yena sarvamidaṃ tatam ।
svakarmaṇā tamabhyarcya
siddhiṃ vindati mānavaḥ ॥ 18.46

श्रेयान्स्वधर्मो विगुणः
परधर्मात्स्वनुष्ठितात् ।
स्वभावनियतं कर्म
कुर्वन्नाप्नोति किल्बिषम् ॥ १८.४७

śreyānsvadharmo viguṇaḥ
paradharmātsvanuṣṭhitāt ।
svabhāvaniyataṃ karma
kurvannāpnoti kilbiṣam ॥ 18.47

सहजं कर्म कौन्तेय
सदोषमपि न त्यजेत्।
सर्वारम्भा हि दोषेण
धूमेनाग्निरिवावृताः ॥ १८.४८

sahajaṃ karma kaunteya
sadoṣamapi na tyajet ।
sarvārambhā hi doṣeṇa
dhūmenāgnirivāvṛtāḥ ॥ 18.48

असक्तबुद्धिः सर्वत्र
जितात्मा विगतस्पृहः।
नैष्कर्म्यसिद्धिं परमां
संन्यासेनाधिगच्छति ॥ १८.४९

asaktabuddhiḥ sarvatra
jitātmā vigataspṛhaḥ ।
naiṣkarmyasiddhiṃ paramāṃ
saṃnyāsenādhigacchati ॥ 18.49

सिद्धिं प्राप्तो यथा ब्रह्म
तथाप्नोति निबोध मे।
समासेनैव कौन्तेय
निष्ठा ज्ञानस्य या परा ॥ १८.५०

siddhiṃ prāpto yathā brahma
tathāpnoti nibodha me ।
samāsenaiva kaunteya
niṣṭhā jñānasya yā parā ॥ 18.50

बुद्ध्या विशुद्धया युक्तो
धृत्यात्मानं नियम्य च।
शब्दादीन्विषयांस्त्यक्त्वा
रागद्वेषौ व्युदस्य च ॥ १८.५१

buddhyā viśuddhayā yukto
dhṛtyātmānaṃ niyamya ca ।
śabdādīnviṣayāṃstyaktvā
rāgadveṣau vyudasya ca ॥ 18.51

विविक्तसेवी लघ्वाशी
यतवाक्कायमानसः।
ध्यानयोगपरो नित्यं
वैराग्यं समुपाश्रितः ॥ १८.५२

viviktasevī laghvāśī
yatavākkāyamānasaḥ ।
dhyānayogaparo nityaṃ
vairāgyaṃ samupāśritaḥ ॥ 18.52

अहङ्कारं बलं दर्पं
कामं क्रोधं परिग्रहम्।
विमुच्य निर्ममः शान्तो
ब्रह्मभूयाय कल्पते ॥ १८.५३

ahaṅkāraṃ balaṃ darpaṃ
kāmaṃ krodhaṃ parigraham ।
vimucya nirmamaḥ śānto
brahmabhūyāya kalpate ॥ 18.53

ब्रह्मभूतः प्रसन्नात्मा
न शोचति न काङ्क्षति।
समः सर्वेषु भूतेषु
मद्भक्तिं लभते पराम् ॥ १८.५४

brahmabhūtaḥ prasannātmā
na śocati na kāṅkṣati ।
samaḥ sarveṣu bhūteṣu
madbhaktiṃ labhate parām ॥ 18.54

भक्त्या मामभिजानाति
यावान्यश्चास्मि तत्त्वतः।
ततो मां तत्त्वतो ज्ञात्वा
विशते तदनन्तरम् ॥ १८.५५

bhaktyā māmabhijānāti
yāvānyaścāsmi tattvataḥ ।
tato māṃ tattvato jñātvā
viśate tadanantaram ॥ 18.55

सर्वकर्माण्यपि सदा कुर्वाणो मद्व्यपाश्रयः । मत्प्रसादादवाप्नोति शाश्वतं पदमव्ययम् ॥ १८.५६	*sarvakarmāṇyapi sadā* *kurvāṇo madvyapāśrayaḥ* । *matprasādādavāpnoti* *śāśvataṃ padamavyayam* ॥ 18.56
चेतसा सर्वकर्माणि मयि संन्यस्य मत्परः । बुद्धियोगमुपाश्रित्य मच्चित्तः सततं भव ॥ १८.५७	*cetasā sarvakarmāṇi* *mayi saṃnyasya matparaḥ* । *buddhiyogamupāśritya* *maccittaḥ satataṃ bhava* ॥ 18.57
मच्चित्तः सर्वदुर्गाणि मत्प्रसादात्तरिष्यसि । अथ चेत्त्वमहङ्कारान् न श्रोष्यसि विनङ्क्ष्यसि ॥ १८.५८	*maccittaḥ sarvadurgāṇi* *matprasādāttariṣyasi* । *atha cettvamahaṅkārān* *na śroṣyasi vinaṅkṣyasi* ॥ 18.58
यदहङ्कारमाश्रित्य न योत्स्य इति मन्यसे । मिथ्यैष व्यवसायस्ते प्रकृतिस्त्वां नियोक्ष्यति ॥ १८.५९	*yadahaṅkāramāśritya* *na yotsya iti manyase* । *mithyaiṣa vyavasāyaste* *prakṛtistvāṃ niyokṣyati* ॥ 18.59
स्वभावजेन कौन्तेय निबद्धः स्वेन कर्मणा । कर्तुं नेच्छसि यन्मोहात् करिष्यस्यवशोऽपि तत् ॥ १८.६०	*svabhāvajena kaunteya* *nibaddhaḥ svena karmaṇā* । *kartuṃ necchasi yanmohāt* *kariṣyasyavaśo'pi tat* ॥ 18.60
ईश्वरः सर्वभूतानां हृद्देशेऽर्जुन तिष्ठति । भ्रामयन्सर्वभूतानि यन्त्रारूढानि मायया ॥ १८.६१	*īśvaraḥ sarvabhūtānāṃ* *hṛddeśe'rjuna tiṣṭhati* । *bhrāmayansarvabhūtāni* *yantrārūḍhāni māyayā* ॥ 18.61
तमेव शरणं गच्छ सर्वभावेन भारत । तत्प्रसादात्परां शान्तिं स्थानं प्राप्स्यसि शाश्वतम् ॥ १८.६२	*tameva śaraṇaṃ gaccha* *sarvabhāvena bhārata* । *tatprasādātparāṃ śāntiṃ* *sthānaṃ prāpsyasi śāśvatam* ॥ 18.62
इति ते ज्ञानमाख्यातं गुह्याद्गुह्यतरं मया । विमृश्यैतदशेषेण यथेच्छसि तथा कुरु ॥ १८.६३	*iti te jñānamākhyātaṃ* *guhyādguhyataraṃ mayā* । *vimṛśyaitadaśeṣeṇa* *yathecchasi tathā kuru* ॥ 18.63

सर्वगुह्यतमं भूयः
शृणु मे परमं वचः ।
इष्टोऽसि मे दृढमिति
ततो वक्ष्यामि ते हितम् ॥ १८.६४

sarvaguhyatamaṃ bhūyaḥ
śṛṇu me paramaṃ vacaḥ ।
iṣṭo'si me dṛḍhamiti
tato vakṣyāmi te hitam ॥ 18.64

मन्मना भव मद्भक्तो
मद्याजी मां नमस्कुरु ।
मामेवैष्यसि सत्यं ते
प्रतिजाने प्रियोऽसि मे ॥ १८.६५

manmanā bhava madbhakto
madyājī māṃ namaskuru ।
māmevaiṣyasi satyaṃ te
pratijāne priyo'si me ॥ 18.65

सर्वधर्मान्परित्यज्य
मामेकं शरणं व्रज ।
अहं त्वा सर्वपापेभ्यो
मोक्षयिष्यामि मा शुचः ॥ १८.६६

sarvadharmānparityajya
māmekaṃ śaraṇaṃ vraja ।
ahaṃ tvā sarvapāpebhyo
mokṣayiṣyāmi mā śucaḥ ॥ 18.66

इदं ते नातपस्काय
नाभक्ताय कदाचन ।
न चाशुश्रूषवे वाच्यं
न च मां योऽभ्यसूयति ॥ १८.६७

idaṃ te nātapaskāya
nābhaktāya kadācana ।
na cāśuśrūṣave vācyaṃ
na ca māṃ yo'bhyasūyati ॥ 18.67

य इदं परमं गुह्यं
मद्भक्तेष्वभिधास्यति ।
भक्तिं मयि परां कृत्वा
मामेवैष्यत्यसंशयः ॥ १८.६८

ya idaṃ paramaṃ guhyaṃ
madbhakteṣvabhidhāsyati ।
bhaktiṃ mayi parāṃ kṛtvā
māmevaiṣyatyasaṃśayaḥ ॥ 18.68

न च तस्मान्मनुष्येषु
कश्चिन्मे प्रियकृत्तमः ।
भविता न च मे तस्मात्
अन्यः प्रियतरो भुवि ॥ १८.६९

na ca tasmānmanuṣyeṣu
kaścinme priyakṛttamaḥ ।
bhavitā na ca me tasmāt
anyaḥ priyataro bhuvi ॥ 18.69

अध्येष्यते च य इमं
धर्म्यं संवादमावयोः ।
ज्ञानयज्ञेन तेनाहम्
इष्टः स्यामिति मे मतिः ॥ १८.७०

adhyeṣyate ca ya imaṃ
dharmyaṃ saṃvādamāvayoḥ ।
jñānayajñena tenāham
iṣṭaḥ syāmiti me matiḥ ॥ 18.70

श्रद्धावाननसूयश्च
शृणुयादपि यो नरः ।
सोऽपि मुक्तः शुभाँल्लोकान्
प्राप्नुयात् पुण्यकर्मणाम् ॥ १८.७१

śraddhāvānanasūyaśca
śṛṇuyādapi yo naraḥ ।
so'pi muktaḥ śubhām̐llokān
prāpnuyāt puṇyakarmaṇām ॥ 18.71

कच्चिदेतच्छ्रुतं पार्थ त्वयैकाग्रेण चेतसा । कच्चिदज्ञानसंमोहः प्रनष्टस्ते धनञ्जय ॥ १८.७२	*kaccidetacchrutaṃ pārtha* *tvayaikāgreṇa cetasā* । *kaccidajñānasaṃmohaḥ* *pranaṣṭaste dhanañjaya* ॥ 18.72
अर्जुन उवाच । नष्टो मोहः स्मृतिर्लब्धा त्वत्प्रसादान्मयाच्युत । स्थितोऽस्मि गतसन्देहः करिष्ये वचनं तव ॥ १८.७३	***arjuna uvāca*** । *naṣṭo mohaḥ smṛtirlabdhā* *tvatprasādānmayācyuta* । *sthito'smi gatasandehaḥ* *kariṣye vacanaṃ tava* ॥ 18.73
सञ्जय उवाच । इत्यहं वासुदेवस्य पार्थस्य च महात्मनः । संवादमिममश्रौषम् अद्भुतं रोमहर्षणम् ॥ १८.७४	***sañjaya uvāca*** । *ityahaṃ vāsudevasya* *pārthasya ca mahātmanaḥ* । *saṃvādamimamaśrauṣam* *adbhutaṃ romaharṣaṇam* ॥ 18.74
व्यासप्रसादाच्छ्रुतवान् एतद्गुह्यमहं परम् । योगं योगेश्वरात्कृष्णात् साक्षात् कथयतः स्वयम् ॥ १८.७५	*vyāsaprasādācchrutavān* *etadguhyamahaṃ param* । *yogaṃ yogeśvarātkṛṣṇāt* *sākṣāt kathayataḥ svayam* ॥ 18.75
राजन्संस्मृत्य संस्मृत्य संवादमिममद्भुतम् । केशवार्जुनयोः पुण्यं हृष्यामि च मुहुर्मुहुः ॥ १८.७६	*rājansaṃsmṛtya saṃsmṛtya* *saṃvādamimamadbhutam* । *keśavārjunayoḥ puṇyaṃ* *hṛṣyāmi ca muhurmuhuḥ* ॥ 18.76
तच्च संस्मृत्य संस्मृत्य रूपमत्यद्भुतंहरेः । विस्मयो मे महान्राजन् हृष्यामि च पुनः पुनः ॥ १८.७७	*tacca saṃsmṛtya saṃsmṛtya* *rūpamatyadbhutaṃhareḥ* । *vismayo me mahānrājan* *hṛṣyāmi ca punaḥ punaḥ* ॥ 18.77
यत्र योगेश्वरः कृष्णो यत्र पार्थो धनुर्धरः । तत्र श्रीर्विजयो भूतिः ध्रुवा नीतिर्मतिर्मम ॥ १८.७८	*yatra yogeśvaraḥ kṛṣṇo* *yatra pārtho dhanurdharaḥ* । *tatra śrīrvijayo bhūtiḥ* *dhruvā nītirmatirmama* ॥ 18.78

CHAPTER 18

LIBERATION

ARJUNA

1 Kṛṣṇa, what is the real difference
between *saṃnyāsa* and *tyāga*?

Arjuna asks this question because both the words – *saṃnyāsa* and *tyāga* – have the same basic meaning: 'to give up.'

KṚṢṆA

2 The seer-sages know that *saṃnyāsa* is
giving up actions driven by selfish desire.
The learned ones define *tyāga* as
giving up attachments to the results of all action.

3 Some thinkers declare that
every action is tainted and should be given up;
others say that *yajña*, *dāna*, and *tapas*
are not to be given up.

Yajña is the *Vedic* fire ritual, which inolves
worship of the divine, interaction, and sharing.
In a broader sense, it refers to a sense of dedication to work.

Dāna is charity that is undertaken with a feeling that it is one's duty to give and includes offering the right gift to the deserving person at an appropriate time, without expecting anything in return.
Tapas refers to austerity, penance, and single-minded focus on work.

4–6 Arjuna,
I shall reveal to you
the ultimate truth about *tyāga*.

First of all, one shouldn't give up
yajña, *dāna*, and *tapas*
because they can sanctify life
when followed wisely.
However, one should do these actions
by giving up attachment and desire for rewards.
Without doubt, this is the best way to act!
Further, note that *tyāga* is of three kinds.

7 It is not right to abandon work
that is meant to be done.

'Work that is meant to be done' refers to one's responsibilities
or to the work that is in tune with one's inherent nature.

When one abandons work
out of delusion –
that *tyāga* is of the nature of *tamas*.

Tamas is the state of deluded lethargy.
It is an extreme form of laziness and stubbornness.

8 One who abandons work
because it is inconvenient,
fearing it will cause exertion –
such a person gains nothing from *tyāga*.
Such *tyāga* is of the nature of *rajas*.

Rajas is the state of relentless activity.
It is an excessive indulgence in luxury.

9 When one engages in work
considering it as a responsibility,
detached and desireless –
that *tyāga* is of the nature of *sattva*.

Sattva is the state of benign goodness.
It is a mindful and balanced mode of existence.

10 Established in *sattva*
and with doubts dispelled,
the wise one renounces.

He doesn't crave for work that is pleasant;
he doesn't avoid work that is unpleasant.

11 As a matter of fact,
one can't give up all actions;
one has to act,
at least to take care of his body.

See 3.5.

But one who gives up desire
for the fruits of action
is said to have relinquished.

'Fruits' of action are the rewards or results of our work.
One should ideally focus on work and not on the result.

[12]For those who are attached to fruits of action,
three kinds of rewards—good, bad, or mixed—
will follow them even upon their death.

'...will follow them even upon their death' refers to the *vāsanas* (residual impact of actions) that we carry to the next life (see 15.8).

There is no such baggage
for those unattached to fruits of action.

[13]The scriptures proclaim that **five factors**
govern the outcome of all actions:
[14]the **situation**,
the **individual**,
the **tools** he has,
how he **uses** the tools,
and **unknown forces**.

'Tools' can refer to knowledge, skills, or resources.

15 Whatever one does
with his body, speech, or mind,
with good or bad intention,
the same five factors
determine the outcome.

16 That being the case,
when one sees himself as the sole cause,
he is truly of limited understanding.
He fails to see the truth.

17 One who is free from ego
and has complete understanding,
even if he kills, he does not kill;
he is not bound.

He is not bound because neither actions nor outcomes affect him.

18 Factors that inspire action are:
the knowable, the knowledge, and the knower.

Action comprises
the individual, the tools, and the act.

19 Knowledge, Action, and Individual
are also of three types,
in accordance with the three *guṇas*.

This is explained in the principles of the *guṇas*.

Guṇas are the inherent tendencies of a human being.

[20]The knowledge that helps one to see
the sole imperishable reality in all beings,
undivided in the divided,
that Knowledge is of the nature of *sattva*.

[21]The knowledge that makes one to see
only division everywhere and
to perceive each individual
as different from all the others,
that Knowledge is of the nature of *rajas*.

[22]The knowledge that drives one
to cling on to an insignificant pursuit
as though it were the only important thing,
without rhyme or reason and
without foundation in the truth,
that Knowledge is of the nature of *tamas*.

[23]Action that is performed as prescribed,
free from attachment, and
without obsession or aversion,
by one who is not affected by the outcome
is of the nature of *sattva*.

[24]Action that is performed
merely for selfish reasons,
with the thought: "I am doing this"
and moreover with undue excitement,
is of the nature of *rajas*.

[25]Action that is undertaken blindly,
not considering one's own ability,
without regard for the consequences,
and leading to loss or injury,
is of the nature of *tamas*.

The loss or injury could be to oneself or to others.

[26]The Individual who is
without any attachments,
endowed with firmness and enthusiasm,
unperturbed by success or failure, and
never indulging in self-praise
is of the nature of *sattva*.

[27]The Individual who is
impure, greedy, overly aggressive,
excessively passionate, and
desires for the rewards of his actions
and is easily affected by their outcomes
is of the nature of *rajas*.

28 The Individual who is
lazy, fickle, wicked, crude, dishonest, depressed,
stubborn, and forever postponing work
is of the nature of *tamas*.

29 Arjuna, let me describe the three kinds of distinctions
that prevail in Intellect and Resolve
as governed by the three *guṇas*.

30 The Intellect that knows
when to act and when to let go,
what to do and what to give up,
what to fear and what not to fear, and
what is bondage and what is liberation,
is of the nature of *sattva*.

31The Intellect that has a wrong notion
of the difference between
dharma and *adharma*,
and what to do and what to abandon,
is of the nature of *rajas*.

Dharma is that which sustains everything. It is the harmony in the universe that sustains the greater good. By definition, *dharma* protects one who protects it. *Adharma* is the opposite of *dharma* – it is that which hinders sustainability.

32The Intellect that is engulfed in darkness,
imagines *adharma* to be *dharma*, and
sees all things contrary to what they truly are,
is of the nature of *tamas*.

33The serenity with which one unites
the *prāṇa*, the senses, and the mind
by pursuing the path of *yoga*,
that Resolve is of the nature of *sattva*.

Prāṇa refers to the 'life-force' of an organism, its sustaining energy. It is also known as the 'vital breath,' for without breathing, there is no life.

34The tenacity with which one vehemently hangs on
to the pursuits of *dharma*, *artha*, and *kāma*,
out of selfish desire for the fruits of action,
that Resolve is of the nature of *rajas*.

Dharma (sustainability principle), *artha* (wealth), and *kāma* (enjoyment) are three of the four *puruṣārthas* (goals of life), the fourth being *mokṣa* (liberation).

[35]The rigidity with which
one is foolishly preoccupied with
sleep, fear, grief, despair, and arrogance,
that Resolve is of the nature of *tamas*.

[36]The pleasure that people seek
to put an end to their pain
is also of three kinds.
Now hear from me what they are.

[37]The right course of action
as conceived by a clear mind
at first seems like poison
but often ends up sweet;
such Pleasure is of the nature of *sattva*.

[38]The Pleasure that arises from
the contact between senses and sensates
is sweet at first but ends up bitter;
it is of the nature of *rajas*.

[39]The Pleasure that comes
from being lazy and careless
is only a delusion from start to end;
it is of the nature of *tamas*.

[40]There is no creature either on earth or elsewhere
that is free from the influence of the *guṇas*,
which are born of *prakṛti*.

Prakṛti refers to nature or environment (see 14.5).

41 Pursuits of *brāhmaṇas*, *kṣatriyas*, *vaiśyas*, and *śūdras* are prescribed in accordance with **their own basic nature**.

Each of us has certain inherent talents and interests, which make us naturally suited to fulfill certain roles.

The classification of individuals into four groups – *brāhmaṇas*, *kṣatriyas*, *vaiśyas*, and *śūdras* – is based on their fundamental aptitudes. This doesn't mean they totally lack other attributes.

42 Serenity, self-discipline, austerity, honesty, purity, forgiveness, knowledge, wisdom, and faith in the almighty are the basic traits of *brāhmaṇas*.

Any individual with natural aptitude for learning, analyzing, researching, teaching, and probing into nature's mysteries is a *brāhmaṇa*.

43 Valor, majesty, firmness, skill, courage, generosity, and lordly disposition are the basic traits of *kṣatriyas*.

Anyone with natural aptitude for warfare, governance, politics, administration, and management is a *kṣatriya*.

44 Farming, raising cattle, and trade are the natural activities of *vaiśyas* as per their nature.

Any individual with natural aptitude for managing money, trading, farming, and skilled labor is a *vaiśya*.

Serving others is the basic trait of *śūdras*.

Anyone with natural aptitude for service and physical work is a *śūdra*.

We are defined by our innate talents and interests; later, our nurturing environment and *gurus* shape us. Who we are has little to do with who we are born to, because every child is an experiment in life.

Some people misunderstood the system of classification of individuals based on natural aptitudes and casted a rigid social structure where one's birth determined what profession one was allowed to take up. In the light of what is said in the *Vedas* and in the *Gītā,* this is an aberration

The system of *varṇa* (social group) is a classification based on the inherent traits of an individual and his chosen profession (see 4.13). Needless to say, a multitude of professions are needed for a healthy society.

45 One attains perfection
when he is committed to his *sva-karma*.
I will tell you how one can find fulfillment
by pursuing one's own profession.

Action aligned to *sva-dharma* (one's inherent temperament) is *sva-karma*.

46 One finds fulfillment
by working in harmony with his natural abilities
and making that as an offering to the One,
who pervades this universe and
from whom all creatures have arisen.

47 Try to excel in your *sva-dharma*,
even if it is less appealing.

It is better than following the *dharma* of others.
You will never feel guilty
if you follow your inherent nature.

Here, '*dharma*' is a reference to the essence of one's personality including his attitude, talent, and nurturing environment. Also see 3.35.

48 It is only natural that
all pursuits have some defect,
just as fire is often obscured by smoke.
But one should never
abandon work suited to one's nature
simply because it is inconvenient.

No pursuit is perfect or ideal – there are always hurdles in the way. When our work is suited to our aptitude and interest, the hurdles seem insignificant, however big they might be. When we work against our own nature, even small hurdles seem big.

49 One who masters himself and
is free from desires and attachments
attains supreme perfection
through renunciation and
transcends all bondages of action.

50 Listen now, as I explain how
one who has attained perfection
also attains *Brahman*.

51 Endowed with clear reasoning and firm self-restraint,
he relinquishes sound and all other sensations
while remaining impartial and selfless.
52 Living in solitude; eating lightly; and
regulating his body, mind, and speech through meditation,
he is established in a state of perfect detachment.
53 Free from ego, aggression, arrogance,
desire, anger, and a sense of possession;
he is at peace with himself and others,
and is fit to become one with *Brahman*.
54 In that Serenity of Oneness,
unmoved by sadness or anxiety,
treating everyone in the same manner,
he gains utmost devotion to the Supreme.
55 He realizes the essential nature of the Supreme
through that ultimate devotion.
After knowing the fundamental truth,
he is united with the Supreme at once.

56 Even while constantly engaged
in worldly activities,
by taking refuge in the Supreme
he will reach that eternal, imperishable state.
Such is the divine grace!

[57–58]With firm understanding,
regard me as the Supreme,
think of me always, and
consciously dedicate your actions to me.
You shall overcome every hurdle by my grace.

But, out of arrogance
if you refuse to listen to me,
you will perish.

[59–60]Even if you say,
"I will not fight"
out of ego or ignorance,
you can't abide by your decision
because you will be forced
by your own nature
to do so against your will.

We are all obliged to act in accordance with our own inherent nature.

[61]Arjuna, the lord resides equally
in the hearts of all beings and
by *māyā* causes them to move about
as though driven by a machine.

Māyā refers to the divine power of illusion.

62 Take refuge in Him alone
with your whole being and
by His grace you will attain
that state of Eternal Peace.

Interestingly, in this verse, Kṛṣṇa refers to the Supreme Being as a separate, higher entity.

63 Thus, I have taught you the wisdom
that is the greatest of all secrets.
Reflect deeply on these teachings
and then do as you please.

64 Listen again to my final words,
the greatest secret of all.

I shall repeat what is good for you
because you are dear to me.

65 Fix your mind on me,
be devoted to me,
make every act an offering to me,
bow down to me, and
you shall certainly come to me;
this I promise,
for you are dear to me.

Here, 'me' is a reference to *ātman* (see 10.20).

[66]Giving up all forms of *dharma*
take refuge in me alone.
I will liberate you from all *pāpas*,
do not grieve!

Here, *dharma* is used in the widest sense of the word – law, virtue, support, duty, path, *etc.* including the various types of *dharma* like *viśeṣa-dharma*, *āpad-dharma*, *mokṣa-dharma*, and so on.

Given that Arjuna is confused and unclear, Kṛṣṇa explains a variety of paths to him and finally offers a simple path to liberation – the path of surrender to the Supreme.
This path is readily accessible to everyone without the need for an organized religion or a mediator; it is free from rules and distinctions.

'Giving up *dharma*' refers to moving beyond it and not violating it. Compared to the divine presence in the universe—the highest *dharma*—and its assurance for ready liberation, all other *dharma*s invariably become insignificant.

[67]Don't share this Sacred Truth with
one who lacks discipline and diligence,
one who doesn't care to listen, or
one who speaks ill of me.

The message is ready for all, but not everyone may be ready or interested; and even if they are ready, they may not have faith in the message.
Advice is best given when sought – else it might not be taken seriously.

[68]But whoever teaches this great secret
with sincerity and devotion
to those who wish to learn it,
he will surely come to me.

[69]Further, none can render more pleasing service to me
than the one who teaches this secret to my devotees,
and no one else on earth is dearer to me.

[70]Whoever earnestly studies this sacred dialog –
I consider him to have honored me
through *jñāna-yajña*.

Jñāna-yajña is the pursuit of knowledge. In other words, making an effort to understand what was taught. This is the respect that one can show to the wise.

[71]Full of reverence and free from malice,
one who merely hears these words
attains liberation and
goes to the happy worlds
of the righteous.

[72]Have you heard this teaching with full attention, Arjuna?
Has your confusion caused by ignorance been clarified?

ARJUNA

[73]Yes! My doubts are cleared.
I am not confused any more.
I am enlightened by your grace, Acyuta!
I stand firm. I will follow your advice.

'Acyuta' is an epithet of Kṛṣṇa which means 'not fallen,' 'stable,' 'fixed,' 'solid,' *etc.*

SAÑJAYA

74 This wonderful dialog
between the two great souls
is so thrilling that
it makes my hair stand.

75 By the gift of Vyāsa,
I saw this supreme *yogic* mystery
being revealed
right in front of my eyes
by the master of *yoga* himself.

Before the war began, sage Vyāsa offered divine vision to Dhṛtarāṣṭra. But the blind king refused to see this terrible war between brothers.

Vyāsa gave the ability of remote viewing to Sañjaya—Dhṛtarāṣṭra's charioteer and counsellor—who could witness the events on the battlefield without leaving the palace and narrate them to the blind king.

76 As I recall again and again
the splendid and sacred dialog
between Kṛṣṇa and Arjuna,
I rejoice over and over again.

77 I am spellbound, O king,
as I recollect Kṛṣṇa's fabulous form.
I rejoice over and over again.

78 I firmly believe that there will be
prosperity, victory, splendor, and justice
with Kṛṣṇa, the lord of *yoga*
and Arjuna, the wielder of the bow
coming together!

Action guided by wisdom leads us to success.
The ideal for life is a combination of spiritual insight and mastery of work.

Epilogue

JUST READING THE text of *Bhagavad-gītā* or intellectually understanding its content is not enough if we aim to reap the full benefit of its wisdom. Sometimes, those who have never read a line of the *Gītā* lead a life that epitomizes it and scholars who give hours of explanation for each verse of the *Gītā* lead a life removed from it. *Practising* the message is vital if we want to attain the wisdom. In other words, we can go through the *Gītā* several times, but it is very important that we let the *Gītā* go through us at least once.

Of course, we can enjoy the *Gītā* merely as poetry or as an intellectual or academic exercise, but if we want to hear the larger voice of a universal consciousness, indeed we have to go beyond reading a book or attending a lecture. We have to verify our understanding in our daily life, see what works and what doesn't, and constantly review our personal philosophy and world view.

We often tend to make our personal view of the world rather static, but when everything is changing how can we remain still? And if we want to indeed achieve Stillness, then we have to transcend the notion of change once and for all. Kṛṣṇa calls this the Supreme State or the state of *Brahman* – a state beyond creation and destruction, growth and decay.

Having read the *Bhagavad-gītā* and having found it to be a fountain of wisdom, we are primarily interested in how the wisdom can help change our own life. For this reason, the peripheral issues around the *Gītā* (Did Kṛṣṇa really exist? Did the war really take place? Did it take place 5,000 years ago? Was the *Gītā* written by a single author? Was the *Gītā* originally part of the text of *Mahā-bhārata*?) go into the background. While these are interesting topics of discussion, since our immediate purpose is to understand the message, we have to take the text at face value and examine it.

A good way to approach the *Gītā* is by trying to understand the mind of Kṛṣṇa. This is easier said than done. The reason is that Kṛṣṇa is a mysterious character. He is an eternal paradox, as famed playwright and poet T P Kailasam captures in his lovely sonnet on Kṛṣṇa –

A woman's witching face, her ways, her eyes;
A panther's frame, its grace, mayhap its heart;
An eerie mastery of ev'ry art;
A honey-tongue that steep'd all truth in lies
And yet could strip all lies in light of **Truth**
A smile that mock'd at plight of friend in Woe;
A breast that bled at sight of fallen foe;
Ador'd and yet afear'd of all, in sooth:

Thou tangl'd mass of man and god and brute,
What mortal mind may con thy rainbow-life
That blazed undimm'd mid storms of human strife,
And glean the wisdom of thy madd'ning flute,
Thy love-lit crimes, thy kindly cruelties,
Thou paradox for all eternities!

Kṛṣṇa, as a person, is extremely happy and playful, but pragmatic. His religion consists of embracing life in totality and enjoying it as a game. He easily manages good and evil since he knows how to live in the world, by looking at things from an overall perspective.

We humans are rather biased in our tastes; we want the cake and eat it too. We want pleasure but no pain, joy but no sorrow, roses but no thorns, peace but no war. Kṛṣṇa points out that these are merely two sides of the same coin. Non-violence has relevance only in the face of violence and Comfort takes on meaning only in the face of discomfort. Worldly life is full of dualities and going beyond the opposites leads us to endless peace. Embracing the world with a sense of connectedness is true spirituality.

There can be no single rule for all of human life; one can merely try to act appropriately in all situations. While brokering for peace, Kṛṣṇa tells Duryodhana that he is about to commit a grave *pāpa* by insisting on war. The same Kṛṣṇa tells Arjuna on the battlefield that he is committing a grave *pāpa* by running away from war. Kṛṣṇa's life and message is filled with such *apparent* contradictions but seen in perspective, the opposing ideas make complete sense. It takes a while for most people to reconcile with the idea that truths can be contradictory because they are at different levels.

Typically religion divides things into 'sacred' and 'profane.' But Kṛṣṇa focuses on a more useful division of what is appropriate and what is not. Thus Kṛṣṇa is able to make statements that are supremely practical and at the same time perfectly spiritual. We must know this if we want to joyfully participate in the game of life. A knowledge of both the material and the spiritual elements helps us sustain our application of wisdom to daily life.

In many ways, the *Bhagavad-gītā* is a unifying text. It doesn't conform solely to any one school of philosophy, be it *advaita* (non-dualism), *viśiṣṭādvaita* (qualified non-dualism), or *dvaita* (dualism). That is why we avoided force-fitting the *Gītā* to any one school.

Kṛṣṇa cuts across class distinctions, mocks at social prejudices, abhors dated traditional practices, and finds convergence for divergent thoughts and beliefs. He declares that the vision of the *Vedas* is inclusive and talks of egalitarianism, but with focus on the inherent strength of an individual. He challenges Arjuna to think differently and not to buy into traditional baggage, by showing him how external factors mean little when greater heights are reached spiritually.

The journey from ignorance to knowledge consists of opening our minds and learning how to entertain an idea without accepting or rejecting it. To blindly accept or reject anything is ignorance. Objective examination of the evidence, experimentation in daily life, carefully listening to the voice of intuition that comes with years of experience – these are some of the ingredients to forming an all-round view of the world around us and attaining supreme bliss.

Om, salutations!
May the spirit of *yajña* flourish!
May the one with the spirit of *yajña* flourish!
May divine grace be upon us!
May divine grace be upon humankind!
May plants be bountiful!
Auspiciousness to the two-footed!
Auspiciousness to the four-footed!
Om, peace, peace, peace!

(from the *Kṛṣṇa-yajur-veda*)

APPENDICES

APPENDIX I

Transliteration Guide

FOR CENTURIES, THE scriptures were learnt in the oral tradition from the *guru* and committed to memory; it was only much later that they were written down. Before 18th century CE, Sanskrit was written in the local writing system in different regions of India. But with the advent of printing technology in India and the widespread distribution of works in Sanskrit, the *deva-nāgarī* script became predominant. By 19th century it had become the standard writing system for Sanskrit. The *deva-nāgarī* script is written from left to right.

Sanskrit has been transliterated using the Latin alphabet for about three hundred years. A commonly used system is the IAST (International Alphabet of Sanskrit Transliteration) which allows for a lossless romanization of Indic scripts. It evolved from earlier schemes, particularly the one developed by the *Tenth International Congress of Orientalists* in 1894.

We have used the IAST scheme to transliterate all Sanskrit words in this book.

Letters of the Sanskrit Alphabet

VOWELS *a ā i ī u ū ṛ ṝ ḷ*

e ai o au aṃ aḥ

CONSONANTS TYPE-1 *k kh g gh ṅ*

c ch j jh ñ

ṭ ṭh ḍ ḍh ṇ

t th d dh n

p ph b bh m

TYPE-2 *y r l v ś ṣ s h*

Pronunciation of the Vowels

a as in away	*ā* as in far	*i* as in it	*ī* as in free
u as in good	*ū* as in mood	*ṛ* as in rhythm	*ṝ* is rri (rolled)
e as in say	*ai* as in sky	*o* as in old	*au* as in owl
aṃ as in hum	*aḥ* is a-huh		

The sound for the vowel *ḷ* doesn't exist in English. It roughly corresponds to the 'l' in bottle.

Pronunciation of the Consonants

TYPE-1	*k* as in kid	*g* as in got	*ṅ* as in song	
	c as in chat	*j* as in joy	*ñ* as in inch	
	ṭ as in ten	*ḍ* as in den	*ṇ* as in end	
	t as in thin	*d* as is then	*n* as in now	
	p as in pat	*b* as in bat	*m* as in mat	

The consonants *kh, gh, ch, jh, ṭh, ḍh, th, dh, ph,* and *bh* are the aspirated versions of the consonants *k, g, c, j, ṭ, ḍ, t, d, p,* and *b* respectively.

TYPE-2	*y* as in yes	*r* as in ran	*l* as in less	*v* as in van
	ś as in shin	*s* as in sit	*h* as in her	

The consonant *ṣ* doesn't exist in English. It approximately sounds like an aspirated version of *ś*.

In some places in the original text of the *Gītā*, one will find apostrophes, like in the last line of 1.21 – *rathaṃ sthāpaya me'cyuta*. According to a rule of forming compound words in Sanskrit, when a word ends in 'e' or in 'o' and is followed by a word that begins with an 'a,' the 'a' is removed and replaced by a silent 'a,' which is denoted by the apostrophe. In the example, *me + acyuta* becomes *me'cyuta*.

APPENDIX 2

ADDITIONAL GĪTĀ VERSES

THE CRITICAL EDITION of the *Mahā-bhārata*—in nineteen volumes—was prepared by a brilliant team of scholars (under the able guidance of Dr. V S Sukthankar) from the *Bhandarkar Oriental Research Institute* (BORI) during the period 1925 to 1966 and it attempts to reconstruct the oldest possible version of the great epic based on the available manuscripts. While the reconstructed *Mahā-bhārata* (called the 'critically constituted text') is given in the main text of the critical edition, footnotes and appendices contain those verses and passages that are found in various manuscripts and which were deemed to be from a later period (and therefore omitted).

Possibly for the very first time, all these verses are being translated into English. We present them chapterwise, giving the original Sanskrit text in both *deva-nāgarī* and IAST in the beginning, followed by the English translation.

CHAPTER I

1. Before the *Mahā-bhārata* verse 6.23.1 [*i.e.*, the first *śloka* of the *Gītā*], K_{0-2}* (as also K_7) has the following passage –

> श्रीरामचन्द्राय नमः । श्रीकृष्णाय नमः । ॐ नमः । अस्य श्रीभगवद्गीतामालामन्त्रस्य भगवान्-वेदव्यास ऋषिः । अनुष्टुप्छन्दः । श्रीकृष्णपरमात्मा देवता । अशोच्यानन्वशोचस्त्वं प्रज्ञावादांश्च भाषसे (*Gītā* 2.11) इति बीजम् । सर्वधर्मान्परित्यज्य मामेकं शरणं व्रज (18.66) इति शक्तिः । अहं त्वां सर्वपापेभ्यो मोक्षयिष्यामि मा शुचः (18.66) इति कीलकम् । कृष्णप्रीत्यर्थं धर्मार्थकाममोक्षार्थे जपे विनियोगः ॥ नैनं छिन्दन्ति शस्त्राणि नैनं दहति पावकः (2.23) इति अङ्गुष्ठाभ्यां नमः । न चैनं क्लेदयन्त्यापो न शोषयति मारुतः (2.23) इति तर्जनीभ्यां नमः । अच्छेद्योऽयम् अदाह्योऽयमक्लेद्योऽशोष्य एव च (2.24) इति मध्यमाभ्यां नमः । नित्यः सर्वगतः स्थाणुरचलोऽयं सनातनः (2.24) इत्यनामिकाभ्यां नमः । पश्य मे पार्थ रूपाणि शतशोऽथ सहस्रशः (11.5) इति कनिष्ठिकाभ्यां नमः । नानाविधानि दिव्यानि नानावर्णाकृतीनि च (11.5)

* This indicates a certain manuscript – its version, orthography, place of preservation, *etc.* *e.g.* **K_0** refers to the Kaśmīrī version / transcript from Śāradā in the *deva-nāgarī* script / stored at the Mirikar Collection of the *Bhārat Itihās Sanshodhaka Mandal* (No. 207) in Poona. For more details, refer to the BORI critical edition.

इति करतलकरपृष्ठाभ्यां नमः । इति करन्यासः ॥ अङ्गन्यासः । नैनं छिन्दन्ति शस्त्राणि नैनं दहति पावकः (2.23) इति हृदयाय नमः । न चैनं क्लेदयन्त्यापो न शोषयति मारुतः (2.23) इति शिरसे स्वाहा । अच्छेद्योऽयमदाह्योऽयमक्लेद्योऽशोष्य एव च (2.24) इति शिखायै वौषट् । नानाविधानि दिव्यानि नानावर्णाकृतीनि च (11.5) इत्यस्त्राय फट् । इत्यङ्गन्यासः ॥*

śrīrāmacandrāya namaḥ । śrīkṛṣṇāya namaḥ । oṃ namaḥ । asya śrībhagavad-gītāmālāmantrasya bhagavānvedavyāsa ṛṣiḥ । anuṣṭupchandaḥ । śrīkṛṣṇa-paramātmā devatā । aśocyānanvaśocastvaṃ prajñāvādāṃśca bhāṣase (G. 2.11) *iti bījam । sarvadharmānparityajya māmekaṃ śaraṇaṃ vraja* (18.66) *iti śaktiḥ । ahaṃ tvāṃ sarvapāpebhyo mokṣaiṣyāmi mā śucaḥ* (18.66) *iti kīlakam । kṛṣṇa-prītyarthaṃ dharmārthakāmamokṣārthe jape viniyogaḥ ॥ nainaṃ chindanti śastrāṇi nainaṃ dahati pāvakaḥ* (2.23) *iti aṅguṣṭhābhyāṃ namaḥ । na cai-naṃ kledayantyāpo na śoṣayati mārutaḥ* (2.23) *iti tarjanībhyāṃ namaḥ । acchedyo'yam adāhyo'yamakledyo'śoṣya eva ca* (2.24) *iti madhyamābhyāṃ namaḥ । nityaḥ sarvagataḥ sthāṇuracalo'yaṃ sanātanaḥ* (2.24) *ityanāmikā-bhyāṃ namaḥ । paśya me pārtha rūpāṇi śataśo'tha sahasraśaḥ* (11.5) *iti kaniṣṭhikābhyāṃ namaḥ । nānāvidhāni divyāni nānāvarṇākṛtīni ca* (11.5) *iti karatalakarapṛṣṭhābhyāṃ namaḥ । iti karanyāsaḥ ॥ aṅganyāsaḥ । nainaṃ chindanti śastrāṇi nainaṃ dahati pāvakaḥ* (2.23) *iti hṛdayāya namaḥ । na cainaṃ kledayantyāpo na śoṣayati mārutaḥ* (2.23) *iti śirase svāhā । acchedyo-'yamadāhyo'yamakledyo'śoṣya eva ca* (2.24) *iti śikhāyai vauṣaṭ । nānāvidhāni divyāni nānāvarṇākṛtīni ca* (11.5) *ityastrāya phaṭ । ityaṅganyāsaḥ ॥*

Salutations to Śrīrāmacandra, Kṛṣṇa, and *Oṃ* (*praṇava*)!
Bhagavān Veda-vyāsa is the *ṛṣi*
for this garland of *mantras*, the *Bhagavad-gītā*.
The *chandas* is Anuṣṭup.
Śrīkṛṣṇa-paramātmā is the deity.
"You grieve for that which you should not
yet you seem to speak words of wisdom" (G. 2.11) is its seed.
"Giving up all forms of *dharma*,
take refuge in me alone" (18.66) is its strength.
"I will liberate you from all *pāpa*,
do not grieve" (18.66) is its promise.

* Typically the अङ्गन्यास ritual involves six elements: ...हृदयाय नमः, ...शिरसे स्वाहा, ...शिखायै वौषट्, ...नेत्रत्रयायै वौषट्, ...अस्त्राय फट्, and दिग्बन्धः. Here the fourth and sixth are missing. However, in other manuscripts like K_7, the others are included.

I offer *japa* of this *mantra* to please Kṛṣṇa and
for the fulfilment of *dharma*, *artha*, *kāma*, and *mokṣa*.
I offer salutations clasping my palms,
invoking these *mantras*
each to the five fingers and palm respectively:
"Weapons do not cleave it, fire does not burn it,
water does not wet it, and wind does not wither it. (2.23)
"It cannot be cut or burnt or drenched or dried.
It is everlasting, all-pervading,
stable, immovable, and primordial. (2.24)
"Arjuna see my forms
by the hundreds or by the thousands
of many colors and shapes." (11.5)
I offer salutations invoking the same (three) *mantras*
to my heart, head, tuft, and space around my head respecively.

followed by these verses:

अथ ध्यानं ।

ॐ पार्थाय प्रतिबोधितां भगवता नारायणेन स्वयं
व्यासेन ग्रथितां पुराणमुनिना मध्ये महाभारते ।
अद्वैतामृतवर्षिणीं भगवतीमष्टादशाध्यायिनीम्
आवर्त्तैरनुसंदधामि भगवद्गीतां भवोन्मोचिनीम् ॥ १
ॐ हृदि विकसितपद्मं सूर्यसोमाग्निबिम्बं
प्रणवमयविकासं यस्य वै निर्विकल्पम् ।
अचलपरमशान्तं ज्योतिराकाशसारं
स भवतु शुभदो मे वासुदेवः प्रतिष्ठः ॥ २
सर्वोपनिषदो गावो
दोग्धा गोपालनन्दनः ।
पार्थो वत्सः सुधीर्भोक्ता
दुग्धं गीतामृतं महत् ॥ ३
ॐ नमोऽस्तु ते व्यास विशालबुद्धे
फुल्लारविन्दायतपद्मनेत्र ।
येन त्वया भारततैलपूर्णः
प्रज्वालितो ज्ञानमयः प्रदीपः ॥ ४

प्रपन्नपारिजाताय
तोत्रवेत्रैकपाणये ।
ज्ञानमुद्राय कृष्णाय
गीतामृतदुहे नमः ॥ ५

atha dhyānaṃ ।
oṃ pārthāya pratibodhitāṃ bhagavatā nārāyaṇena svayaṃ
vyāsena grathitāṃ purāṇamuninā madhye mahābhārate ।
advaitāmṛtavarṣiṇīṃ bhagavatīmaṣṭādaśādhyāyinīm
āvarttairanusaṃdadhāmi bhagavadgītāṃ bhavonmocinīm ॥ 1
oṃ hṛdi vikasitapadmaṃ sūryasomāgnibimbaṃ
praṇavamayavikāsaṃ yasya vai nirvikalpam ।
acalaparamaśāntaṃ jyotirākāśasāraṃ
sa bhavatu śubhado me vāsudevaḥ pratiṣṭhaḥ ॥ 2
sarvopaniṣado gāvo
dogdhā gopālanandanaḥ ।
pārtho vatsaḥ sudhīrbhoktā
dugdhaṃ gītāmṛtaṃ mahat ॥ 3
oṃ namo'stu te vyāsa viśālabuddhe
phullāravindāyatapadmanetra ।
yena tvayā bhāratatailapūrṇaḥ
prajvālito jñānamayaḥ pradīpaḥ ॥ 4
prapannapārijātāya
totravetraikapāṇaye ।
jñānamudrāya kṛṣṇāya
gītāmṛtaduhe namaḥ ॥ 5

Thus we meditate:
[1]*Bhagavad-gītā* taught to Arjuna by Bhagavān Nārāyaṇa himself,
presented in the middle of the *Mahā-bhārata* by the ancient sage Vyāsa.
Goddess *Gītā*, mother of eighteen chapters
showers the *amṛta* of *advaita* on us!
I repeatedly study the *Gītā* for relief from
the illusion of manifestation.

[2]*Oṃ*! May Vāsudeva be auspicious to me!
He is the one with a lotus blossoming in the heart;

he has the form of Sūrya, Soma, and Agni;
he is the elaboration of *Oṃ*;
he is unfathomable, immovable, and
is endowed with Supreme peace;
his glow is essence of space!

[3]All the *Upaniṣads* are cows;
the milker is Kṛṣṇa, the son of the cowherd;
Arjuna is the calf;
the wise and the pure drink the milk (which is)
the Supreme, immortal *amṛta* of the *Gītā*.

[4]*Oṃ*! Salutations to Vyāsa,
the one with the great intellect,
with eyes like the fully-blossomed lotus, and
through whom the lamp of wisdom is
fuelled by the oil of the *Bhārata*!

[5]Salutations to Kṛṣṇa, who grants us all our desires!
He wields the whip in one hand and a staff in another.
He is in *jñāna-mudra*. He is milker of the *amṛta* of the *Gītā*.

In $Ś_1$ we find the lines –

अथ गीता लिख्यते । श्रीगणेशाय नमः ।
atha gītā likhyate । śrīgaṇeśāya namaḥ ।

Thus the *Gītā* is written. Salutations to Śrīgaṇeśa!

In K_5 –

अतः परं गीता लिख्यते ।
ataḥ paraṃ gītā likhyate ।

Thus the Supreme *Gītā* is written.

In D_1 –

अथ गीता ।

atha gītā ।

Thus, the *Gītā* (begins).

In D_2 –

अतः परं गीता भविष्यति । ॐ नमो नारायणाय । श्रीकृष्णाय नमः ।

ataḥ paraṃ gītā bhaviṣyati । *oṃ namo nārāyaṇāya* । *śrīkṛṣṇāya namaḥ* ।

Thus the Supreme *Gītā* will be (uttered).
Oṃ! Salutations to Nārāyaṇa and Śrīkṛṣṇa!

In G_2 –

श्रीकृष्णाय नमः । श्रीमते रामानुजाय नमः । हरिः ॐ शुभमस्तु ।

śrīkṛṣṇāya namaḥ । *śrīmate rāmānujāya namaḥ* । *hariḥ oṃ śubhamastu* ।

Salutations to Śrīkṛṣṇa and to Śrī Rāmānujācārya!
Hari *Oṃ*! Let auspiciousness prevail!

followed by:

85*†	कृष्णं कमलपत्राक्षं	*kṛṣṇaṃ kamalapatrākṣaṃ*
	पुण्यश्रवणकीर्तनम् ।	*puṇyaśravaṇakīrtanam* ।
	वासुदेवं जगद्योनिं	*vāsudevaṃ jagadyoniṃ*
	नौमि नारायणं हरिम् ।	*naumi nārāyaṇaṃ harim* ।
1*	नारायणं नमस्कृत्य	*nārāyaṇaṃ namaskṛtya*
	नरं चैव नरोत्तमम् ।	*naraṃ caiva narottamam* ।
	देवीं सरस्वतीं चैव	*devīṃ sarasvatīṃ caiva*
	ततो जयमुदीरयेत् ।	*tato jayamudīrayet* ।

[85*] Salutations to Kṛṣṇa, whose eyes are as wide as a lotus leaf
We attain *puṇya* when we listen to his glory!
Salutations to Vāsudeva, the primary cause of the universe!
I bow down to him who is Nārāyaṇa and Hari!

† This indicates an additional verse or passage in a given volume of the BORI critical edition. We use the numbering as given in the *Bhīṣmaparvan* (Volume 7) for easy cross-referencing.

[1*]Having saluted Nārāyaṇa—
the human and the divine—
and *Devī* Sarasvatī –
May *Jaya* be narrated!

and finally:

श्रीकृष्णाय नमः । श्रीवेदव्यासाय नमः । ॐ

śrīkṛṣṇāya namaḥ । śrīvedavyāsāya namaḥ । oṃ

Salutations to Śrīkṛṣṇa
and to Śrī Vedavyāsa! *Oṃ*!

2. After 6.23.7 [*i.e.*, *Gītā* 1.7], in $Ś_3$ D_6 we find the line –

86* सैन्ये महति ये सर्वे नेतारः शूरसंमताः ।

sainye mahati ye sarve netāraḥ śūrasaṃmatāḥ ।

[86*]In this great army, all war-leaders are of valorous resolve!

while in D_5 we find:

सैन्ये महति ये सर्वे ते नराः सर्वसंमताः ।

sainye mahati ye sarve te narāḥ sarvasaṃmatāḥ ।

In this great army, all your men hold the same opinion!

Chapter 2

3. After verse 6.24.11, Ś K_6 $C_{ā, b, g, k}$ has the verse –

87* त्वं मानुष्येणोपहतान्तरात्मा
विषादमोहाभिभवाद्विसंज्ञः ।
कृपागृहीतः समवेक्ष्य बन्धून्-
अभिप्रपन्नान्मुखमन्तकस्य ।

tvaṃ mānuṣyeṇopahatāntarātmā
viṣādamohābhibhavādvisaṃjñaḥ ।
kṛpāgṛhītaḥ samavekṣya bandhūn-
abhiprapannānmukhamantakasya ।

[87*]Your inner being has been subdued by human instincts
Your sorrow and attachment have
rendered you unconscious!

Discard your misplaced compassion
and see your relatives, who have entered
the mouth of Time!

4. After verse 6.24.48, Ś K_6 $C_{ā, g, k}$ has the verse –

88*	यस्य सर्वे समारम्भा	*yasya sarve samārambhā*
	निराशीर्बन्धनास्त्विह ।	*nirāśīrbandhanāstviha* ।
	त्यागे यस्य हुतं सर्वं	*tyāge yasya hutaṃ sarvaṃ*
	स त्यागी स च बुद्धिमान् ।	*sa tyāgī sa ca buddhimān* ।

88* One who performs all undertakings
selflessly and without earthly ties
and one whose *tyāga* is itself his ritual offering –
he is indeed a renunciate and he is truly wise!

[This verse is a variation of 3.203.43. The first *pāda* is identical to *Gītā* 4.19.]

Chapter 3

5. After verse 6.25.37, in Ś K_6 D_3 $C_{ā, b, k}$ we find the following verses –

89*	अर्जुन उवाच ।	*arjuna uvāca* ।
	भवत्येष कथं कृष्ण	*bhavatyeṣa kathaṃ kṛṣṇa*
	कथं चैव विवर्धते ।	*kathaṃ caiva vivardhate* ।
	किमात्मकः किमाचारस्-	*kimātmakaḥ kimācāras-*
	तन्ममाचक्ष्व पृच्छतः ।	*tanmamācakṣva pṛcchataḥ* ।
	श्रीभगवानुवाच ।	*śrībhagavānuvāca* ।
	एष सूक्ष्मः परः शत्रुर्-	*eṣa sūkṣmaḥ paraḥ śatrur-*
	देहिनामिन्द्रियैः सह ।	*dehināmindriyaiḥ saha* ।
	सुखतन्त्र इवासीनो	*sukhatantra ivāsīno*
	मोहयन्पार्थ तिष्ठति ।	*mohayanpārtha tiṣṭhati* ।
	कामक्रोधमयो घोरः	*kāmakrodhamayo ghoraḥ*
	स्तम्भहर्षसमुद्भवः ।	*stambhaharṣasamudbhavaḥ* ।
	अहंकारोऽभिमानात्मा	*ahaṃkāro'bhimānātmā*
	दुस्तरः पापकर्मभिः ।	*dustaraḥ pāpakarmabhiḥ* ।
	हर्षमस्य निवर्त्यैष	*harṣamasya nivartyaiṣa*
	शोकमस्य ददाति च ।	*śokamasya dadāti ca* ।
	भयं चास्य करोत्येष	*bhayaṃ cāsya karotyeṣa*
	मोहयंस्तु मुहुर्मुहुः ।	*mohayaṃstu muhurmuhuḥ* ।

स एष कलुषः क्षुद्रश्-	*sa eṣa kaluṣaḥ kṣudraś-*
छिद्रप्रेक्षी धनञ्जय ।	*chidraprekṣī dhanañjaya* ।
रजःप्रवृत्तो मोहात्मा	*rajaḥpravṛtto mohātmā*
मनुष्याणामुपद्रवः ।	*manuṣyāṇāmupadravaḥ* ।

ARJUNA

[89*] O Kṛṣṇa, how does this (desire) exist
and how does this grow?
What part of it is innate and
what part is from conduct?
Please reveal this to me!

KṚṢṆA

This is a subtle and powerful enemy of humans.
With the senses, it bewitches humans
by the illusions of comfort, O Pārtha!
It is a ghastly thing, full of lust and anger.
It originates from stupidity and reckless joy.
One who is arrogant and conceited
becomes incorrigible
owing to sinful actions.
This suppresses our joy, grants sorrow, and invokes fear.
Again and again, it deludes us!
This (Desire) is tainted, vile,
and forever seeking vulnerabilities,
O Dhanañjaya!
That illusory being
—endowed with *rajas*—
is a catastrophe for humankind!

CHAPTER 4

Nil

Chapter 5

6. After verse 6.27.17, $Ś_{2,3}$ K_6 has the verse –

90* स्मरन्तोऽपि मुहुस्त्वेतत्-
स्पृशन्तोऽपि स्वकर्मणि ।
सक्ता अपि न सज्जन्ति
पङ्के रविकरा इव ।

smaranto'pi muhustvetat-
spṛśanto'pi svakarmaṇi ।
saktā api na sajjanti
paṅke ravikarā iva ।

[90*] While he is engaged in his work,
he comes in contact with *karma* in thought and deed;
although he is attached, he is detached
just like sun-rays in the mire!

Chapter 6

7. After the first half of verse 6.28.37, we find the following verse in Ś K_6 (line 2 only) $C_{ā, b, k}$ –

91* लिप्समानः सतां मार्गं
प्रमूढो ब्रह्मणः पथि ।
अनेकचित्तो विभ्रान्तो
मोहस्यैव वशं गतः ।

lipsamānaḥ satāṃ mārgaṃ
pramūḍho brahmaṇaḥ pathi ।
anekacitto vibhrānto
mohasyaiva vaśaṃ gataḥ ।

[91*] Clinging to the path of the noble
(if one is) perplexed the path of *Brahman*,
will he not be deluded by multiple distractions
and fall into the trap of attachment?

8. After verse 6.28.47, we find the following verse in $Ś_1$ –

92* भगवन्नामसंप्राप्ति-
मात्रात्सर्वमवाप्यते ।
फलिताः शालयः सम्यग्-
वृष्टिमात्रेऽवलोकिते ।

bhagavannāmasaṃprāpti-
mātrātsarvamavāpyate ।
phalitāḥ śālayaḥ samyag-
vṛṣṭimātre'valokite ।

[92*] Attaining merely the name of the Supreme,
one attains everything (just as)
rice grains reach fruition merely at a glance of rain.

[This is just the *saṃgrahaśloka* ('summary verse') to *adhyāya* 6 in C_g.]

CHAPTER 7

9. In verse 6.29.23, after the first three *pādas*,

{A} we find in $Ś_2$ K_6 $C_ā$ –

93*	...सिद्धान्यान्ति सिद्धव्रताः । भूतान्भूतयजो यान्ति...	*...siddhānyānti siddhavratāḥ* । *bhūtānbhūtayajo yānti...*

93* Those who adhere to a vow of perfection attain the *siddhas*.
Those who worship elemental spirits attain them!

{B} we find in $Ś_6$ $C_ā$ –

94*	पितॄन्यान्ति पितृव्रताः । भूतानि यान्ति भूतेज्या	*pitṝnyānti pitṛvratāḥ* । *bhūtāni yānti bhūtejyā*

94* Those who worship the *pitṛs* go to the *pitṛs*.
Those who worship elemental spirits attain those spirits.

[which is identical to the second and third *pādas* of *Gītā* 9.25.]

10. After verse 6.29.30 [*i.e.*, end of Chapter 7], we find in $Ś_1$ –

95*	स्फुटं भगवतो भक्तिर्- विहिता कल्पमञ्जरी । साधनेच्छासमुचितां येनाशां परिपूरयेत् ।	*sphuṭaṃ bhagavato bhaktir-* *vihitā kalpamañjarī* । *sādhanecchāsamucitāṃ* *yenāśāṃ paripūrayet* ।

95* Their aspirations are fulfilled when –
their *bhakti* towards the Supreme is clear,
their aggregation of thoughts are reined, and
their practice and desire are appropriate.

CHAPTER 8

11. After verse 6.30.11, we find in D_1 –

96*	सर्वे वेदा यत्पदमामनन्ति तपांसि सर्वाणि च यद्वदन्ति । यदिच्छन्तो ब्रह्मचर्यं चरन्ति तत्ते पदं संग्रहेण ब्रवीमि ।	*sarve vedā yatpadamāmananti* *tapāṃsi sarvāṇi ca yadvadanti* । *yadicchanto brahmacaryaṃ caranti* *tatte padaṃ saṃgraheṇa bravīmi* ।

(SEE *Kaṭhopaniṣad* 1.2.15 and also the second half of *Gītā* 8.11)

96* All the *Vedas* praise that state and all *tapas* speaks of it.
Those who desire to reach that state lead a life of *brahmacarya*.
I will tell you in essence how one reaches there.

12. After the first half of verse 6.30.22, we find in $Ś_{3-6}$ K_6 C_k –

97*	यं प्राप्य न पुनर्जन्म लभन्ते योगिनोऽर्जुन ।	*yaṃ prāpya na punarjanma* *labhante yogino'rjuna* ।

97* The *yogins* who attain it (*i.e.*, the state of *Puruṣa*)
are not born again, Arjuna!

13. After verse 6.30.28, in $Ś_1$ we find the verse –

98*	सर्वतत्त्वगतत्वेन विज्ञाते परमेश्वरे । अन्तर्बहिर्न सावस्था न यस्यां भासते विभुः ।	*sarvatattvagatatvena* *vijñāte parameśvare* । *antarbahirna sāvasthā* *na yasyāṃ bhāsate vibhuḥ* ।

98* He knows the Supreme Lord
as being present in all philosophies;
whether within or outside, there is nowhere
that the Supreme does not exist!

[This is just the *saṃgrahaśloka* to *adhyāya* 8 in C_g.]

Chapter 9

14. After verse 6.31.5, in D_3 we find –

99*	सर्वगः सर्ववश्चाद्यः सर्वकृत्सर्वदर्शनः । सर्वज्ञः सर्वदर्शी च सर्वात्मा सर्वतोमुखः ।	*sarvagaḥ sarvavaścādyaḥ* *sarvakṛtsarvadarśanaḥ* । *sarvajñaḥ sarvadarśī ca* *sarvātmā sarvatomukhaḥ* ।

99* (I am) all-pervading and the first among all;
(I am the one who) does everything, perceives everything,
knows everything, and sees everything;
(I am) the *ātmā* in everyone and
(I am the one) facing all directions!

15. After verse 6.31.6, we find in $Ś_{3-6}$ K_6 $Ñ_1$ D_5 $C_{ā,g,k}$ –

100* एवं हि सर्वभूतेषु चराम्यनभिलक्षितः । भूतप्रकृतिमास्थाय सहैव च विनैव च ।

evaṃ hi sarvabhūteṣu
carāmyanabhilakṣitaḥ ।
bhūtaprakṛtimāsthāya
sahaiva ca vinaiva ca ।

[100*] Similarly, I move about in all beings without being perceived
Having taken recourse to the fundamental nature of beings,
I am with them and I am without them!

Chapter 10

16. After 6.32.38, in K_5 D_3 we find with a remark "त्यक्तं च" ("*tyaktaṃ ca*") –

101* ओषधीनां यवश्चास्मि धातूनामस्मि काञ्चनम्
सौरभेयो गवामस्मि स्नेहानां सर्पिरप्यहम्
सर्वासां तृणजातीनां दर्भोऽहं पाण्डुनन्दन ।

oṣadhīnāṃ yavaścāsmi dhātūnāmasmi kāñcanam
saurabheyo gavāmasmi snehānāṃ sarpirapyaham
sarvāsāṃ tṛṇajātīnāṃ darbho'haṃ pāṇḍunandana ।

"And left out" –

[101*] I am barley among herbs, I am gold among metals.
Among cattle, I am the bull.
Among oils, I am clarified butter (ghee).
Of different kinds of grass, I am Darbha,
O son of Pāṇḍu!

Chapter 11

17A. After the first half of the verse 6.33.27, we find in $Ś_1$ –

102* सहस्रसूर्यात*संनिभानि तथा जगद्ग्रासकृतक्षणानि ।

*sahasrasūryāta***saṃnibhāni*
tathā jagadgrāsakṛtakṣaṇāni ।

[102*] Resembling thousand suns and
swallowing the worlds instantaneously.

17B. After the verse 6.33.27, we find in Ś$_{1,3-5}$ K$_6$ D$_3$ C$_k$ –

103*	नानारूपैः पुरुषैर्वध्यमाना	*nānārūpaiḥ puruṣairvadhyamānā*
	विशन्ति ते वक्त्रमचिन्त्यरूपम् ।	*viśanti te vaktramacintyarūpam* ।
	यौधिष्ठिरा धार्तराष्ट्राश्च योधाः	*yaudhiṣṭhirā dhārtarāṣṭrāśca yodhāḥ*
	शस्त्रैः कृत्ता विविधैः सर्व एव ।	*śastraiḥ kṛttā vividhaiḥ sarva eva* ।
	त्वत्तेजसा निहता नूनमेते	*tvattejasā nihatā nūnamete*
	तथा हीमे त्वच्छरीरं प्रविष्टाः ।	*tathā hīme tvaccharīraṃ praviṣṭāḥ* ।

[103*] Different kinds of men to be slayed
are entering your jaws of unimaginable form,
warriors belonging to both Yudhiṣṭhira and Dhṛtarāṣṭra
severed by different kinds of weapons
are readily killed by your brilliance and
are entering your body (getting digested).

18. After the first half of the verse 6.33.39, we find in Ś$_{1,3-6}$ K$_6$ D$_3$ C$_ā$ –

104*	अनादिमानप्रतिमप्रभावः	*anādimānapratimaprabhāvaḥ*
	सर्वेश्वरः सर्वमहाविभूते ।	*sarveśvaraḥ sarvamahāvibhūte* ।

[104*] Eternal lord of all, of immeasurable power
and every conceivable great splendour.

19. After the first half of the verse 6.33.40, we find in Ś$_{1,3-6}$ K$_6$ D$_3$ C$_k$ –

105*	न हि त्वदन्यः कश्चिदपीह देव	*na hi tvadanyaḥ kaścidapīha deva*
	लोकत्रये दृश्यतेऽचिन्त्यकर्मा ।	*lokatraye dṛśyate'cintyakarmā* ।

[105*] Besides you, there is no other Deity of inconceivable deeds
that can be seen in the three worlds!

20. After the verse 6.33.44,
{A} we find in Ś$_{1,3-6}$ K$_6$ D$_3$ C$_{ā,k}$ –

106*	दिव्यानि कर्माणि तवाद्भुतानि	*divyāni karmāṇi tavādbhutāni*
	पूर्वाणि पूर्वेऽप्यृषयः स्मरन्ति ।	*pūrvāṇi pūrve'pyṛṣayaḥ smaranti* ।
	नान्योऽस्ति कर्ता जगतस्त्वमेको	*nānyo'sti kartā jagatastvameko*
	धाता विधाता च विभुर्भवश्च ।	*dhātā vidhātā ca vibhurbhavaśca* ।

तवाद्भुतं किं नु भवेदसह्यं	*tavādbhutaṃ kiṃ nu bhavedasahyaṃ*
किं वाशक्यं परतः कीर्तयिष्ये ।	*kiṃ vāśakyaṃ parataḥ kīrtayiṣye* ।
कर्तासि सर्वस्य यतः स्वयं वै	*kartāsi sarvasya yataḥ svayaṃ vai*
विभो ततः सर्वमिदं त्वमेव ।	*vibho tataḥ sarvamidaṃ tvameva* ।
अत्यद्भुतं कर्म न दुष्करं ते	*atyadbhutaṃ karma na duṣkaraṃ te*
कर्मोपमानं न हि विद्यते ते ।	*karmopamānaṃ na hi vidyatc te* ।
न ते गुणानां परिमाणमस्ति	*na te guṇānāṃ parimāṇamasti*
न तेजसो नापि बलस्य नर्द्धेः ।	*na tejaso nāpi balasya narddheḥ* ।

[106*]The *ṛṣis* of the past have previously acknowledged
your divine and marvelous deeds!
There is no other doer like you in the whole world.
You are the creator and the cause of the world.
Your wonders have no equal –
who can truly sing your glory?
You do everything singlehandedly.
You pervade all this.
Your deeds are marvelous,
extraordinary, and incomparable.
Your qualities, strength, splendor,
and fame are immeasurable.

{B} we find in $Ñ_1$ –

107*	इमानि कर्माणि तवाद्भुतानि	*imāni karmāṇi tavādbhutāni*
	कृतानि पूर्वे मुनयो वदन्ति ।	*kṛtāni pūrve munayo vadanti* ।
	न ते गुणानां परिमाणमस्ति	*na te guṇānāṃ parimāṇamasti*
	न तेजसश्चापि बलस्य विष्णो ।	*na tejasaścāpi balasya viṣṇo* ।

[107*]The *ṛṣis* of the past have spoken of your all those marvelous deeds.
O Viṣṇu, your qualities, strength, and splendor are immeasurable!
[*Cf.* lines 1, 2, 11, 12 of 106*.]

Chapter 12

Nil

Chapter 13

21A. Before the verse 6.35.1, we find in $Ś_{1.3}$ $K_{0-3,5,6}$ $Ñ_1$ $B_{1,3,4}$ Da_1 Dn_1 $D_{1-4,6}$ T G M_2 C_g [*Cf.* 109*] –

108*	अर्जुन उवाच ।	*arjuna uvāca* ।
	प्रकृतिं पुरुषं चैव	*prakṛtiṃ puruṣaṃ caiva*
	क्षेत्रं क्षेत्रज्ञमेव च	*kṣetraṃ kṣetrajñameva ca* ।
	एतद्वेदितुमिच्छामि	*etadveditumicchāmi*
	ज्ञानं ज्ञेयं च केशव ।	*jñānaṃ jñeyaṃ ca keśava* ।

Arjuna

[108*] Keśava! I wish to learn about –
prakṛti, *puruṣa*, *kṣetra*, *kṣetrajña*,
knowledge, and its purpose.

21B. After the verse 6.35.1, we find in K_6 [*Cf.* 108*] –

109*	प्रकृतिं पुरुषं चैव	*prakṛtiṃ puruṣaṃ caiva*
	क्षेत्रं क्षेत्रज्ञमेव च ।	*kṣetraṃ kṣetrajñameva ca* ।
	एतत्ते कथयिष्यामि	*etatte kathayiṣyāmi*
	ज्ञानं ज्ञेयं च भारत ।	*jñānaṃ jñeyaṃ ca bhārata* ।

[109*] Arjuna! I will tell you about –
prakṛti, *puruṣa*, *kṣetra*, *kṣetrajña*,
knowledge, and its purpose.

Chapters 14–17

Nil

Chapter 18

22. After the first half of the verse 6.40.47, we find in $Ś_{4,5}$ K_{0-6} D_3 (see the second half of *Gītā* 3.35) –

110*	स्वधर्मे निधनं श्रेयः	*svadharme nidhanaṃ śreyaḥ*
	परधर्मोदयादपि ।	*paradharmodayādapi* ।

[110*] It is meritorious to die upholding one's *dharma*,
even if the *dharma* of others is profitable.

23A. After the verse 6.40.78 [*i.e.*, end of Chapter 18], in Ñ1 we find –

111*	भगवद्भक्तियुक्तस्य	*bhagavadbhaktiyuktasya*
	तत्प्रसादात्मबोधतः ।	*tatprasādātmabodhataḥ* ।
	सुखं बन्धविमुक्तिः स्याद्-	*sukhaṃ bandhavimuktiḥ syād-*
	इति गीतार्थसंग्रहः ।	*iti gītārthasaṃgrahaḥ* ।

[111*] Being diligently devoted to the Supreme,
through Divine grace
one gains knowledge of the Self and
thus overcomes the bondage of mortal comforts.
This indeed is the essence of *Bhagavad-gītā*.

[This seems to have been the *saṃgrahaśloka* to *Gītā adhyāya* 18 in C_g.]

23B. After Chapter 6.40 [*i.e.*, at the end of the *Gītā*], in $Ś_1$ K_{0-1} we find the following lines; in case of K_2 B_{2-4} Dn D_{4-8}, these lines come after 113* –

112* षड्शतानि सविंशानि श्लोकानां प्राह केशवः ।
अर्जुनः सप्तपञ्चाशत्सप्तषष्टिस्तु संजयः ।
धृतराष्ट्रः श्लोकमेकं गीताया मानमुच्यते ।

ṣaṭśatāni saviṃśāni ślokānāṃ prāha keśavaḥ ।
arjunaḥ saptapañcāśatsaptaṣaṣṭistu saṃjayaḥ ।
dhṛtarāṣṭraḥ ślokamekaṃ gītāyā mānamucyate ।

[113*] The *Bhagavad-gītā* is said to consist of 620 verses spoken by Kṛṣṇa,
57 verses by Arjuna, 67 verses by Sañjaya,
and just one verse by Dhṛtarāṣṭra.

The popular version of the *Gītā* has 574 verses by Kṛṣṇa,
84 by Arjuna, 41 by Sañjaya, and one verse by Dhṛtarāṣṭra.

23C. After the chapter 6.40, we find in K_2 B_{2-4} Dn D_{3-5} –

113*	वैशंपायन उवाच ।	*vaiśaṃpāyana uvāca* ।
	गीता सुगीता कर्तव्या	*gītā sugītā kartavyā*
	किमन्यैः शास्त्रविस्तरैः ।	*kimanyaiḥ śāstravistaraiḥ* ।
	या चेयं पद्मनाभस्य	*yā ceyaṃ padmanābhasya*
	मुखपद्माद्विनिःसृता ।	*mukhapadmādviniḥsṛtā* ।
	सर्वशास्त्रमयी गीता	*sarvaśāstramayī gītā*
	सर्वदेवमयो हरिः ।	*sarvadevamayo hariḥ* ।

सर्वतीर्थमयी गङ्गा	*sarvatīrthamayī gaṅgā*
सर्ववेदमयो मनुः ।	*sarvavedamayo manuḥ* ।
गङ्गा गीता च गायत्री	*gaṅgā gītā ca gāyatrī*
गोविन्देति हृदि स्थिते ।	*govindeti hṛdi sthite* ।
चतुर्गकारसंयुक्ते	*caturgakārasaṃyukte*
पुनर्जन्म न विद्यते ।	*punarjanma na vidyate* ।

VAIŚAMPĀYANA

[113*] *Gītā* is a great song and must be sung (studied)!
Beyond it, what other *śāstra* do we really need?
Gītā has come to us straight from
the lotus mouth of Padmanābha!
Among all *śāstras*, it is *Gītā*;
among all deities, it is Hari;
of all *tīrthas*, it is Gaṅgā; and
of all the knowledge, it is (the one given by) Manu.

A *tīrtha*(*-kṣetra*) is a pilgrimage centre; a sacred place on the banks of a river.

If Gaṅgā, *Gītā*, Gāyatrī, and Govinda
are established in one's heart (*i.e.*, dear to one),
by association with these four G-s,
one will not be born again!

In other words, one will be liberated from the cycles of birth and death.

and at the end of chapter 6.40 D_5 *repeats* 6.22, 17–22.

23D. After 112* we find in B_{2-4} Dn D_{4-8} –

114*	भारतामृतसर्वस्व-	*bhāratāmṛtasarvasva-*
	गीताया मथितस्य च ।	*gītāyā mathitasya ca* ।
	सारमुद्धृत्य कृष्णेन	*sāramuddhṛtya kṛṣṇena*
	अर्जुनस्य मुखे हुतम् ।	*arjunasya mukhe hutam* ।

[114*] Among all the ambrosias in the *Mahā-bhārata* epic,
Gītā is the essence, churned by Kṛṣṇa and offered to Arjuna.

23E. After 112* in K_{0-2} we find the following segment –

अर्जुन उवाच ।	*arjuna uvāca* ।
यदेतन्निष्कलं ब्रह्म	*yadetanniṣkalaṃ brahma*
व्योमातीतं निरञ्जनम् ।	*vyomātītaṃ nirañjanam* ।
कैवल्यं केवलं शान्तं	*kaivalyaṃ kevalaṃ śāntaṃ*
शुद्धमत्यन्तनिर्मलम् ॥ १	*śuddhamatyantanirmalam* ॥ 1
अप्रतर्क्यमविज्ञेयं	*apratarkyamavijñeyaṃ*
विनाशोत्पत्तिवर्जितम् ।	*vināśotpattivarjitam* ।
ज्ञानयोगविनिर्मुक्तं	*jñānayogavinirmuktaṃ*
तज्ज्ञानं ब्रूहि केशव ॥ २	*tajjñānaṃ brūhi keśava* ॥ 2
श्रीभगवानुवाच ।	*śrībhagavānuvāca* ।
सर्वतोज्योतिराकाशं	*sarvatojyotirākāśaṃ*
सर्वभूतगुणान्वितम् ।	*sarvabhūtaguṇānvitam* ।
सर्वतःपरमात्मानम्	*sarvataḥparamātmānam*
अक्षयं परमं पदम् ॥ ३	*akṣayaṃ paramaṃ padam* ॥ 3
अनादिनिधनं देवं	*anādinidhanaṃ devaṃ*
महाज्योतिरतिध्रुवम् ।	*mahājyotiratidhruvam* ।
अत्यन्तपरमं स्थानं	*atyantaparamaṃ sthānaṃ*
शब्दादिगुणवर्जितम् ॥ ४	*śabdādiguṇavarjitam* ॥ 4
यत्तत्परतरं ज्योतिः	*yattatparataraṃ jyotiḥ*
ध्रुवात्परतरं स्थितम् ।	*dhruvātparataraṃ sthitam* ।
आचतुर्युगमद्यापि	*ācaturyugamadyāpi*
कथितं न हि कस्यचित् ॥ ५	*kathitaṃ na hi kasyacit* ॥ 5
आत्मदेहे मया सृष्टा	*ātmadehe mayā sṛṣṭā*
प्रकृतिः क्षेत्रमेव च ।	*prakṛtiḥ kṣetrameva ca* ।
सकलं तु भवेत्क्षेत्रं	*sakalaṃ tu bhavetkṣetraṃ*
निष्कलं परमं पदम् ॥ ६	*niṣkalaṃ paramaṃ padam* ॥ 6
अर्जुन त्वत्प्रसादेन	*arjuna tvatprasādena*
शृण्वन्तु मुनिसत्तमाः ।	*śṛṇvantu munisattamāḥ* ।
अद्य मुक्ता महाबाहो	*adya muktā mahābāho*
त्वत्प्रसादाद्धनंजय ॥ ७	*tvatprasādāddhanaṃjaya* ॥ 7
प्रमाणं वेदतत्त्वानां	*pramāṇaṃ vedatattvānāṃ*
सांख्यादीन्यभियोगिनाम् ।	*sāṃkhyādīnyabhiyoginām* ।
तेषां न विद्यते निष्ठा	*teṣāṃ na vidyate niṣṭhā*
सर्वैः पाषण्डिभिः सह ॥ ८	*sarvaiḥ pāṣaṇḍibhiḥ saha* ॥ 8
कथितं च मया ज्ञानं	*kathitaṃ ca mayā jñānaṃ*
देवानामपि दुर्लभम् ।	*devānāmapi durlabham* ।
विश्वरूपमयं दिव्यं	*viśvarūpamayaṃ divyaṃ*
भैरवग्रन्थिबिन्दुना ॥ ९	*bhairavagranthibindunā* ॥ 9

अप्रकाशमिदं प्रश्नं	*aprakāśamidaṃ praśnaṃ*
यन्मया कथितं तव ।	*yanmayā kathitaṃ tava* ।
वाङ्मयं सर्वशास्त्राणाम्	*vāṅmayaṃ sarvaśāstrāṇām*
अतिसूक्ष्मं चराचरम् ॥ १०	*atisūkṣmaṃ carācaram* ॥ 10
नाग्निर्वायुर्न चाकाशं	*nāgnirvāyurna cākāśaṃ*
न क्षितिर्नापि वा जलम् ।	*na kṣitirnāpi vā jalam* ।
न मनोबुद्ध्यहंकारं	*na manobuddhyahaṃkāraṃ*
गूढार्थं कथितं तव ॥ ११	*gūḍhārthaṃ kathitaṃ tava* ॥ 11
अनित्यो नित्यतां याति	*anityo nityatāṃ yāti*
यदा भावं न पश्यति ।	*yadā bhāvaṃ na paśyati* ।
शून्यं निरञ्जनाकारं	*śūnyaṃ nirañjanākāraṃ*
निर्वाणं ध्रुवमव्ययम् ॥ १२	*nirvāṇaṃ dhruvamavyayam* ॥ 12
पुरुषं निर्गुणं साक्षात्	*puruṣaṃ nirguṇaṃ sākṣāt*
सर्वतश्चैव तिष्ठति ।	*sarvataścaiva tiṣṭhati* ।
सर्वं तत्स्यात्परं ब्रह्म	*sarvaṃ tatsyātparaṃ brahma*
बुद्धिश्चास्य न बुध्यति ॥ १३	*buddhiścāsya na budhyati* ॥ 13
प्रतिभावप्रयत्नेन	*pratibhāvaprayatnena*
हरिं त्रैलोक्यबान्धवम् ।	*hariṃ trailokyabāndhavam* ।
दशमं चाङ्गुलं व्याप्य	*daśamaṃ cāṅgulaṃ vyāpya*
चाशाबाह्यं व्यवस्थितम् ॥ १४	*cāśābāhyaṃ vyavasthitam* ॥ 14
जीवो यत्र प्रलीयेत	*jīvo yatra pralīyeta*
सा कला षोडशी स्मृता ।	*sā kalā ṣoḍaśī smṛtā* ।
तया सर्वमिदं व्याप्तं	*tayā sarvamidaṃ vyāptaṃ*
त्रैलोक्यं सचराचरम् ॥ १५	*trailokyaṃ sacarācaram* ॥ 15
तच्चिन्त्यं तेन वै ज्ञानं	*taccintyaṃ tena vai jñānaṃ*
तदत्राद्या उपासते ।	*tadatrādyā upāsate* ।
ब्रह्मणैव हि विख्यातं	*brahmaṇaiva hi vikhyātaṃ*
वेदान्तेषु प्रकाशितम् ॥ १६	*vedānteṣu prakāśitam* ॥ 16
वेदेषु वेदमित्याहुः	*vedeṣu vedamityāhuḥ*
वेदधाम परं मतम् ।	*vedadhāma paraṃ matam* ।
तत्परं विदितं यस्य	*tatparaṃ viditaṃ yasya*
स विप्रो वेदपारगः ॥ १७	*sa vipro vedapāragaḥ* ॥ 17
आहुतिः सा परा ज्ञेया	*āhutiḥ sā parā jñeyā*
सा च संध्या प्रतिष्ठिता ।	*sā ca saṃdhyā pratiṣṭhitā* ।
गायत्री सा परा ज्ञेया	*gāyatrī sā parā jñeyā*
अजपा नाम विश्रुता ॥ १८	*ajapā nāma viśrutā* ॥ 18
तपस्यथ तथा वेदे	*tapasyatha tathā vede*
मुनिभिः समुपास्यते ।	*munibhiḥ samupāsyate* ।
तां कलां योऽभिजानाति	*tāṃ kalāṃ yo'bhijānāti*
स कलाज्ञोऽभिधीयते ॥ १९	*sa kalājño'bhidhīyate* ॥ 19

यां ज्ञात्वा मुच्यते जन्तुः	*yāṃ jñātvā mucyate jantuḥ*
गर्भजन्मजरादिभिः ।	*garbhajanmajarādibhiḥ* ।
परिज्ञानेन मुच्यन्ते	*parijñānena mucyante*
नराः पातककिल्बिषैः ॥ २०	*narāḥ pātakakilbiṣaiḥ* ॥ 20
इडा भगवती गङ्गा	*iḍā bhagavatī gaṅgā*
पिङ्गला यमुना नदी ।	*piṅgalā yamunā nadī* ।
तयोर्मध्ये तृतीया तु	*tayormadhye tṛtīyā tu*
तत्प्रयागमनुस्मरेत् ॥ २१	*tatprayāgamanusmaret* ॥ 21
इडा वै वैष्णवी नाडी	*iḍā vai vaiṣṇavī nāḍī*
ब्रह्मनाडी तु पिङ्गला ।	*brahmanāḍī tu piṅgalā* ।
सुषुम्णा चैश्वरी नाडी	*suṣumṇā caiśvarī nāḍī*
त्रिधा प्राणवहा स्मृता ।	*tridhā prāṇavahā smṛtā* ।
ब्रह्मा विष्णुर्महादेवो	*brahmā viṣṇurmahādevo*
रेचकः पूरकुम्भकः ॥ २२	*recakaḥ pūrakumbhakaḥ* ॥ 22
सक्रान्तिविषुवच्चैव	*sakrāntiviṣuvaccaiva*
योऽभिजानाति विग्रहम् ।	*yo'bhijānāti vigraham* ।
नित्ययुक्तः स योगीशो	*nityayuktaḥ sa yogīśo*
ब्रह्मविद्यां प्रपद्यते ॥ २३	*brahmavidyāṃ prapadyate* ॥ 23
इडा वै गार्हपत्यस्तु	*iḍā vai gārhapatyastu*
पिङ्गलाहवनीयकः ।	*piṅgalāhavanīyakaḥ* ।
सुषुम्णा दक्षिणाग्निस्तु	*suṣumṇā dakṣiṇāgnistu*
ह्येतदग्नित्रयं स्मृतम् ॥ २४	*hyetadagnitrayaṃ smṛtam* ॥ 24
तस्य मध्ये स्थितं ज्योतिः	*tasya madhye sthitaṃ jyotiḥ*
सोममण्डलमेव च ।	*somamaṇḍalameva ca* ।
सोममण्डलमध्यस्थं	*somamaṇḍalamadhyasthaṃ*
तन्मध्ये सूर्यमण्डलम् ॥ २५	*tanmadhye sūryamaṇḍalam* ॥ 25
सूर्यमण्डलमध्यस्थो	*sūryamaṇḍalamadhyastho*
ज्वलत्तेजो हुताशनः ।	*jvalattejo hutāśanaḥ* ।
हुताशनस्य मध्ये तु	*hutāśanasya madhye tu*
निर्धूमाङ्गारवर्चसम् ॥ २६	*nirdhūmāṅgāravarcasam* ॥ 26
तत्रास्थितो महात्मासौ	*tatrāsthito mahātmāsau*
योगिभिस्तु प्रगीयते ।	*yogibhistu pragīyate* ।
सुगीतं चैव कर्तव्यं	*sugītaṃ caiva kartavyaṃ*
मन एकाग्रचेतसा ॥ २७	*mana ekāgracetasā* ॥ 27
शिवो बिन्दुः शिवो देवो	*śivo binduḥ śivo devo*
घर्घरामृतवर्चसा ।	*ghargharāmṛtavarcasā* ।
निखिलं पूरयेद्देहं	*nikhilaṃ pūrayeddehaṃ*
विषदाहज्वरापहम् ॥ २८	*viṣadāhajvarāpaham* ॥ 28

सर्पवत्कुटिलाकार-
सुषुम्णावेष्टितां तनुम् ।
मकारवेष्टितां कृत्वा
मातृवत्परियोजयेत् ॥ २९

sarpavatkuṭilākāra-
suṣumṇāveṣṭitāṃ tanum ।
makāraveṣṭitāṃ kṛtvā
mātṛvatpariyojayet ॥ 29

त्रिस्थानं च त्रिमात्रं च
त्रिब्रह्म च त्रिरक्षरम् ।
अर्धमात्रं च यो वेत्ति
स भवेद्वेदपारगः ॥ ३०

tristhānaṃ ca trimātraṃ ca
tribrahma ca trirakṣaram ।
ardhamātraṃ ca yo vetti
sa bhavedvedapāragaḥ ॥ 30

सर्वतःपाणिपादं तत्
सर्वतोक्षिशिरोमुखम् ।
निर्मलं विमलाकारं
शुद्धस्फटिकसंनिभम् ॥ ३१

sarvataḥpāṇipādaṃ tat
sarvatokṣiśiromukham ।
nirmalaṃ vimalākāraṃ
śuddhasphaṭikasaṃnibham ॥ 31

अर्जुन उवाच ।
स्थावरं जंगमं चैव
यत्किंचित्सचराचरम् ।
जीवो जीवति जीवेन
स जीवः केन जीवति ॥ ३२

arjuna uvāca ।
sthāvaraṃ jaṃgamaṃ caiva
yatkiṃcitsacarācaram ।
jīvo jīvati jīvena
sa jīvaḥ kena jīvati ॥ 32

श्रीभगवानुवाच ।
मुखनासिकयोर्मध्ये
प्राणः संचरते सदा ।
आकाशं पिबते नित्यं
स जीवस्तेन जीवति ॥ ३३

śrībhagavānuvāca ।
mukhanāsikayormadhye
prāṇaḥ saṃcarate sadā ।
ākāśaṃ pibate nityaṃ
sa jīvastena jīvati ॥ 33

काकीमुखं ककारान्तं
मकारं चेतनानुगम् ।
अकारस्य तु लुप्तस्य
कोऽर्थः संप्रतिपद्यते ॥ ३४

kākīmukhaṃ kakārāntaṃ
makāraṃ cetanānugam ।
akārasya tu luptasya
ko'rthaḥ saṃpratipadyate ॥ 34

तावत्पश्येत्खगाकारं
खकारं तु विचिन्तयेत् ।
खमध्ये कुरु चात्मानम्
आत्ममध्यं च खं कुरु ॥ ३५

tāvatpaśyetkhagākāraṃ
khakāraṃ tu vicintayet ।
khamadhye kuru cātmānam
ātmamadhyaṃ ca khaṃ kuru ॥ 35

खमध्ये च प्रवेष्टव्यं
खं च ब्रह्म सनातनम् ।
आत्मानं खमयं कृत्वा
न किंचिदपि चिन्तयेत् ॥ ३६

khamadhye ca praveṣṭavyaṃ
khaṃ ca brahma sanātanam ।
ātmānaṃ khamayaṃ kṛtvā
na kiṃcidapi cintayet ॥ 36

ऊर्ध्वशून्यमधःशून्यं
मध्येशून्यं निरामयम् ।
त्रिशून्यं योऽभिजानाति
स भवेत्कुलनन्दनः ॥ ३७

ūrdhvaśūnyamadhaḥśūnyaṃ
madhyeśūnyaṃ nirāmayam ।
triśūnyaṃ yo'bhijānāti
sa bhavetkulanandanaḥ ॥ 37

अमात्रशब्दरहितं	*amātraśabdarahitaṃ*
स्वरव्यञ्जनवर्जितम् ।	*svaravyañjanavarjitam* ।
बिन्दुनादकलातीतं	*bindunādakalātītaṃ*
यस्तं वेद स वेदवित् ॥ ३८	*yastaṃ veda sa vedavit* ॥ 38
संप्राप्ते ज्ञानविज्ञाने	*saṃprāpte jñānavijñāne*
ज्ञेये च हृदि संस्थिते ।	*jñeye ca hṛdi saṃsthite* ।
लब्धशान्तपदे भावे	*labdhaśāntapade bhāvc*
न योगो न च धारणा ॥ ३९	*na yogo na ca dhāraṇā* ॥ 39
वेदादौ यः सुरः प्रोक्तो	*vedādau yaḥ suraḥ prokto*
वेदान्ते च प्रतिष्ठितः ।	*vedānte ca pratiṣṭhitaḥ* ।
तस्य प्रकृतिलीनस्य	*tasya prakṛtilīnasya*
यः परः स महेश्वरः ॥ ४०	*yaḥ paraḥ sa maheśvaraḥ* ॥ 40
ना नावार्थी भवेत्तावत्	*nā nāvārthī bhavettāvat*
यावत्पारं न गच्छति ।	*yāvatpāraṃ na gacchati* ।
उत्तीर्णे तु परे पारे	*uttīrṇe tu pare pāre*
किं नावा वै प्रयोजनम् ॥ ४१	*kiṃ nāvā vai prayojanam* ॥ 41
दूरस्थो नापि दूरस्थः	*dūrastho nāpi dūrasthaḥ*
पिण्डस्थः पिण्डवर्जितः ।	*piṇḍasthaḥ piṇḍavarjitaḥ* ।
अमलो निर्मलः सूक्ष्मः	*amalo nirmalaḥ sūkṣmaḥ*
सर्वव्यापी निरञ्जनः ॥ ४२	*sarvavyāpī nirañjanaḥ* ॥ 42
अर्जुन उवाच ।	*arjuna uvāca* ।
अक्षराणि समात्राणि	*akṣarāṇi samātrāṇi*
सर्वे बिन्दुसमाश्रिताः ।	*sarve bindusamāśritāḥ* ।
बिन्दुर्भिद्यति नादेन	*bindurbhidyati nādena*
स नादः केन भिद्यते ॥ ४३	*sa nādaḥ kena bhidyate* ॥ 43
श्रीभगवानुवाच ।	*śrībhagavānuvāca* ।
ओंकारध्वनिनादेन	*oṃkāradhvaninādena*
वायुः संहरणान्तिकम् ।	*vāyuḥ saṃharaṇāntikam* ।
निरालम्भस्तु निर्देहो	*nirālambhastu nirdeho*
यत्र नादो लयं गतः ॥ ४४	*yatra nādo layaṃ gataḥ* ॥ 44
अर्जुन उवाच ।	*arjuna uvāca* ।
बाह्येन व्यापितं व्योम	*bāhyena vyāpitaṃ vyoma*
व्योम चाननुनासिकम् ।	*vyoma cānanunāsikam* ।
अधश्चोर्ध्वं कथं चैव	*adhaścordhvaṃ kathaṃ caiva*
कण्ठे चैव निरञ्जनः ॥ ४५	*kaṇṭhe caiva nirañjanaḥ* ॥ 45

श्रीभगवानुवाच ।	*śrībhagavānuvāca* ।
अनूष्ममव्यञ्जकमस्वरं यत्	*anūṣmamavyañjakamasvaraṃ yat*
तत्तालुकण्ठेष्वनुनासिकं च ।	*tattālukaṇṭheṣvanunāsikaṃ ca* ।
अरेफजातं शुभमूष्मवर्जितं	*arephajātaṃ śubhamūṣmavarjitaṃ*
न दुष्कराणां कुरुते कदाचित् ॥ ४६	*na duṣkarāṇāṃ kurute kadācit* ॥ 46
आकाशमप्यनाकाशं	*ākāśamapyanākāśaṃ*
पुरुषत्वे प्रतिष्ठितम् ।	*puruṣatve pratiṣṭhitam* ।
शब्दं गुणमिवाकाशं	*śabdaṃ guṇamivākāśaṃ*
निःशब्दं ब्रह्म चोच्यते ॥ ४७	*niḥśabdaṃ brahma cocyate* ॥ 47
सर्वगं सर्वबोधादि	*sarvagaṃ sarvabodhādi*
वासनाजालवर्जितम् ।	*vāsanājālavarjitam* ।
इन्द्रियाणां निरोधेन	*indriyāṇāṃ nirodhena*
देहे पश्यन्ति मानवाः ॥ ४८	*dehe paśyanti mānavāḥ* ॥ 48
देहे नष्टे कुतो बुद्धिः	*dehe naṣṭe kuto buddhiḥ*
ज्ञानं विज्ञानमेव च ।	*jñānaṃ vijñānameva ca* ।
ज्ञानं विज्ञानयुक्तं च	*jñānaṃ vijñānayuktaṃ ca*
रक्षणीयं प्रयत्नतः । ४९	*rakṣaṇīyaṃ prayatnataḥ* । 49
छिन्नमूलस्य वृक्षस्य	*chinnamūlasya vṛkṣasya*
यथा जन्म न विद्यते ।	*yathā janma na vidyate* ।
ज्ञानदग्धशरीरस्य	*jñānadagdhaśarīrasya*
पुनर्देहो न विद्यते ॥ ५०	*punardeho na vidyate* ॥ 50
गीताः सुगीताः कर्तव्याः	*gītāḥ sugītāḥ kartavyāḥ*
किमन्यैः शास्त्रसंग्रहैः ।	*kimanyaiḥ śāstrasaṃgrahaiḥ* ।
याः पुरा पद्मनाभस्य	*yāḥ purā padmanābhasya*
मुखपद्मविनिःसृताः ॥ ५१	*mukhapadmaviniḥsṛtāḥ* ॥ 51
गीतागङ्गोदकं पीत्वा	*gītāgaṅgodakaṃ pītvā*
पुनर्जन्म न विद्यते ।	*punarjanma na vidyate* ।
सर्वशास्त्रमयी गीता	*sarvaśāstramayī gītā*
सर्वधर्ममयो हरिः ॥ ५२	*sarvadharmamayo hariḥ* ॥ 52
सर्वतीर्थमयी गङ्गा	*sarvatīrthamayī gaṅgā*
सर्वपापक्षयंकरी ।	*sarvapāpakṣayaṃkarī* ।
सर्वभोगमयश्चायं	*sarvabhogamayaścāyaṃ*
सर्वमोक्षमयो ह्ययम् ॥ ५३	*sarvamokṣamayo hyayam* ॥ 53
गकारपूर्वाश्चत्वारो	*gakārapūrvāścatvāro*
रक्षन्ति महतो भयात् ।	*rakṣanti mahato bhayāt* ।
गीता गङ्गा च गायत्री	*gītā gaṅgā ca gāyatrī*
गोविन्दो हृदि संस्थिताः ॥ ५४	*govindo hṛdi saṃsthitāḥ* ॥ 54

स्नातो वा यदि वास्नातः
शुचिर्वा यदि वाशुचिः ।
यः स्मरेत्पुण्डरीकाक्षं
स बाह्याभ्यन्तरे शुचिः ॥ ५५
स गच्छेत्तत्क्षणात्प्रायो
ब्रह्ममूर्ते नमोऽस्तु ते ।
गीतासारं पठेद्यस्तु
विष्णुलोके महीयते ॥ ५६
एतत्पुण्यं पापहरं
धन्यं दुःस्वप्ननाशनम् ।
पठतां शृण्वतां चैव
विष्णोर्माहात्म्यमुत्तमम् ॥ ५७

snāto vā yadi vāsnātaḥ
śucirvā yadi vāśuciḥ ।
yaḥ smaretpuṇḍarīkākṣaṃ
sa bāhyābhyantare śuciḥ ॥ 55
sa gacchettatkṣaṇātprāyo
brahmamūrte namo'stu te ।
gītāsāraṃ paṭhedyastu
viṣṇuloke mahīyate ॥ 56
etatpuṇyaṃ pāpaharaṃ
dhanyaṃ duḥsvapnanāśanam ।
paṭhatāṃ śṛṇvatāṃ caiva
viṣṇormāhātmyamuttamam ॥ 57

ARJUNA

[1]What is that one (and only)
spotless, untainted, peaceful,
and the absolute *Brahman*
that transcends the skies
and is perfectly pure?

[2]O Keśava!
Teach me *jñāna yoga* for liberation –
it is hard to comprehend by logic and difficult to know;
it is devoid of death and rebirth.

KṚṢṆA

[3](*Brahman*) completely illuminates space;
it is the *guṇa* in all beings, it is eternal,
it is the Supreme *ātman*, it is the Supreme State.

[4]The Supreme is without beginning and without end,
the greatest illumination, utterly unwavering,
possessed of the highest state, and
free from the attributes of sound and other sensations.

[5]It is the greatest illumination,
whose state is higher than even the pole star;
throughout the four *yugas*,
no one has been able to speak of it!

[6]In my body, I have created *prakṛti* and *kṣetra*.
The manifest one is called *kṣetra*
while the unmanifest is the Supreme state.

The original uses the terms *sakalam* (manifest, qualified, with attributes) and *niṣkalam* (unmanifest, beyond qualification, transcending attributes).

[7]Arjuna on your account let the *munis* (sages) listen.
Now they are liberated on your account, O mighty-armed!

[8]For the *yogins*, *Vedānta* and *Sāṅkhya* are authorities.
Pāṣaṇḍins (those who reject authority of *Vedas*)
will never gain that discipline (wisdom).

[9]The knowledge I have imparted (to you)
is unavailable to even the *devas*.
The divine universal form (you saw)
is a mere speck of the cosmic focal point.

In the *pratyabhijñā-śaiva-darśana* and other *śākta* traditions, the *bhairavi-granthi* is a type of focal point or an object of meditation.

[10]The review I presented to you is not commonly known.
Vedānta is extremely subtle among
all the literature and all the *śāstras* in this world.

[11]Neither fire, wind, space, earth, water
nor mind, intellect, ego are aware of the
subtle knowledge I have imparted to you.

12When impermanent becomes permanent,
when (illusion of) manifestation vanishes, and
when imperishable Supreme is seen as formless,
nirvāṇa is guaranteed!

13Formless *puruṣa* (Supreme) is
as though established in everything.
Everything is the Supreme *Brahman* –
and it is not grasped by the intellect!

14By means of *pratibhāva* (a type of *tapas*),
(know) Hari, the friend of the three worlds!
He pervades (the universe) and
is established (in a state) beyond desire!

15Know this: the *jīva* dissolves in
the sixteenth phase (*i.e.* the unmanifest).
In that (unmanifest) everything is occupied –
the animate and the inanimate in the three worlds.

The moon has *ṣoḍaṣa-kalā* or sixteen phases; starting from the *pratipat* (first day of the lunar fortnight) until the *pūrṇimā* (full moon), we have fifteen phases of the moon. The sixteenth phase is the *amāvāsyā* (new moon) and this represents the unseen, unmanifest. This verse simply suggests that the whole of the manifest world lies in the unmanifest *Brahman*.

16That (*Brahman*) should be meditated upon
and worshipped as foremost –
that alone is wisdom.
Brahman is brought to light (revealed)
and celebrated in the *Vedānta*.

17Of all the bodies of knowledge,
Veda is said to be the supreme.
It is said to be the supreme abode of knowledge.

Those who know it to be so
are sages and masters of *Veda*!

[18]Performing *sandhyā-vandanam* is to be known
as superior to offering *āhuti* (oblations).
Gāyatrī mantra of great fame is to be known
as superior to performing *sandhyā-vandanam*.

[19]Practice *tapas* and know that
which the *munis* have hailed in the *Vedas*.
One who knows *kalā*
is considered a *kalājña*.

In the *pratyabhijñā-śaiva-darśana*, the term *kalā* refers to
Supreme, power, or omnipotence.

[20]By knowing that (wisdom), one is
liberated from rebirth and old age.
By the selfsame wisdom, humans are
liberated from grave calamities.

[21]*Iḍā* is the divine river Gaṅgā,
piṅgalā is the river Yamunā.
In between them is the third
(River Sarasvatī is *suṣumnā*)
and one should recollect that as Prayāga.

Iḍā, *piṅgalā*, and *suṣumnā* are the three *nāḍis*
(energy channels, particular vessels of the body).
The *suṣumnā* is said to lie between *iḍā* and *piṅgalā*.

[22]*Iḍā* is *vaiṣṇavī-nāḍi*,
piṅgalā is *brahma-nāḍi*, and
suṣumnā is *īśvarī-nāḍi*;
these three are considered to carry *prāṇa*.

Brahmā-Viṣṇu-Mahādeva are
recaka, *pūraka*, and *kumbhaka*.

Vaiṣṇavī means 'of Viṣṇu' and *īśvarī* means 'of Śiva.'
Prāṇa refers to the 'life-force' of an organism, its sustaining energy;
it is also known as the 'vital breath,' for without breathing, there is no life.
Recaka (breathing out), *pūraka* (breathing in), and *kumbhaka* (holding the breath)
are the three parts of the *prāṇāyāma* ('breath control') cycle.

23 One who knows solstice and equinox
as embodiment (of the Supreme),
such steadfast master of *yoga*
gets the knowledge of the Supreme.

24 The three *agnis* – *gārhapatya*, *āhavanīyaka*, and *dakṣiṇā* –
should be considered as *iḍā*, *piṅgalā*, and *suṣumnā*.

In a *yajña*, typically there are three kinds of *agni* (sacred fire)
and they are raised in altars of different shapes – *gārhapatya* (circular),
āhavanīya (square-shaped), and *dakṣiṇa* (semicircular).

25 The light amidst them is indeed the orb of the moon.
Amidst the moon's orb is the orb of the sun.
26 The glowing fire in the middle of sun's orb is *hutāśana*.
In the middle of *hutāśana* (fire) is smokeless glow of coal.

27 Situated amidst those fires a great soul resonates with *yoga*.
Being in tune with that is essential for single-pointed conscience.

28 Śiva is the *bindu*, Śiva is the deity;
the splendour of the flood of *amṛta*
completely fills the body and
destroys poison, thirst, and fever.

In the *pratyabhijñā-śaiva-darśana*, the term *bindu* refers to
a point of focus or the object of meditation.
This verse basically says that when the *Kuṇḍalinī* is awakened,
worldly affictions are destroyed.

29 (*Kuṇḍalinī*) in the body is coiled up like a serpent
and enclosed in *suṣumnā*.
It must be wrapped in the '*ma*'-*kāras*
and we should associate it with like a mother.

The *pañca-makāras* (five 'm's) of the *tantra* tradition are – *mantra* (prayer), *mudra* (hand gesture), *māṃsā* (meat), *madya* (alcohol), and *maithuna* (sex).
In some lists, *matsya* (fish) is included instead of *mantra*.

30 Three positions, three *mātrās*,
three *brahmas*, and three *akṣarams*.
One who knows the (three-and-a-)half *mātrā*
become learned in the *Veda*.

This verse is a reference to *Oṃ* (*praṇava*), the single syllable that denotes *Brahman*.
The primordial sound *Oṃ* is made up of four parts.
The first three parts of *Oṃ* – '*a*,' '*u*,' and '*m*' – emanate from the navel, chest, and head respectively (*i.e.*, three positions).
Mātrā is the shortest recognizable syllabic utterance and *Oṃ* comprises three *mātrās* ('*a*,' '*u*,' and '*m*').
'Three *brahmas*' possibly refers to the presiding deities of the three *mātrās*.
Akṣaram typically refers to 'syllable' but it is also used to denote 'letter' and *Oṃ* comprises three *akṣarams* as well.
The fourth part, which is silence, accounts for half a *mātrā* and so, one who knows these three-and-a-half *mātrās* of *Oṃ* is said to know the *Vedas*, for *Brahman* is the essence of *Veda*.

31 With hands, legs, eyes,
head, and mouth everywhere,
(*Brahman* is) resplendent and spotless,
resembling a pure gemstone.

ARJUNA

32 The moving and the motionless
and all beings that exist, animate and inanimate –
live off other living beings;
but how indeed does he (the wise one) live?

KṚṢṆA

33 *Prāṇa* constantly moves about
in the region between the mouth and the nose
Forever consuming *ākāśa* (sky)
from that, he (the wise one) lives.

This is the literal translation of the verse; the meaning is obscure.

34 Starting with '*kā-kī*,' ending with '*ka-kā*,'
and including '*ma*' – thus one follows consciousness
When '*a*' is missing, what meaning can indeed be given?

This is the literal translation of the verse; the meaning is obscure.

35 Thus, he should see the form of a bird and
indeed must meditate on '*kha*' (sky, sense organs)
Place the self in '*kha*' and place the '*kha*' in the self!

36 One should enter into the core of
'*kha*' (sky, sense organs).
'*Kha*' is the Eternal *Brahman*!
Having made the self pervaded by '*kha*'
do not think about anything else!

This is perhaps a suggestion that *Brahman* is subtle like the sky.

37 Vacant above, vacant below, and
entirely nothing in between.
The one who knows these three voids
indeed becomes a joy to his clan!

This perhaps suggests the unmanifest nature of *Brahman*.

38 He truly knows who knows
that which is beyond *bindu-nāda-kalā*

and that which is without
mātrā, *śabda*, *svara*, and *vyañjana*.

In the *pratyabhijñā-śaiva-darśana*, the term *bindu* refers to
'focus' or 'concentration,' and is associated with Śiva
while *nāda* refers to 'expanse' or 'ripples' and is associated with Śakti.
Kalā refers to Supreme, power, or omnipotence.
This verse suggests one who who truly knows
transcends the letter and grasps the spirit.

39 One who has attained wisdom
and the knowledge to apply it,
one who has the knowable
(object of knowledge)
firmly residing in his heart, and
one who has attained
the emotional state of peace –
such a person needs
neither *yoga* nor meditation!

40 He, Maheśvara, who is hailed
as a *sura* in the *Vedas*
and is established in *Vedānta* –
one who is immersed in his nature
indeed transcends (the material world)!

41 Until one has to cross (the ocean of *saṃsāra*)
he is not desirous of a boat.
And what indeed is the use of a boat
after one has transcended the Ultimate?

42 It is far away yet near. It is together yet separate.
It is pure, subtle, and without taint!
The stainless (*Brahman*) is all-pervading!

This is similar to verse 13.15.

ARJUNA

[43]All the *akṣaras* along with the *mātrās*
are dependent on *bindu*.
That *bindu* is cleft by means of *nāda*
How is that *nāda* cleft?

KṚṢṆA

[44]Through the sound of *oṃkāra*
the *prāṇa-vāyu* is annihilated.
Transcending body and ritual,
nāda attains dissolution.

This speaks of transcending *bindu-nāda-kalā*.

ARJUNA

[45]The inner space is wrapped by the external
and is not in the *anunāsika*.
How indeed is it untainted
being present neither above (*i.e.*, palate, nose)
nor below (*i.e.*, chest, navel) the throat?

The five sources of sound in the human body are – *nābhī* (navel), *hṛt* (chest), *kaṇṭha* (throat), *rasana* (tongue, palate), and *nāsa* (nose).
Anunāsika refers to nasal sounds.
The meaning of this verse is obscure.

KṚṢṆA

[46]He never utters the difficult sounds
that are not *ūṣma* (*śa*, *ṣa*, *sa*, *ha*)
that are neither consonants nor vowels,
neither *tālavya* (palatal) nor *kaṇṭhya* (guttural)
nor *anunāsikas* (nasal),
neither with the '*ra*' nor with the auspicious *ūṣma*.

This possibly suggests that the *Brahman* is beyond any sort of utterance.

[47]Both *ākāśa* (subtle) and not *ākāśa* (gross)
are established in the *puruṣa*;
śabda (sound) is the quality of the sky
but the *Brahman* is said to be beyond
śabda and other traits!

[48]When people restrain their senses
they see within their own bodies
the all-pervading, all-wise (*Brahman*)
that is free of the web of *vāsanas*.

Vāsana is the residual impact of actions that we carry from one life to the next.

[49]If the body is destroyed,
where indeed is intellect,
wisdom or applied knowledge?
One must strive to protect (the self)
through wisdom and applied knowledge.

[50]Just as a tree whose roots are severed
does not have rebirth (does not regrow)
similarly, when the body is burnt
by the fire of wisdom
one does not take on another body.

[51]*Gītā* is a great song
and must be sung (studied)!
Beyond it, what other *śāstra*
do we really need?
During ancient times,
the *Gītā* sprung from
the lotus-mouth of Padmanābha.

This is similar to the first part of 113* (see *pp.* 404–5).

[52]By the (study of) the *Gītā* and
drinking the sacred water of the Gaṅgā
one is not reborn.

In other words, one will be liberated from the cycles of birth and death.

The *Gītā* is the quintessence of all *śāstras*
Kṛṣṇa is the quintessence of *dharma*.

[53]Gaṅgā is pervaded by the spirit of all *tīrthas*;
it washes away all *pāpa*
It is the essence of all enjoyments
and it is pervaded by *mokṣa*.

[54]The four ancient G-s
protect one from grave danger –
Gītā, Gaṅgā, Gāyatrī, and Govinda –
when they are established in the heart.

This is similar to the last part of 113* (see *pp*. 404–5).

[55]Whether one has bathed or not
whether one is pure or impure
the one who remembers Viṣṇu
becomes cleansed both within and outside!

[56]Salutations to you, the embodiment of *Brahman*!
The one who studies this essence of *Gītā*
attains at once the realm of Viṣṇu
and find everlasting bliss!

[57](He attains the highest)
who studies or even hears
the greatness of Viṣṇu's glory;

it is (a great) *puṇya*,
it demolishes all *pāpa*,
it is auspicious, and
it destroys bad dreams!

~

BY NO MEANS is this section a comprehensive translation of the Critical Edition of the *Bhagavad-gītā* edited by Shripad Krishna Belvalkar, which contains several other details, *e.g.* the specific variations in the different manuscripts. That said, this is a humble attempt to translate into English major passages and all additional verses of the *Gītā* that fall outside the ambit of the critically constituted text.

Many additional verses are from the Northern Recension, especially from the Kaśmīrī version, which appears to have been influenced by the *pratyabhijñā-śaiva-darśana*, one of the schools of Indian philosophy that includes elements of mysticism.

Among these additional *Gītā* verses, a few of them are invocatory in nature and a few others are valuable for their imagery, but the bulk of the verses are rather mystical and obscure; while they are not opposed in spirit to the philosophy of the *Gītā*, they don't add much to the understanding of the *Gītā* and appear superfluous. That said, these verses offer us a glimpse into how the different retellings of the epic added on to Kṛṣṇa's wartime counsel to Arjuna.

APPENDIX 3

Glossary

Some Important Concepts in Hinduism

Harmony • Truth is one, the Supreme is one; people call it by various names. Different people have different perspectives and so in a broad sense, there are as many religions as there are people. Hinduism is pluralistic, tolerant, and encompasses diverse paths. It emphasizes on conduct more than creed. And everyone is free to practice it.

Inner Voice • Hinduism encourages introspection and offers an intuitive approach to learning. It considers personal experience more real than knowledge gained by reading or listening. True happiness lies within; embark on that inward journey and listen to the inner voice.

Nurture • Life supports life, so avoid causing harm. Some Hindu groups stress on vegetarianism but it is not a must for a Hindu. Enjoy all blessings (food, wealth, relationships, fame, *etc.*) with gratitude and detachment; don't be greedy after another's share.

Dharma • Support what is right, for the greater good. This is a necessity and is the basis of sustaining harmony. Not supporting *dharma* is akin to chopping branches of a tree under which one is taking shade.

Unity • All living beings and non-living objects are inter-connected; they are essentially manifestations of *brahman*. The world is one family.

Inner Strength • One should neither degrade oneself nor be pretentious. One should elevate oneself by one's own efforts – this is a personal responsibility. A little effort in the right direction goes a long way and also no effort ever goes waste.

Supreme • One becomes sustained if one knows the sustaining power of the Supreme (God, *Brahman*). When things get out of control, the Supreme incarnates into an earthly form to set things right. One can worship the Supreme as a god with pretty much any form, or as a formless spirit. On the whole, it is more important to respect the divine presence in the universe. Thus, Hinduism readily appeals to both theists and agnostics.

Mokṣa • It is the highest goal of life and it refers to 'liberation from cycles of birth and death,' 'going beyond the dualities,' 'being in perfect Bliss,' and 'becoming one with *Brahman*.' There are numerous paths and varied opportunities for attaining *mokṣa*, including: *karma-yoga* (selfless action), *jñāna-yoga* (path of knowledge), *bhakti-yoga* (devotion), *prapatti* (surrender to Supreme), *rāja-yoga* (control of body, mind, and intellect), *dhyāna* (meditation), and *japa* (repetition of a *mantra*, a sacred word or verse used for prayer or meditation).

The other goals of life are *Dharma* (sustainability principle, good deeds, moral law), *Artha* (wealth, means to fulfil desires), and *kāma* (enjoyment, pleasures, desires). To achieve the goals of life, it is best to stay close to one's own attitudes and aptitudes.

Some Important Terms in the Gītā

ātman • Inner, higher self of an individual; also refers to 'soul' or 'spirit.'

avatāra • Incarnation; usually refers to incarnation of the Supreme. History has shown that during a great crisis, someone rises to the occasion, assumes leadership, and brings about change. In the *Bhagavad-gītā*, Kṛṣṇa presents the concept of *avatāra* without any limitations of space or time.

brahman • The imperishable, supreme being. *Brahman* is the source and sustainer of the entire universe; there is nothing beyond *brahman*.

brahmacarya • Following the path of *brahman*. It refers to leading a life of purity and not letting the mind wander around trivial things.

dāna • Charity that is undertaken with a feeling that it is one's duty to give and includes offering the right gift to the deserving person at an appropriate time.

deva • Class of divine beings who reside in *deva-loka* (higher realm). The elements and forces of nature such as wind, water, fire, earth, space, time, sun, moon, stars, planets, rain, oceans, mountains, plants, animals, *etc.* are also personified as *devas*.

dharma • That which sustains everything; refers to harmony in the universe that sustains greater good. By definition, *dharma* protects one who protects it. The word '*dharma*' has many different meanings; depending on the context, it can mean one or more of the following – virtue, moral principle, righteousness, religion, law, duty, path, state, *etc.*

guṇa • In general, refers to the inherent tendencies or traits of a human being. In the context of *guṇa-traya* ('three traits') it represents three types of *guṇa* – *Sattva* (benign goodness), *Rajas* (restless activity), and *Tamas* (deluded lethargy). Often these *guṇa-traya* are simply referred to as *guṇa*.

guru • Remover of darkness and ignorance, spiritual guide, or teacher.

karma • Action; includes all spheres of work. *Karma* is also the work that is suited to *guṇa*. In general, *karma* refers to all the activities associated with origin, sustenance, and destruction, including the creative impulse that brought all creation into existence and keeps it going. *Karma* also refers to the consequences of our actions (SEE *vāsana*).

karma-yoga • Path of selfless action.

mantra • Sacred utterances or verses that are recited in rituals and prayers or silently repeated during meditation. *Mantra* also refers to the formative thought behind the recited verses.

māyā • The divine power of illusion.

naraka • A transient place where people are punished for their immoral deeds; they stay there until they receive the full course of punishments. Can be loosely translated as 'hell.' Opposite of *svarga*.

om • The most sacred sound in Hinduism; this single-syllable word represents the Supreme and the universe. '*Om*' has four parts: '*a*,' '*u*,' '*m*,' and silence. The '*a*' represents birth, '*u*' represents growth, '*m*' represents letting go, and the silence represents immortality.

pāpa • Evil, sin, guilt, crime, misfortune, *etc*. Opposite of *puṇya*.

prakṛti • Material nature or surrounding environment; the source of the five elements and the body, including the five senses, mind, ego, intellect, *guṇa*, and *prāṇa*.

prāṇa • The 'vital force' or 'life energy' of an organism. It is also known as the 'vital breath,' for without breathing, there is no life. The *prāṇa* is distributed all over the body as it energizes all the cells.

puṇya • Righteous, just, auspicious, *etc*. in general. Typically refers to 'religious merit' or 'virtuous action.' Opposite of *pāpa*.

puruṣa • It is the Supreme Spirit; same as *Brahman*. It is the basis of one's feeling of being alive and the associated experiences of pleasures and pains.

rajas • The trait of restless activity. SEE *guṇa*.

sāṅkhya • It the path of reasoning (or knowledge). It is also one of the six classical schools of Indian philosophy.

saṃnyāsa • Giving up actions driven by selfish desire. A *saṃnyāsin* is one who follows the path of *saṃnyāsa* – *i.e.* renouncing the rewards of an action and not the action itself. The idea of a *saṃnyāsin* in the *Bhagavad-gītā* is different from the typical image of an old man who has given up everything and has fully retired from active life.

sattva • The trait of benign goodness. SEE *guṇa*.

svarga • A transient place where people are rewarded for their good deeds; they stay till they receive the full course of rewards. Can be loosely translated as 'heaven.' Opposite of *naraka*.

tamas • The trait of deluded lethargy. SEE *guṇa*.

tapas • Austerity, penance, and single-minded focus on work.

varṇa • Basic traits of individuals—determined by their *guṇa* and *karma*—that influence the roles they play in a society. The four categories according to the principle of *varṇa* are *brāhmaṇas* (scholars/teachers), *kṣatriyas* (warriors/administrators), *vaiśyas* (traders/artisans), and *śūdras* (workers/laborers).

vāsana • Residual impact of actions. In other words, the consequences of one's *karma*. The soul carries experiences from previous births, which to some extent influence the present life – for better or for worse, depending on the experiences.

yajña • Vedic fire ritual that involves worship of the divine, interaction, and sharing. Fire is raised in closed altars made of bricks, with the top portion open to air. Agni (sacred fire) exists in three forms: *gārhapatya*, *dakṣiṇa*, and *āhavanīya*, and fires are raised in three altars, one for each *agni*. Agni is both a deity as well as the medium to deliver the offerings made to other deities. Deities to be worshipped are invoked during the *yajña*. Clarified butter (fuel for the fire), medicinal herbs, twigs of the pīpal tree (*Ficus religiosa*), and other offerings (milk, grains that are fried and then cooked, juice of the *soma* plant, animals, *etc.*) are put in the fire, accompanied by reciting specific *mantras* from the *Vedas*. Typically, sixteen *ṛtviks* (loosely, 'priests' or 'officiators') preside over rituals in a *yajña*. Metaphorically, *yajña* refers to 'an act of self-dedication' or 'service above self.'

yoga • Form of physical and mental discipline. In a broader sense, *yoga* can mean 'union with the Supreme,' 'contemplation,' 'oneness of body and mind,' 'path,' or 'the path of action.' It is also one of the six classical schools of Indian philosophy. A *yogin* is one who practices *yoga*.

yuga • Age or epoch. The four *yugas* are – Satya-*yuga*, Tretā-*yuga*, Dvāpara-*yuga*, and Kali *yuga*. Together these four *yugas* make a *mahā-yuga* (Great Age) that spans 4,320,000 human years.

Foundational Works of Hinduism

ॐ

Śruti

Four *Vedas* [Foremost revealed scriptures of Hinduism]

Ṛg-veda	***Yajur-veda***	***Sāma-veda***	***Atharva-veda***
	Kṛṣṇa- *Śukla-*		

The four sections of each *Veda*

Saṃhitā	***Brāhmaṇa***	***Āraṇyaka***	***Upaniṣad**** (*Vedānta*)

Smṛti

Six *Vedāṅgas* [Auxiliary disciplines to understand the *Vedas* thoroughly]

Śikṣā	***Vyākaraṇa***	***Chandas***	***Nirukta***	***Jyautiṣa***	***Kalpa***
					Dharma-sūtra *Gṛhya-sūtra* *Śrauta-sūtra* *Śulba-sūtra*

Four *Upavedas* [Secular treatises that are studied along with the *Vedas*]

Āyur-veda	***Artha-veda***#	***Gāndharva-veda***	***Sthāpatya-veda***

Itihāsa [Epic literature based on history]

Rāmāyaṇa	***Mahā-bhārata***

Purāṇa [Old episodes and stories]

18 *Mahā-purāṇas*	**18 *Upa-purāṇas***

Smṛtis, *Āgamas*, and other works

Bhagavad-gītā*

A beautiful harmony of various concepts

Texts of the three *Nāstika-darśanas*

Six *Āstika-darśanas* [Classical schools of Indian philosophy]

Sāṅkhya	***Yoga***	***Nyāya***	***Vāiśeṣika***	***Mīmāṃsā***	***Vedānta***
					Brahma-sūtra* of Bādarāyaṇa

Some sources give this as ***Dhanur-veda***

* *Prasthāna-trayī*

Glossary

Important Characters in the Mahā-bhārata

Abhimanyu • Son of Arjuna and Subhadrā (Kṛṣṇa's sister). He was just sixteen when he was killed in the *Mahā-bhārata* war. He was married to Uttarā (Virāṭa's daughter) and fathered Parīkṣit, who inherited the throne after the Pāṇḍavas retired.

Arjuna • SEE *p.* 28.

Aśvatthāmā • Son of Droṇa and Kṛpī (Kṛpa's sister). He was among the few survivors from the Kaurava army. He killed the sons of the Pāṇḍavas while they were sleeping and also tried to kill Uttarā who was then pregnant with Parīkṣit.

Bharata • Famous ancestor of the Pāṇḍavas and Kauravas. The name of the epic (*Mahā-bhārata*) is derived from King Bharata.

Bhīma • Second of the five Pāṇḍava brothers. His immense strength (equal to a thousand elephants) and fierce nature especially scared Duryodhana.

Bhīṣma • SEE *p.* 26.

Dhṛṣṭadyumna • Son of Drupada and a student of Droṇa. He was the commander-in-chief of the Pāṇḍava army on the first day of war.

Dhṛtarāṣṭra • Blind son of Vyāsa, born of Ambikā after the death of her husband, Vicitravīrya. Since Dhṛtarāṣṭra was blind, his younger brother Pāṇḍu ascended the throne. However, after Pāṇḍu's untimely death he became the caretaker king. He was the father of the Kauravas.

Draupadī • Daughter of Drupada and wife of the five Pāṇḍavas.

Droṇa • SEE *p.* 26.

Drupada • King of Pāñcāla and a staunch ally of the Pāṇḍavas; he was respected as the seniormost king in their side. He was also a sworn enemy of Droṇa.

Duryodhana • SEE *p.* 27.

Gāndhārī • Daughter of the king of Gāndhāra, wife of Dhṛtarāṣṭra, and mother of the Kauravas.

Janamejaya • Son of Parīkṣit (Abhimanyu's son and Arjuna's grandson). Vaiśampāyana (Vyāsa's disciple) recited the *Mahā-bhārata* to him.

Jayadratha • King of Sindhu and husband of Duśśalā (only daughter of Dhṛtarāṣṭra). He fought on the side of the Kauravas in the war and was killed by Arjuna.

Karṇa • Son of the unmarried Kuntī from her union with Sūrya (the Sun deity). He became the chief support and best friend of Duryodhana, who made him the king of Aṅga. He was killed by Arjuna in the war.

Kṛpa • Son of Sage Śaradvān, raised by King Śantanu. Along with Droṇa he taught martial arts to the Kauravas and Pāṇḍavas. Kṛpa survived the war and was later appointed as the preceptor of King Parīkṣit.

Kṛṣṇa • SEE *pp*. 28–29.

Kuntī • Daughter of Śūrasena (grandfather of Kṛṣṇa) and the first wife of Pāṇḍu. When she was still a baby, her father gave her away to his close friend King Kuntibhoja, who had no children. She was named Pṛthā at birth but was called 'Kuntī' as she was raised by Kuntibhoja. Yudhiṣṭhira, Bhīma, and Arjuna are her sons from Pāṇḍu. She had a son, Karṇa, before her marriage.

Kuru • Famous ancestor of the Pāṇḍavas and Kauravas and founder of the Kuru dynasty. He performed many noble deeds in the vast plains of his kingdom, which came to be known as Kurukṣetra. It was revered as a sacred land by his descendants.

Nakula • Fourth of the five Pāṇḍava brothers. Son of Pāṇḍu and his second wife Mādrī.

Pāṇḍu • Son of Vyāsa, born of Ambālikā, Vicitravīrya's widow. Pāṇḍu ascended the throne because his elder brother was blind but soon retired to the forest because of a curse and subsequently died. He had two wives: Kuntī and Mādrī. His sons are the Pāṇḍavas.

Parīkṣit • Son of Abhimanyu and Uttarā. He was born after his father's death in the war. The Pāṇḍavas installed him as king when they retired to the forest after ruling for thirty-six years.

Sahadeva • Last of the five Pāṇḍava brothers. Son of Pāṇḍu and his second wife Mādrī.

Sañjaya • SEE *p*. 27.

Satyavatī • Mother of Vyāsa (from Sage Parāśara); later became wife of Śantanu and gave birth to Vicitravīrya and Citrāṅgada.

Śakuni • Brother of Gāndhārī and advisor to Duryodhana. For the sake of Duryodhana and his brothers, he orchestrated many devious schemes to destroy the Pāṇḍavas.

Śantanu • Famous king of the Kuru dynasty. He was the father of Bhīṣma from his first marriage to Gaṅgā. Later he married Satyavatī.

Glossary

Family Tree

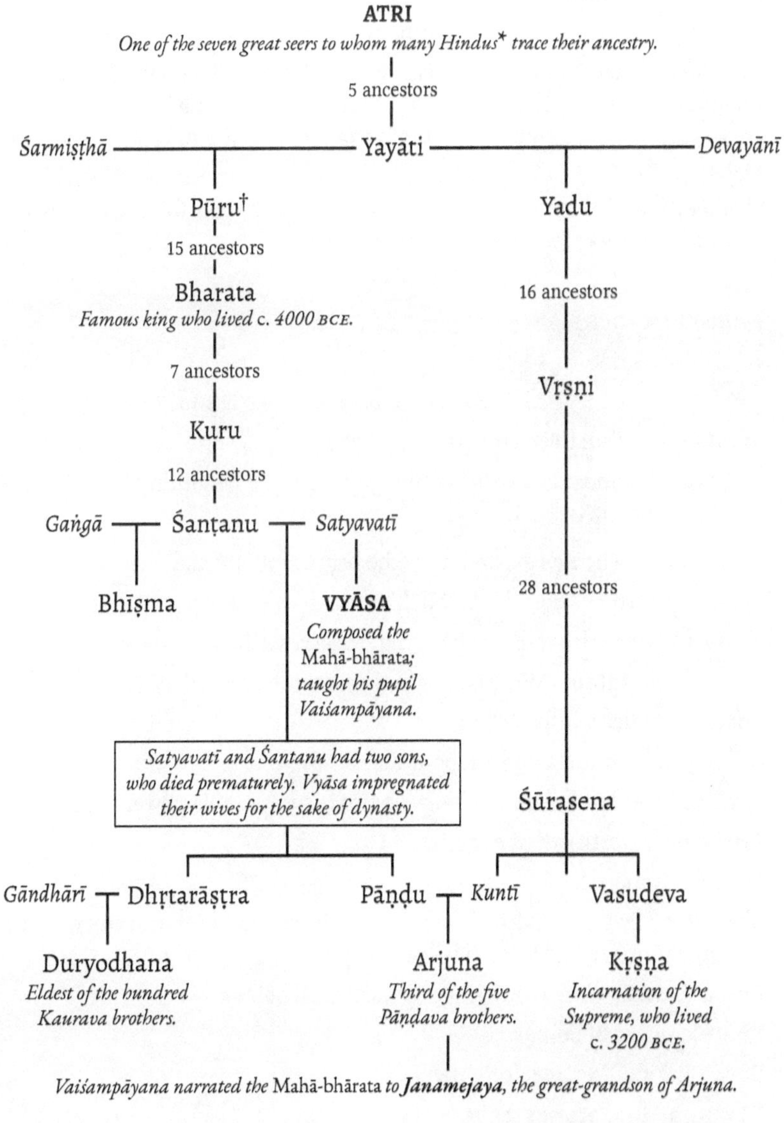

Legend

SAGES Men *Women* *Notes* Ancestors

* *For example, of the translators of this work, Koti traces his ancestry back to Āṅgīrasa while Hari traces his ancestry back to Atri.*

† *Not to be confused with Purūravas, the great-grandfather of Yayāti.*

Śikhaṇḍī • Son of Drupada who was a woman in his previous life (Ambā) and a sworn enemy of Bhīṣma.

Vasudeva • Kṛṣṇa's father and brother of Kuntī.

Vaiśampāyana • Student of Vyāsa, from whom he learned the original version of the *Mahā-bhārata*. He later narrated it to King Janamejaya, the great-grandson of Arjuna. Vaiśampāyana was also the first teacher of the *Kṛṣṇa-yajur-veda*.

Virāṭa • King of Matsya, where the Pāṇḍavas spent their final year in exile. He fought the war on the side of the Pāṇḍavas.

Vyāsa • SEE *p.* 25.

Yudhiṣṭhira • SEE *p.* 28.

A Few Epithets of Kṛṣṇa in the Gītā

Acyuta • Immaculate, changeless, unshaken

Ādideva • Foremost god, primal god, god from the beginning

Ādikarta • Original creator

Ādyam • One who has existed from the beginning, primal one

Ajam • Unborn, without birth, birthless

Akṣaram • Imperishable, unchanging, indestructible

Anādimadhyantam • Without beginning, middle, or end

Ananta • Endless, infinite

Aprameyam • Immeasurable, boundless

Apratimaprabhāva • Unmatched valor, of incomparable power

Arisūdana • Destroyer of enemies

Avināśī • Imperishable

Bhagavān • God, blessed lord, endowed with six attributes (infinite wealth, splendor, strength, knowledge, glory, and renunciation).

Bhūtabhāvana • One who brings welfare to all beings

Bhūteśa • Lord of beings

Deva • The shining one, lord, deity

Devavara • Best of gods, chosen of gods

Devadeva • Lord of lords

Deveśa • King of lords

Map of Ancient India

Gāndhāra
Madra
Kurukṣetra
Hastināpura
Indraprastha
Kuru
Himālayas
Sindhū
Sarasvatī
Matsya
Pāñcāla
Mathurā
Yamunā
Sindhū
Gaṅgā
Mithila
Aṅga
Prayāgā
Kāśī
Dvārakā
I N D I A
N
Sri
Lanka
Legend
Kingdoms Cities Rivers

Dharmagopta • Defender of *dharma*
Divyam • Divine, heavenly
Gururgarīyān • Most venerable teacher
Govinda • Friend of cows, chief herdsman, delighter of the senses
Hari • Lord Viṣṇu, stealer of hearts
Hṛṣīkeśa • Lord of the senses, one with bristling hair
Īśamīḍyam • Adorable one
Jagannivāsa • Cosmic guardian, abode of the universe
Jagatpati • Lord of the universe
Janārdana • Protector of men
Kamalapatrākṣa • Lotus-eyed
Keśava • Lord of creation, preservation, and dissolution
Keśinisūdana • Killer of demon Keśin
Kṛṣṇa • Dark, one who attracts
Mādhava • Personification of sweetness, god of fortune
Madhusūdana • Killer of demon Madhu, destroyer of ignorance
Mahābāhu • Mighty-armed
Mahātman • Great soul
Parabrahma • Supreme *Brahman*
Paramam • Supreme
Parameśvara • Supreme lord
Parandhāma • Supreme abode
Pavitram • Purifier
Prabhu • Lord, master
Puruṣa • Spirit, all-encompassing person, supreme lord
Puruṣottama • Supreme spirit, highest among men
Sahasrabāhu • Thousand-armed
Śāśvatam • Permanent, eternal
Vārṣṇeya • A descendent of the Vṛṣṇi clan
Vāsudeva • Lord of the world, soul of the universe, son of Vasudeva
Vibhu • All pervading, omnipresent

Viśṇu • All-pervading

Viśvamūrti • Embodiment of the universe who has all forms

Viśvarūpa • Embodiment of the universe

Viśveśvara • Lord of the universe

Yādava • A descendent of the Yādava clan

Yogeśvara • Master of *yoga*

A Few Epithets of Arjuna in the Gītā

Anagha • Sinless, free from *pāpa*

Arjuna • Free, plain, having no binding

Bhārata • A descendent of King Bharata

Bharataśreṣṭha • Best of the Bhāratas

Bharatarṣabha • Bull (chief) among the Bhāratas

Bharatasattama • Best of the Bhāratas

Dehabhṛtāṃvara • Supreme among humans

Dhanañjaya • Conqueror of wealth, vanquisher of Kubera

Guḍākeśa • Conqueror of sleep, one with thick hair

Kaunteya • Son of Kuntī

Kirīṭin • Adorned with a crown

Kurunandana • The joy of the Kurus, choice son of the Kurus

Kurupravīra • Great hero of the Kurus

Kurusattama • Best of the Kurus

Kuruśreṣṭha • Best of the Kurus

Mahābāhu • Mighty-armed

Pāṇḍava • Son of Pāṇḍu

Parantapa • Scorcher of enemies

Pārtha • Son of Pṛthā (Kuntī)

Puruṣarṣabha • Bull (chief) among men

Puruṣavyāghra • Tiger among men

Savyasācin • Ambidextrous archer

Tāta • Son, father; Kṛṣṇa addresses Arjuna as 'my son' out of affection.

APPENDIX 4

INFLUENCE OF THE GĪTĀ

THE INFLUENCE OF the *Bhagavad-gītā* has not been limited to a single period in history or a single place in the world; it has not been bound to a single school of philosophy or a single sect of people. It transcends all boundaries and distinctions.

"If all the *Upaniṣads* are cows, Kṛṣṇa, the cowherd boy, milks them. Arjuna is the calf, and the pure ones are the partakers of the milk, which is the Supreme *Gītā*."
VAIṢṆAVĪYA-TANTRA-SĀRA (TRADITIONAL)

"Though engaged in the performance of worldly duties, one who is regular in the study of the *Gītā* becomes free. He is the happy man in this world. He is not bound by *karma*."
VARĀHA-PURĀṆA (TRADITIONAL)

"From a clear knowledge of the *Bhagavad-gītā* all the goals of human existence become fulfilled. *Bhagavad-gītā* is the manifest quintessence of all the teachings of the *Vedic* scriptures."
ŚANKARĀCĀRYA (*c.* 7th century CE)
Indian saint, philosopher, and perpetuator of *Advaita* philosophy

"The *Bhagavad-gītā* was spoken by Lord Kṛṣṇa to reveal the science of devotion to God which is the essence of all spiritual knowledge."
RĀMĀNUJĀCĀRYA (1017–1137)
Indian philosopher, social reformer, and perpetuator of *Viśiṣṭādvaita* philosophy

"The *Maha-bhārata* has all the essential ingredients necessary to evolve and protect humanity and that within it. The *Bhagavad-gītā* is the epitome of the *Mahā-bhārata* just as ghee is the essence of milk and pollen is the essence of flowers."
MADHVĀCĀRYA (1238–1317)
Indian philosopher, theologian, and perpetuator of *Dvaita* philosophy

"[In the story of the *Maha-bhārata*]...there is a discourse, which was given by Lord Kṛṣṇa to Arjuna, of Vyāsa's intelligence, after churning the sea of

the *Vedas*. Men of dispassion seek it, the saints constantly enjoy it, and the adepts rejoice in it... It is heard eagerly by the devotees and is highly esteemed in the three worlds... It is called the *Bhagavad-gītā*..."
SANT JÑĀNEŚVAR (1275–96)
Indian saint, poet, philosopher, and *yogi* of the Nātha tradition

"I advise everyone to follow the instructions of the *Bhagavad-gītā* as spoken by Lord Kṛṣṇa."
CAITANYA MAHĀPRABHU (1486–1533)
Indian ascetic, social reformer, and chief proponent of *Gauḍīya Vaiṣṇavism*

"The *Bhagavad-gītā* teaches us that one attains union with God through knowledge, love and action. These three must develop together... this is integral *yoga*."
SAMARTHA RĀMADĀS (1608–1682)
Indian saint, poet, and spiritual teacher

"I hesitate not to pronounce the Geeta a performance of great originality, of a sublimity of conception, reasoning, and diction almost unequalled; and a single exception, amongst all the known religions of mankind."
WARREN HASTINGS (1754–1826)
British official and first Governor-General of British India

"This episode of the Mahabharata was the most beautiful; perhaps the only true philosophical song existing in any known tongue... the deepest and loftiest thing the world has to show."
WILHELM VON HUMBOLDT (1767–1835)
Prussian minister of education, philosopher, and linguist

"In the Bhagavad Gita Krishna thus raises the mind of his young pupil Arjuna when, seized with compunction at the sight of the arrayed hosts... Krishna leads him to this point of view [the world is the empty delusion of Maya], and the death of thousands can no longer retrain him; he gives the sign for battle."
ARTHUR SCHOPENHAUER (1788–1860)
German philosopher and author

"I read more of the Bhagavat Geeta and felt how surpassingly fine were the sentiments; these, or selections from this book should be included in a Bible for Mankind."
AMOS BRONSON ALCOTT (1799–1888)
US-American author, teacher, and philosopher

"I owed a magnificent day to the Bhagavat Geeta. It was the first of books; it was as if an empire spoke to us, nothing small or unworthy, but large, serene, consistent, the voice of an old intelligence which in another age and climate had pondered and thus disposed of the same questions which exercise us."
RALPH WALDO EMERSON (1803–82)
US-American transcendentalist philosopher and poet

"It is a wonderful book and has greatly excited my curiosity to know more of the religious literature of the East."
JOHN GREENLEAF WHITTIER (1807–92)
US-American Quaker poet and social activist

"In the morning I bathe my intellect in the stupendous and cosmogonal philosophy of the Bhagvat-Geeta, since whose composition years of the gods have elapsed, and in comparison with which our modern world and its literature seem puny and trivial..."
HENRY DAVID THOREAU (1817–62)
US-American transcendentalist philosopher and author

"...probably the most beautiful book which has ever come from the hand of man."
ÉMILE-LOUIS BURNOUF (1821–1907)
French orientalist, author, and racialist

"In plain but noble language it unfolds a philosophical system... blending as it does the doctrine of Kapila, Patanjali, and the *Vedas*."
EDWIN ARNOLD (1832–1904)
English poet, journalist, and translator

"What is the significance of the *Gita*? It is what you get by repeating the word ten times. It is reversed into '*tagi*' – a person who has renounced everything for god."
RAMAKRISHNA PARAMAHAMSA (1836–86)
Indian ascetic and spiritual teacher

"Among the priceless teachings that may be found in the great Hindu poem of the Mahabharata, there is none so rare and priceless as this, 'The Lord's Song'."
ANNIE BESANT (1847–1933)
Irish theosophist and author

"*Bhagavad-gītā* is one of the most brilliant and pure gems of our ancient sacred books. It would be difficult to find a simpler work in Sanskrit literature or even in all the literature of the world than the *Gītā*, which explains to us in an unambiguous and succinct manner the deep, and sacred principles of the sacred science of the self (*ātman*), after imparting to us the knowledge of the human body and the cosmos, and on the authority of those principles acquaints every human being with the most perfect and complete condition of the self..."
BAL GANGADHAR TILAK (1856–1920)
Indian nationalist, social reformer, and freedom-fighter

"I believe that in all the living languages of the world, there is no book so full of true knowledge and yet so handy. To my knowledge, there is no book in the whole range of the world's literature as high above as the *Bhagavad-gītā*, which is the treasure-house of *dharma* not only for the Hindus but for all mankind."
MADAN MOHAN MALAVIYA (1861–1946)
Indian freedom-fighter, social reformer, and founder of *Benaras Hindu University*

"In order to approach a creation as sublime as the Bhagavad-Gita with full understanding, it is necessary to attune our soul to it."
RUDOLF STEINER (1861–1925)
Austrian philosopher, artist, literary scholar, and founder of Anthroposophy

"The Bhagavad Gita represents one of the highest flights of the conditioned spirit to its unconditioned Source ever achieved."
ELIZABETH LOUISA MORESBY A.K.A LILY ADAMS BECK (1862–1931)
British novelist and fantasy writer

"...a magnificent flower of Hindu mysticism."
COUNT MAURICE MAETERLINCK (1862–1949)
Belgian essayist, poet, and playwright

"A great landmark in the history of religion is here... religions of fear and of temptations were gone forever, and in spite of the fear of hell and temptation of enjoyment in heaven, came the grandest of ideals, love for love's sake, duty for duty's sake, work for work's sake... The human race will never again see such a brain as his who wrote the *Gītā*."
SWAMI VIVEKANANDA (1863–1902)
Indian spiritual leader, social reformer, and founder of the *Ramakrishna Mission*

"The Bhagavad-Gita and the Upanishads contain such godlike fullness of wisdom on all things that I feel the authors must have looked with calm remembrance back through a thousand passionate lives, full of feverish strife for and with shadows, ere they could have written with such certainty of things which the soul feels to be sure."
Æ GEORGE RUSSELL (1867–1935)
Anglo-Irish poet, painter, and author

"The Bhagavad Gita is one of the noblest scriptures of India, one of the deepest scriptures of the world... with many meanings, containing many truths..."
CHARLES JOHNSTON (1867–1935)
English civil servant and scholar

"...one of the greatest of the religious phenomena of the world... the earliest and still the greatest monument of Hindu religion."
EDWARD JOSEPH THOMAS (1869–1958)
British author, librarian and Pali scholar

"I find a solace in the Bhagavad-Gita that I miss even in the Sermon on the Mount. When doubts haunt me, when disappointments stare me in the face, and I see not one ray of hope on the horizon, I turn to Bhagavad-Gita and find a verse to comfort me; and I immediately begin to smile in the midst of overwhelming tragedies."
M K GANDHI (1869–1948)
Indian politician, freedom-fighter, and leader of the civil disobedience movement

"...the work in which Arjuna engages himself as a result of the *Gītā* teaching is stupendous in its magnitude, being no less than setting right the world which is running off the rails."
M HIRIYANNA (1871–1950)
Indian philosopher, Sanskrit professor, and author

"...a true scripture of the human race, a living creation rather than a book, with a new message for every age and a new meaning for every civilization."
SRI AUROBINDO (1872–1950)
Indian nationalist, author, philosopher, and spiritual teacher

"The charm of the Bhagavad-Gītā is due to this idea of spiritualised activity which springs only from the highest motives... The Bhagavad-Gītā

has a sphinx-like character. It contains such marvellous phrases about inner detachment from the world, about the attitude of mind which knows no hatred and is kind, and about loving self-devotion to God, that we are wont to overlook its non-ethical contents. It is not merely the most read but also the most idealised book in world-literature."
ALBERT SCHWEITZER (1875–1965)
German-French physician, philosopher, and musician

"The idea that man is like unto an inverted tree seems to have been current in bygone ages. The link with Vedic conceptions is provided by Plato in his *Timaeus* in which it states: 'Behold we are not an earthly but a heavenly plant.' This correlation can be discerned by what Krishna expresses in chapter 15 of Bhagavad-Gita."
CARL GUSTAV JUNG (1875–1961)
Swiss psychiatrist and founder of Analytical Psychology

"Uncounted millions have drawn from it comfort and joy. In it they have found an end to perplexity, a clear, if difficult, road to salvation."
ARTHUR WILLIAM RYDER (1877–1938)
US-American professor, translator, and author

"The marvel of the Bhagavad-Gita is its truly beautiful revelation of life's wisdom which enables philosophy to blossom into religion."
HERMAN HESSE (1877–1962)
German-Swiss poet, painter, and author

"...probably the most important single work ever produced in India; this book of eighteen chapters is not, as it has been sometimes called, a 'sectarian' work, but one universally studied and often repeated daily from memory by millions of Indians of all persuasions."
ANAND KENTISH COOMARASWAMY (1877–1947)
Indian historian, art philosopher, and metaphysician

"The *Gītā* is one of the most authoritative sources of Hindu doctrine and ethics, and is accepted as such by Hindus of all denominations. A study of even selections from it, strengthened by earnest meditation, will enable young men and women to understand the religion of our fathers, which is the background of all the noble philosophy, art, literature and civilization that we have inherited."
CHAKRAVARTHI RAJAGOPALACHARI (1878–1972)
Indian lawyer, statesman, author, and last Governor-General of India

"...Bhagavad-Gita, perhaps the most beautiful work of literature of the world."
COUNT HERMANN KEYSERLING (1880–1946)
German aristrocrat, philosopher, author, and philanthropist

"...a work of imperishable significance... gives us profound insights that are valid for all times and for all religious life."
JAKOB WILHELM HAUER (1881–1961)
German indologist, teacher, and author

"Some people think of the *Bhagavad-gītā* as a scripture for *dharma* alone, *i.e.* its aim is to exhort men to do their work. This is not the right summary. It is primarily a scripture for liberation. The main idea of the *Gītā* is to teach man the ways to work himself out of all his miseries."
SUBRAMANYA 'BHARATI' (1882–1921)
Indian poet, social reformer, and freedom fighter

"Our ancestors have referred to the *Gītā* as a *mokṣa-śāstra*. Indeed it is a path to liberation but it is also a treatise on living well... Essential lessons on improving one's life gradually can be found in the *Bhagavad-gītā*. A healthy respect for one's life, enthusiasm to perform one's *sva-dharma*, courage in the face of adversity, and faith that brings solace during moments of doubt – are some of the treasures that we can take from the *Gītā*."
D V GUNDAPPA (1887–1975)
Indian author, journalist, poet, polymath, and founder of *Gokhale Institute of Public Affairs*

"Is the *Gītā* an interpolation? The question has no meaning in the light of the explanation I have given you of the structure and the meaning of the *Mahābhārata*. The *Gītā* is in fact the heart's heart of the *Mahābhārata*, and the *Mahābhārata* is a sort of a necessary commentary on the *Gītā*."
V S SUKTHANKAR (1887–1943)
Indian polymath, Sanskrit scholar, and the editor of the Critical Edition of the *Mahābhārata*

"The *Gītā* is a gospel for the whole world. It is meant for the generality of mankind."
SWAMI SIVANANDA SARASWATI (1887–1963)
Indian physician, spiritual teacher, and founder of *The Divine Life Society*

"...the noblest of scriptures and the grandest of sagas..."
KANHAIYALAL MANEKLAL MUNSHI (1887–1971)
Indian freedom fighter, lawyer, politician, and founder of *Bharatiya Vidya Bhavan*

"...*Gītā* appeals to us not only by its force of thought and majesty of vision, but also by its fervor of devotion and sweetness of spiritual emotion."
SARVEPALLI RADHAKRISHNAN (1888–1975)
Indian philosopher, teacher, statesman, and former President

"...very thankful for having had the opportunity to study the Bhagavad Gita and the religious and philosophical beliefs, so different from my own."
THOMAS STEARNS ELIOT (1888–1965)
American-British poet and dramatist

"The Bhagavad-Gita deals essentially with the spiritual foundation of human existence. It is a call of action to meet the obligations and duties of life; yet keeping in view the spiritual nature and grander purpose of the universe."
JAWAHARLAL NEHRU (1889–1964)
Indian politician and first Prime Minister of independent India

"...no other didactic poem is in a position, like the Gita, to combine – absolutely free from the hard limitations of a narrow-minded dogmatism – such a variety of views and to offer to the readers of the most different schools and directions poetical pleasure, ethical teaching and religious edification."
HELMUTH VON GLASENAPP (1891–1963)
German Indologist, religious scholar, and author

"...words of spiritual guidance that are timeless in their applicability..."
PARAMAHANSA YOGANANDA (1893–1952)
Indian *yogi*, spiritual teacher, and author

"...the most systematic statement of spiritual evolution. It is one of the most clear and comprehensive summaries of perennial philosophy ever revealed; hence its enduring value is subject not only to India but to all of humanity."
ALDOUS HUXLEY (1894–1963)
English essayist, author, and philosopher

"...everything stated in the *Gītā* is meant to be tested in the life of every man; it is intended to be verified in practice."
VINOBA BHAVE (1895–1982)
Indian spiritual teacher and social reformer

"For almost everyone the Bhagavad-Gita is the book *par excellence*."
LOUIS RENOU (1896–1966)
French Indologist, professor, and author

"The greatness of the *Bhagavad Gītā* is the greatness of the universe, but even as the wonder of the stars in heaven only reveals itself in the silence of the night, the wonder of this poem only reveals itself in the silence of the soul."
JUAN MASCARÓ (1897–1987)
Spanish author, translator, and professor

"...the mental quintessence and successful synthesis of the various systems of religion and philosophy, it offers a unique epitome of the high culture of prehistoric India."
PAUL BRUNTON (1898–1981)
British philosopher, mystic, traveler, and author

"It is impossible to do justice to the profound insights and philosophical majesty of the Bhagavad Gita as a whole. The Gita shows the way to live a complete and satisfying life."
HORACE ALEXANDER (1899–1989)
English Quaker, diplomat, author, and ornithologist

"We knew the world would not be the same. A few people laughed, a few people cried, most people were silent. I remembered the line from the Hindu scripture, the Bhagavad-Gita. Vishnu is trying to persuade the Prince that he should do his duty and to impress him takes on his multi-armed form and says, 'Now I am become Death, the destroyer of worlds.' I suppose we all thought that, one way or another."
J. ROBERT OPPENHEIMER (1904–67)
US-American theoretical physicist and scientific director of the *Manhattan Project*

"Which other religion has its God say, as Krishna does in the Bhagavad Gita, 'All paths lead to me'?"
ROBERT CHARLES ZAEHNER (1913–74)
British religious historian and intelligence officer

"The hero of the Bhagavad-Gītā [Krishna] is doubly heroic: he is a warrior and a saint, a man of action and a quietest philosopher."
OCTAVIO PAZ (1914–98)
Mexican author, poet, and diplomat

"The Gita can be seen as the main literary support for the great religious civilization of India, the oldest surviving culture in the world. It brings to the West a salutary reminder that our highly activistic and one-sided culture is faced with a crisis that may end in self-destruction because it lacks the inner depth of an authentic metaphysical consciousness."
THOMAS MERTON (1915–68)
US-American Trappist monk, poet, author, and social critic

"When such a perfect combination of both science and philosophy is sung to perfection that Krishna was, we have in this piece of work an appeal both to the head and heart."
SWAMI CHINMAYANANDA (1916–93)
Indian journalist, social reformer, and spiritual teacher

"...a complete guide to practical life. It provides all that is needed to raise the consciousness of man to the highest possible level."
MAHARISHI MAHESH YOGI (1917–2008)
Indian spiritual teacher and founder of Transcendental Meditation

"The Bhagavad Gita is both supremely realistic and extremely idealistic, certainly the most acute, penetrating depiction of human nature and true morality, however remote it may seem from our own."
AMAURY DE RIENCOURT (1918–2005)
French historian and author

"It answers all moral concerns and needs of the world, be it man's quest for inner peace, his need for belonging to the rest of the human and natural community, his concern for the environment, or his attitude towards work and... death."
ATAL BIHARI VAJPAYEE (1924–2018)
Indian freedom-fighter, poet, and former Prime Minister of India

"I was fortified by the Bhagavad Gita which taught that if one were morally right, one need not hesitate to fight injustice."
BÜLENT ECEVIT (1925–2006)
Turkish politician, journalist, poet, and former Prime Minister of Turkey

"The *Gītā* is the greatest harmonizer of yogas... once the *Gītā* is made the guiding star of your life, the way you act will be *karma yoga*, the way you feel will be *bhakti yoga*, the way you reason will be *jñāna yoga*. What you do

will be in line with *dharma*; what you feel will foster *prema*; what you think will reveal *satya*."
SATYA SAI BABA (1926–2011)
Indian spiritual leader and social reformer

"...the Gita's popularity and authority have been unrivalled."
JOHANNES VAN BUITENEN (1928–79)
American indologist, professor, and author

"...the quest for Truth is the quest for God. This is the core teaching of all religions. The scientist's motivation is to seek the very kind of truth that Krishna speaks about in the Bhagavad Gita."
HARVEY COX (B. 1929)
US-American theologian, author, and professor of divinity

"The first psychological scripture... long before Freud, Adler and Jung."
OSHO RAJNEESH (1931–90)
Indian mystic, philosopher, and spiritual teacher

"The Bhagavad Gita is *par excellence* the book of democracy; that is what gives it its peculiar radiance. It unites all men in the same principle which "resides in all hearts". If Krishna makes no distinction between races, castes, sects, he also shows us how men, nations, can sink in the typhoon of unchained passions. The message of the Gita is a universal call to democracy, liberty for the peoples, liberty for each individual. The great affirmation of the Bhagavad Gita is that every individual, whatever he may be, rich or poor, can and must raise himself on life's path and that he has a right to his emancipation, social, intellectual, and spiritual."
LOUIS REVEL (20TH CENTURY)
French Indologist and author

"In the middle of our fast-paced life, the *Gita* will provide an oasis. It is a practical guide for several dimensions of life... It encourages debate and keeps our minds open. Anybody who is inspired by the *Gita* will always be compassionate by nature and democratic in temperament."
NARENDRA MODI (B. 1950)
Indian politician and Prime Minister of India

APPENDIX 5

REFERENCES

BOOKS, ARTICLES, AND WEB-PAGES

Alexander, Horace. Consider India: An Essay in Values. Asia Publishing House, 1961

Anantharangacharya, N. S. *Srimadgītā Bhāṣya*. Bangalore: Ramanuja Seva Trust, 1993

Anantharangacharya, N. S. *Gītāmṛta*. Bangalore: Deshika Sukti Prakashana, 1978

Antonov, Vladimir. Bhagavad Gita: With Commentaries. Trans. Nikolenko, Mikhail. Ontario: New Atlanteans, 2008

Armstrong, Jeffrey (aka Kavindra Roshi). The Bhagavad Gita Comes Alive: A Radical Translation. Vancouver: Vedic Academy of Sciences and Arts (VASA) Publishers, 2020

Arnold, Edwin. The Song Celestial or Bhagavad-Gita. New York: Truslove, Hanson & Comba, 1900. 16 Oct. 2008 <*http://www.yogamovement.com/texts/gita.html*>

Aurobindo, Sri. Essays on the Gita. Pondicherry: Sri Aurobindo Ashram, 1997

Barnett, Lionel D. Bhagavad-gītā or The Lord's Song. London: J. M. Dent & Sons, 1905

Besant, Annie. The Bhagavad Gītā: The Lord's Song. London: Theosophical Publishing House, 1895

Beck, L. Adams. The Story of Oriental Philosophy. New York: Farrar & Rinehard, 1928

Berry, Thomas. Religions of India. New York: Columbia University Press, 1996

Bharathi, Subramanya. *Bhagavad Gītai*. 12 Feb. 2011 <*http://www.scribd.com/doc/8051489/Bhagavad-Gita-Tamil-By-Bharathiar*>

Bhattacharya, Pradip. The Mahabharata in Arabic and Persian. 24 Feb. 2011 <*http://www.boloji.com/history/048.htm*>

Bhattacharya, Pradip. The First Bengali Mahabharata. 8 Apr. 2011 <*http://mahabharata-resources.org/variations/kabism.html*>

Bhave, Vinoba. Talks on the Gita. Sarva Seva Sangh Prakashan, 1970

Bolle, Kees W. The Bhagavadgītā: A New Translation. Berkeley: University of California Press, 1979

Brunton, Paul. Indian Philosophy and Modern Culture. E. P. Dutton & Co. Inc., 1939

Burgess, Ebenezer. Translation of the Sûrya-Siddhânta. New Haven: American Oriental Society, 1860. 23 Feb. 2011 <*http://books.google.com/books?id=jpE7AAAAcAAJ*>

Chidbhavananda, Swami. The Bhagavad Gita. Tirupparaitturai: Sri Ramakrishna Tapovanam, 1972

Chinmayananda, Swami. Sreemad Bhagawad Geeta: Hinduism at a Glance. Bangalore: N. M. Sirur, 1958

Chinmayananda, Swami. The Holy Geeta. Mumbai: Central Chinmaya Mission Trust, 1996

Coomaraswamy, Ananda K. Hinduism and Buddhism. Mountain View: Golden Elixir Press, 2011

Coulson, Michael. Sanskrit: An Introduction to the Classical Language. Gomrich, Richard & Benson, James, eds. London: Hodder & Stoughton Publishers, 2001

Datta, Amaresh. The Encyclopaedia Of Indian Literature. Volume One (A To Devo). Sahitya Akademi, 2006. 8 Apr. 2011 <*http://books.google.com/books?id=ObFCT5_taSgC&dq=The+Encyclopaedia+Of+Indian+Literature&source=gbs_navlinks_s*>

De, Soumen. "The Historical Context of The Bhagavad Gita and Its Relation to Indian Religious Doctrines." Exploring Ancient World Cultures: Essays on Ancient India. 1996. 14 Oct. 2008 <*http://eawc.evansville.edu/essays/de.htm*>

De Riencourt, Amaury. The Soul of India. Honeyglen Publishing Ltd, 1986

Debroy, Bibek. The Bhagavad Gita. New Delhi: Penguin, 2005

Desai, Mahadev. The Gospel of Selfless Action or The Gita According to Gandhi. Ahmedabad: Navjivan Publishing House, 1956

Dharma, Krishna. The Great Spiritual Epic of All Time: Mahabharata. Badger: Torchlight Publishing Inc, 2005

Divecha, Acharya Vishnu K. Gītā Explained Word-by-Word. Acharya Vishnu K Divecha, 2004

Dowson, John. A classical dictionary of Hindu mythology and religion, geography, history, and literature. Calcutta-Allahabad-Bombay-New Delhi: Rupa & Co., 1987

Durant, Will. The Case for India. New York: Simon and Schuster, 1930

Dutt, Guru K. Hindu Culture. Hind Kitabs, 1951

Easwaran, Eknath. The Bhagavad Gita: Translated for the Modern Reader. Tomales: Nilgiri Press, 1985

Fosse, Lars Martin. The Bhagavad Gita. 1st ed. New York: YogaVidya.com, 2007 21 Oct. 2008 <*http://www.yogavidya.com/Yoga/BhagavadGita.pdf*>

Freke, Timothy. Lao Tzu's Tao Te Ching. London: Piatkus, 1999

Galav, T. C. Philosophy of Hinduism - an Introduction: Universal Science-Religion. T. C. Galav, 1992

Gambhirananda, Swami. Bhagavad Gītā (With the commentary of Śaṅkarācārya). Mayavati: Advaita Ashrama, 1984

Ganguli, Kisari Mohan. The Mahabharata of Krishna-Dwaipayana Vyasa. Calcutta: Bharata Press, 1883–96. 19 Oct. 2008 <*http://www.sacred-texts.com/hin/maha/index.htm*>

Giri, Swami Nirmalananda. Srimad Bhagavad Gita: The Holy Song of God. Atma Jyoti Ashram. 2004. 10 Oct. 2008 <*http://www.atmajyoti.org/pdfs/gita_full.pdf*>

Gopalacharya, Srinivasa Chakravarthy. Samskrita-Kannada Dictionary. Bangalore Press, 1997

Goswami, Satsvarupa Dasa. Readings in Vedic Literature: The Tradition Speaks for Itself. Bhaktivedanta Book Trust, 1985

Govindacharya, A. Ṣrī Bhagavad-Gītā (with Ṣrī Rāmānujāchārya's Viṣishtadvaita-commentary). Madras: Vaijayanti Press, 1898

Goyandka, Jayadayal. Śrīmad Bhagavadgītā. Trans. Editorial staff of the Kalyana-Kalpataru. 1st ed. Gorakhpur: Gita Press, 1969

Goyandka, Sriharikrishnadas. Śrīmadbhagavadgītā (Śrīrāmāṇuja-bhāṣya hindī anuvāda sahit). Gorakhpur: Gita Press, 1952

Griffith, Ralph T. H. The Hymns of the Rig Veda. 17 Jan. 2010 <*http://www.sacred-texts.com/hin/rigveda/index.htm*>

Gundappa, D. V. *Jīvana-dharma-yoga*. Bangalore: Directorate of Kannada and Culture, 1990

Gupta, Prashant and Gupta, M. D. The Bhagawad-Gita. New Delhi: Dreamland Publications.

Harrison, Paul. "A history of pantheism and scientific pantheism." Bhagavad Gita – the Song of God. 1996. 13 Oct. 2008 <*http://members.aol.com/Heraklit1/gita.htm*>

Harshananda, Swami. All About Gītā. Bangalore: Ramakrishna Math, 1993

Hawley, Jack. The Bhagavad Gita – A Walkthrough for Westerners. Novato: New World Library, 2001

Hegde, Krishnananda. Bhagavad Gita: The Dialogue. Udupi: Rashtrakavi Govinda Pai Research Centre, 2006

Hooker, Richard. Bhagavadgita. 15 Oct. 2008 <*http://www.wsu.edu/~dee/TEXT/gita.rtf*>

Hubert, Paul. Histoire de la Bhagavad-Gîtâ: ses diverses éditions de 1785 à nos jours. Adyar-Paris, 1949

Huchzermeyer, Wilfried & Zimmermann, Jutta. The Bhagavad Gita as a Living Experience. Herndon: Lantern Books, 2002. 11 Oct. 2008 <*http://books.google.com/books?id=CiGSLOJPBz4C*>

Iyengar, Masti Venkatesa. Srimat Bhagavadgita: A Study. Bangalore: Jeevana Karyalaya, 1978

Jackson, Carl T. The Oriental Religions and American Thought (Nineteenth-Century Explorations). London: Greenwood Press, 1981

Johnson, W. J. The Bhagavad Gita. New York: Oxford University Press, 2008

Johnston, Charles. Bhagavad Gita: "The Song of the Master". New York: The Quarterly Book Department, 1908

Jyotirmayananda, Swami. Srimad Bhagavad Gita. Vishva Hindu Parishad of America, 1986

Kaushik *et al.* *Srimanmahaabhaarata*. Volumes 13 and 14. Bangalore: Bharata Darshana Prakashana, 1977

Keay, John. India Discovered: The Recovery of a Lost Civilization. HarperCollins Publishers Ltd, 2001

Kosambi, D. D. Myth and Reality: Studies in the Formation of Indian Culture. 4 Jan. 2009 <*http://vidyaonline.org/arvindgupta/mythandreality.pdf*>

Krishnananda, Swami. A Short History of Religious and Philosophic Thought in India. Sivanandanagar: The Divine Life Society, 1970

Krishnaraj, Veeraswamy. Bhagavadgita in Sanskrit, Transliteration, and Translation. New York: iUniverse, 2009

Lal, P. The Bhagavadgita. New Delhi: Roli Books, 1994

Maeterlinck, Maurice. The Great Secret. San Diego: The Book Tree, 2003

Maharshi, Ramana. Sri Maharshi Gita. 10 Oct. 2008 <*http://www.atmajyoti.org/gi_bhagavad_gita_maharshi.asp*>

Mascaró, Juan. The Bhagavad Gita. Middlesex: Penguin Books, 1962

Merton, Thomas. Thoughts on the East. New York: New Directions Publishing Corporation, 1995

Miller, Barbara Stoler. The Bhagavad-Gita: Krishna's Counsel in Time of War. New York: Bantam Books, 1986

Mitchell, Stephen. Bhagavad Gita. New York: Three Rivers Press, 2000

Morgan, Les. Translating the Bhagavadgītā: A Workbook for Sanskrit Students. Los Angeles: Mahodara Press, 2017

Mohanraj, V. M. The Warrior and the Charioteer: a Materialistic Interpretation of the Bhagavadgita, Including a New Translation of the Poem. New Delhi: Leftword Books, 2005

References

Mookerji, Radha Kumud. Ancient Indian Education: Brahmanical and Buddhist. Motilal Banarsidass, 1990

Munshi, K. M. Bhagavad Gita and Modern Life. Bombay: Bharatiya Vidya Bhavan, 1947

Nabar, Vrinda & Tumkur, Shanta. The Bhagavadgītā. Hertfordshire: Wordsworth Classics, 1997

Narale, Ratnakar. Gita As She Is – in Vyasa's Own Words. Volume 1 – Chapters 1, 2 & 12. Toronto: Hindu Institute of Learning, 2007

Narale, Ratnakar. Gitopanishad. Toronto: Pustak Bharati (Books India), 2015

Natarajan, S. Main Currents in India Culture. Hyderabad: Indo-Middle East Cultural Studies, 1960

Nath, D. History of the Koch Kingdom 1515-1615. Mittal Publications, 1989

Nehru, Jawaharlal. A Discovery of India. New Delhi: Oxford University Press, 2002

Osho. Inner War and Peace: Timeless Solutions to Conflict from the Bhagavad Gita. Watkins, 2006

Osho. Krishna: The Man and His Philosophy. New Delhi: Jaico Book House, 2004

Pai, Roopa. The Gita for Children. New Delhi: Hachette India, 2015

Parthasarathy, A. Bhagavadgita. Bombay: A. Parthasarathy, 2008

Patri, Umesh. Hindu Scriptures and American Transcendentalists. South Asia Books, 1987

Paz, Octavio. In Light of India. Trans. Eliot Weinberger. Orlando:Harcourt, 1995

Piparaiya, Ram K. The Bhagavad Gita: Your Charioteer in the Battlefield of Life. Mumbai: Aridhi Indusvista, 1999

Powell, Barbara. Windows into the Infinite: A Guide to the Hindu Scriptures. Fremont: Asian Humanities Press, 1996

Prabhavananda, Swami & Isherwood, Christopher. The Song of God: Bhagavad Gita. New York: Mentor Books, 1951

Prabhupada, A. C. Bhaktivedanta Swami. Bhagavad-Gita As It Is. Los Angeles: The Bhaktivedanta Book Trust, 1983

Prasad, M. G. Garland - An Anthology of Vedic Hinduism. Flushing: Foundation for Arts and Sciences from India (ARSI), 2001

Prasad, Ramananda. The Bhagavad Gītā. New Delhi: Motilal Banarsidass, 1996

Radhakrishnan, Sarvepalli. The Bhagavadgītā. London: George Allen and Unwin, 1948

Raghavachar, S. S. Ramanuja on the Gita. Calcutta: Advaita Ashrama, 1998

Rai, Lala Lajpat. The Message of the Bhagawad Gita. Bombay: Hindusthan Press, 1923

Rajagopalachari, Chakravarthi. Bhagavad-Gita. 4th ed.
Madras: Federation of International Fellowships, 1941

Ramachandra, Magdal. Shashvata Dharma in Srimad Bhagavad Gita or
The Lord's Science of Eternal Religion. Bangalore: Magdal Ramachandra, 1954

Ramanujam, Saroja. Srimad-Bhagavad-Gita. Volumes 1–3.
16 Mar. 2011 *<http://www.srihayagrivan.org/html/ebook057.htm>*
<http://www.srihayagrivan.org/html/ebook058.htm>
<http://www.srihayagrivan.org/html/ebook059.htm>

Ramanujananda, Swami. Divine Nectar (Gita in Verse). Trissur: Ramakrishna Math, 1994

Ramaswamy, S R. Evolution of the Mahabharata and Other Writings on the Epic.
Tr. Ravikumar, Hari and Bharadwaj, Arjun with Balakrishna, Sandeep.
Bengaluru: Prekshaa Pratishtana, 2019

Ranade, R. D. The Bhagavadgītā as a Philosophy of God-Realization. 3rd ed.
Bombay: Bharatiya Vidya Bhavan, 1982

Ranganathananda, Swami. The Charm and Power of The Gita.
Calcutta: Advaita Ashrama, 2001

Ranganathananda, Swami. Universal Message of the Bhagavad Gītā: An Exposition of the Gītā in the Light of Modern Thought and Modern Needs. Volumes 1–3.
Calcutta: Advaita Ashrama, 2000

Rao, P. Nagaraja. Introduction to Vedanta. 2nd ed. Bombay: Bharatiya Vidya Bhavan, 1960

Rao, S. R. The Lost City of Dvaraka. New Delhi: Aditya Prakashan, 1999

Rau, S. Subba. The Bhagavad-Gita (According to Sri Madhwacharya's Bhasyas). Madras, 1906
10 Aug. 2021 *<https://archive.org/details/MadhvacaaryaBhagavadgigtabhashya1906>*

Ravindra, Ravi. The Bhagavad Gita: A Guide to Navigating the Battle of Life.
Boulder: Shambala, 2017

Ravindra, Ravi. Yoga and the Teaching of Krishna.
Chennai: The Theosophical Publishing House, 1998

Renou, Marie-Simone. The India I Love. New York: Tudor Publishing Company, 1968

Revel, Louis. The Fragrance of India: Landmarks for the world of tomorrow.
Allahabad: Kitabistan, 1946

Roy, Dilip Kumar. The Bhagavad Gita: A Revelation. New Delhi: Hind Pocket Books, 1993

Ryder, Arthur W. The Bhagavad Gita. Kessinger Publishing, 2004

Sankaranarayanan, S. Śrīmadbhagavadgītā with Gītārthasangraha of Abhinavagupta. Parts 1 & 2. Tirupati: Sri Venkateswara University Oriental Research Institute, 1985

Sargeant, Winthrop. The Bhagavadgita. Albany: State University of New York Press, 1984

Sarma, D. S. The Bhagavad Gita. Mumbai: Bharatiya Vidya Bhavan, 2003

Sarma, D. S. What is Hinduism?. Madras: G. S. Press, 1939

Sastry, Alladi Mahadev. The Bhagavad Gita: With the Commentary of Sri Sankaracharya. Madras: Samata Books, 1979

Schweig, Graham M. Bhagavad Gita: The Beloved Lord's Secret Love Song. 1st ed. New York: HarperSanFrancisco, 2007

Schweitzer, Albert. Indian Thought and its Development. London: Rodder and Stougkton, 1936

Sharma, N. Ranganatha. Gītārthaprakāśa. Mysore: Geetha Book House, 1997

Singh, H. L. The Treasury of Hinduism. Robin Books, 2002

Singhal D. P. India and World Civilization. Pan Macmillan Limited, 1993

Sivananda, Swami. Bhagavad Gita. Shivanandanagar: The Divine Life Society, 2000 17 Oct. 2008 <*http://www.dlshq.org/download/bgita.pdf*>

Somanathananda, Swami. *Gitaabhaavadhaare*. Mysore: Ramakrishna Ashrama, 1993

Stanford, Ann. The Bhagavad Gita: A New Translation. New York: Harder and Harder, 1970

Sukthankar, V S. On the Meaning of the Mahābhārata. Bombay: The Asiatic Society of Bombay, 1957

Swami, Purohit. The Bhagavad Gita. 10 Oct. 2008 <*www.thebigview.com/download/bhagavad-gita.pdf*>

Swamiji, Sugunendra Teertha. *Srimadbhagavadgita*. Udupi: Suguna Samsath, 1991

Swarupananda, Swami. Srimad Bhagavad Gita. Almora: Advaita Ashrama, 1909.

Tadatmananda. Bhagavadgita: A Lyrical Translation for Singing, Chanting, and Recitation. Saylorsburg: Arsha Vidya Gurukulam, 1997

Tapasyananda, Swami. Bhagavad Gītā: The Scripture of Mankind. Madras: Sri Ramakrishna Math

Telang, Kâshinâth Trimbak. The Bhagavadgîtâ: With the Sanatsugâtîya and the Anugîtâ. Volume 8, The Sacred Books of the East. Oxford: The Clarendon Press, 1882. 11 Oct. 2008 <*http://www.sacred-texts.com/hin/sbe08/index.htm*>

Thompson, George. The Bhagavad Gita: A new translation.
New York: Northpoint Press, 2008

Thoreau, Henry David. Walden; or, Life in the Woods. Stilwell: Digireads.com, 2005

Tilak, Bal Gangadhar. Srimad Bhagavadgītā Rahasya or Karma Yoga Sastra.
Trans. Sukthankar, B. S. 10th ed. Poona: Tilak Brothers, 2000

Tokunaga, Muneo. The Mahabharata in Sanskrit. Smith, John D., ed.
20 Oct. 2008 <*http://www.sacred-texts.com/hin/mbs/index.htm*>

Tomlin, E. W. F. Great Philosophers of the East. London: Arrow Books, 1959

V, Jayaram. The Bhagavadgita: Complete Translation (Word to word Translation & Commentary). New Albany: Pure Life Vision, 2011

Van Buitenen, J. A. B. The Bhagavadgītā in the Mahābhārata.
Chicago and London: University of Chicago Press, 1981

Vedavyasa, E. Astronomical Dating of the Mahabharata War.
Delhi: Agam Kala Prakashan, 1986

Veerabhadrappa, B. V. The Bhagavadgita: A Rational Enquiry.
Trans. Sastry, D. K. Seetharama. Bangalore: Navakarnataka Prakashana, 2004

Versluis, Arthur. American Transcendentalism and Asian Religions.
New York: Oxford University Press, 1993

Vireśwarānanda, Swāmī. Śrīmad Bhagavad Gītā: With the Gloss of Śrīdhara Swāmī.
3rd ed. Madras: Sri Ramakrishna Math, 1972

Vivekananda, Swami. My India, the India Eternal.
Calcutta: The Ramakrishna Mission Institute of Culture, 1996

Wadiyar, Sri Jayachamaraja. The Gītā and Indian Culture. New Delhi: Orient Longmans, 1963

Yardi, M. R. *Jnaneshwari*. Pune: Bharatiya Vidya Bhavan, 1995.
18 Oct. 2008 <*http://www.bvbpune.org/contents1.html*>

Yogananda, Sri Sri Paramahansa. God Talks With Arjuna: The Bhagavad Gita.
Volumes 1 & 2. Kolkata: Yogoda Satsanga Society of India, 2002

Yogi, Maharishi Mahesh. Maharishi Mahesh Yogi on the Bhaqavad-Gita: a New Translation and Commentary: Chapters 1-6. New York: Viking Penguin, 1990

Zaehner, Robert Charles. The Bhagavad-Gītā: With a Commentary Based on the Original Sources. New York: Oxford University Press, 1973

Gītārtha-Saṅgraham of Yāmunācārya.
16 Mar. 2011 <*http://srivaishnavism.yuku.com/topic/466*>

Gītādhāturūpāvaliḥ: A Collection of All Verb Declensions used in Bhagavad Gita. Ed. Vishwasa, H R. New Delhi: Samskrita Bharati, 2020

Holy Gītā Ready Reference: Your Doorway to the Bhagavad Gītā. Veliyanad: Chinmaya International Foundation, 2005

Kailāsam Kṛtigaḷu: Collected Works of T. P. Kailasam (1884–1946). Mysore: Institute of Kannada Studies, 1987

Mahabharata in Oriya – Sarala Mahabharat. 8 Apr. 2011 <*http://www.hindu-blog.com/2008/05/mahabharata-in-oriya-sarala-mahabharat.html*>

Sri Jnanadeva's Bhāvārtha Dīpikā otherwise known as Jnāneshwarī ज्ञानेश्वरी. Tr. Bhagwat, Ramchandra Keshav. 2nd ed. Madras: Samata Book, 1979

Srimadbhagavadgita (with multiple commentaries). Ed. Paṇs'īkar, Wāsudev Laxmaṇ Shāstrī. 2nd ed. Bombay: Nirṇaya-Sāgar Press, 1936

Śrīmad-bhagavad-gītā with the "Jñānakarmasamuccaya" commentary of Ānanda [vardhana]. Ed. Belvalkar, Shripad Krishna. Poona: Bilvakuñja Publishing House, 1941

The Best of Hiriyanna (A selection of papers by Prof. M. Hiriyanna on Sanskrit Language and Literature, Indian Aesthetics, and Indian Philosophy). Mason: W.I.S.E. Words Inc. (in collaboration with Prekshaa Pratishtana, Bangalore), 2018

The Bhagavadgītā (relevant parts of the Bhīṣmaparvan of the BORI Edition of the Mahābhārata). Cr. Ed. Belvalkar, Shripad Krishna. Poona: Bhandarkar Oriental Research Institute, 1968

The Bhagavadgītā or The Song Divine. Gorakhpur: Gita Press, 1975

The Bhagavad-gita with Eleven Commentaries. Cr. Ed. Sadhale, Shastri Gajanana Sambhu. Volumes 1–3. Bombay: The "Gujarati" Printing Press, 1935–38

The Call of the Gita. Madras: Sri Ramakrishna Math, 1983

The Complete Works of Swami Vivekananda. 18 Feb. 2011 <*http://www.ramakrishnavivekananda.info/vivekananda/complete_works.htm*>

The Wisdom of India. Ed. Lin Yutang. London: Michael Joseph, 1948

Vedanta Deshika's Prabandham on Bhagavad-Gita. 16 Mar. 2011 <*http://www.freeonlinebook.net/Others/28029/Gitartha-Sangraham*>

Audio Tapes

Bhadragiri, Sant Keshavadas. Shrimad Bhagavadgeetha.

Saraswathi, Swami Dayananda. Ten Essential Verses of the Bhagavad Gita.

Shankar, Sri Sri Ravi. Contradictions in the Bhagavad Gita.

Sukhabodhananda, Swami. Gita Talks.

Documentaries

Joseph Campbell and The Power of Myth. Episodes 1-6. Feat. Campbell, Joseph. Exec. Ed. Moyers, Bill. Public Broadcasting Service, 1988

Root of All Evil?. Dir. Barnes, Russell. Feat. Dawkins, Richard. Prod. Clements, Alan and Kidd, Deborah. 2006.

The Naked Truth: Exposing the Deceptions About the Origins of Modern Religions. Feat. Partridge, Derek and Maxwell, Jordan with Jenkins, Bill. Writ. Maxwell, Jordan. International Research and Educational Society, 1991

Websites

About.com: Hinduism. <*http://hinduism.about.com*>

Gita Supersite. <*https://www.gitasupersite.iitk.ac.in/*>

Hindu Website. <*http://www.hinduwebsite.com*>

Hindu Wisdom. <*http://www.hinduwisdom.info*>

Śrīmad Bhagavad-Gītā: For Everyone In All The Worlds. <*http://www.bhagavad-gita.org*>

The Bhagavad Gita: The Divine Song of God. <*http://www.bhagavad-gita.us*>

Wikipedia: The Free Encyclopedia. <*http://en.wikipedia.org*>

Others

<*http://www.atomicarchive.com/Movies/Movie8.shtml*>

<*http://wikimapia.org/1025255/Niranam*>

<*http://www.vnn.org/world/9804/07-1732/index.html*>

Harijan 24-8-1934

Hindustan Times – 11 Mar. 2021

Sathya Sai Speaks II

The Telegraph, Calcutta – 14 Nov. 2002

READERS' PRAISE FOR THE NEW BHAGAVAD-GITA

"This innocuously simple translation actually clarifies the correct meaning and spirit... [for] certain critically important verses. I strongly recommend a study of Koti and Hari's The New Bhagavad-Gita to anyone who is interested in understanding the ancient wisdom in the Gita."
NARAYAN SRINIVASAN (Flower Mound, TX, USA)

"...indeed simple, lively, complete and laudable."
RATNAKAR NARALE PhD (Toronto, Canada)

"Simple, lucid exposition contributes an engaging reading experience. A great presentation of India's timeless wisdom."
KANNIKS KANNIKESWARAN (Cincinnati, OH, USA)

"This translation provides priceless insight that evades the boundary of religion and embraces the realm of spirituality and the very essence of life."
CHARLES BEST (Los Angeles, CA, USA)

"...they have...succeeded in translating 'The Song of God' as it is. I recommend this book to anyone who is interested in knowing, learning, and practicing the art of living."
JWALA PRASAD MD (Cincinnati, OH, USA)

"I have read other translations and summaries of the Gita, but none has been as helpful as this. This translation gives the reader easy access to understanding the text without being simplistic. Not only does this interpretation provide a clear, accessible reading of the Gita, but it allows the reader a depth of insight into Hinduism as a whole. This is an excellent resource for teaching Hindu scripture to a Western audience."
MATT STRAUSS (Cincinnati, OH, USA)

"I would definitely recommend this book to my teenage daughter and other teenagers who would like to be introduced to this wonderful Indian practical spiritual guide given to us more than 5,000 years ago."
SRIRAMA BHAIRI PhD (San Diego, CA, USA)

"It was a special treat for me to read The New Bhagavad-Gita. It is written in simple English, easy to read and understand the complex story of Bhagavad Gita."
PROF. JNANENDRA K BHATTACHARJEE (Oxford, OH, USA)

"[The authors] have successfully poured the essence of the Gita by virtue of resurrection of its quintessential values and philosophy."
SHANTESH HEDE (Mumbai, India)

"I seriously recommend to anyone who is curious about Hinduism, or is just trying to understand better their Indian friends. Grab it, read it once, and then discuss it, reflect on it, and then read it again."
PEDRO POBLETE LASERRE (Temuco, Chile)

"I carry this around every day and even after many readings, each page has something new to offer every time it is read."
RAVIKIRAN PRABHU (Bengaluru, India)

"The authors have distilled the 'eternal wisdom' of Gita into a simply superb concoction. I thoroughly enjoyed this book."
G HARISH MD (Charleston, WV, USA)

"As I read through the first few pages, I was assured that this is the right book for a broad spectrum of readers... from a neophyte to a strong believer who is in search of the true essence of the Gita."
SOUJANYA REDDY (Singapore)

"Gita is not [just] for old age...but to practice every day...
and we really feel now that way."
SOHINI and SOUMYA PALDE (Blue Ash, OH, USA)

"The way you have led us to Bhagavad-Gita,
we would never have gotten to it this way..."
MINATI and AMAR BHATTACHARYA (Cincinnati, OH, USA)

"It is not easy to take a powerful work like the the Gita
and translate it for a modern audience. The authors have
worked very hard, to keep it simple and contemporary
while staying sincere to the core message."
SEEMA EMBAR (Atlanta, GA, USA)

"I have started looking at things very differently...
become a changed person."
KANTHI MURALI (Cincinnati, OH, USA)

"My life and perspective are irreversibly changed.
For the better."
RASHMI BALAKRISHNA (Mason, OH, USA)

Koti Sreekrishna PhD (*b.* 1953, Bangalore) earned his doctorate from the *Indian Institute of Science* in 1978. After being a Research Fellow at *The Baylor College of Medicine* (Houston, TX) and *University of Kentucky* (Lexington, KY) he worked at *Phillips Petroleum Company*, *Marion Merrel Dow*, and *Procter and Gamble Company*. His interests include philosophy, inter-religious dialogue, and studying the Hindu scriptures. He has previously (co-)authored books related to Indian philosophy. He is currently the Religious Counselor of *Hindu Society of Greater Cincinnati*, where he earlier served in the Executive Council for several years. He has given temple tours and made presentations on Hinduism to local universities, schools, and churches. He has moderated courses on *Gita* and Hinduism at OLLI, *University of Cincinnati*. He is a distinguished Toastmaster.

Hari Ravikumar BE (*b.* 1984, Bangalore) is a writer, translator, editor, violinist, and designer. In the past, he has worked as a software coder, content manager, teacher/trainer, and product strategist. He has (co-) written and (co-)edited over twenty books, mostly related to Indian culture and philosophy. He is one of the contributing editors of the online journal *Prekshaa* and works in an advisory capacity with *Abhinava Dance Company*, *Edyoulead Life India*, *Lakshminarayana Global Centre of Excellence*, *Pramiti* school, and *Samvit Research Foundation*. He has a lasting interest in philosophy, music, literature, films, and education pedagogy.

www.ingramcontent.com/pod-product-compliance
Lightning Source LLC
Chambersburg PA
CBHW050846150626
46549CB00012B/34
* 9 7 9 8 8 9 3 5 6 3 8 3 2 *